Encountering John

Encountering Biblical Studies
Walter A. Elwell, General Editor and New Testament Editor
Eugene H. Merrill, Old Testament Editor

Encountering the Old Testament: A Christian Survey
Bill T. Arnold and Bryan E. Beyer

*Readings from the Ancient Near East: Primary Sources
for Old Testament Study*
Bill T. Arnold and Bryan E. Beyer, editors

*Encountering the New Testament: A Historical
and Theological Survey*
Walter A. Elwell and Robert W. Yarbrough

*Readings from the First-Century World: Primary Sources
for New Testament Study*
Walter A. Elwell and Robert W. Yarbrough, editors

*Encountering the Book of Genesis: A Survey of Its Content
and Issues*
Bill T. Arnold

*Encountering the Book of Psalms: A Literary and Theological
Introduction*
C. Hassell Bullock

Encountering the Book of Isaiah
Bryan E. Beyer

*Encountering John: The Gospel in Historical, Literary,
and Theological Perspective*
Andreas J. Köstenberger

Encountering the Book of Romans
Douglas J. Moo

Encountering the Book of Hebrews: An Exposition
Donald A. Hagner

Encountering John

The Gospel in Historical, Literary, and Theological Perspective

Andreas J. Köstenberger

Baker Academic

A Division of Baker Book House Co
Grand Rapids, Michigan 49516

Published by Baker Academic
a division of Baker Book House Company
P.O. Box 6287, Grand Rapids, MI 49516-6287

Paperback edition published 2002

Printed in the United States of America

Library of Congress Cataloging-in-Publication Data

Köstenberger, Andreas J., 1957–
    Encountering John : the Gospel in historical, literary, and theological perspective / Andreas J. Köstenberger.
        p.   cm.—(Encountering biblical studies)
    Includes bibliographical references and index.
    ISBN 0-8010-2150-2 (cloth)
    ISBN 0-8010-2603-2 (paper)
    1. Bible. N.T. John Textbooks.   I. Title.   II. Series.
BS2616.K67   1999
226.5'07—dc21   99-34290

Photo acknowledgments:

John McRay: 122, 158, 179.

Chris Miller: 25, 26, 54, 64, 68, 69, 72, 73, 74, 85, 86, 87, 88, 89, 91, 94, 96, 97, 98, 100, 101, 102 (2), 103, 109, 114, 118, 137, 176, 177, 178 (2), 181, 192, 211.

An instructor's manual for this book is available from Baker Academic.

For information about Baker Academic, visit our web site:
www.bakeracademic.com

For my children
Lauren, Tahlia, and David
With prayer and thanksgiving

Like arrows in the hand of a warrior,
So are the children of one's youth.
How blessed is the man
whose quiver is full of them.

Psalm 127:4–5a

Contents in Brief

Contents

List of Sidebars, Tables, Maps, and Excursuses

Editor's Preface

The strength of the church and the vitality of the individual Christian's life are directly related to the role Scripture plays in them. Early believers knew the importance of this and spent their time in fellowship, prayer, and the study of God's Word. The passing of two thousand years has not changed the need, but it has changed the accessibility of many of the Bible's ideas. Time has distanced us from those days, and we often need guidance back into the world of the Old and New Testaments.

To that end Baker Book House is producing two separate but related series of biblical textbooks. The design of these new series is to put us back into the world of the biblical text, so that we may understand it as those early believers did and at the same time see it from and for our own day, thus facilitating the application of its truths to our contemporary situation.

Encountering Biblical Studies consists of undergraduate-level texts, and two surveys treating the Old and New Testaments provide the foundation for this series. Accompanying these survey texts are two collateral volumes of readings, which illuminate the world surrounding the biblical text. Built on these basic survey texts are upper-level college texts covering the books of the Bible that are most frequently offered in the curriculum of Christian colleges.

A related series, titled Engaging Biblical Studies, provides graduate-level treatments for introduction and theology courses.

Complementing both levels of textbooks is a set of standard reference books that may be consulted for answers to specific questions or more in-depth study of biblical ideas. These reference books include *Baker Commentary on the Bible, Baker Topical Guide to the Bible, Baker Encyclopedia of the Bible, Baker Theological Dictionary of the Bible,* and *Evangelical Dictionary of Theology.*

Encountering and Engaging Biblical Studies series are written from an evangelical point of view, in the firm conviction that the Scripture is absolutely true and never misleads us. It is the sure foundation on which our faith and life may be built because it unerringly leads willing readers to Jesus Christ.

Walter A. Elwell
General Editor

Publisher's Preface

Bible courses must be considered the heart of the curriculum for Christian colleges and evangelical seminaries. For Christians the Bible constitutes the basis for both our spiritual and our intellectual lives—indeed for *all* of life. If these courses are fundamental to Christian education, then the textbooks used for these courses could not be more crucial.

Baker Book House is launching two separate but related series of volumes for college- and seminary-level Bible courses. Encountering Biblical Studies consists of undergraduate texts, while Engaging Biblical Studies represents graduate-level treatments.

In these two series, Baker will publish texts that are clearly college-level, and introductory and biblical theology texts that are explicitly seminary-level. The textbooks for the basic college survey courses and for the more advanced college courses on individual Bible books will be designed expressly for this purpose. They will not be written for laypeople or pastors and seminarians, nor will they be primarily reference books. Rather, they will be pedagogically oriented textbooks written with collegians in mind.

Texts for the seminary courses in Old Testament and New Testament introduction and biblical theology will induct the student into graduate-level study of the Testaments, even while remembering that many seminarians are preparing for ministry rather than for further graduate study and a career in academia.

Encountering John is part of the college-level Encountering series, and it attempts to build on the basic survey text, *Encountering the New Testament: A Christian Survey* (Walter A. Elwell and Robert W. Yarbrough). While the survey text is written for college freshmen, this John volume is intended for upper-level collegians.

Rather than providing a sustained exegetical analysis of each verse in John, this volume surveys the entire book with an emphasis on drawing out its theological message and its practical significance for collegians. It consists of appropriate introduction and survey material with the necessary critical, historical, literary, hermeneutical, and background concerns woven within the exposition of the biblical text.

Guiding Principles

As part of the developing of this volume, the series editors, author, and publisher established the following principles:

1. It must reflect the finest in evangelical scholarship of our day.
2. It must be written at a level that most of today's upper-level collegians can understand.
3. It must be pedagogically sound. This extends not only to traditional concerns like study and review questions, chapter objectives and summaries for each chapter, but also the manner in which the material is presented.
4. It must include appropriate illustrative material such as photographs, maps, charts, graphs, figures, and sidebars.
5. It must seek to winsomely draw in the student by focusing on biblical teaching concerning crucial doctrinal and ethical matters.

Goals

The goals for *Encountering John* fall into two categories: intellectual and attitudinal. The intellectual goals are to (1) present the factual content of the Gospel, (2) introduce historical, geographical, and cultural background, (3) outline primary hermeneutical principles, (4) touch on critical issues (e.g., why some people read the Bible differently), and (5) substantiate the Christian faith.

The attitudinal goals are also fivefold: (1) to make the Bible a part of students' lives, (2) to instill in students a love for the Scriptures, (3) to make them better people, (4) to enhance their piety, and (5) to stimulate their love for God. In short, if this text builds a foundation for a lifetime of Bible study, the authors and publisher will be amply rewarded.

Overarching Themes

Controlling the writing of *Encountering John* have been three essential theological themes: God, people, and the gospel as it relates to individuals. The notion that God is a person—one and three—and a transcendent and immanent Being has been woven throughout the text. Moreover, this God has created people in his image who are fallen but still the objects of his redemptive love. The gospel is the means, the active personal power that God uses to rescue people from darkness and death. But the gospel does more than rescue—it restores. It confers on otherwise hopeless sinners the resolve and strength to live lives that please God, because they walk in the love that comes from God.

Features

The publisher's aim has been to provide an exceptionally unique resource on the one hand but not merely trendy on the other. Some of the distinguishing features we hope will prove helpful to the professor and inspiring to the student include the following:

- Liberal use of illustrations—photographs, figures, tables, charts.
- Sidebars and excursuses exploring exegetical, ethical, and theological issues of interest and concern to modern-day collegians.
- Chapter outline and objectives presented at the opening of each chapter.
- Study questions at the end of each chapter.
- A helpful glossary.
- An annotated bibliography.

To the Student

The Underlying Purpose of This Book

This book has been written with you, the student, in mind from beginning to end. The one question that guided the inclusion of material in this volume was: What would I want my students to know about the Gospel of John? In this I have sought to pursue a twofold purpose: to nurture you spiritually and to increase your knowledge by providing you with helpful information on John's Gospel. In the writing of this book, primary emphasis was given to the text of the Gospel itself. Where appropriate, I have included references to helpful secondary literature.

The goal of a book such as the present one must be to understand the history and story of Jesus as it was written by John himself. This involves giving careful attention to repeated key words as well as to major themes such as "Jesus as the Christ," "believing," or "eternal life." At the same time, I have made an effort to relate John's teaching to the rest of Scripture. For John did not write in a vacuum. He consciously built on Old Testament revelation, and he seems to have presupposed his readers' familiarity with the gospel tradition.

Didactic Features Included in This Book

Let me briefly familiarize you with some of the didactic features of this book. I trust this will help you make the most of your study of John's Gospel. At the beginning of each chapter, you will find Chapter Outlines providing you with a road map of the chapter's contents. The Chapter Objectives are designed to structure your learning as you work through the present volume. Take note of them before you read the chapter. Then return to them when you're done working through the material. See whether you are able to accomplish the stated objectives.

At the end of each chapter, you will also find several Study Questions that will help reinforce the major content that has been covered in that particular section of the book. Try to answer these questions from your recollection of what you've read. Then check yourself by looking through the relevant section in that chapter.

Finally, let me refer you to several resources gathered together at the end of the present volume. First, you will find a Glossary of important theological terms used throughout this book. If you are not sure about the meaning of a particular word as you read through a given chapter, check the listing in the Glossary. Then go back and see whether this helps you understand the statement made in the text. Second, I have provided an Annotated Select Bibliography for further reading. This includes the most helpful commentaries as well as other important studies on various aspects of John's Gospel.

Third, you will notice a section titled Tools for Study consisting of a list of (1) Proper Names, (2) Place Names, and (3) Important Theological Terms in John's Gospel. To my knowledge, this kind of material has never before been published in such a format. It is, however, extremely useful for the study of important geographical features, key characters, and significant themes in John's Gospel. Professors may want to assign one character study (e.g. Peter) and one theme study (e.g. the "world") as major assignments in a course on Johannine Theology.

Fourth, ten substantive excursuses on Johannine themes are gathered at the end of this volume. Professors could have their students read one excursus each per chapter (e.g., chs. 5–14).

Special Instructions Pertaining to the Tools for Study

A few additional comments on the Tools for Study may help. Most importantly, while the listings are all in English (with the transliteration of the original Greek term in brackets, as well as the number of occurrences in John's Gospel in relation to the NT as a whole), they are based on the actual use of a given Greek word. This will greatly enhance the accuracy of your findings. Consider the following example. The word *mimnēskomai* ("to remember") occurs three times in John's Gospel. But while the Greek term used is one and the same, the NIV uses three different English renderings: "remembered" in 2:17; "recalled" in 2:22; and "realize" in 12:16. Only a Greek-based tool such as the one provided in the present volume will enable you to trace *John's* use of words, not just the translation equivalents in a given contemporary English version. And that, of course, is what we're after—to grow in our understanding of what *John himself* has written.

One word of caution may be appropriate here as well. For completeness' sake, I have chosen to provide exhaustive listings of all the included terms. Not all instances of a given word may, however, be equally relevant in the study of a particular term. Consider, for instance, the varied use of the word *menō* ("remain," "stay") in your study of discipleship. Also, keep in mind that not every listing under a given proper name may refer to the same person. Thus "Judas (*not* Iscariot)" is listed under "Judas" together *with* Judas Iscariot. Or, three different Josephs are included under the heading "Joseph." The same

observation applies to "Mary," with the additional caution that the one person not included is the most famous of them all, Jesus' mother, for the simple reason that she is not called "Mary" in John's Gospel! By the way, John, the author of the present Gospel, likewise does not identify himself by the name of John; the simple designation "John" belongs, in the present Gospel, to John the Baptist. The author's favorite self-reference, "the disciple Jesus loved," can be traced by looking at the listings of "disciple" (*mathētēs*) or "to love" (*agapaō* as well as *phileō*).

Finally, let me encourage you to look up as many of the references listed in the Tools for Study in the Gospel itself. Needless to say, the gloss provided for a given occurrence of a term is partial. What is more, if taken by itself and thus out of context, it may be positively misleading. I don't want anyone to accuse me of heresy, just because the listing of John 3:17 under "God" reads "For God did not send his Son" or the listing of John 3:3 under "kingdom" has "no one can see the k. of God"! In sum, I have provided the tools, but you must make sure that you use them properly, which includes studying a given word in context.

Enough said. May the present volume acquaint you better with an exciting portion of God's revealed word, and may you enjoy the ride!

Author's Preface

It is my joy to say thank you to a few special people who made the present work possible. As always, pride of place belongs to my wife Marny, who has encouraged me in my writing while being faithfully devoted to raising three small children in the nurture and admonition of the Lord. I am also most thankful to President Paige Patterson and Dean Russ Bush at Southeastern Baptist Theological Seminary for their active support of my writing ministry. Thanks are also due Jim Weaver of Baker Book House for his gracious invitation to contribute to the present series.

I can do no better than express my wish for the reception of this volume in John's own words: "I have no greater joy than to hear that my children are walking in the truth" (3 Jn 4). By Christ's mercy, may this be true for our children Lauren, Tahlia, and David, to whom the book is affectionately dedicated. And may it be true for everyone who takes Jesus at his word when he said: "If anyone chooses to do God's will, he will find out whether my teaching comes from God or whether I speak on my own" (Jn 7:17). For "whoever comes to me I will never drive away" (Jn 6:37).

Before You Begin . . .

It's not a good idea to embark on a journey without a good map of the area. Likewise, we had better not plunge into our exploration of John's Gospel without some brief words of orientation. This is why the opening chapters of this book are so important. In Part 1, Encountering the Gospel of John: Come On In!, we will discuss the triad governing the study of John's Gospel: history, literature, and theology. How did John's Gospel come to be? How does the evangelist's message unfold? And what are the major themes addressed in this remarkable work? Different answers have been given to these crucial questions, and this has led to vastly differing interpretations of John's Gospel.

Regarding history, recent years have seen a remarkable erosion of belief in the traditional view that the apostle John wrote the Gospel named after him. An alternative hypothesis holds that the Gospel is the product of a "Johannine school," "circle," or "community," which traced its origins back to the apostle but which in the Fourth Gospel provided a history of its own existential struggles in terms of the history of Jesus. But what about ancient church tradition? And does this view not alter radically the way in which John's Gospel has traditionally been understood? Of course it does! That's why it's so important to consider carefully at the outset which approach to the Fourth Gospel does most justice to the text as it reflects the intention(s) of its author(s).

Regarding literature, we must first ask what kind of writing we have in the case of John's Gospel. What is a Gospel? What kind of Gospel is John's Gospel? These are questions of literary genre that will have crucial implications for interpretation. Also, the rise of narrative criticism in the secular arena has had a large impact on scholarship on John as well. As a result, numerous studies on John's literary artistry have appeared in recent years. However, while these works have doubtless led to a refined understanding of certain surface phenomena of the Fourth Gospel, it is troubling that many of these studies show little interest in historical or theological concerns. Some of those embarking on literary investigations of John's Gospel may hope thus to find a way out of the impasse caused by a highly skeptical use of the so-called historical-critical method. Others may not share evangelical presuppositions regarding the nature of Scripture, the deity of Christ, or the substitutionary atonement, but nonetheless consider John's Gospel to be a work of literature deserving of study. Our problem with this kind of reductionism is simply this: since John is at the core a *religious* book with a *spiritual* message, and since Christianity is at the core a *historical* religion, an investigation of John's Gospel in mere literary terms can never understand its true character and message.

While historical setting and literary aspects of John are thus important, these are merely the vehicles for John's theological message. And this message is bound up inextricably with who Jesus is and what we are to do about him. John's explicitly stated purpose is quite clear: "Jesus did many other signs in the presence of his disciples, which are not recorded in this book. But these are written that you may believe that the Christ, the Son of God, is Jesus, and that by believing you may have life in his name" (20:30–31; author's own translation). John's stated purpose must set the agenda for our study of this Gospel. We must therefore trace out Jesus' signs that were selected by the evangelist in order to instill faith in his readers. In particular, we must determine how these signs show that Jesus is in fact the Christ, the Son of God. And we must celebrate and proclaim anew John's revolutionary claim that believing in Jesus, and in him alone, for salvation imparts eternal life, not merely in some future life, but already in the here and now.

Part
1

Encountering
the Gospel of John:
Come On In!

John's Gospel is deep enough
for an elephant to swim
and shallow enough
for a child not to drown.

—Attributed to Augustine

1 History: How John's Gospel Came to Be

The man who saw it has given testimony,
    and his testimony is true.
He knows that he tells the truth,
    and he testifies so that you also may believe.
                                    —John 19:35

Outline

- **Authorship**
  Internal Evidence
  External Evidence
- **Place and Date of Writing, Audience, Occasion, and Purpose**

Objectives

After reading this chapter, you should be able to

1. Analyze internal and external evidence for the Johannine authorship of John's Gospel.
2. Identify the place and date of writing of John's Gospel.
3. Provide an integrative discussion of John's audience, occasion, and purpose.

What is the life-setting of John's Gospel, the historical matrix out of which the message of the Fourth Gospel was born? The first question that arises is that of authorship. Two kinds of evidence can aid us in determining the answer to this crucial question: external evidence (information provided outside the Gospel, such as comments by the ancient Fathers) and internal evidence (data supplied by the text of John's Gospel itself). Traditionally, conservative interpreters have begun with a discussion of the external evidence. But some have objected to this procedure, arguing that to proceed thus causes us to have our minds already made up when we finally come to the Gospel. It is, of course, naive to believe that anyone can approach John's Gospel free from presuppositions. But the objection is still valid to some extent. We will therefore begin by discussing the internal evidence from John's Gospel and only then take a look at the external evidence.

Authorship

Internal Evidence

"The Word became flesh and made his dwelling among us. *We have seen his glory,* the glory of the One and Only, who came from the Father, full of grace and truth" (1:14): this is the opening testimony of John's Gospel. Who are the "we" who have seen Jesus' glory? We are given the answer on the heels of John's narration of Jesus' first sign: "This, the first of his miraculous signs, Jesus performed at Cana in Galilee. He thus revealed *his glory,* and *his disciples* put their faith in him" (2:11). At the very outset, John's Gospel thus claims to represent apostolic eyewitness testimony regarding Jesus' earthly ministry.

But which apostle was responsible for writing this account? Here we are helped by information provided at the very end of the Gospel. There Jesus, after dealing with Peter, is shown to converse with the so-called disciple whom Jesus loved (cf. 21:20). And then we are told the following: "This is the disciple who testifies to these things and who wrote them down. We know that his testimony is true"

(21:24). Thus we know that the man who wrote the Gospel was none other than the "disciple whom Jesus loved"—but who is he? He is first mentioned as such in 13:23 at the Last Supper in the Upper Room, reclining next to Jesus. Thus he must be one of the Twelve. At the same time, he cannot be any of the disciples named in chapters 13–16, that is, Peter, Philip, Thomas, Judas Iscariot, or Judas the son of James.

The "disciple whom Jesus loved" meets us again at the foot of the cross, where he is given charge of Jesus' mother (19:26–27) and becomes a firsthand witness of the crucifixion, asserting in language closely resembling that of 21:24, "The man who saw it has given testimony, and his testimony is true. He knows that he tells the truth, and he testifies so that you also may believe" (19:35). Finally, the "disciple whom Jesus loved" is shown at the empty tomb in chapter 20. All that is said about his reaction when he goes inside the tomb is that he "saw and believed" (20:8). As in the Upper Room, the "disciple whom Jesus loved" is here associated closely with the apostle Peter. This is also the case in the final chapter of John's Gospel, where the "disciple whom Jesus loved" alerts Peter that the figure on the other side of the shore is "the Lord" (21:7).

Since Peter and the "disciple whom Jesus loved" are here mentioned as part of a group of only seven disciples who go fishing by the Sea of Galilee, the "disciple whom Jesus loved" must be one of the following mentioned in 21:2: "Simon Peter, Thomas (called Didymus), Nathanael from Cana in Galilee, the sons of Zebedee, and two other disciples." Since it is part of this Gospel's characterization of the "disciple whom Jesus loved" that he is not named, he cannot be Simon Peter, Thomas (see already above), or Nathanael (= Bartholomew?); but he must be either one of the two sons of Zebedee or one of the two "other disciples." If he is one of the two sons of Zebedee, he can hardly be James, since according to 21:23 there was a rumor in the early church that the "disciple whom Jesus loved" would not die but James was martyred in A.D. 42 according to Acts 12:2 ("He [Herod Agrippa I] had James, the brother of John, put to death with the sword").

We may recapitulate: the author is

- an apostle
- the "disciple whom Jesus loved"
- one of the Twelve but cannot be Peter, Philip, Thomas, Judas Iscariot, or Judas the son of James
- one of the seven in John 21:2, but not Simon Peter, Thomas, or Nathanael
- either John the son of Zebedee (but not James his brother) or one of the two "other disciples" mentioned in 21:2

This means that, from the apostolic lists found in the **Synoptics** and Acts, only the following apostles remain (Andrew, Peter's brother, is an unlikely candidate owing to 1:40; see below):

- Matthew (Levi)
- Simon the Zealot
- James the son of Alphaeus
- John the son of Zebedee

Of these, Matthew is highly unlikely, because he is credited with writing another Gospel. Equally implausible are the obscure figures of Simon the Zealot and James the son of Alphaeus, whom, to my knowledge, no one has ever suggested as possible authors of John's Gospel. Which leaves John the son of Zebedee.

This conclusion from the internal evidence of the Fourth Gospel is corroborated also by data supplied by the Synoptic Gospels as well as Paul. It has already been pointed out that Peter and the "disciple whom Jesus loved" are regularly featured side by side in John's Gospel. The question is obvious: which is the disciple whom the other New Testament writings show to be closely associated with Peter in ministry in the early years of the church? The answer could not be more unambiguous: it is John the son of Zebedee (Lk 22:8; Acts 3–4; 8:14–25; Gal 2:9). Thus we are able to conclude that the internal evidence of John's Gospel, corroborated by evidence from the rest of the New Testament, points unequivocally to John the son of Zebedee as the author of John's Gospel. Apparently, this

also was the conclusion of the early Fathers, who unanimously support Johannine authorship (see the discussion of external evidence below).

But if this is the case, why did John not identify himself *explicitly* as the Gospel's author? Here we can only speculate. To begin with, it must be pointed out that while John's Gospel is formally anonymous, so are the other canonical Gospels. Thus the only difference between the Synoptics and John is that the author of John's Gospel features himself also in a prominent position in the narrative (see esp. 21:24). Why does he do this? One obvious answer is: historical fact. If John the son of Zebedee was the author of John's Gospel, he was not only one of the Twelve, but even one of three apostles who constituted Jesus' "inner circle": Peter, James, and John. Consider the following evidence:

—Peter, James, and John are amazed by the miraculous catch of fish recorded in Luke 5:8–10; there James and John are identified as Peter's "partners" or "associates" (*koinōnoi*) in fishing.

—Peter, James, and John are mentioned first in the apostolic lists in Mark 3:16–17 and Matthew 10:2 = Luke 6:14 (where Andrew's name is mentioned together with Simon Peter); and Acts 1:13.

—Peter, James, and John alone are witnesses of Jesus' raising of Jairus's daughter from the dead, one of only three raisings from the dead in all four Gospels combined (Mk 5:37; Lk 8:51).

—Peter, James, and John alone are witnesses of Jesus' transfiguration (Mk 9:2; Mt 17:1; Lk 9:28).

—Peter, James, and John, together with Andrew, ask Jesus privately about the end times in Mark 13:3 and are given an extensive response by Jesus.

—Peter, James, and John alone accompany Jesus as he withdraws to pray in the Garden of Gethsemane (Mk 14:33).

Interestingly, John's Gospel is silent regarding this "inner circle." There is no apostolic list, and there are no accounts of the transfiguration, the raising of Jairus's daughter, Jesus' end-time discourse, or Gethsemane. The most pertinent information is found in 1:35–42, the account of Jesus' calling of his first disciples. There two disciples, both followers of John the Baptist, are called to follow Jesus: one is Andrew, Simon Peter's brother; the other is unnamed. In light of the close association between Peter/Andrew and the sons of Zebedee in the Synoptics (cf., e.g., Lk 5:8), it is likely that this unnamed disciple vis-à-vis Andrew was one of the sons of Zebedee, and could very possibly have been John.

Thus historical evidence shows that John the son of Zebedee, the author of John's Gospel, was one of only three disciples in Jesus' "inner circle." This would certainly explain why the author of John's Gospel, John, features himself in a prominent role in his Gospel: it was required by historical fact. At the same time, it is not surprising that John would seek to avoid doing anything that would steal the spotlight from Jesus. Thus he invented the self-designation "the disciple whom Jesus loved." While this reconstruction has been challenged in recent years, it has not been refuted and remains the most plausible explanation of the available data.

But what does it matter? Is it not possible to accept John's Gospel regardless of who wrote it and to benefit from its lofty portrayal of Christ and its manifold lessons on what it means to follow him? Clearly, this is possible. And it must be acknowledged that affirming John the son of Zebedee as the author of John's Gospel is not an issue of biblical inerrancy or inspiration, since the fourth evangelist falls short of making such identification explicit. Nevertheless, holding John the son of Zebedee to be the author of John's Gospel matters a great deal. For Johannine authorship safeguards the Gospel's character as apostolic eyewitness testimony (which, as has been shown, is clearly suggested by the Gospel's internal evidence).

This, in turn, is highly significant in light of the unique, foundational, and authoritative function awarded apostolic teaching in the early church (cf. Acts 2:42; Eph 2:20; cf. also Jn 14:26; 15:27; 16:13). Therefore it does matter whether the author of John's Gospel was an apostolic eyewitness or an anonymous member of a late-first-century sect (as is proposed by the

Johannine community hypothesis), whether John's Gospel is a mainstream apostolic writing or a sectarian fringe document (for a brief critique of the "Johannine community hypothesis," see Appendix 1). Therefore it was necessary to present a thorough account of the Gospel's internal evidence, which turned out to be decidedly in favor of apostolic authorship.

External Evidence

Owing to its philosophical nature and universal language, John's Gospel was a favorite among the Gnostics (on which, see ch. 2 below). This is already borne out by the fact that the first known commentary written on John's Gospel was penned by a Gnostic, Heracleon. But when the church father Irenaeus used John's Gospel in order to *refute* Gnostic teaching in the second half of the second century A.D., the Gospel's place in the church's canon had been cemented once and for all. Claiming as his informant none other than Polycarp, himself a disciple of the late apostle John, Irenaeus writes, "John the disciple of the Lord, who leaned back on his breast, published the Gospel while he was resident at Ephesus in Asia" (*Adv. Haer.* 3.1.2). This early Father thus identified the author of John's Gospel unambiguously with John the apostle who is called "the disciple whom Jesus loved" in John 13:23 and later passages.

Echoing these sentiments, Clement of Alexandria remarks that "John, last of all, . . . composed a spiritual Gospel" (quoted by Eusebius, *H.E.* 6.14.7). From the end of the second century on, the church is virtually unanimous in attributing the Fourth Gospel's authorship to John, the son of Zebedee.

Those who question this attribution usually take their point of departure from Papias, quoted by Eusebius (*H.E.* 3.39.4–5), who is alleged to have referred to a second John other than the apostle, one "John the elder," whom they suggest as possible author of John's Gospel. But Papias may simply refer to John "the aforementioned elder" when distinguishing between deceased eyewitnesses of Jesus' ministry and those still alive.[1] Moreover, it strains credulity to believe that John's Gospel was written by a vir-

diaspora

proselytes

Dominus et Deus

tual unknown in the early church. Matthew was an apostle, Mark the associate of Peter (and Paul), and Luke the associate of Paul. Should we reject authorship of John's Gospel by the apostle John in favor of authorship by a "John the elder" of whom nothing is known apart from an obscure and dubious reference in Eusebius's rendition of Papias? This can hardly be considered to be the preferable alternative.

Thus we conclude that both internal and external evidence cohere in suggesting John, the son of Zebedee, to be the author of the Gospel that bears his name.

Place and Date of Writing, Audience, Occasion, and Purpose

Now that we have established the apostolic character of John's Gospel, we must investigate John's presumed provenance (place of writing), date, audience, occasion, and purpose. Since these questions are interrelated, they will be discussed jointly.

Regarding the place of writing, mention has already been made of the information supplied by the church father Irenaeus that "John . . . published the Gospel

The pavement, crushed from falling stones, speaks of the A.D. 70 destruction of the Jewish temple in Jerusalem.

while he was resident at Ephesus in Asia." No other location has the support of the early Fathers. But just because John *wrote* his Gospel in Ephesus does not mean that he wrote it to a church (or communities of believers) *in* Ephesus, or even if this was his primary audience, that he wrote his Gospel *exclusively* to the Ephesian churches. We will explore this issue more fully below in our discussion of the Gospel's audience.

Regarding the date of writing, the period subsequent to the destruction of the temple in Jerusalem seems likely. As will be argued in greater detail below, John's emphasis on Jesus' replacement of the temple and Jewish feasts probably represents an effort to exploit the temple's destruction evangelistically in an effort to reach **diaspora** Jews and Gentiles attracted to Judaism **(proselytes)**.[2] If so, a date after A.D. 70, but not *immediately* in the aftermath of the traumatic events in Jerusalem, seems most likely. Also, the reference to Peter's martyrdom in 21:19 seems to indicate that this event had already taken place at the time of writing. Since Peter was martyred around A.D. 65, this, too, points to a date toward the last decades of the first century A.D. This would place the time of composition in the reign of the Roman emperor Domitian (A.D. 81–96). Most fascinating is the fact that coins of that time period have been found that identify Domitian as **"Dominus et Deus"**

The Arch of Titus near the Colosseum commemorates this Roman general's triumph at the occasion of the fall of Jerusalem in A.D. 70.

(Lord and God), the precise equivalent of Thomas's confession of Jesus as "my Lord and my God" in 20:28. Thus 20:28 may represent a not-so-thinly veiled allusion to Christians' confession vis-à-vis that required by the Roman emperor of John's day. For these reasons a date in the A.D. 80s seems most likely.

Regarding the Gospel's audience, we note both the universal character of John's Gospel and the emphasis on the Jews' rejection of Jesus in the first half of John's Gospel. Taken together, these elements point to Jews and Gentiles attracted to Judaism in the dispersion (diaspora), the larger Greco-Roman world of the end of the first century A.D. Richard Bauckham has recently argued persuasively that all four canonical Gospels were "Gospels for all Christians."[3] John thus was written, not merely to the Ephesian churches, even less merely to segments of the "Johannine com-

munity" or a Jewish parent synagogue from which the sectarians had been expelled, but to the church at large. After all, John's Gospel is a *Gospel*, heralding the universal good news of salvation in Christ.

We sum up our findings thus far: John probably wrote his Gospel in the A.D. 80s in Ephesus, primarily to diaspora Jews and Gentiles attracted to the Jewish faith, but ultimately to the church at large. But what was the occasion for his writing, and which purpose did he pursue by authoring the Gospel? It is to this question that we must now turn.

We already alluded to the fact that the destruction of the Jerusalem temple left a gaping void in Jewish life, especially in Palestine, but also in the diaspora. Judaism without a temple meant Judaism without a fully operational sacrificial system, including the priesthood. This situation was similar to that of the Babylonian exile (starting in 606/586 B.C.), which led to the development of local cells of instruction and worship, that is, synagogues. How would Judaism cope with the destruction of the temple this time? As it turns out, the major development was that of rabbinic Judaism led by the Pharisees. But it took decades, if not centuries, for rabbinic Judaism to become the dominant force in Judaism. Certainly at the time John wrote his Gospel, the recent traumatic

events in Palestine provided a window of opportunity.[4]

The question of what would now become of Judaism was in everyone's mind. John's answer is clear: he hoped to encourage diaspora Jews and proselytes to turn to Jesus, the Messiah who fulfilled the symbolism embodied in the temple and the Jewish feasts. For John, the temple's destruction thus becomes an opportunity for Jewish evangelism. He invites

Is John's Gospel an Anonymous Work?

The author of a recent essay on rhetoric in John's Gospel assesses the nature of this work as follows: "With regard to the Gospel, it is possible that the allusions to the 'beloved disciple' in the Gospel of John are a literary device to refer obliquely to the author, with the further possibility that the 'beloved disciple' is the Johannine reference to the apostle John, the son of Zebedee, so named in the synoptic tradition. This scenario would correspond to the early external attestation that the Gospel is written by the apostle John. In the end, however, the Gospel of John must be regarded as an anonymous text" (Dennis L. Stamps, "The Johannine Writings," in *Handbook of Classical Rhetoric in the Hellenistic Period 330 B.C.–A.D. 400*, ed. Stanley E. Porter [Leiden: Brill, 1997], 611).

David R. Beck, the author of a recent volume entitled *The Discipleship Paradigm: Readers and Anonymous Characters in the Fourth Gospel* (Leiden: Brill, 1997), takes a similar approach, following the highly influential work by R. Alan Culpepper, *The Anatomy of the Fourth Gospel: A Study in Literary Design* (Philadelphia: Fortress, 1983). Are these authors right? Is it really adequate to classify John's Gospel simply as an anonymous text (and nothing more) and then to explore the literary features of this work in a somewhat detached, anesthetized fashion? This certainly does seem to follow the "aesthetic turn" in biblical studies so ably chronicled by Kevin J. Vanhoozer in his perceptive essay "A Lamp in the Labyrinth: The Hermeneutics of 'Aesthetic' Theology," *Trinity Journal* 8 (1987): 25–56.

The place to start in an assessment of this question is at an understanding of the Gospel **genre**. It appears that while the author of such

a work did not explicitly identify himself—perceiving himself as the servant of the larger Christian community in writing his Gospel—this does not make the document he produces "anonymous" the way the term would be understood in modern parlance. For literally the term means "without a name," which may not merely imply that no name is attached to a given work, but also that the author of this particular document is genuinely unknown to its recipients or others. But while "anonymous" may be a fitting label in the first sense of the term, it is hardly adequate in the second sense. In fact, as the label "Gospel according to John," attached early in the second century, clearly attests, the author (or at least the person on whose authority the work rested) was not an unknown among the early Christians.

Should we then read John's Gospel as an "anonymous" work? What about statements such as the one in John 1:14 that "we have seen his glory"? What about the assurance given to the readers of the Gospel that "the man who saw it [i.e., Jesus' crucifixion] has given testimony, and his testimony is true. He knows that he tells the truth, and he testifies so that you also may believe" (19:35; cf. 21:24)? A depersonalized, "literarily correct" reading of John's Gospel hardly does justice to such intensely personal, experiential appeals. No, the sheer absence of a name attached to John's Gospel does not by itself render this work "anonymous." Rather, we should read this work as an apostolic account of a close eyewitness of the events surrounding Jesus' earthly ministry. This kind of reading alone can truly claim to use the Gospel as it was intended to be used by the one who wrote it.

Study Questions

1. Set forth the various pieces of internal evidence for Johannine authorship from John's Gospel in consecutive logical order.

2. Briefly sketch the external evidence for the Johannine authorship of John's Gospel.

3. Discuss the place and date of writing of John's Gospel as well as its audience, occasion, and purpose.

Key Words

internal evidence

external evidence

Synoptics

Johannine community hypothesis

diaspora

proselytes

Dominus et Deus

genre

his countrymen to take another look at Jesus, the crucified and risen Messiah, the Son of God. This, of course, would have been true to Paul's motto: "first for the Jew, then for the Gentiles" (Rom 1:16; Acts). This does not mean that John's Gospel was an evangelistic document written *directly* to unbelievers.[5] Rather, John probably wrote in order to equip believers to proclaim the message of Jesus the Messiah among their unbelieving audiences.

Also, the fact that John may have written primarily to nonmessianic Jews and proselytes does not mean that the Gospel was limited to such. The universal character of John makes the unmistakable point that Christianity is, and has become, a universal religion, and that salvation is by faith, not by joining Jews in *their* worship and religious practice. The implication for interested Jews is that they are invited to join the new messianic community made up of Jews and Gentiles, but that they must do so not on Jewish terms but on universal terms, that is, faith in Jesus as "the way, the truth, and the life."

We conclude therefore that John's occasion for writing was the destruction of the temple in Jerusalem, which he considered to be an opportunity to present Jesus as filling the void left thereby. John's purpose for writing his Gospel was (indirect) Jewish evangelism. One last point must be made: Some may cite the increasingly strained relations between Christians and Jews after A.D. 70 as evidence that it is unlikely that John, a Christian, sought to evangelize Jews. But to the contrary, it is unthinkable that John, himself a Jew, would ever have given up seeking to convert his fellow-Jews to his unshakable conviction that Jesus was in fact the Messiah and that "no one comes to the Father except through him."

Finally, does this mean that the Gospel is not directly relevant for us? Not at all. But we must first learn to appreciate John's Gospel in its original context in order to understand John's message authentically and appropriately. In God's providence, then, the Gospel's audience is not *limited* to its first readers and intended recipients; it also extends to us. And in God's providence, we may benefit from John's Gospel by deriving spiritual insights from it not even envisioned by John himself. This is entirely legitimate, yet these insights must still be informed and constrained by the Gospel John actually wrote. We, too, should use John's Gospel in an evangelistic context rather than merely for the purpose of our own edification. And just as in John's day, it is of crucial importance today that Jesus, and Jesus alone, is the universal Savior, the one and only way provided by God for us to have our sins forgiven, to be saved, and to experience eternal life.

2 Literature: Mapping John's Story

It was just before the Passover Feast. Jesus knew that the time had come for him to leave this world and go to the Father. Having loved his own who were in the world, he now showed them the full extent of his love.

—John 13:1

Outline

- **The Recent Rise of Literary Criticism in Biblical Studies**
- **What Is a Gospel?**
- **What Is the Outline of John's Gospel?**
- **What Are the Major Structural Components of John's Gospel?**

Objectives

After reading this chapter, you should be able to

1. Correct distortions in a purely or predominantly literary approach to John's Gospel.
2. Identify the proper genre of John.
3. Sketch out the structure and major literary motifs of John's narrative.

historical-critical method

The Recent Rise of Literary Criticism in Biblical Studies

Recent years have seen increasing attention being devoted to literary aspects of John's Gospel. John's Gospel is not alone in this regard. The science of literary criticism as practiced in nonbiblical studies has invaded the exegetical enterprise, often to the extent of overshadowing traditional historical and theological concerns. Several factors may account for this phenomenon:

1. a growing disenchantment with the limitations of the so-called **historical-critical method:** it became clear that while the historicity of events recorded in Scripture is important, it is reductionistic to limit exegesis (biblical interpretation) to the assessment of the historicity of certain events alone; the study of various literary aspects of biblical narratives can helpfully supplement the historical-critical method

2. an impasse regarding historical questions in biblical scholarship: it became apparent that consensus was elusive regarding matters such as the authorship of John's Gospel; so why not choose agnosticism in this regard, agree to disagree, leave historical concerns aside altogether, and move on to an area of investigation that appears to offer almost limitless potential for fruitful exploration, that of the study of a biblical book "as literature"

3. the meteoric rise of postmodernism in reaction to the perceived flaws of modernism: a preoccupation with factual historicity and absolute, objective, propositional truth must give way, it was argued, to more dynamic models of knowing, focusing instead on subjective experience, the cultural relativity of various interpretive communities, and other factors; once the author was dethroned as determinative for interpretation, the isolated text proved patent to interpretations by interpreters of various stripes and backgrounds[1]

What should be our response to the rising dominance of literary criticism in biblical studies? We may express concern regarding the following developments spawned by literary methods:

1. Recent years have witnessed a deplorable deemphasis on theology. Literature is a medium, a vehicle to convey a message. Once the study of the medium (the literary art of the fourth evangelist) has overshadowed the apprehension of the message (John's desire to lead his readers to faith; 19:35; 20:31), biblical priorities have been reversed.

2. Inherent in much of literary criticism is also an illegitimate dichotomy between literature and history. As already mentioned, the literary study of biblical narratives has often become an avenue for avoiding the historical dimensions of the text of Scripture. But here we must say with Paul that, if Christ has not been raised, our faith is futile, and we are still in our sins: "If only for this life we have hope in Christ, we are to be pitied more than all men" (1 Cor 15:17, 19). Christianity is a historical religion, not merely an exercise in art appreciation. Scripture is not merely world literature, a classic document of Western civilization, it is divine revelation that confronts readers with their sin and need for salvation and forgiveness, calling upon them to make a choice that has eternal ramifications: to receive Christ's free gift of salvation or to reject it. Readers of Scripture are not merely dispassionate literary critics—they are existentially addressed and engaged by the biblical message and must act in response to it rather than merely revel in interesting plot lines, masterful characterization, or various other instances of skillful literary techniques employed by the biblical authors.

In a culture where the medium is the message and image is frequently more important than substance, it is, of course, not surprising that the literary study of Scripture is elevated above historical and theological concerns. But faithfulness to the intentions of the authors of Scripture

aretalogy

Midrash

demands that the historical and theological dimensions of biblical narratives are given their due and the literary investigation of a given text be kept in proper perspective. This said, a proper appreciation of the literary devices used by John or other biblical authors will indeed be useful to enhance our appreciation of John's Gospel.

Now before we delve into a discussion of how John's Gospel came to be, we must establish some basic ground rules on how to study this work. In a seminal work on the subject written in 1967, E. D. Hirsch points to the crucial importance of genre in interpretation.[2] Genre, simply put, is the kind of literature a work represents: novel, science fiction, romance, biography, historical narrative, or the like. In keeping with Hirsch's insight, we must therefore first ask, and attempt to answer, the following questions: What is a Gospel? And what kind of Gospel is the Gospel of John?

What Is a Gospel?

The Greek word for gospel is *euangelion,* which means "good news." The Hebrew *basar,* "bear (good) tidings," is found frequently in the Old Testament (e.g. Ps 95:1; Is 40:9; 52:7; 61:1). Jesus referred to the gospel of the kingdom of God, Christians used the term to refer to the good news of salvation in Christ. Mark opens his Gospel with the words, "The beginning of the gospel about Jesus Christ, the Son of God." This may be the first time *euangelion* is used not merely for a spoken message but for a written work (a "Gospel") that contains the story of how this good news came about through the life, death, and crucifixion of Jesus. Toward the end of the first or at the beginning of the second century A.D., titles were given to the canonical Gospels: "Gospel according to Matthew," "Gospel according to Mark," and so on.[3] This kind of designation reflects early church belief that there is only *one* gospel but that there are four canonical *versions* of this gospel, the Gospels "according to" the four evangelists. In the middle of the second century, Justin uses the word "Gospel" for the canonical accounts of Jesus' ministry (*Apol.* 1.66; *Dial.* 10.2).

The question has been asked whether the genre "Gospel" is a unique Christian invention or, if not, which other ancient kind of writing provides a parallel type of literature. The following possibilities have been suggested:

1. Greek **aretalogy:** stories of miraculous deeds of a godlike hero
2. Jewish **Midrash:** legendary expansions of historical narrative
3. Greco-Roman biography: accounts of the lives of great political or other leaders

Some have suggested that the Gospel of Mark, for example, presents Jesus as a "divine man" along the lines of Greco-Roman culture. Others have argued that the first few chapters of Matthew, for example, represent Midrash, that is, expansions of Old Testament materials with reference to the early years of Jesus' life. But by far the most frequent suggestion is that the Gospels fit the pattern of Greco-Roman biography. What are we to make of this suggestion?

First of all, it is true that Gospels, like ancient biographies, portray significant events in the life of an important person. But unlike biographies, Gospels are anonymous, lack literary pretension, and combine teaching and action in a preaching-oriented work. Also, ancient biographies recount the deeds of a person only as a means of illuminating his essence. We may thus call Gospels biographies with unique aspects, or a unique genre with points of contact with ancient biography (as well as other genres). As one standard work has it, "the uniqueness of the Person on whom they focus has forced the evangelists to create a literary form that is without clear parallel."[4]

A perceptive refinement of this position has recently been advocated by Swartley, who argues that the closest genre parallel for the Gospels is in fact Old Testament historiography (the writing of history), that is, works such as the books of Samuel, Kings, or Chronicles.[5] Similar to the Gospel narratives of Jesus, these accounts of portions of the history of Israel include the interpretation of the significance of these events from a divine perspective.

In the end, we must allow the four writers of the canonical Gospels to write their own story. The question is therefore not merely, "What is a Gospel?" but "Which kind of Gospel did John write?" And at this point it is striking that John, in keeping with the conventions of ancient biographies, recounts the deeds of a person primarily as a means of illuminating his essence.

What Is the Outline of John's Gospel?

How does John write his Gospel? Unlike the other canonical Gospels, he does not aim at a fairly detailed account of events of Jesus' ministry. Rather, John is highly selective. The major convictions underlying the writing of John's Gospel can be listed as follows:

1. Jesus' uniqueness: his deity as well as his humanity
2. Jesus' messiahship: Jesus is the Messiah promised in the Old Testament
3. the new messianic community: Israel, the old covenant community, is replaced by the new covenant community made up of believers in Jesus the Messiah

According to his purpose statement in 20:30–31, John selects certain signs performed by Jesus to prove that Jesus is in fact the Messiah. We may diagram the structure of John's Gospel, with a focus on these signs, as follows:

Prologue (1:1–18)

I. **The Book of Signs (1:19–12:50): The Signs of the Messiah**

   A. Inaugural Signs (1:19–4:54)
   1. Changing water into wine (2:1–11): "first sign" in Cana of Galilee
   2. Temple cleansing (2:14–17): one of Jesus' Jerusalem signs (cf. 2:23; 3:2)
   3. Healing of the nobleman's son (4:41–54): "second sign" in Cana of Galilee

   B. Signs amidst Mounting Controversy (chs. 5–10)

   4. Healing of lame man (5:1–15)
   5. Feeding of multitude (6:1–15)
   6. Healing of blind man (ch. 9)
      Inclusion: no signs by John the Baptist, but his witness concerning Jesus is true (10:40–42)

   C. The Climactic Sign (11:1–12:19)
   7. Raising of Lazarus (ch. 11)

   D. Conclusion: The Dawning Age of the Gentiles (12:20–36) and the Signs of the Messiah Rejected by the Old Covenant Community (12:37–50)

II. **The Book of Glory (chs. 13–20): Jesus' Passion and Preparation of the New Covenant Community**

   A. The Cleansing and Instruction of the New Covenant Community, including Jesus' Final Prayer (chs. 13–17)
   B. The Passion Narrative (chs. 18–19)
   C. The Resurrection Appearances and the Commissioning of Jesus' Disciples (ch. 20)
   D. Conclusion: The Signs of the Messiah Witnessed by the New Covenant Community (20:30–31)

Epilogue (ch. 21)

By way of strategic overview, we may trace the compositional flow of John's Gospel as follows.

What Are the Major Structural Components of John's Gospel?

The Prologue sets John's entire Gospel into the framework of the eternal, preexistent Word-become-flesh in Jesus (1:1–18). The first half of John's narrative portrays Jesus as Messiah by selecting seven representative signs (1:19–12:50; cf. 20:30–31). John also marshals Jesus' seven **"I am" sayings** (6:25–59; 8:12 = 9:5; 10:7, 9, 11; 11:25; 14:6; 15:1) and several witnesses: John (the Baptist; 1:7–8, 15, 32, 34; 3:32; 5:33); the Samaritan woman (4:39); Moses (chs. 5, 9); the Father (5:37; 8:16); Jesus himself, including his own works (3:11; 5:36; 8:14, 18; 10:25, 32, 37–38; 13:21; 18:37); the

farewell discourse

Paraclete

Spirit and the disciples (15:26–27); and the fourth evangelist (19:35; 21:24).

According to John, all these witnesses support the notion that Jesus is in fact the Messiah and the Son of God. In the Synoptics, it is Jesus who is on trial. John reverses this pattern: it is actually the world that is on trial, and all the above characters are on the witness stand, testifying to Jesus' messianic identity while convicting the world (including "the Jews") of its guilt of sin and unbelief.

But what kind of Messiah is Jesus? John skillfully interweaves three portraits that complement one another:

1. Jesus is the one who came into the world and returned to the place from where he came (descent-ascent): this aspect of John's Christology focuses on the otherworldly origin and divinity of Jesus
2. Jesus is the sent Son: here the emphasis lies on the closeness and uniqueness of relationship sustained by Jesus and God the Father
3. Jesus is the eschatological (end-time) shepherd-teacher: the Old Testament (e.g., Ezek 34) predicted that Yahweh (one of the names for God in the Old Testament) would visit, care for, and teach his people; in fact, he would send his servant David (the Son of David) to accomplish this mission; as it turns out, this eschatological shepherd-teacher is Jesus

Study Questions

1. Raise appropriate cautions regarding the rise of literary criticism in biblical studies in recent years.

2. Discuss and critique the various suggestions of genre parallels to the canonical Gospels.

3. Provide a basic outline of the Book of John with emphasis on the Johannine signs.

4. Identify and trace other important structural components of John throughout the Gospel.

In developing his presentation of Jesus' messianic identity, John traces people's (esp. "the Jews'") response to Jesus' claims by featuring characters in his Gospel asking representative questions or confessing Jesus as Messiah. This device serves the purpose of leading the readers of John's Gospel to arrive at the conclusion stated in 20:31: "Jesus is the Christ, the Son of God." Thus in 1:41, Andrew tells Peter: "We have found the Messiah." In 4:29, the Samaritan woman tells her countrymen: "Come, see a man who told me everything I ever did. Could this be the Christ?" In 7:26 and 31, the crowd at the Feast queries, "Here he is, speaking publicly, and they are not saying a word to him. Have the authorities really concluded that he is the Christ? . . . When the Christ comes, will he do more miraculous signs than this man?" In 10:24, the Jews confront Jesus: "How long will you keep us in suspense? If you are the Christ, tell us plainly." And in 11:27, Martha confesses, "I believe that you are the Christ, the Son of God, who was to come into the world."

Overall, while the first portion of John's Gospel (chs. 1–12) portrays the earthly Jesus' (failed) mission to the Jews, the second part (chs. 13–21) presents the exalted Jesus' mission with and through his new messianic community. The **farewell discourse** (chs. 13–17) tells of the cleansing (footwashing and Judas's departure; ch. 13) and preparation of the messianic community (instructions concerning the coming **Paraclete** and his ministry to the disciples; chs. 14–16) as well as Jesus' final prayer on behalf of his own (ch. 17). John's passion narrative (chs. 18–19) shows Jesus' death both as providing atonement for sin (cf. already 1:29, 36; 6:48–58; 10:15, 17–18), though largely drained of notions of shame and humiliation (contrast the Synoptics), and as a station on Jesus' return to the Father (e.g. 13:1; 16:28).

The account of the crucifixion and burial of Jesus is followed by the narration of his resurrection appearances and commissioning of his disciples (ch. 20). Jesus, the Sent One par excellence (9:7), is now the one who sends his new messianic community (20:21–23). The disciples are to depend on Jesus and to obey him the way he depended on and obeyed the Father

Paraclete

during his earthly mission. The disciples are taken into the life of the Godhead, which is characterized by perfect love and unity (chs. 14–17), and are appointed partners in the proclamation of salvation and forgiveness in Christ (15:15–16; 20:21–23). The purpose statement in 20:30–31 reiterates the major motifs of the entire narrative: the "signs"; believing; (eternal) life; and Jesus as Christ and Son of God.

The concluding chapter portrays the relationship between Peter and the "disciple whom Jesus loved" in terms of differing yet equally valid roles of service within the community of believers.

Key Words

historical-critical method

aretalogy

Midrash

"I am" sayings

farewell discourse

Paraclete

3 Theology: John's Major Themes

> But that John, last of all, conscious that the outward facts had been set forth in the Gospels, was urged on by his disciples, and, divinely moved by the Spirit, composed a spiritual Gospel.
>
> —Eusebius (*H. E.* 6.14.7), referring to Clement of Alexandria

Outline

Objectives

After reading this chapter, you should be able to

1. Compare and contrast John and the Synoptic Gospels.
2. Delineate the conceptual background of John.
3. Identify and trace the major themes of John's Gospel.

aphoristic

symbolic
discourses

eschatology

We've looked at the historical setting of John, and we've looked at John's literary dimension. We now turn to the pinnacle of the study of John's Gospel, the apprehension of its theological message. Three topics will be particularly significant in this regard: first, a comparison between John and the Synoptics; second, the identification of the conceptual background of John's Gospel; and third, an investigation of major Johannine themes.

John and the Synoptics

Differences and Similarities

It does not take a genius to discover that John's Gospel differs markedly from the Synoptic Gospels (Matthew, Mark, Luke). Consider the following material found in the Synoptics but not in John:

- narrative parables
- Jesus' teaching on the kingdom of God
- **aphoristic** sayings (with few exceptions)[1]
- the eschatological discourse
- the Sermon on the Mount, including the Lord's Prayer
- an account of Jesus' baptism by John
- an account of the institution of the Lord's Supper
- an account of the Transfiguration
- an account of Jesus' temptation by Satan
- an account of Gethsemane
- demon exorcisms

On the other hand, John has the following "substitutes":

- **symbolic discourses** (such as on the vine and the branches in ch. 15) for narrative parables
- teaching on (eternal) life rather than the kingdom of God
- extended discourses rather than aphoristic sayings
- an emphasis on realized **eschatology** rather than an eschatological discourse
- the farewell discourse (chs. 13–17) but not the Sermon on the Mount

- accounts of Jesus' interaction with John the Baptist, of Jesus as the "Bread from Heaven," or of scenes in the Upper Room, but not accounts of Jesus' actual baptism or his institution of the Lord's Supper
- Satan as Jesus' chief antagonist working through Judas the betrayer but no demon exorcisms

How Do We Account for These Differences?

Traditionally, the explanation for these striking differences has been that John wrote to supplement the Synoptics. As Clement of Alexandria stated, John was "conscious that the outward facts had been set forth in the [Synoptic] Gospels." More recently, the theory that John wrote independently of the Synoptics has gained ground. If this means that John did not make extensive use of the Synoptics as he wrote, or even that he did not let his agenda be set by the other Gospels, this seems almost self-evident in light of the different approaches taken. However, if this means that John was unaware of the existence of these Gospels or that he had never read them, this raises the question where John must have been located, especially if he wrote considerably later than the Synoptists, so that he remained unaware of or unexposed to these other Gospels. Certainly if the author of John's Gospel was John, the son of Zebedee, this is unimaginable. Only if the Fourth Gospel is presented as a sectarian document entirely outside the mainstream of apostolic Christianity can such a position be maintained.

Arguably, John's Gospel contains traces of acquaintance with the Synoptic tradition (if not the actual written Gospels) with which John expects his readers to be familiar. Note, for example, 1:40, where Andrew is called "Simon Peter's brother," even though Peter had not yet been mentioned. Or consider 3:24: "(This was before John [the Baptist] was put in prison)." This assumes that John's readers know of the Baptist's imprisonment toward the end of his life; but his Gospel has made no mention of it whatsoever up to that point. John 4:44 is another instance, where the evangelist interjects that Jesus himself had pointed out that a prophet has no honor in his own country, apparently expecting his readers' familiarity with this saying. But it is not recorded in his own Gospel; it is rather found in Mark 6:4 = Matthew 13:57 = Luke 4:24.

Or note 11:1–2, where John, in providing background information regarding the raising of Lazarus, identifies Bethany as "the village of Mary and her sister Martha" and proceeds as follows: "This Mary, whose brother Lazarus now lay sick, was the same one who poured perfume on the Lord and wiped his feet with her hair," an event not mentioned until the following chapter in this Gospel. Does John expect his readers to have read Luke's account of "distracted Martha" and "devoted Mary" at this point (Lk 10:38–41)? Or is he simply expecting them to be familiar with Synoptic tradition? In any case, he assumes a basic familiarity on part of his readers with the Gospel story. Likewise, John casually mentions "the Twelve" (6:67) and notes that Judas the betrayer was "one of the Twelve" (6:71), even though he has not previously used the term "Twelve" in his Gospel.

Conclusion and Implications

We conclude that John was certainly familiar with Synoptic tradition and probably also one or several of the Synoptic Gospels, but that he saw fit not to let them set his agenda. In this sense, then, John wrote independently. As Clement of Alexandria puts it, John "composed a spiritual Gospel." By this Clement did not mean to imply that the other Gospels are unspiritual, but that John is more overtly interested in the *theological* underpinnings of Jesus' person and work than are the Synoptics.

This is borne out, for example, by John's transposition of Synoptic miracles (*dynameis*, works of power) into "signs" (*sēmeia*, significant acts that may or may not actually be "miraculous"). For John, what is significant is not Jesus' amazing deeds in and of themselves. Rather, all of Jesus' "works" point to the essence of who Jesus is—the Christ, the Son of God. In the style of ancient biographies, John recounts the deeds of a person (in this case, Jesus) primarily as a means of illuminating his essence. Other instances of this approach include John's emphasis on Jesus' preexistence and the seven "I am sayings."

What should therefore be our proper approach to John's Gospel? First and foremost, we should not read it with constant reference to how it supplements the Synoptic Gospels—that would be to reduce John's Gospel to the menial task of filling in gaps in the other Gospel writings. If John did not write his Gospel with the intention of providing a mere complement to the Synoptics, we should respect his desire and treat his Gospel accordingly. A more satisfying approach is therefore to "let John be John" and to let John himself set his own agenda.

There remain significant common elements between John and the Synoptics: both are Gospels; both focus on Jesus' earthly ministry culminating in his crucifixion, burial, and resurrection; and both have as their "minor theme" the question of what it means to be Jesus' disciple and to follow him. But John and the Synoptics should be regarded as independent witnesses to the same Jesus in whom the gospel centers, complementary portraits in "stereo" (or "quadro") of one and the same person and history.

The Conceptual Background of John's Gospel

In chapter 1, we identified the time period following the destruction of the Jerusalem temple in A.D. 70 as the most likely scenario underlying the writing of John's Gospel. We have suggested that John sought to fill the void left by the events of A.D. 70 with his presentation of Jesus as the replacement for the temple and the fulfillment of the symbolism of the various Jewish feasts. The primary purpose for this was shown to be (Jewish) mission, John's desire to persuade particularly diaspora Jews and proselytes that the Messiah and Son of God is in fact Jesus. It remains here simply to tie in this presumed historical background with John's conceptual framework.

The problem is that frequently John's historical background and theological themes are not interrelated. Either John is believed to be the apostle who presents his theological (religious) views regarding

parallelomania

God-fearers

Jesus, without adequate attention being given to the circumstances leading to the writing of his Gospel. Or the life-setting of John's Gospel is dwelt upon to the extent that the Gospel's background overwhelms John's theological message. In fact, however, it is John's contemporary situation that provides the occasion for him to frame his account the way he does. The historical context and John's purpose for writing combine to influence his choice of particular theological terms in order for him to achieve his desired goal.

Two Approaches: History-of-Religions and Salvation-Historical

Two major approaches to ascertaining John's background can be identified: the history-of-religions model and the salvation-historical school of thought. In its purest form, the history-of-religions model utilizes a comparative religions approach that views Scripture from essentially an evolutionary vantage point. The history of Israel, the life of Jesus, and the development of the early church are viewed in terms of the evolution of human religious consciousness.

When proponents of this approach turn to the study of John's Gospel, their primary interest is directed toward identifying possible parallels in other religious movements contemporary with the writing of John's Gospel. Suggestions range from various Hellenistic sources (Mandaean literature, Hermetic writings) to Qumran (Dead Sea Scrolls) to Jewish wisdom literature. But as Samuel Sandmel has pointed out so trenchantly, we must beware of **parallelomania,** drawing conclusions regarding conceptual backgrounds from surface parallels that may not actually have led John to frame his theological message the way he did.[2]

Ultimately, it is not isolated parallels but the entire fabric of John's text that must be studied in this regard. And here one of the most helpful recent works is a book by John Pryor entitled *John: Evangelist of the Covenant People.* Pryor, following a salvation-historical approach, adduces the following parallels:

1. the use of "his own" with reference to Israel in 1:11 and with regard to Jesus' followers in 13:1

2. the claim that Jesus' glory "dwelt among us" (that is, the new messianic community), in allusion to God's dwelling among his old covenant people Israel (1:14)
3. the insistence that Jesus' sonship is unique (e.g., 1:14, 18; 3:16, 18)
4. the Fourth Gospel's portrayal of Jesus as the Mosaic Prophet, even though Jesus exceeds both Moses and Abraham categories (1:17; 8:58)
5. the implication of 1:51 that Jesus replaces Israel as the place where God's glory is revealed
6. the patterning of the farewell discourse in John 13–17 after the Book of Deuteronomy
7. John's adaptation of the covenantal terminology and patterns found in the primary texts of Judaism, that is, Exodus and Deuteronomy (e.g. to love, obey, live, know, and see in 14:15–24)
8. the insistence of 15:1 that Jesus is the "true" vine embodying the true Israel
9. the use of "shepherd" and "flock" imagery for the relationship between Jesus and a community that transcends Jewish ethnic lines
10. the "creation" of the new messianic community by Jesus' breathing the Spirit on it (20:22)[3]

What this list makes clear is that John was steeped in Old Testament concepts and that he consciously related events in the life of Jesus to previous events in the history of Israel. John viewed history as the plane on which God's plan of salvation unfolded, progressively unveiled and pursued in Old Testament times, but dramatically escalated in the coming of Jesus the Messiah. Even diaspora Jews and proselytes, as well as other interested Gentiles (the so-called **God-fearers**) would have sufficient acquaintance with the Old Testament record to be able to understand John's conceptual background rooted in the history of Israel and the Old Testament Scriptures.

John's Theological Message in Its Historical Context

But we must not stop here. It is only part of our task to identify John's conceptual background. We must also determine John's immediate historical context which led him to frame his theological

logos

message as is evident in his Gospel. And this is where data converge in the period following A.D. 70 where the argument could be singularly persuasive that Jesus, and Jesus alone, matched the fabric of Old Testament information regarding the coming Messiah, including direct prediction, typological patterns, and other hints of things to come. As Richard Bauckham has argued, John's Gospel must not be confined to a "Johannine community" or even to the Ephesian church; it is a universal document that is "for all Christians."[4]

Moreover, it is a document that is not merely designed to edify those who already believe but rather primarily seeks to provide believers with a tool for evangelism. Jesus' vision of the church as "one flock" under "one shepherd" (10:16) had the potential of healing both the trauma recently experienced by the Jewish nation and the strained relationship between Jews and Gentiles. John's Gospel is engaged in mission, even at a time when Rome persecutes Christians and Jewish synagogues expel Christians from their midst. As a Christian as well as a Jew, John could do no less—as did Paul, he had "great sorrow and unceasing anguish" in his heart for the people of Israel and believed that the saving message of the gospel of Jesus Christ must be proclaimed among all, "that whoever believes in him shall not perish but have eternal life" (3:16).

Major Themes

God

God is known in John's Gospel primarily in two ways: as "the one who sent" Jesus (e.g., 5:37) and as the Father of the Son (e.g., 5:17–23). This already indicates that God himself is not the direct focus of attention in John's Gospel. This distinction belongs to Jesus. For the Jews already believed in God; the issue was whether they would believe that Jesus was the Messiah and Son of God. Thus Jesus' relationship with God becomes the inevitable focal point. While Jesus claims oneness with God (e.g., 10:30–39), "the Jews" cast doubts on his paternity, possibly even insinuating that he may be an illegitimate child (8:41). In the end, John's readers must make up their mind: is

Jesus' claim that he came from God and is one with him accurate? If so, Jesus must be worshiped as God and Lord; if not, he is a false Messiah and deserved to die. As C. S. Lewis said, Jesus is either lunatic, liar, or Lord[5]—with this statement John would have agreed wholeheartedly.

The Christ

The entire purpose of John's Gospel is tied up with Christology. John seeks to demonstrate that Jesus is the Son of God, the Christ (cf. 20:30–31). It is to this end that he presents seven selected signs (chs. 2–11). "The Jews" don't believe, so Jesus focuses his final hours on working with the twelve (minus Judas), his new messianic community (chs. 13–17, 20–21).

The striking opening of John's Gospel establishes a connection between God's act of creation through his Word and his act of providing salvation through the incarnate Word, Jesus. The background for this **logos** Christology is probably the Old Testament understanding that God sends his Word to accomplish his purposes (cf. Is 55:10–11) which is seen as hypostatized in Jesus. The term "logos" appears in John in a christological sense only in the Prologue and functions as an umbrella term for Jesus in the rest of the Gospel (on Jesus' preexistence, see also 8:58; 17:5).

Jesus is presented as the Son of the Father, a formulation that later became important for the church's development of its trinitarian theology. Jesus employs here a metaphor rooted in Jewish life, that is, the sending of a son by his father. A son, especially one's firstborn, could be uniquely trusted to be faithful in carrying out his father's commission.[6]

While the designation of Jesus as Son blends elements of his humanity and deity, other elements of John's Christology focus more explicitly on Jesus' divine nature. Among these are:

1. Jesus as the preexistent "Word" (1:1, 14) as well as other claims to Jesus' preexistence (8:58; 12:41; 17:5)
2. Jesus' "signs" (e.g., 2:11)
3. Jesus' "I am sayings," which allude to the Old Testament name of God (cf. esp. Ex 3:14; Is)
4. Jesus' possession of supernatural knowledge (1:48: Nathanael under the fig tree; 2:19: nature of Jesus' death; cf.

Table 3.1
The Spirit in John's Gospel

Passage in John	Designation	Role
14:17	another Paraclete, the Spirit of truth	with you and in you
14:26	the Paraclete, the Holy Spirit	teach, bring to remembrance
15:26	the Paraclete, the Spirit of truth	bear witness to Jesus
16:7	the Paraclete	convict the world
16:13	the Spirit of truth	guide into all truth; declare things to come

ecce homo

lifted-up sayings

substitutionary atonement

also 12:24; 11:14: Lazarus's death; 13:38: Peter's denials; 21:18–19: nature of Peter's death)

5. Thomas's confession of Jesus as "my Lord and my God" (20:28), a mirror image of the designation awarded to the Roman emperor at the time of writing

Nevertheless, while John emphasizes Jesus' deity and preexistence, he does not therefore neglect to present Jesus as thoroughly human:

1. he has a human family (1:45; 2:12; 6:42; 7:3–8; 19:25–26)
2. he is worn out and thirsty (4:6–7; 19:28)
3. he weeps when he loses a friend (11:33, 35)
4. he is perceived by others as a man (Pilate: "*ecce homo*," 19:5)
5. he dies (19:30) and is buried (19:38–42)[7]

There is, of course, much common ground with the Synoptic Gospels. As do Mark, Matthew, and Luke, John portrays Jesus as the Christ, the Son of God (20:30–31), as well as the Son of Man (on which see esp. the **lifted-up sayings** in 3:14; 8:28; and 12:31–32).

Salvation

Some have argued that John, in good Gnostic style, teaches salvation by revelation.[8] These scholars argue that the concept of a **substitutionary atonement** is foreign to John's thought. However, several passages in John's Gospel refute this claim: John the Baptist's designation of Jesus as "the Lamb of God" (1:29, 36); Caiaphas's prophecy that Jesus would die

"for the people" (11:49–52); and references to Jesus' death in chapters 6 and 10 in terms of a vicarious sacrifice.

It must be admitted that John generally *presupposes* rather than explicitly *develops* the concept of a substitutionary atonement as he does with regard to many other features of the Synoptic Gospels. It is also true that John presents Jesus as the final *revelation* of God. Nevertheless, it is illegitimate to argue that the cross functions in John *solely* as the revelation of God's love and not also as redemptive. If so, we may ask, why did God have to reveal himself in such a gruesome way when only revelation, not substitutionary atonement, was at stake?[9]

Another important aspect of John's soteriology is the universality of salvation provided in Jesus. Jesus is "the Savior of the world" (4:42) and offers salvation to "everyone who believes" (e.g., 3:16).

The Spirit

Of all the Gospels, John has the most explicit teaching on the Holy Spirit (see esp. chs. 14–16). The term *paraklētos* (perhaps meaning "advocate" or "helping presence") is only used in this Gospel to designate the Holy Spirit. The context for Jesus' teaching on the Holy Spirit in John's Gospel is Jesus' own imminent "departure" from his disciples. The emphasis lies on the continuity between Jesus' teaching and the Holy Spirit's mission of explaining that teaching. Rather than acting independently, the Holy Spirit thus subordinates himself and his mission to Jesus.

The chart above illustrates John's teaching on the Spirit.

Table 3.2
Life and Kingdom in John and the Synoptics

New Testament Book	Life	Kingdom	Total
Matt	7	55	62
Mark	4	20	24
Luke	5	46	51
John	36	5	41
Acts	8	8	16
Paul	37	14	51
Hebrews	2	3	5
James	2	1	3
Peter	4	1	5
1–3 John	13	0	13
Jude	2	0	2
Rev	23	9	32
Total	**143**	**162**	**305**

Only three designations are used for the Spirit: (1) the Paraclete ("helping presence"); (2) the Holy Spirit (focusing on the Spirit's holiness); and (3) the Spirit of truth (focusing on the Spirit's truthfulness). The functions of the Spirit vary: they include (1) indwelling believers; (2) teaching and guiding believers; and (3) witnessing to and convicting the world.

John's teaching on the "procession" of the Spirit from the Father and the Son (14:26: "whom the Father will send in my name"; 15:26: "whom I will send to you from the Father") has provided the raw material for the patristic teaching on this subject, which at one point even led to a split between the Western and Eastern churches.

The New Covenant Community

The word "church" (*ekklēsia*) does not occur in John's Gospel, but neither does it occur in any of the other Gospels, except for two references in Matthew (16:18; 18:17). John's **ecclesiology** is centered on Jesus as the replacement of Israel (ch. 15), with Jesus' followers pictured as branches of Jesus, the new vine (cf. Is 5:1–7; 27:2–6; Jer 2:21; Ez 15; 19:10–14; Hos 10:1; Ps 80:9–16). Another metaphor for the church in the Gospel of John is that of a flock (chs. 10, 17; 21:15–23; cf. Ps 23; Is 40:11; Jer 23:1; Ez 34:11).

Generally, the key to understanding John's teaching on the church lies in seeing the important typological Old Testament connections. Jesus replaces Israel, and the twelve become his new messianic community. As such they function as representatives of all believers. At the same time, there remains a distinction between the apostolic eyewitnesses of Jesus' ministry and later believers (cf. 15:27; 17:20). Interestingly, there is throughout the Gospel a gradual building from physical following to a spiritual following of Jesus that is not constrained by limits of time and space (cf. 1:35–51; 8:12; 13:34–35).

Some have pointed out that John focuses especially on the need for *individual* believers to put their faith in Jesus. While this is true, however, John balances the necessity of personal faith with teachings on the corporate dimension of the church. He emphasizes the need for mutual love and unity in order for the church's mission to the world to be successful (e.g., 13:34–35; 15:12–13; 17:20–26).

Those who subscribe to the Johannine community hypothesis have at times cast the community behind the Fourth Gospel as a sect set apart from the mainstream of orthodox historic Christianity. However, there is a strong emphasis on mission in John's Gospel (cf. esp. 3:16; 17:18; 20:21). There are also passages in John that envision the inclusion of the Gentiles in God's community (10:16; 11:52; 12:32; 17:20).

Finally, we should note John's singling out of the term "to believe" (*pisteuō*) as the central core of his teaching on requirements for membership in Jesus' messianic community. The term occurs more often in John than in all the other Gospels combined.

Last Things

Many have drawn attention to the "realized eschatology" of John's Gospel. According to John, we can have eternal life *now* and already *have* passed from death over into life. Some have taken this to mean that John did not believe in Christ's second coming. But this is clearly not true. There are several references in John's Gospel to God's judgment on the last day (e.g., 3:36; 5:21, 28–29, 39; 6:40, 54; 12:25). Also, the Gospel ends with Jesus' charge to his disciples to follow him "until I return" (21:22, 23).

John demonstrably has a sense of redemptive history. His eschatological dualism is not a Gnostic-style dualism (between matter and spirit) but reflects the Jewish distinction between "this age" and "the age to come." At the same time, John clearly accentuates the need for people to make a decision concerning

Christ *now* in light of eternal realities at stake. This sharpens his evangelistic appeal and lends urgency to his missionary call.

What in the Synoptic Gospels is described in terms of the kingdom of God finds expression in John through the terminology of "(eternal) life." As George Ladd points out, "[W]hile the idiom is different, and we are not to identify the Kingdom of God and eternal life, the underlying theological structure is the same, though expressed in different categories."[10] Table 3.1 (see p. 41) illustrates the Johannine substitution of the more generic, universal term "(eternal) life" for the more historically and ethnically constrained term "kingdom of God."

Note especially the total reversal between the number of occurrences of life and kingdom in the Synoptic Gospels and John. Note also that Paul, similar to John, features life much more frequently than kingdom. As might be expected, the Johannine Epistles and the Book of Revelation display the same pattern as John's Gospel.

Summary

In this chapter, we have attempted to get an overall sense of John's theology. This involved (1) a brief comparative analysis of John's Gospel in relation to the Synoptics; (2) a determination of the most likely conceptual background of John's Gospel; and (3) a tracing of some of the most important theological themes found in John. While it remains for the balance of this book to explore these motifs in greater detail, this initial synthesis will help us to look for these distinctive Johannine themes.

We may briefly summarize our conclusions:

(1) While John almost certainly knew of the existence of the Synoptic Gospels and probably read one or all of them, he clearly did not use them to any significant extent in writing his own account; John and the Synoptics should therefore be regarded as independent witnesses to the same Jesus in whom the gospel cen-

---

Study Questions

1. Which material is found in the Synoptic Gospels but not in John, and what are the Johannine equivalents of Synoptic teaching?

2. What is the predominant conceptual background of John, and how can it be demonstrated from specific passages in John's Gospel?

3. Briefly summarize some of the major Johannine themes: God, the Christ, salvation, the Spirit, the new covenant community, and last things.

ters, complementary portraits of one and the same person and history.

(2) John was steeped in Old Testament concepts and consciously related events in the life of Jesus to previous events in the history of Israel; the apostle sought to fill the void left by the events of A.D. 70 with his presentation of Jesus as the replacement of the temple and the fulfillment of the symbolism of the various Jewish feasts in an effort to persuade particularly diaspora Jews and proselytes that the Messiah and Son of God was in fact Jesus.

(3) We summarized John's teaching on major subjects as follows:

- God: God is featured as the sender of Jesus and as the Father of the Son.
- the Christ: Jesus is presented as both human and divine; he is the preexistent, incarnate Word; the Son of God, Son of Man, and Christ; the Son of the Father; the signs-working "I am"; and as the Savior.
- salvation: Jesus' death is cast as redemptive, as "for others," that is, as substitutionary atonement; at the same time, Jesus' death also reveals God's love for a sinful world; Jesus' death is not (primarily) portrayed as a shameful, painful event; John rather views it as merely a station on Jesus' way back to the Father and as the place and the hour where God is glorified.
- the Spirit: the Spirit is presented as "another helping presence" similar to Jesus; he will teach and guide Jesus' followers and, through them, convict the world of its sin of unbelief in Jesus; the Spirit will also empower the disciples' mission and provide continuity with the earthly mission of Jesus.
- the new covenant community: Jesus is the replacement for Israel, and his new messianic community is characterized

by one thing only: faith in Jesus the Messiah; in keeping with Old Testament imagery, believers in Jesus are depicted as Jesus' "flock" and "branches" of Jesus, the new vine; the new messianic community is to be characterized by mutual love and unity in order for its mission to the world to go forth unhindered.

- last things: eternal life is available through Jesus already in the here and now, not just in the afterlife; at the same time, Jesus will be God's agent on the final day of judgment; believers are to follow him until he returns; the Synoptic teaching on the kingdom of God is replaced by John's teaching on eternal life.

After exploring the history, literature, and theology of John's Gospel, we are now ready to embark on a more detailed exploration of this rich book. Fasten your seat belts!

Key Words

aphoristic

symbolic discourses

eschatology

parallelomania

God-fearers

logos

ecce homo

lifted-up sayings

substitutionary atonement

ecclesiology

Part

2

Encountering the Word

John 1:1–18

The Word became flesh.

—John 1:14

4 The Incarnation of the Word

John 1:1–18

> Your word is truth.
> —John 17:17

Outline

Objectives

After reading this chapter, you should be able to

1. Explain the function of John's Prologue.
2. Analyze the significance of John's use of the term "Word."
3. Trace the literary structure of the Prologue of John's Gospel.
4. Explain the theological concept of the Incarnation.

Why a Prologue? The Prologue's Function in John's Gospel

Think of John's Prologue as a kind of foyer to the Gospel. In it John introduces the most important themes he will develop in the rest of his work. These are the glasses through which John wants his readers to see Jesus. Among the evangelists, Mark wins the prize for brevity: "The beginning of the gospel about Jesus Christ, the Son of God" (Mk 1:1). Matthew and Luke both preface their account of Jesus' ministry with a genealogy (Mt 1:1–17; Lk 3:23–38) and a birth narrative, including also a variety of remarkable events surrounding Jesus' birth as well as further information regarding Jesus' growing-up years (Mt 1:18–2:23; Lk 1:5–2:52). In addition to this, Luke crafts an impressive literary preface to his work: "In as much as many have undertaken to compile an account of the things accomplished among us . . ." (Lk 1:1–4; NASB).

But as with the rest of his Gospel, John goes his own way. He supplies neither a genealogy nor a birth narrative of Jesus; as a matter of fact, he gives absolutely no

---

Table 4.1

Important Terms Introduced in John's Prologue

The following important terms are introduced in John's Prologue (in order of first appearance):

God (*theos;* 1:1, 2, 6, 12, 13, 18)
life (*zōē;* 1:4)
light (*phōs;* 1:4, 5, 7, 8, 9)
darkness (*skotia;* 1:5)
to send (*apostellō;* 1:6)
John the Baptist (*Iōannēs;* 1:6, 15)
to believe (*pisteuō;* 1:7, 12)
witness (*martyreō:* 1:7, 8, 15; *martyria:* 1:7)
truth (*alēthinos:* 1:9; *alētheia:* 1:14, 17)
the world (*kosmos;* 1:9, 10)
to know (*ginōskō;* 1:10)
born of God (*ek theou egennēthēsan;* 1:13)
glory (*doxa;* 1:14)
only begotten (*monogenēs;* 1:14, 18)
the Father (*patēr;* 1:14, 18)
Moses (*Mōuseōs;* 1:17)
to see (*horaō;* 1:18)

The following important terms are used only in John's Prologue but not in the rest of the Gospel:

the Word *(logos)* as a christological designation (1:1, 14)
to tabernacle (*skenoō;* 1:14)
grace (*charis;* 1:14, 16, 17)
fullness (*plērōma;* 1:16)
to explain (*exēgeomai;* 1:18)

---

omniscience

Table 4.2
The Frequency of Important Terms First Introduced in the Prologue in John's Gospel as a Whole

Important term	First ref. in Jn	Frequency in Jn	Frequency in NT
life (zōē)	1:4	36	135
light (phōs)	1:4	23	73
witness (martyreō/martyria)	1:7	47	113
believe (pisteuō)	1:7	98	241
world (kosmos)	1:9	78	185
truth, true (alētheia, etc.)	1:14	56	181
glory (doxa/doxazō)	1:14	42	227
father (patēr)	1:14	136	413*

*These references are not just to "the Father" but include all references to the Greek word *patēr*. Nevertheless, a large number of passages do in fact refer to "the Father."

information regarding Jesus' upbringing or early years. Rather, John takes us back to eternity past, prior to creation. At first, it sounds as if John is retelling the story of creation itself: "In the beginning was the Word . . ." (1:1; cf. Gn 1:1: "In the beginning God created"). But soon it becomes clear that John is not merely recounting a past event; he heralds the news that something of equal, or even greater, import than creation has taken place—the incarnation of the Word: "The Word became flesh" (1:14).

This, then, is how John wants us to read his account of the life, death, and resurrection of Jesus:

1. in universal, cosmic terms (space): Jesus' coming has an impact on the entire world, not merely on God's chosen people, the Jews (cf. 1:11–12).
2. in eternal terms (time): Jesus was not merely a "divine man," a mere human being with an unusual sense of the divine—he was himself God (1:1), one with the preexistent Creator as the Word through whom everything that is came into being (1:3).
3. in essential terms (being): greater than any one of Jesus' numerous miracles

(called "signs" by John), greater than any one of Jesus' teachings (featured in John in several extended discourses) is the fact of who Jesus *is:* being precedes doing, essence precedes action. In one of his great "I am sayings," the Johannine Jesus declares himself to *be* the way, the truth, and the life (14:6); and he does not merely raise others from the dead and himself come back to life—he *is* the resurrection (11:25).

John's Prologue thus has a function similar to the first two chapters of the Old Testament Book of Job. There the readers are told something neither Job's friends nor even Job himself knew as the story progressed: that it was Satan who had asked permission from God to afflict Job (Job 1:6–12; 2:1–7). This piece of information places the readers of the book of Job in the privileged position of **omniscience**: they are given the interpretive clue to the unfolding events by the "omniscient" narrator. Thus they are able to learn the spiritual lessons God has for them.

Similar in John: what none of the characters in John's Gospel knew at the outset (neither the Pharisees nor even Jesus' own disciples)—that Jesus is the preexis-

49

Table 4.3
Significant Words Used Only Once in John's Gospel

to "tabernacle" (skēnoō; 1:14)
fullness (plērōma; 1:16)
Israelite (Israelitēs; 1:47)
wrath (orgē; 3:36)
salvation (sōteria; 4:22)
Savior (sōtēr; 4:42)
to hope (elpizō; 5:45)
abundant (perissos; 10:10)
blasphemy (blasphemeia; 10:33)
meeting [of the Sanhedrin] (synedrion; 11:47)
to prophesy (prophēteuō; 11:51)
example (hypodeigma; 13:15)
messenger (apostolos; 13:16)
Satan (Satanas; 13:27)
to overcome (nikaō; 16:33)
judgment seat (bēma; 19:13)

---

tent, incarnate Word from the Father—John's readers are told at the very beginning of his narrative. As in the case of Job, this helps the reader to view the actions of the Gospel's characters in light of the information supplied in the Prologue. The Prologue is thus a very important device used by the evangelist to lead (at least some of) his readers to "believe that Jesus is the Christ, the Son of God" and to "have life in his name" (20:31).

Why "the Word"? An Exploration of Possible Backgrounds

What is the message conveyed by John's use of the term "Word"? What is the function of this characterization within the context of John's Gospel as a whole? And why does John use *this* expression rather than one of several other possible designations for Jesus?

The Message Conveyed by the Term "Word" in John's Prologue

To begin with, the idea underlying "Word" is that of divine self-expression, of divine speech. According to the psalmist, God's creation provides telling testimony of who God is:

> The heavens declare the glory of God;
> The skies proclaim the work of his hands.
> Day after day they pour forth speech;
> night after night they display knowledge.
> There is no speech or language
> where their voice is not heard.
> Their voice goes out into all the earth,
> their words to the ends of the world
> (Ps 19:1–4a).

God's Word is also the vehicle for divine action: in the beginning God spoke, and everything that is came into being:

> And God said, "Let there be light," *and there was light.*
> And God said, "Let the water under the sky be gathered to one place, and let dry ground appear." *And it was so* (Gn 1:3, 9; cf. Gn 1:11, 15, 24, 30).

The Word may therefore be depicted as God's effective speech or self-expression. What is more, Jesus is characterized by John as God's final revelation: the Law (the expression of God's character and

Stoicism

will for his people) was given through Moses, grace and truth came through Jesus Christ (1:17). Jesus, the unique God who is in the bosom of the Father, has explained him (1:18). And the word of John the Baptist (simply called "John" in this Gospel) witnesses to the truth of who Jesus is (1:6–8, 15).

The Function of the Term "Word" in John's Gospel as a Whole

As is commonly known among students of this Gospel, the term "Word," used as a christological title, occurs only in the Prologue (1:1, 14). In the rest of John's narrative, Jesus is called "Son of God," "Son of Man," or "Christ," to name but a few other designations. But while Jesus' preexistence is implied also in the body of John's Gospel (e.g., 8:58; 17:5), it is only in the Prologue that he is he called "the Word." How can we explain this phenomenon?

The most probable explanation is that John wants his readers to understand the expression "the Word" as a christological umbrella term for the entire Gospel. The characterization of Jesus as "the Word" is designed to encompass his entire ministry as it is narrated in the remainder of John's account. All of Jesus' "works" and "words" flow from the eternal fount of Jesus' eternal existence as "the Word." Everything Jesus does is therefore revelation, works as well as words, because everything that Jesus says and does points beyond mere external appearances to who Jesus *is*. This is the profound theological point made by John's Prologue, and it sets the account of Jesus' ministry in a much more explicitly theological (even philosophical) context than do the other Gospels.

The expression "Word" is also broader than John's favorite term for Jesus in the remainder of his Gospel, that of "Son." For "Son" strikes a personal, relational, familial note, connotations not present in the term "Word." That Jesus is the Son underscores the intimacy of Jesus' relationship with God (e.g., 5:20). In the context of John's sending Christology, Jesus' sonship also lends authority and legitimacy to his mission ("the Father who sent me"). But the expression "the Word" is more comprehensive than "Son." Jesus says it best: "Anyone who has seen me

has seen the Father" (14:9b). What is affirmed in the most general sense in John's Prologue is thus fleshed out in greater detail in the body of John's Gospel: that Jesus came to show us who God is (revelation; 1:18), including the demonstration of God's redemptive love for the world (salvation; 3:16).

The Background of the Term "Word" in John's Prologue

Before we discuss the background of the term "Word" in John's Prologue, we must register an important qualification, the distinction between John's conceptual background and his desire to contextualize, that is, to communicate his message to his contemporary audience. This desire to contextualize his message may have led John to use a term that had currency among his readers in order to persuade them of the relevance of his gospel.

Yet even if John used the term "Word" because it served his purpose of communicating to a Hellenistic (-Jewish) audience, this does not mean that he used the expression in the way in which it was commonly used in the world of his day; the background for this term may rather lie in John's own thought world. In that case, John, while using a term familiar to his audience, would have filled this expression with a new, different meaning, thus correcting and challenging his readers' worldview. The significance of these observations will become clear in the following discussion.

Three major backgrounds for the term "Word" (Greek: *logos*) in John have been proposed: (1) Greek philosophy (**Stoicism, Philo**); (2) the "Word" as the personification of Wisdom in wisdom literature *(sophia)*; and (3) the Word of God in the Old Testament. We will consider these seriatim.

Greek Philosophy

Did John borrow his Logos doctrine from Stoic philosophy, either directly or through Philo (a Hellenistic-Jewish philosopher from Alexandria, Egypt)? In Stoic thought, Logos was Reason, the impersonal rational principle governing the universe. This principle was thought to pervade the entire universe and was indeed the only god recognized by the Stoics (roughly equivalent to *theos*, God). According to Stoicism, human beings must live in keeping with this Reason. A spark of universal Reason was thought to reside within people, at least within the best and wisest of them. For the Stoic, Reason must be obeyed at all costs; without it, life is devoid of dignity and meaning. Zeno, the founder of this school of thought (ca. 336–263 B.C.), wrote that "destiny is the concatenated causality of things, or the scheme according to which the kosmos is directed."[1] Zeno believed that "the General Law, which is Right Reason, pervading everything, is the same as Zeus, the Supreme Head of the government of the universe."[2]

In keeping with the distinction between conceptual background and contextualization drawn above, it is probable that John was aware of the Stoic concept of the Logos. It is equally clear, however, that this doctrine does not constitute John's primary conceptual framework, for the following reasons:

1. in John, unlike the Stoics, *logos* and *theos* are not identical; for the Stoics, logos was god; in John's case, things are not quite as simple; to be sure, according to John "the Word was God" (1:1c); but the Word also was *"with God"* (1:1b)—which implies a plurality within the Godhead and militates against a simplistic identification of the Word (*logos*) and God (*theos*).

2. the Stoic Logos is the supreme principle, an abstraction of logic; but John's interest lies in historical events, not mere metaphysical theory.

3. if John, the author of the Gospel, is none other than John the son of Zebedee, a Palestinian Jew, then a Jewish conceptual framework is much more likely, a fact that is borne out by the Jewish background of many other elements in John's Gospel.

Personified Wisdom

Second, should the personification of Wisdom in wisdom literature be identified as the most likely background of John's Logos doctrine? Consider the words of Wisdom in Proverbs 8:22–31:

The LORD brought me forth as the first
of his works,
before his deeds of old.

Table 4.4
Parallels between Exodus 33–34 and John 1:14–18

Exodus 33–34	John 1:14–18
Israel finds grace in Yahweh's sight (33:14)	disciples receive "grace instead of grace" (1:16)
no one can see Yahweh's face and live (33:20)	no one has seen God at any time (1:18)
Yahweh's glory passes by Moses (33:23; 34:6–7)	the disciples beheld the Word's glory (1:14)
Yahweh abounds in lovingkindness and truth (34:6)	Jesus is full of grace and truth (1:14,17)
Yahweh dwelt in a tent (33:7)	the Word "tented" among the disciples (1:14)
Moses was given the Law (34:27–28)	the Law was given through Moses (1:17)
Moses, mediator between Yahweh, Israel (34:32–35)	Jesus, mediator between God and man (1:17–18)

Stoicism

apocryphal

I was appointed from eternity,
from the beginning, before the
world began . . .
. . . when he marked out the foundations
of the earth.
Then I was the craftsman at his side.
I was filled with delight day after day,
rejoicing always in his presence,
rejoicing in his whole world
and delighting in mankind.

A whole corpus of **apocryphal** wisdom literature built further on the notion expressed in the biblical Book of Proverbs that Wisdom was at God's side at creation (cf. Sir 1:1–10; Wis Sol). On the face of it, the parallels between the characterization of wisdom in Proverbs 8 and John's Logos concept seem impressive. Wisdom, like John's Logos, claims preexistence and participation in God's creative activity. Wisdom, like the Logos, is depicted as vehicle of God's self-revelation, in creation as well as the Law. And did not even Paul draw this parallel when he called Christ the "wisdom of God"? (1 Cor 1:30). Surface parallels abound—but do these prove to be true parallels at closer scrutiny?

In a seminal presidential address, delivered in 1961 to the learned Society of Biblical Literature, the Jewish scholar Samuel Sandmel issued his now classic warning against parallelomania.[3] Sandmel observes that those who claim to detect parallels between two writings tend to make the following three assumptions: (1) a *surface* parallel is a *true* parallel; (2) the parallel points to *literary dependence* (in the present case, between Proverbs or apocryphal wisdom literature and John's Prologue); and (3) this literary dependence goes *in a certain direction: John* is dependent on *apocryphal wisdom literature* rather than the other way around. Sandmel does not discourage the search for parallels; he is merely concerned that surface parallels not be mistaken for true ones. He concludes that closer scrutiny of alleged parallels may reveal (1) a true parallel that is (a) significant or (b) insignificant; (2) a seeming parallel that is so only imperfectly; and (3) statements that can be called parallels only by taking them out of context. In our present quest to determine the most likely background of Logos in John's Prologue, in which of these categories

should we place the personification of Wisdom in wisdom literature?

It must be kept in mind that the question is not merely what may appear to be a parallel to you and me. The question is rather: What did *John, the author,* have in mind as he penned his Prologue? Also, we must show not only the *possibility* that personified Wisdom was in John's mind as he wrote. We must show that this is *probable* and more likely than any of the alternatives. Closer scrutiny reveals that, despite the above mentioned surface similarities, John's Logos doctrine differs from personified Wisdom in some significant respects: (1) wisdom literature does not present Wisdom as a second person of the Godhead but merely as a divine attribute already present at creation; Jesus, on the other hand, is portrayed not merely as "with God" (1:1, 2), but as himself God (1:1); (2) Wisdom is not really cast as a person—it is merely a concept that is *personified*, a common literary device; but in John, the exact opposite procedure is at work: Jesus, *a real person,* is presented in *conceptual terms* as the Word; (3) the stubborn fact remains that John does not use the term "wisdom" *(sophia)* but the expression "the Word" *(logos).*

The least that can be said, then, is that John's Logos doctrine transcends the notion of personified Wisdom in some significant ways, so significant in fact that one wonders if personified wisdom constitutes the primary background of John's Logos concept. Still, if no closer parallel can be found, it may be necessary to conclude that personified Wisdom constitutes at least a remote parallel to the characterization of Logos in John.

The Word of God in the Old Testament

Reference has already been made to the parallels between the creation account in Genesis 1 and John 1. Consider the following evidence:

1. the identical opening phrase, "In the beginning," in both books, clearly a deliberate effort on John's part to echo the creation narrative and the opening phrase in the Hebrew canon of Scripture

The Granite mountains of Sinai near modern Eilat provide a majestic reminder of Moses' giving of the Law to Israel.

2. the presence of other significant terminology found in Genesis 1 also in John 1, such as "light" and "darkness" or "life"

3. the preponderance of Old Testament parallels in the entire Prologue, including further references to Israel's wilderness wanderings in the Book of Exodus (1:14: he "dwelt"—lit. "tented"—among us, an allusion to the tabernacle) or to God's appearance to Moses, including the giving of the Law (1:17–18). Consider, for example, the list of parallels between Exodus 33–34 and John 1:14–18 in table 4.4.[4]

This impressive list already constitutes presumptive evidence for an Old Testament background for John's Logos concept. As we look for Old Testament passages where the notion of the Word of God is developed beyond the initial mention in Genesis 1, we are drawn particularly to Isaiah 55:9–11:

> As the heavens are higher than the
>   earth,
>   so are my ways higher than your
>   ways
>   and my thoughts than your thoughts.
> As the rain and the snow
>   come down from heaven,
> and do not return to it
>   without watering the earth
> and making it bud and flourish,
>   so that it yields seed for the sower
>   and bread for the eater,
> so is my word that goes out from my
>   mouth:
>   It will not return to me empty,
> but will accomplish what I desire

and achieve the purpose for which I sent it.

Here, then, is God's personified Word (not Wisdom): (1) it is sent by God in order to accomplish a particular divine purpose; (2) it unfailingly accomplishes this purpose; (3) and it returns to God who sent it after accomplishing its mission. It is hard to imagine a closer conceptual and even verbal parallel to John's depiction of Jesus as the divine Word. In conformance with the Isaianic paradigm, Jesus in John habitually refers to God as "the Father who sent me," claims to carry out his Father's will and to do his works while on earth (4:34), and returns to the Father after having completed the work God has given him to do (17:4).

As a detailed comparison shows, Isaiah 55:9–11 matches the message conveyed by the term "Word" in John's Prologue very closely indeed.[5] In both instances, God's Word is portrayed as effective speech. It is more than a mere utterance; it inexorably leads to action in accordance with God's will. Arguably, Isaiah's portrayal of the personified Word of God thus provides the conceptual framework for John's theology of the Logos. This is further supported by the fact that John frequently uses motifs from the Book of Isaiah in his Gospel (cf. esp. 12:38 quoting Is 53:1; 12:40 quoting Is 6:10; and 12:41 alluding to Is 6:1–4).

One final point should be noted: Just because we have identified Isaiah's theology of the Word of God (exemplified

Did the Darkness Not "Understand" or "Overcome" the Light? (Jn 1:5)

Since the Greek word underlying the phrase "the darkness has not understood/overcome it [the light]" in John 1:5, *katalambanō,* can mean either "understand" or "overcome" depending on the context, the existing English translations show a considerable amount of indecisiveness (as well as variation) on how this term is rendered. Consider the following sampling:

NIV: "the darkness has not understood [footnote: or overcome] it"

NASB: "the darkness did not comprehend [footnote: or overpower] it"

NKJV: "the darkness did not comprehend [footnote: or overcome] it"

NLT: "the darkness can never extinguish it"

NET: "the darkness has not mastered it"

ISV: "the darkness has never put it out"

RSV: "the darkness has not overcome it"

Among the above versions, the first three favor the sense "understand" (though each include a footnote giving the alternative rendering) while the next four prefer an equivalent of "overcome." How are we to sort out this rather unsettled situation? What is at issue here? First, it must be said that part of the difficulty lies with John's simultaneous use of "light" and "darkness" in a literal and figurative sense. Verse 3 refers plainly to the creation, which saw the creation of light, the distinction between light and darkness, and the creation of life (cf. vv. 4–5). This literal level thus still resonates very plainly in the present verse.

At the same time, John already prepares the reader for the enfleshment of the preexistent Word through whom everything was created, who himself is the "Light" (1:7–9). And as it turned out, the world in its spiritual darkness failed to embrace the light out of preference for its evil ways (1:10–11; cf. 3:19–21). Thus it is clear that, at least later in the Prologue (1:10–11), John indicates that the (world in its) "darkness" did not *understand* the light. The question remains, however, if the earlier passage in verse 5 should already be read this way. After all, we should beware of imposing our knowledge of a later passage onto an earlier one.

If, in fact, the literal level of light and darkness is judged still to resonate in verse 5 rather distinctly, it stands to reason that literal darkness can hardly be said to "understand" literal light. On the other hand, it makes perfect sense for literal darkness not to *overcome* literal light. Quite to the contrary, as experience tells, literal light overcomes literal darkness. Hence the analogy with the spiritual realm suggests itself that Jesus, the Light of the World, likewise overcame the world's spiritual darkness. As he tells his disciples toward the end of his ministry, "I have overcome *(nikaō)* the world" (16:33).

If we are therefore correct in assuming that the *primary* meaning of *katalambanō* in John 1:5 is "overcome," John would start out on a triumphant note: Jesus, "the Light," triumphed over the world's darkness. Perhaps decisive in favor of this interpretation is the close parallel statement in 12:35: "Walk while you have the *light,* before *darkness* overtakes *(katalambanō)* you" (NIV). Note how here even the NIV (which has opted for "understand" in 1:5) renders the same word, *katalambanō,* with "overtake" (that is, "overcome"). That, on a secondary level, the darkness's lack of *understanding* may already begin to resonate in verse 5 as well (in preparation of 1:10–11), need not be ruled out. But we believe that a strong case can be made for the primacy of the meaning "overcome" in 1:5.

in passages such as Is 55:9–11) as the conceptual background for John's Logos doctrine, this does not mean that John merely took over this theology without further refinement or development. To the contrary: while the Word of God in Isaiah remains a hypostatization (personification) of God's Word, John's Logos refers to an actual historical person, the incarnate Lord Jesus Christ. Thus John utilizes a concept he has found in Isaiah and applies it to Jesus in construing his own dis-

---

"In Order That You Might Believe": The Importance of Believing in John's Gospel

Apart from "Jesus" (241 times) and "Father" (136 times), there is no theologically significant word that occurs more frequently in John's Gospel than the word "believe" (*pisteuō;* 98 times). John's ninety-eight instances compare to eleven in Mark, fourteen in Matthew, and nine in Luke. Thus Merrill Tenney seems to be justified in calling John "the Gospel of belief." Another interesting observation is that while John uses the *verb* "to believe" almost a hundred times, he does not once use the corresponding *noun* (*pistis,* "faith"). It appears therefore that John's primary purpose is to engender in his readers the *act* of believing, of placing their trust in Jesus Christ.

Note the prominence of "believing" in John's purpose statement: "Jesus did many other miraculous signs in the presence of his disciples, which are not recorded in this book. But these are written that you may believe that Jesus is the Christ, the Son of God, and that by believing you may have life in his name" (20:30–31). The central verse of John's prologue, too, includes a reference to believing: "Yet to all who received him, to those who believed in his name, he gave the right to become children of God" (1:12). And John's summary indictment of the Jews at the end of his "Book of Signs" is that "Even after Jesus had done all these miraculous signs in their presence, they still would not believe in him" (12:37).

Thus, in a sense, John divides all of humanity into two classes of people: those who believe that the Messiah is Jesus, and those who don't. Those who do have eternal life, those who don't will be condemned at the last judgment. Those who believe walk in the light, those who don't walk in darkness. To adapt Shakespeare, we may sum up John's message as follows: "To believe or not to believe—*that's* the question." Space does not permit to trace all ninety-eight references to believing in John's Gospel. But as you do, you will see that the struggle between believing and not believing provides the entire narrative with its inner dynamic, suspense, and drama. May you and I be among those who believe.

One final word of caution should be registered. The word "believe" (similarly to the term "disciple") in John does not necessarily refer to "saving faith." Context must decide. Thus the Jews who had "believed" in Jesus in 8:31 turn out in the ensuing interchange to be "children of the devil" (!), just as "many of his [Jesus'] *disciples*" desert Jesus (6:60) and no longer follow him (6:66). Likewise, when many "believe in Jesus' name" on account of his signs in Jerusalem, Jesus does not "entrust himself" (a play on words) to them (2:23–25). In other words, he did not necessarily trust their "conversion." Then there are secret believers in Jesus such as Joseph of Arimathea; sincere inquirers such as Nicodemus; there is "doubting Thomas"—truly reality is messier than you or I might like it to be. All this is to say that "believe" in John's Gospel does not necessarily refer to saving faith. The term is more fluid. Occasionally, initial faith turns out to be spurious, while at other times it must be confirmed by a more definitive commitment.

Note: On the important contemporary implications of this issue, see esp. D. A. Carson, "Reflections on Christian Assurance," *Westminster Theological Journal* 54 (1992): 1–29.

tinctive Christology. As is frequently the case with New Testament writers' use of the Old Testament, John draws from existing sources, but he does so not slavishly but with a considerable degree of originality and imagination.

Why Poetry? The Literary Structure of John's Prologue

While there is some disagreement as to whether the Prologue is original with John (as seems to be supported by the close coherence between the Prologue and the rest of John's Gospel) or whether he adapted a preexisting hymn to suit his purposes (inserting sections on John the Baptist in vv. 6–8 and 15?), John's Prologue represents one of the most beautiful and carefully crafted poetic portions of the entire New Testament.

The macrostructure of the opening section of John's Gospel reveals a chiastic pattern, with the Word's incarnation at the center, framed by references to John the Baptist's witness:

A **The Word's activity in creation (1:1–5)**

  B John's witness concerning the light (1:6–9)

    C The incarnation of the Word (1:10–14)

  B' John's witness concerning the Word's preeminence (1:15)

A' **The final revelation brought by Jesus Christ (1:16–18)**

In the opening lines of the Prologue, John proceeds by introducing a new concept at the end of one line and by taking up this concept at the beginning of the subsequent line (synthetic parallelism). This is obscured in English translation, which cannot always follow original word order, but is brought out clearly when English word order is made to conform to that of the original Greek:

> In the beginning was the *Word*,
> and the *Word* was with *God*,

and *God* [emphasized in the original] was the Word (1:1).

Closure is brought to this opening assertion by concluding this first section the way it began: with the phrase "in the beginning":

> He was with God in the beginning (1:2).

The poetic parallelism (now in antithetical fashion) continues in the following statement:

> Through him *all things were made;*
> without him *nothing was made* that has been made (1:3).

After this, the staircase parallelism resumes:

> In him was *life,*
> and that *life* was the *light* of men.
> The *light* shines in the *darkness,*
> but the darkness has not overcome it (1:4–5).

Even though English poetry utilizes rhyme rather than parallel ideas, the rhythmic cadence found in the original shines through even in translation. The following verses (1:6–9), narrating John the Baptist's witness to "the light," break the stitching pattern of verses 1–5 (similarly, v. 15); in the subsequent verses, the parallelism is not always as obvious as in the opening verses, but a similar pattern is sustained until the conclusion of the Prologue.

Another possible chiasm may be detected in the sequence found in 1:14–18:

A **the One and Only (1:14)**

  B full of grace and truth (1:14)

    C grace instead of grace (1:16)

  B' grace and truth (1:17)

A' **God the One and Only (1:18)**

In relation to God's theophanies during Israel's wilderness wanderings, this section highlights God's covenant faithfulness and truthfulness to his promises that culminated in the apostles' (the "we" in v. 14) beholding of God's glory in his Son Jesus Christ.

Gnosticism

From a literary perspective, there may be two climactic statements in this section: (1) the assurance at the center of the Prologue that "to all who received him, to those who believed in his name, he gave the right to become children of God" (v. 12); and (2) the concluding assertion that "No one has ever seen God, but God the One and Only, who is at the Father's side, has made him known" (v. 18). The central claim draws attention to the universal salvific impact of Jesus' coming into the world; the final exclamation point underscores the decisive eschatological revelation brought through Jesus.

Why the Incarnation? Reflections on a Crucial Doctrine

The wonderful, amazing truth of Jesus' incarnation is nowhere taught more clearly than in the fourteenth verse of John's Prologue: "The Word became flesh." John's message is clear: Jesus' incarnation represents an event as important as creation. For the world is dark, fallen, and sinful, with not even God's chosen people being exempt (1:10–11). Man's need is for spiritual rebirth (1:13; cf. 3:3, 5); and no one but the preexistent Word-become-flesh in Jesus could fill this need. In the words of John the Baptist, he is "the Lamb of God, who takes away the sin of the world" (1:29; cf. 1:36). Thus the purpose of the incarnation is Jesus' substitutionary atonement.

One movement threatening the early church denied every single one of these tenets: **Gnosticism.** Its name derives from the Greek word for "knowledge," *gnōsis,* because it was people's mystical communion with the divine and knowledge of esoteric spiritual secrets, not atonement for human sin, that was considered to constitute salvation. Hence even incipient Gnostic thought denied all of the following:

1. *Jesus' incarnation:* since Gnosticism was founded on the conventional Greek dualism between matter (considered evil) and spirit (alone considered good), it was judged to be an im-

---

"One and Only God" or "One and Only Son"? The Textual Issue of John 1:18

One of the most striking references to Jesus as God, besides 1:1 and 20:28, is the reference to him as "the One and Only God" in John 1:18. As a closer look reveals, however, manuscripts are divided as to whether John actually wrote "the One and Only God" *(monogenēs theos)* or "the one and only Son" *(monogenēs huios).* Which is the probable original reading?

First, to use one of the principles of textual criticism, the "harder reading" is doubtless "God the One and Only." It is clearly more likely that a later scribe sought to soften such blatant ascription of deity to Jesus by changing "God" to "Son"—thus conforming 1:18 to the later reference to Jesus as God's "one and only Son" in 3:16 and 18 (cf. also 1 John 4:9)—than for him to change "Son" to "God."

Second, the recent acquisition of two very early papyrus manuscripts, p66 and p75, both of which read "One and Only God" *(monogenēs theos),* has tilted the evidence decidedly in the way of this reading as probably being original (the important Codices Sinaiticus and Vaticanus also read this way). Still, the fact that the Codex Alexandrinus (A) has "one and only Son" *(mono-*

genēs huios) cautions against dogmatism.

For these reasons, it is likely that John actually referred to Jesus as "the One and Only God." While this is indeed a striking designation, following, as it does, on the heels of John's entire Prologue, it is certainly credible. For as Jesus affirms later in John's Gospel, "I and the Father are one" (10:30).

Note: Compare the discussion in Bruce M. Metzger, *A Textual Commentary on the New Testament,* 2nd ed. (New York: United Bible Societies, 1994), 169–70.

Study Questions

1. Why does John's Prologue identify Jesus as "the Word"?

2. How does the depiction of Jesus as "the Word" relate to John's Gospel as a whole?

3. What was the purpose of the incarnation?

possibility for God (who is spirit) to take on evil matter; thus the Gnostic did not acknowledge Jesus as "come in the flesh" (cf. 1 Jn 4:1–3; 2 Jn 7).

2. *human sinfulness:* the body was considered to be the prison of the soul, a prison that could, however, be escaped through spiritual communion with the divine; Gnostics claimed in effect "to be without sin" (1 Jn 1:8, 10).

3. *the need for atonement:* it follows from the Gnostic denial of human sinfulness that this early Christian heresy did not see any need for an atoning sacrifice to be brought on behalf of sinners (1 Jn 2:2; 4:10).

The pronouncement of John's Gospel that, in Jesus, the Word (which was God) had become flesh (that is, a human being), was therefore diametrically opposed to the claims of Gnosticism. A Gnostic would have had nothing but scorn in response to John's claim of Jesus' incarnation.

On the one hand, John alone among the Gospels teaches the incarnation of the Word (at least in those terms). On the other hand, John makes no reference to the virgin birth (cf. Mt 1:18, 20, 23; Lk 1:35).[6] Matthew seeks to show Jesus' descendance from Abraham and David (Mt 1:1, 2, 6, 16–17); Luke traces Jesus' genealogy even back to Adam (Lk 3:37). But John surpasses them both: he shows Jesus' origin to reach back all the way to eternity past, making him equal to God.

This has led some to claim that John represents the pinnacle of New Testament Christology: Jesus himself, it is argued, never claimed to be the Messiah; he was elevated to such a position only by his later followers. Gradually, those interpreters contend, the Christian "myth" grew, and the human Jesus came to be worshiped as God, with preexistence attributed to him only at this later stage of christological development. But Paul can write already in A.D. 57,

> yet for us there is but one God,
>   the Father,
>   from whom all things came
>   and for whom we live;
> and there is but one Lord, Jesus
>   Christ,
>   through whom all things came
>   and through whom we live
> (1 Cor 8:6).

Thus John's "high" Christology does not require one to place the writing of the Fourth Gospel toward the end of the canonical process; worship of Jesus as co-equal with the Father was an early, not a late, development in the early church.[7]

Finally, why did Jesus become a man (echoing the title of Anselm's famous treatise *Cur Deus Homo?*). This side of heaven, we will never be able fully to explain this mystery. But one thing is clear: the incarnation was necessary for our salvation. Paul says as much when he writes, "God made him who had no sin to be sin *for us*, so that *in him* we might become the righteousness of God" (2 Cor 5:21). And the author of Hebrews comments, "But we see Jesus, who was made a little lower than the angels, now crowned with glory and honor because he suffered death, so that by the grace of God he might taste death *for everyone*. In bringing many sons to glory, it was fitting that God, for whom and through whom everything exists, should make the author of their salvation perfect through suffering" (Hb 2:9–10). And again, "Since the children have flesh and blood, he too shared in their humanity so that by his death he might destroy him who holds the power of death—that is, the devil—and free those who all their lives were held in slavery by their fear of death" (Hb 2:14–15). In order to free humankind from the power of death and sin, Jesus had to become a man, albeit sinless, so that the death of this innocent God-man was able to atone for our sin. As Paul has it, "For what the law was powerless to do in that it was weakened by the sinful nature, God did

Key Words

incarnation

omniscience

Stoicism

apocrypha

Gnosticism

by sending his own Son in the likeness of sinful man to be a sin offering" (Rom 8:3).

At this early stage in John's Gospel, and at this early stage in the present book, may those of us who know Christ pause to marvel at the wonder of the incarnation. And may those who do not, fall on their knees, acknowledge their sinfulness and need for a Savior, and thank Jesus personally for what he has done for us on the cross, fully assured that Jesus' promise is true that if anyone comes to him, he will in no way reject him (6:37).

Part

3

Encountering the Earthly Jesus: The Mission to the Jews (Including Seven Signs)

John 1:19–12:50

Even after Jesus had done all these miraculous signs in their presence, they still would not believe in him.

—John 12:37

5 Jesus' Early Ministry (Part 1): Signs ##1–2

John 1:19–2:25

The Lord will surely comfort Zion
    and will look with compassion on all her
    ruins;
he will make her deserts like Eden,
    her wastelands like the garden of the
    Lord.
Joy and gladness will be found in her,
    thanksgiving and the sound of singing.

—Isaiah 51:3

**Supplemental Reading: Isaiah
52:13–53:12; Genesis 28:10–22**

Outline

• **The Testimony of John the Baptist
  (1:19–34)**
• **The First Disciples (1:35–51)**
• **The First Sign: Turning Water into
  Wine at the Wedding at Cana (2:1–12)**
• **The Second Sign: The Cleansing of the
  Temple (2:13–25)**

Objectives

**After reading this chapter, you should
be able to**

1. Discuss John's depiction of the ministry
   of John the Baptist.
2. Compare John's account of Jesus' calling
   his first disciples with the Synoptic
   parallels.
3. Identify the function of Jesus' first two
   signs in John's Gospel as a whole.

John the Baptist administered a baptism of repentance to his fellow-Jews at various locations alongside the Jordan River.

The Testimony of John the Baptist (1:19–34)

After his magnificent introduction, John gets down to earth and sets Jesus' ministry in historical perspective. Similar to the Synoptic Gospels, he links the beginning of Jesus' ministry with that of John the Baptist. In the Prologue, John's readers were already told

1. that John had been "sent from God" (1:6)
2. that he had come as a witness to "the light" in order that all might believe through him (1:7)
3. that he himself was not "the light" but that he merely witnessed to the light (1:8)
4. that John acknowledged the preeminence/preexistence of the Word-become-flesh and of the One and Only from the Father (1:15)

A survey of all the passages pertaining to John the Baptist in John's Gospel (1:6–8, 15, 19–37, 40; 3:22–36; 4:1–3; 5:33–36; 10:40–42) yields the following emphases in the Baptist's witness regarding Jesus.

In perfect humility, John readily acknowledges that not even he himself knew who the Messiah was (1:31, 33). But when he saw the Spirit descend and remain on Jesus, he knew that Jesus was the one who would baptize with the Holy Spirit (1:33; cf. Mk 1:8; Mt 3:11; Lk 3:16; Acts 1:5). Indeed, Jesus is "the Lamb of God, who takes away the sin of the world" and "the Son of God" (1:29). And at once the Baptist refers two of his disciples to Jesus (1:35).

After this, the Baptist disappears from the scene for a while. Jesus calls his first disciples, performs his first sign at the wedding at Cana, cleanses the Jerusalem temple, and, still in Jerusalem, engages in nightly conversation with "the Teacher of Israel," Nicodemus. After this, Jesus and his disciples journey to the Judean countryside where they baptize; John the Baptist, too, is still engaged in a ministry of baptism. For, as we are told by the evangelist in a parenthetical statement, "this was before John was put in prison" (3:24). This is one of several instances in John where the readers are assumed to have a basic familiarity with the gospel story (cf. 1:40; 4:44; 6:67; 11:2).

Again, John reiterates that he is not the Christ but sent before him, and that he is merely the "friend of the bridegroom" (the "best man" in a wedding), not the bridegroom himself (3:28). John knows his role; he knows when it is time to make room for the one whose ministry he has come to prepare: "He must become greater; I must become less" (3:30). For "whoever believes in the Son has eternal life, but whoever rejects the Son will not see life, for God's wrath remains on him" (3:36).

And with this final verdict, the Baptist disappears from the scene. He is mentioned only once more in John's Gospel, when Jesus withdraws in the face of mounting opposition to the place where John had been baptizing and many were saying, "Though John never performed a miraculous sign, all that John said about this man [Jesus] was true" (10:40–42).

The First Disciples (1:35–51)

Starting in verse 29, John links his narrative sequence with the expression "the next day"; in verse 35, it is "the next day" again. Starting with John the Baptist's testimony in 1:19–28, we can therefore reconstruct an entire week of ministry:

Day 1: John's testimony regarding Jesus (1:19–28)

Day 2: John's encounter with Jesus (1:29–34; "the next day")

Day 3: John's referral of two disciples to Jesus (1:35–39; "the next day")

Table 5.1
John the Baptist as a Witness to Jesus in John's Gospel

1. Jesus is the Light: "*He came as a witness to testify* concerning that light, so that through him all men might believe. He himself was not the light; he came only as a witness to the light" (1:6–8).
2. Jesus is preeminent: "*John testifies* concerning him. He cries out, saying, 'This was he of whom I said, "He who comes after me has surpassed me because he was before me"'" (1:15).
3. Jesus is the Son of God: "Then *John gave this testimony:* 'I saw the Spirit come down from heaven as a dove and remain on him. . . . I have seen and *I testify* that this is the Son of God'" (1:32–34).
4. John gave temporary testimony to the truth: "You have sent to John and *he has testified* to the truth. . . . John was a lamp that burned and gave light, and you chose for a time to enjoy his light. I have testimony weightier than that of John" (5:33–36).
5. John's testimony was completely true: "Though John never performed a miraculous sign, *all that John said about this man was true*" (10:41).

As in the Prologue, John is cast in the ensuing narrative as a witness to Jesus. Remarkably, John resists any labels of greatness for himself. When a delegation from Jerusalem inquires regarding his own identity, he denies being the Christ (1:20), Elijah (1:21), or the Prophet (1:21). Rather, he is the figure predicted in Isaiah, "a voice crying in the wilderness, 'Make straight the way of the Lord'" (1:23; Is 40:3; cf. Mk 1:3; Mt 3:3; Lk 3:4). Why, then, does he baptize? John baptizes merely with water, preparing the way for the one whose shoelaces he is not worthy to untie, in order to announce his coming to Israel (1:26–28, 31).

Table 5.2
Who John (the Baptist) Was Not

1. The Christ (1:20, 25): The Old Testament predicted the coming of God's "anointed" king, the Son of David. John considered his ministry to be merely preparatory for this Messiah (1:23 citing Is 40:3; cf. Mk 1:3 par.). He himself was not the Christ, nor did he claim to be.
2. Elijah (1:21, 25): Elijah did not die (2 Kgs 2:11) and was expected to return to announce the end; in this sense, John was not Elijah. In a different sense, however, Jesus observes that John was indeed "Elijah" (Mt 11:14; 17:10–13), in fulfillment of the prophecy of Malachi 4:5 (cf. Lk 1:17).
3. The Prophet (1:21, 25): Moses forecast the coming of a prophet like himself in Deuteronomy 18:15, 18. John also denied being this prophet who was eagerly expected by the Jewish people in his day.

---

inclusio

Day 4: Andrew's introduction of his brother Peter to Jesus (1:40–42)

Day 5: Philip and Nathanael follow Jesus (1:43–51; "the next day")

Day 7: Wedding at Cana (2:1–11; "on the third day")

Thus John is found to open his Gospel with an account of Jesus' first week of ministry, culminating in his "first sign" at Cana.

And what a week of work it turns out to be! John the Baptist's testimony triggers a chain reaction, issuing in a whole string of followers attaching themselves to Jesus. John's initial witness causes Andrew and an unnamed disciple (John the son of Zebedee?) to follow Jesus (1:35, 40); Andrew's witness recruits his brother Peter (1:41–43); Jesus calls Philip, who is from the same town as Andrew and Peter, that is, Bethsaida, to follow him (1:44); and Philip brings Nathanael (1:45–51), who is probably identical with the Bartholomew linked with Philip in the Synoptic apostolic lists (Mt 10:3; Mk 3:18; Lk 6:14). Nathanael's skepticism regarding Jesus, which is overcome by a demonstration of Jesus' true identity, is later mirrored (an **inclusio**)[1] by the "conversion" of "doubting Thomas" (20:24–29).

A comparison with the call narratives in the Synoptic Gospels raises at least two questions. First, how is it that in John disciples follow Jesus immediately while in the Synoptics they follow him only at a later point in time (cf. Mt 4:18–22; 9:9; Mk 1:16–20; 2:13–14; Lk 5:1–11, 27–28)? And second, how is it that John's initial chapter abounds with high christological confessions while the Synoptic Gospels (esp. Mark) focus on the disciples' failure to understand Jesus' true identity? At first glance, these contradictions seem to be irreconcilable. At a closer look, however, the opposite turns out to be the case. John and the Synoptics are found to complement each other in ways that enhance the significance of both accounts.

First, we may take up the question of disciples' instantaneous following of Jesus in John. If we did not have the Synoptics, we would not know that a period of preparation had preceded the disciples' eventual decision to leave their families, homes, and careers behind in order to follow Jesus. This would make their

---

Table 5.3
Agreements between John's Gospel and the Synoptics in Portraying John the Baptist

1. John the Baptist is identified as the figure predicted in Isaiah, "a voice crying in the wilderness, 'Make straight the way of the Lord'" (Is 40:3 referred to in Mk 1:3; Mt 3:3; Lk 3:4; Jn 1:23).
2. John the Baptist was baptizing with water, but Jesus would baptize with the Holy Spirit (Mk 1:8; Mt 3:11; Lk 3:16; Acts 1:5; Jn 1:33).

Chronology of Jesus' Ministry in John's Gospel*

Time	Location/Event	John
Origins (1:1–18)		
Eternity past	The Word was with God	1:1–18
Initial ministry (1:19–2:12) (A.D. 29–30?)		
	Baptist near Jordan	1:19–34
	Calling of first disciples	1:35–51
	Cana wedding	2:1–12
First Passover and first full year of ministry (2:13–4:54) (A.D. 30–31?)		
March/April	First Passover (Jerusalem)	2:13–3:21
	Baptist near Jordan	3:22–36
December?	Samaria	4:1–45
	Cana healing	4:46–54
Second year of ministry (ch. 5) (A.D. 31–32?)		
[March/April	Passover not recorded in John?]	
Sept./Oct.?	Jerusalem Sabbath controversy	5:1–47
Second Passover and third full year of ministry (6:1–11:54) (A.D. 32–33?)		
March/April	Second Passover recorded in John (Galilee)	6:1–21
	Synagogue of Capernaum	6:22–71
Sept./Oct.	Tabernacles (Jerusalem)	7:1–52; 8:12–59
Oct./Nov.?	Healing of blind man, Good shepherd discourse	9:1–10:21
mid-Dec.	Dedication (Jerusalem)	10:22–39
Jan.?	Withdrawal to area near Jordan	10:40–42
Feb./March?	Raising of Lazarus (Bethany)	11:1–54
Third Passover and Passion week (11:55–21:25) (A.D. 33?)		
March/April	Third Passover recorded	11:55–20:31
April/May	Resurrection appearance (Galilee)	21

*Note that these dates are tentative, representing merely the most plausible reconstruction of the sequence of events. For a helpful treatment, see Harold W. Hoehner, *Chronological Aspects of the Life of Christ* (Grand Rapids: Zondervan, 1977).

Table 5.4
The Son of Man in John's Gospel (in order of first reference)

1. The Son of Man has descended from heaven and will return in glory (1:51; 3:13; 6:62).
2. The Son of Man must be "lifted up" and thus be glorified; he is the one who gives his flesh and blood for the life of the world (3:14; 6:53; 8:28; 12:23, 34; 13:31).
3. The Son of Man is the eschatological judge (5:27).
4. The Son of Man as a self-reference of Jesus (6:27; 9:35).

misunderstanding

Even though he had been born in Bethlehem, Jesus was identified with his hometown of Nazareth and was a frequent target of prejudice, even from fellow-Galileans.

decision appear rash and not adequately considered. Here the Synoptics provide helpful background. For they tell us of earlier encounters between disciples and Jesus that culminated in their decision to follow Jesus. On the other hand, it must be remembered that John never claims to provide exhaustive information. He does not deny earlier encounters; he just chooses not to record them but to focus exclusively on Jesus' climactic call of certain disciples to follow him. And he does so in a way that it becomes clear that some of Jesus' first disciples had been

disciples of John the Baptist, thus emphasizing the continuity between their respective ministries.

Second, what are we to make of the high christological confessions in John 1 when compared with the **misunderstanding** theme in the Synoptics? Again, at first glance there seems to be a discrepancy. Here are some of the designations applied to Jesus in John 1:

Lamb of God (1:29, 36; by John the Baptist)

Son of God (1:34; by John the Baptist)

Messiah (1:41; by Andrew)

the one foretold in the Law and the Prophets (1:45; by Philip)

Son of God, king of Israel (1:49; by Nathanael)

But two things must be kept in mind: to begin with, John supplies a credible motive why these men would make the dramatic decision to leave everything behind to follow Jesus: they were convinced that he was the Messiah, the Son of God, the king of Israel, the one foretold by the Law and the Prophets.

Also, just because John the Baptist and some of Jesus' first followers utter these initial lofty confessions does not mean they fully understood the import of what they were saying. An analogy may help. Sometimes my five-year-old daughter makes statements that leave me in utter amaze-

Jesus' pronounce-ment, "I saw you while you were still under the fig tree," convinced Nathanael that he was the Son of God and the King of Israel.

This point is not only made in John's Gospel, where the disciples frequently are caught in misunderstanding; it is also evident from the Synoptic Gospels, where Peter, moments after confessing Jesus as the Christ, the Son of the living God, "rebukes" Jesus for suggesting that he (Jesus) would have to die—a crucified Messiah? an impossibility! And moments after being commended for his spiritual insight, Peter is called "Satan" by his Lord (cf. Mt 16:13–28). Which raises the question: when Peter confessed Jesus to be the Messiah in the first place, how accurate was his understanding of the nature of Jesus' messiahship, if he is immediately thereafter shown to be adamantly opposed to the idea that the Messiah must be crucified? The answer: his insight was genuine, but still incomplete. The christological confessions in John 1 should be viewed in the same light.

ment in light of the apparent spiritual insight they reveal. But usually it becomes eventually clear that my daughter spoke better than she knew. Or perhaps she had some initial grasp of the truth, but the insight still must become part of her experience to become fully hers. The same is true for Jesus' first followers: there was some real initial insight that caused them to leave everything behind to attach themselves to Jesus. But as time revealed, this insight still needed to be confirmed and tested.

Before we move on to John 2, three other important issues in 1:35–51 must first be addressed. First, what does John the Baptist mean when he calls Jesus the

Jesus' Display of Supernatural Knowledge

While John presents Jesus as the Word "become flesh" (1:14), that is, as thoroughly human, he nonetheless makes clear that Jesus displayed *his divine glory* while on earth. This, of course, includes what Jesus simply calls his "works" (but what John terms his "signs"), arresting and amazing acts of Jesus designed to evoke faith among those in his audience. Jesus' deity is also given expression through glimpses of his supernatural insight (one might also call this "divine omniscience") scattered throughout John's entire Gospel. Consider the following instances of Jesus' display of this divine attribute:

Jesus "saw" Nathanael under the fig tree (1:48)
Jesus knows that his time has not yet come (2:4)
Jesus foretells the nature of his own death (violent death by crucifixion, including three-day interim between crucifixion and resurrection: 2:19; 6:51; 10:15, 17, 18; 12:24; 15:13; cf. 18:32; and the "lifted up sayings" in 3:14; 8:28; and 12:32)
Jesus knows the Samaritan woman's immoral background (4:17–18)
Jesus knows the identity of his betrayer (6:70; 13:10–11)
Jesus knows the purpose of the blind man's and Lazarus's sicknesses (9:3; 11:4)
Jesus knows that Lazarus has

died (11:14)
Jesus foretells Peter's three denials (13:38)
Jesus foretells Peter's martyrdom (21:18–19)

John therefore holds in admirable balance Jesus' humanity and deity. Nevertheless, he makes clear that it is precisely because Jesus was *more* than just a man that he got into trouble with the Jewish authorities. And he also provides a plausible rationale why Jesus' followers chose to leave everything behind and follow him. They saw him as more than just another Jewish rabbi. He was the Messiah (1:41; cf. 1:45), the Son of God, and the King of Israel (1:49).

Table 5.5
The Seven Signs of Jesus in John's Gospel

1. The changing of water into wine	2:1–11
2. The temple cleansing	2:13–22
3. The healing of the nobleman's son	4:46–54
4. The healing of the lame man	5:1–15
5. The feeding of the multitude	6:1–15
6. The healing of the blind man	9:1–41
7. The raising of Lazarus	11:1–44

Aqedah

rabbi

**Map 5.1
Galilee**

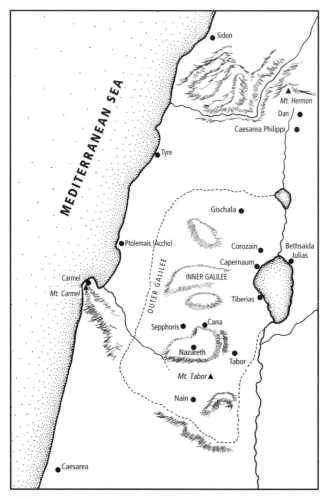

all, like sheep, have gone astray, each of us has turned to his own way; and the LORD has laid on him the iniquity of us all." One also thinks of the lamb provided by God for Abraham when he was ready to offer up his son of promise, Isaac, in obedience to God's command (called **Aqedah;** Gn 22:13). This is especially suggestive since John 3:16 probably alludes to this scene, highlighting one important difference: what Abraham was spared from doing at the last minute, God actually did—he gave his unique son (cf. also Rom 8:32).

Finally, one thinks of Paul's statement that "Christ, our Passover lamb, has been sacrificed" (1 Cor 5:7). This is the climax to which John's Gospel inexorably builds: Jesus is the Bread of Life (he will give his flesh for the life of the world) (6:51); he is the Good Shepherd who lays down his life for his sheep (10:15); and his sacrifice is shown to fulfill Passover symbolism (19:14, 31). We have already commented on John's profound reflection on Jesus' incarnation. John's teaching on the substitutionary atonement rendered by Jesus goes hand in hand with this earlier teaching. For it is in the flesh that Christ suffered vicariously for us; Jesus' humanity was an indispensable prerequisite for his cross-work on our behalf.

A second issue is of interest here: the consistent depiction of Jesus as a Jewish religious teacher, a **rabbi,** in John's Gospel. There are eight instances where Jesus is addressed as rabbi in John (1:38, 49; 3:2; 4:31; 6:25; 9:2; 11:8; 20:16). The designation is used by Jesus' first followers (1:38), Nathanael (1:49), Nicodemus (3:2), his disciples (4:31; 9:2; 11:8), and the multitudes (6:25). Interestingly, John translates the Hebrew (Aramaic) term *rabbi* in the first and last instance into Greek (*didaskalos* = teacher; 1:38; 20:16) but otherwise leaves the original term *rabbi*. The Synoptic writers, on the other hand, especially Luke, prefer the Greek term *didaskalos*. This indicates that, contrary to common prejudice, John is very concerned to preserve reliable historical information regarding Jesus. But what is even more important, all four Gospel writers agree that Jesus was first and foremost perceived by his contemporaries as a religious teacher, a rabbi.[2]

"Lamb of God"? In 1:29, John adds that, as the Lamb of God, Jesus "takes away the sin of the world." This clearly refers to substitutionary atonement. One is reminded of the sacrificial lamb of Isaiah 53. In Isaiah 53:6, the prophet writes, "We

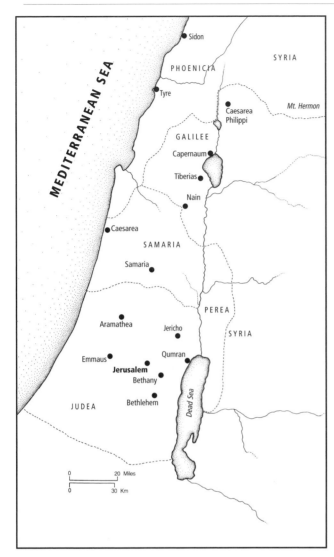

**Map 5.2
Palestine in
Jesus' Day**

---

apocalyptic

expectations for the reader of John's Gospel as he or she continues to follow John's narrative.

In the present case, the "greater things" Jesus promises to Nathanael are bound up with greater revelation: "you shall see heaven open, and the angels of God ascending and descending on the Son of Man." An "open heaven" was the dream of every Jewish **apocalyptic.** This spawned an entire genre of literature in the intertestamental period where enigmatic figures such as Enoch (who, according to Gn 5:24, was translated to heaven without dying) are depicted as traversing heaven and reporting what they see (1 Enoch is quoted in Jude 14–15). But, as Jesus himself asserts in John 3:13, "No one has ever gone into heaven except the one who came from heaven—the Son of Man." This Son of Man, in turn, is none other than the mysterious figure of Daniel 7:13, "one like a son of man, coming with the clouds of heaven." What Jesus claims is that he is that Son of Man prophesied in Daniel, the one who has seen God and has explained him (cf. Jn 1:18), the one who was "lifted up" at the cross (Jn 3:14; cf. 8:28; 12:32) and the one who will return in all his glory (Mt 26:64).

Jesus' words to Nathanael echo Genesis 28:12, the passage regarding Jacob's ladder, "with its top reaching to heaven, and *the angels of God were ascending and descending* on it." When Jacob awoke from his dream, he exclaimed, "How awesome is this place. This is none other than the house of God; this is the gate of heaven" (Gn 28:17). And he called that place Bethel, which means "house of God." What Jesus tells Nathanael, then, is that he himself will be the place of much greater divine revelation than that given at previous occasions. Jesus will mediate greater revelation than Abraham (8:58), Jacob (cf. also 4:12–14), Moses (1:17–18; 5:45–47; 9:28–29), and Isaiah (12:37–41). In this, John's argument is remarkably similar to that of the Book of Hebrews.

As the incarnate Word, Jesus is the Lamb of God providing atonement for sin; a rabbi, a Jewish religious teacher; and, as the Son of Man, the place of superior revelation. In all these things, the latter part of John 1 further develops John's empha-

The third and last issue pertains to the enigmatic reference at the end of the chapter, where Jesus comments to Nathanael, "You believe because I told you I saw you under the fig tree. You shall see greater things than that. . . . I tell you the truth, you shall see heaven open, and the angels of God ascending and descending on the Son of Man" (1:50–51). This is one of several references in John's Gospel to "greater things" to come. In 5:20, Jesus maintains that the Father "will show him even greater things than these," referring to his participation in the final judgment. And in 14:12, Jesus predicts that believers after his death will do "even greater things than these, because I am going to the Father." These pronouncements raise

sis in the Prologue that Jesus is the pre-existent Word become flesh through whom God dwelt among his people.

The First Sign: Turning Water into Wine at the Wedding at Cana (2:1–12)

In his concluding purpose statement, John writes that he recorded several of Jesus' signs in order to engender faith in his readers (20:30–31). The first is Jesus' turning water into wine at the wedding of Cana (2:11). Interestingly, John numbers another, later sign as "the second sign" Jesus performed in Cana (4:54). This brings Jesus' first ministry circuit to a close that spans chapters 2 through 4 (an inclusio). A complete list of Jesus' signs in John's Gospel is in table 5.5 (p. 70).

It is apparent that all of Jesus' signs occur in the first part of John's Gospel, which deals with Jesus' public ministry to the Jews. In human terms, this ministry turns out to be a failure, as John makes clear in his summary statement in 12:37: "Even after Jesus had done all these miraculous signs in their presence, they still would not believe in him." While Jesus' disciples see in Jesus' signs a reflection of the glory of God (2:11), the very same signs reveal the hardening of the Jewish leadership in its rejection of Israel's Messiah (cf., e.g., 2:13–22; 9:1–41; 11:1–44).

What the two events narrated in John 2 share in common is that they present Jesus as the restorer of Israel. In the first instance, the wedding at Cana, Jesus is shown to fill up the depleted resources of Judaism; in the second instance, the temple cleansing, Jesus cleanses the temple, the center of Jewish worship, from any activity unworthy of the true worship of God.

It is fitting that the insignificant village of Cana in Galilee becomes the site of Jesus' first sign. For Jesus chose obscurity over fame (Mt 4:5–7; Lk 4:9–12), and came, not to be served, but to serve others (Mk 10:45). The fact that Cana is also Nathanael's hometown (cf. 21:2) ties 2:1–11 in with the end of chapter 1. The way John tells the story (and information such as that there

Large water jars were used by the Jews for a variety of purposes, including ceremonial washing.

According to the Jewish historian Josephus, Herod the Great began the reconstruction of the Jerusalem temple in 20/19 B.C.

were six stone water jars suggests eyewitness recollection), the entire event served as a foil for Jesus' revelation that his "time had not yet come" (2:4; cf. later 7:30; 8:20; and the arrival of the "hour" in 12:23, 27; 13:1; 17:1). Nevertheless, Jesus finds a way not to "blow his cover": he performs a miracle "behind the scenes," without stealing the spotlight that properly belonged to the bride and groom, selflessly meeting the need of the hour.

That need, as Jesus' mother informs him, is for more wine. And Jesus gets to work. When he is done, an amazing miracle has been performed, a feat unparalleled in any of the Gospels. But what for human eyes is "miraculous" in the sense that natural laws are suspended is mere "work" for Jesus, albeit work that displays the glory of God in Jesus' humanity. As Augustine pointed out long ago, "He who made the wine at this wedding does the same thing every year in the vines. As the water which the servants put into the water-pots was turned into wine by the Lord, so that which the clouds pour down is turned into wine by the same Lord."[3]

Nevertheless, Jesus does not merely content himself with producing mediocre wine; he creates wine of superior quality. In a fine display of Johannine irony, the evangelist records the master of the banquet's reproach of the bridegroom for saving the best wine for last (when the wedding guests' taste had long been dulled by prolonged consumption of drink). This emphasis on the spectacular nature of Jesus' signs becomes a regular feature of John's narration. When Jesus heals the royal official's son in chapter 4, he does not even come to Capernaum to lay hands on the boy but performs the healing *long-distance*. In his healing of a lame man of chapter 5, Jesus does not merely restore the use of the man's legs; the man had been lame *for thirty-eight years*. When Jesus gives sight to a blind man, the man turns out to have been blind *from birth*. And when Jesus hears of Lazarus's sickness, he waits for two more days, by which time his friend has died. When Jesus arrives at the scene, he is faced not merely with the challenge of raising a dead man, but of restoring life to one *who had been dead for four days*, one day more than when a man's spirit left his corpse according to contemporary Jewish belief.

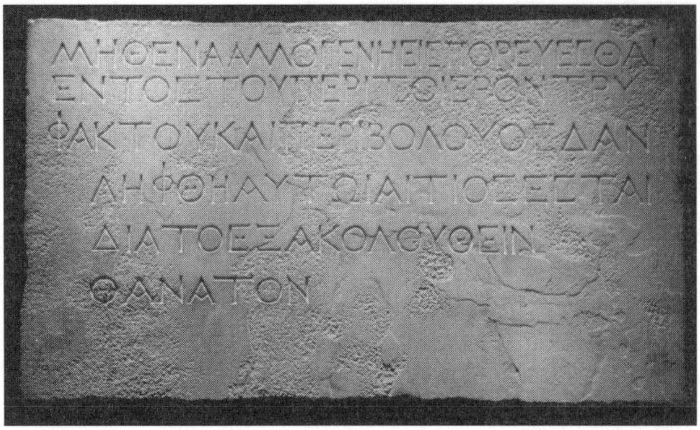

Foreigners who entered the inner sanctuary of the temple were subject to the death penalty

The superior quality of Jesus' revelation exposes the depth of Jewish (and human) unbelief: if eyewitnesses of *those* kinds of miracles fail to be persuaded of Jesus' true identity, nothing will change their minds; and God is justified when he pronounces their judgment.

Second Temple

The Second Sign: The Cleansing of the Temple (2:13–25)

The Jerusalem temple was a symbol of Jewish national and religious identity. The original temple, built by Solomon, had been destroyed by the Babylonians. But Zerubbabel had rebuilt the temple, and this **Second Temple** had been completed forty-six years prior to Jesus' first Jerusalem Passover. However, in keeping with Jesus' prediction (Mk 13:1–2 par.), it was destroyed again, this time by the Romans, in A.D. 70, shortly after reconstruction of the entire temple area had been completed. At the time of Jesus' ministry, the temple, once glorious symbol of God's presence in the midst of his people, had deteriorated into a place of religious profiteering and perfunctory ritual (2:14–16). The predicted destruction of the temple was a clear sign of God's disapproval of Israel's apostasy from the true worship of Yahweh.

It is against this backdrop that Jesus' rather striking action of cleansing the temple must be understood. What may at first appear to be a rather impetuous outburst of uncontrolled anger is cast by John as an outflow of genuine spiritual zeal. Thus Jesus is shown to typify the pronouncement of Psalm 69:9: "Zeal for your house consumes me" (quoted in Jn 2:17). What is it that provokes Jesus' authoritative display of driving the merchants and moneychangers from the temple area? In part, Jesus' actions are directed against the subversion of religious worship into commerce. This is made clear in the Synoptic

Map 5.3: The Jerusalem Temple

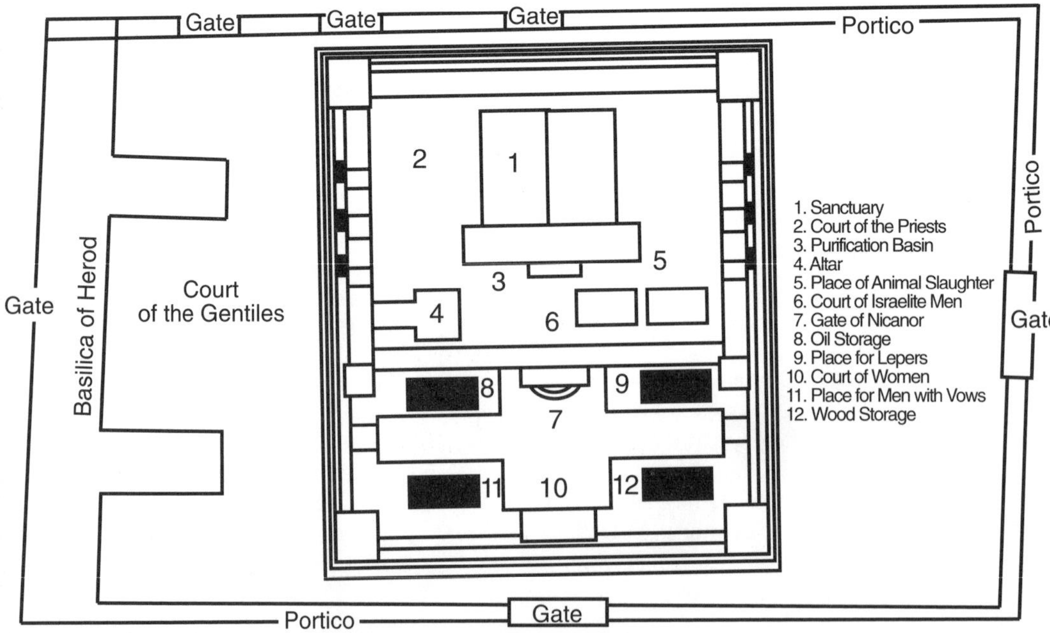
Gate
Gate
Gate
Portico
Portico
Gate
Gate
Basilica of Herod
Court of the Gentiles
1
2
3
4
5
6
7
8
9
10
11
12
1. Sanctuary
2. Court of the Priests
3. Purification Basin
4. Altar
5. Place of Animal Slaughter
6. Court of Israelite Men
7. Gate of Nicanor
8. Oil Storage
9. Place for Lepers
10. Court of Women
11. Place for Men with Vows
12. Wood Storage
Portico
Gate

accounts of a temple cleansing, where Jesus is quoted as charging that these merchants had made the temple "a den of robbers" (Mk 11:17 par.). We quote the context of Jeremiah 7:11 from which this allusion is taken in full:

> Will you steal and murder,
>   commit adultery and perjury,
> burn incense to Baal
>   and follow other gods you have not
>   known,
> and then come and stand before me in
>   this house, which bears my Name,
>   and say, "We are safe"—safe to do
>   all these detestable things?
> Has this house, which bears my Name,
>   become a den of robbers to you?
> But I have been watching! declares the
>   LORD (Jer 7:9–11).

What becomes clear from this quote is God's personal association with the temple. Twice the phrase "this house, which bears my Name" is repeated. What Jesus therefore conveys by his cleansing of the temple is that God's holiness and purity cannot tolerate the consistent defilement of "his house," the temple—judgment is inevitable. In prophetic style, Jesus' cleansing of the temple provides a symbolic act that points to the inner meaning of Jesus' crucifixion and bodily resurrection, which render him the replacement of the temple in the life and worship of his people (2:19–21).[4]

But there is one other important abuse that is targeted by Jesus' display of righteous outrage: the fact that the temple had in Jesus' day become a Jewish "nationalistic stronghold," a place where Gentile worship was obstructed rather than facilitated and encouraged.[5] This was contrary to the vision underlying Solomon's construction of the original temple (cf. 1 Kgs 8:41–43). As the prophet Isaiah expresses God's desire, "My house will be called a house of prayer *for all nations*," not merely Israel (Is 56:7). By selling sac-

Table 5.6
Major Archaeological Finds Relating to John's Gospel

Site or Artifact	Location	Passage in John
Inscription re: Gentile entrance of temple courts	Jerusalem	2:14–17
Herod's temple	Jerusalem	2:20
Remains of Samaria	Samaria	4:4
Jacob's well	Nablus	4:5–6
Pool of Bethesda	Jerusalem	5:2
Ancient fishing boat	Galilee	6:22–24; 21:8
Early synagogue	Capernaum	6:59
Pool of Siloam	Jerusalem	9:7
Tomb of Lazarus	Bethany	11:38
Caiaphas' family tomb	Jerusalem	11:49; 18:13–14
Pilate inscription	Caesarea	18:29
Stone pavement	Jerusalem	19:13
Skeletal remains of crucified man	Jerusalem	19:18
Garden tomb	Jerusalem	19:41–42*

*This listing does not imply endorsement as the likely site of Jesus' tomb. The Garden tomb rather provides a setting not dissimilar to the kind of tomb Jesus would have been laid in.

doublet

rificial animals and setting up their currency exchange in the court of the Gentiles, the outer court of the temple, the merchants in effect torpedoed Gentile worship in the only place where it was possible. And *that* flew in the face of God's, and Jesus', desire for the temple to become a place of worship, not just for Israel, but for people from all the nations.

Students of the Gospels are familiar with one particular puzzle presented by the temple cleansing: John's account is found at the beginning of Jesus' ministry, while the Synoptic Gospels place Jesus' cleansing of the temple at the end of Jesus' ministry, at the inception of Jesus' final week in Jerusalem culminating in his crucifixion (Mk 11:12–19 par.). Do we have to do here with a so-called **doublet,** an

instance where a certain type of event occurred more than once during Christ's ministry? This is certainly possible, as Mark's inclusion of two feedings of the multitudes makes clear (Mk 6:30–44; 8:1–13). Or does John, or do the Synoptic writers, rearrange their material, with one or the other following a topical rather than chronological arrangement?

Space does not permit a full treatment of this issue. We can merely state and briefly defend our conclusion. In short, it seems more likely that Jesus cleansed the temple twice, and that John only records the first instance while the Synoptic writers only report the second. For in both John and the Synoptics, Jesus' cleansing of the temple is closely interwoven with the chronology immediately preceding

The Coming of Jesus' "Hour"

One of the devices by which drama is built in John's Gospel is the repeated references to the coming of Jesus' "hour." Throughout the first major portion of the Gospel, Jesus emphatically maintains that *his hour has not yet come* (2:4; 7:6, 8; 7:30 = 8:20). When the Jews seek to arrest him (or even when the people want to make him king), he consistently eludes their grasp (6:15; 7:44; 8:59; 10:39; 11:53). For God has extended his providential hand of protection (cf. 8:20: "yet no one seized him, because his time had not yet come"). Also, Jesus regularly withdraws in order not to be seized before his time has come (6:15; 10:40–42; 11:54; cf. 11:8).

The tone changes dramatically at the very end of chapter 12 with Jesus' solemn announcement that his "hour" has now come (12:23). In the Johannine equivalent to the

Synoptic account of Gethsemane, there follows a brief struggle. Should Jesus ask to be rescued from this hour? No, he must go through it, for our sake (cf. 12:27). The farewell discourse reflects the settled conviction that Jesus' "hour" has now come (13:1; 16:32; 17:1; cf. 16:21).

What is Jesus' "hour"? It is the time of his crucifixion, at which he triumphantly exclaims, "It is finished!" (19:30; cf. 17:4). The work of salvation has been accomplished by the Lamb of God who takes away the sin of the world, God's sinless substitute dying for the transgressions of the people. The Gospel's entire theology of atonement culminates in this moment. Jesus is the Bread of Life who gives his flesh for the life of the world (6:51). He is the Good Shepherd who lays down his life for the sheep

(10:15). He is the Savior of the world (4:42).

Jesus' keen awareness of when his hour has or has not yet come highlights his messianic consciousness and his closeness and dependence on God. Jesus, "God the One and Only," is the one who is "at the Father's side" throughout his entire earthly sojourn (1:18). Even when his disciples leave him, Jesus knows that "I am not alone, for my Father is with me" (16:32). As we draw close to God, and he to us, may we grow in our sense of God's presence in our lives. May it be our "food" to do the will of God (4:34). May we be able to say at the end of our days, "I have brought you glory on earth by completing the work you gave me to do" (17:4). In the words of the psalmist, "Teach us to number our days aright, that we may gain a heart of wisdom" (Ps 90:12).

and following this event, so that it is difficult to extricate it from the fabric of the narrative sequence in the respective Gospels. In John, the cleansing of the temple takes place after Jesus' first sign at the wedding at Cana, and after a few days' stay in Capernaum, Jesus' base for ministry (2:12). The summary section in 2:23–25 and Nicodemus's visit with Jesus follow on the heels of the temple cleansing, and it appears from John that the arrangement is not merely topical but chronological.

The same observation can be made regarding the Synoptic account of the temple cleansing. In Mark's narrative, for instance, the temple cleansing is said to take place on the day following the triumphal entry ("the next day," Mk 11:12) and is sandwiched between Jesus' cursing of the fig tree and the disciples' comments on its having withered the following morning (Mk 11:20). It is hard to imagine how Mark could have tied in the temple cleansing more closely with immediately preceding and subsequent events in Jesus' ministry.

Moreover, maintaining the reality of *two* cleansings of the temple has the advantage of explaining why the witnesses at Jesus' trial could not remember exactly what Jesus had said at the occasion of the first temple cleansing: by that time, the event had happened three years ago (cf. Mk 14:57–58; Mt 26:60–61)! For the claim of these false witnesses that Jesus had said, "I will destroy this man-made temple and in three days will build another" has no equivalent in the Synoptic account of Jesus' temple cleansing just a few days earlier; but it coheres closely with Jesus' statement recorded in John 2:19, "Destroy this temple, and I will raise it again in three days." (Of course, even there the

The Significance of Jewish Festivals in John's Gospel

Three different Jewish festivals are featured in John's Gospel:

the Feast of Passover (2:13; 6:4; 11:55ff.), which was celebrated in March or April
the Feast of Tabernacles (Booths; 7:2), which took place in September or October
the Feast of Dedication (Hanukkah; 10:22), which occurred in November or December

The fact that John records three Passovers (four, if the "feast of the Jews" in 5:1 is another Passover) enables us to trace Jesus' ministry over a period of two to three years (note also that John may not record one Passover featured in the Synoptic Gospels). Attendance at the three great pilgrim feasts—Passover, Pentecost, and Tabernacles—in Jerusalem was expected of all Jewish males if at all possible. In keeping with this requirement, John portrays Jesus as attending many of the major Jewish festivals in Jerusalem, even though he was headquartered in Galilee and opposition toward him gradually mounted in the capital. Of the three festivals mentioned in John's Gospel, only the Passover and Tabernacles are biblical feasts. The Feast of Dedication, mentioned only in passing, commemorated the rededication of the Jewish temple in 164 B.C.

As you read John's Gospel, allow each mention of a particular feast to give you a sense of chronology and timing as you see Jesus' ministry—and people's response to it—unfold. Note also how John presents Jesus as the fulfillment, even replacement, of these feasts. His body is the temple (2:21); he is the light of the world and the living water to which the Feast of Tabernacles pointed (7:38–39; 8:12; 9:5); and he is God's Passover lamb (1:29, 36). These festivals were a focal point in Jewish religious and national life, commemorating, as it were, God's mighty acts of deliverance and provision for the nation. By placing himself squarely in this context, himself an observant Jew, Jesus staked the unmistakable claim of embodying himself God's final, greatest act of deliverance and provision for his people.

Table 5.7
References to "Feasts of the Jews" in the Gospel of John

Name of Feast	Reference in John	Time celebrated
Passover	2:13, 23	March–April
"A feast of the Jews"	5:1	?
Passover	6:4	March–April
Tabernacles (Booths)	7:2	September–October
Dedication (Hanukkah)	10:22	November–December
Passover	11:55–12:1	March–April

witnesses got it wrong: Jesus did not say he himself would destroy the temple, but he "dared" his opponents to destroy the temple *of his body* [2:21] which he knew they would in fact do, but his "temple" would prove to be indestructible, as evidenced by his resurrection.)

If this interpretation is correct, Jesus would have cleansed the temple twice, at the beginning as well as at the end of his ministry. What is more, since John 6 indicates that Jesus spent the middle Passover of his public ministry in Galilee, Jesus would have cleansed the temple *at every occasion* he was in Jerusalem at the Passover recorded by John (though John only includes the first of these occasions). His holiness and righteousness could not bear to see how God's house was desecrated, *whenever* he observed such abuse. One final observation confirms the accuracy of our interpretation: the statement in John 2:20 that "it has taken forty-six years to build this temple," together with the fact that historical records show that Herod the Great began the project of restoring the temple in the eighteenth year of his reign, that is, 20–19 B.C. (Josephus, *Ant.* 15.380), and finished it one and a half years later in 18/17 B.C. (Josephus, *Ant.* 15.421) places the dates for 2:13–22 at A.D. 29/30. And this date applies more likely to the beginning than the end of Jesus' ministry, since Luke 3:1 assigns the beginning of the Baptist's ministry to the fifteenth year of Tiberius (A.D. 29).[6]

Study Questions

1. Briefly summarize the first week of Jesus' ministry recorded in John 1:19–2:11 and show how John here begins to flesh out his presentation of Jesus as the preexistent, incarnate Word in the Prologue.

2. Pinpoint the role of John the Baptist in relation to Jesus according to John.

3. Describe the essence of Jesus' first sign at the wedding at Cana.

4. Explain the significance of Jesus' cleansing of the temple, including a discussion of the question of whether John and the Synoptics record one or two temple cleansings.

Conclusion

John 1:19–2:11 presents one entire week of Jesus' ministry, taking its point of departure from the ministry of John the Baptist and culminating in Jesus' "first sign" in Cana of Galilee. Jesus' first followers indicate why they chose to attach themselves to Jesus: they believe Jesus to be the Christ, the Son of God (cf. 20:30–31).

Also, Jesus is identified at the very outset of John's Gospel as the Lamb of God (1:29, 36), providing substitutionary atonement for "the sin of the world," and as the place of superior revelation, surpassing Jacob's vision of a ladder reaching into heaven at Bethel (1:50–51). Jesus' cleansing of the temple, finally, constitutes another sign (2:18), this time in Jerusalem (cf. 2:23; 3:2), portraying Jesus as the restorer of true worship to Israel and the replacement of the temple in the life of God's people. With this, the stage is set for Jesus' encounters with Nicodemus and the Samaritan woman in the following chapters, an unlikely pair of contrasts which it remains for us to explore in the following chapter.

Key Words

inclusio

misunderstandings

Aqedah

rabbi

apocalyptic

Second Temple

doublet

asides

6 Jesus' Early Ministry (Part 2): Sign #3

John 3:1–4:54

Every valley shall be raised up,
  every mountain and hill made low;
the rough ground shall become level,
  the rugged places a plain.
And the glory of the LORD will be revealed,
  and all mankind together will see it.
For the mouth of the LORD has spoken.

—Isaiah 40:4–5

Supplemental Reading: Ezekiel 36:22–38; Jeremiah 31:31–34

Outline

- Jesus and Nicodemus (3:1–21)
- The Testimony of John the Baptist (3:22–36)
- Jesus and the Samaritan Woman (4:1–42)
- The Third Sign: The Healing of the Nobleman's Son (4:43–54)

Objectives

After reading this chapter, you should be able to

1. Explain the relationship between Jesus' two signs in Cana of Galilee.
2. Compare and contrast Jesus' encounters with Nicodemus and the Samaritan woman.
3. Demonstrate the undercurrent of people's rejection of Jesus in both Galilee and Jerusalem by analyzing their response to Jesus' signs.

Chapters 3 and 4 feature Jesus' encounters with two individuals who could not be more different: he a Jew, she a Samaritan; he a respected member of the Sanhedrin, the Jewish ruling council, she ostracized from society to the extent that she must draw water at the communal well in the heat of the noon hour when no one else would be there (cf. Gn 24:11); he a rabbi, a Jewish religious teacher, she steeped in folklore and religious ignorance; he a man, she a woman. The sheer fact that John chooses to place these two encounters side by side has a powerful impact on the reader. Let's read on and explore the message John seeks to convey by those two narratives.

Jesus and Nicodemus (3:1–21)

While oral and written communication share certain features, there are also important differences. In a personal face-to-face conversation, the tone of a given statement, a person's facial expression, or an accompanying gesture may be an important part of the interchange. When such a living interaction is reduced to writing, a large part of these aspects of communication is invariably lost. This does not mean that written forms of communication are necessarily indeterminate or inescapably ambiguous in meaning. It does mean, however, that understanding the particular interaction conveyed in written form may be rendered more difficult.

A case in point is Jesus' conversation with Nicodemus. Was Nicodemus's tone condescending when he said to Jesus, "Rabbi, we know you are a teacher who has come from God" (3:2)? It is hard to be sure. For the decisive clues present in oral communication, such as tone of voice or facial expression, are lacking once the conversation has been reduced to writing. We are left with the challenge of drawing probable inferences from the available textual data. In the present case, we discover that Jesus responds by not responding at all. Cutting right through Nicodemus's initial platitudes, he immediately confronts him with his need for a spiritual rebirth.[1] Later in the conversation, Jesus chides Nicodemus by saying, "You are Israel's teacher [cf. Nicodemus calling Jesus a "teacher come from God" in 3:2] and do you not understand these things? I tell you the truth, *we* speak of what *we know*, and *we* testify to what *we* have seen" (3:11). It seems that, finally, at that point Jesus returns Nicodemus's initial comment in kind by echoing his phrase "we know."

One other aspect, largely invisible in the text because largely implicit, should be drawn out. It is the fact that Jesus and Nicodemus are here engaged in what might be called an acute power struggle. Like it or not, the two men found themselves on two opposite ends of the spectrum as far as formal didactic authority within Judaism is concerned. Regarding Jesus, people asked in amazement, "How did this man get such learning without having studied?" (7:15). Since Jesus had never attached himself as a disciple to a Jewish rabbi, he was considered to be self-taught and without formal authority (cf. Mt 7:29); the same charge was leveled later against his disciples (Acts 4:13). Nicodemus, on

The Double *Amēn* in John's Gospel

There are twenty-five instances of the double *amēn* in John's Gospel. The first one is in 1:51; three are found in the present narrative (3:3, 5, 11), which underscores the authoritative tone with which Jesus spoke to Nicodemus. Jesus' words to the Jews likewise contain several instances of the double *amēn* each (5:19, 24, 25; 6:26, 32, 47, 53; 8:34, 51, 58; 10:1, 7; 12:24). The same can be said of Jesus' final words to his disciples (13:16, 20, 21, 38; 14:12; 16:20, 23; 21:18). In every instance, Jesus uses this phrase to introduce a weighty, authoritative pronouncement. The term *amēn* comes from the Hebrew "it is firm." In the Old Testament, it is regularly used by a second party confirming the truth of a given statement. But in a startling break with common Jewish usage, Jesus used this term to introduce *his own* pronouncements. Notably, while the Synoptics have a single *amēn*, John uses the phrase twice.

the other hand, was a powerful member of the Jewish ruling council called Sanhedrin (see sidebar, p. 185). As John's entire Gospel makes clear, the relationship between Jesus and the Jewish leadership of his day was essentially characterized by a struggle for control over the masses (hence the title "Escalating Conflict" for John 5–12). What may look rather innocent and pale on the written page was probably much more charged and poignant when it actually happened.

Now to the substance of the interchange. Rather than responding in kind to Nicodemus's complimentary remarks, Jesus confronts the "Teacher of Israel" with his need for regeneration: "I tell you the truth, no one can see the kingdom of God unless he is born again" (3:3). The phrase "I tell you the truth," distinctive to John's Gospel, reflects a double *amēn*,

signaling an authoritative pronouncement about to be made (see sidebar, p. 82). "To see the kingdom of God" is a thoroughly Jewish phrase, attesting to John's accuracy in historical detail. It is one of only two contexts (the other one is Jesus' statement to Pilate that his kingdom is not of this world in 18:36) where the phrase "kingdom of God" is used in John's Gospel.[2] For Nicodemus, as for every believing Jew, "seeing the kingdom of God" was a major aspiration, even expectation. For Jesus to assert spiritual rebirth as a precondition must have startled his rabbinic counterpart.

But should it have? While Nicodemus fails to understand the true meaning of Jesus' words, objecting that it would be impossible for a person to be literally born a second time (3:4; see also v. 9), the sharpness of Jesus' rebuke (3:10) suggests that

Irony in John's Gospel

As do the Synoptic writers, John occasionally flashes a sense of humor, using a literary device called "irony." While there is a certain overlap with the Johannine misunderstanding theme, irony is a distinct feature. In fact, not every misunderstanding is an instance of irony. What the following instances of Johannine irony have in common is that in each case it is hard for the reader to keep a straight face. Likewise, one wonders whether even John the evangelist had a smile on his face when he recorded the following ironic statements.

The first one belongs to Nicodemus. When Jesus talked about his need for spiritual rebirth, he responded: "How can a man be born when he is old? Surely he cannot enter a second time into his mother's womb to be born!" (3:4).

Another case of irony can be detected in the Jews' puz-

zlement regarding Jesus' statement that they would look soon for him but would not be able to find him: "Where does this man intend to go that we cannot find him? Will he go where our people live scattered among the Greeks, and teach the Greeks?" (7:35).

Or consider John's record of the crowd's confusion regarding Jesus' origin: "Does not the Scripture say that the Christ will come from David's family and from Bethlehem, the town where David lived?" (7:42). Little did they know that what they considered an obstacle to faith in Jesus as Messiah (thinking he came from Galilee) was in fact further proof that that's precisely who he was.

Once again, the Jews can't figure out what Jesus means when he says that they will look for him unsuccessfully: "Will he kill himself? Is that

why he says, 'Where I go, you cannot come'?" (8:22).

For those of us who would do well to lighten up once in a while, John serves as a good example. By virtue of his considerable discernment, he saw the fine ironies of life in which those of us get caught who are blind to spiritual truth. And while he went to great lengths in order to persuade others that Jesus is the Christ, he was not above occasionally having a good laugh along the way.

Note: Want to check out some more instances of Johannine irony for yourself? Try 2:9–10, 20; 7:28; the entire ch. 9, esp. 9:29, 30–34; 11:50; 18:38 (cf. 14:6); 19:15. For a book-length treatment of this feature of John's Gospel, see Paul D. Duke, *Irony in the Fourth Gospel* (Atlanta: John Knox, 1985).

Nicodemus could legitimately be expected to understand the personal need for regeneration. But where in the Hebrew Scriptures is this taught? Ezekiel's vision of the valley of dry bones raised to life (Ez 37) may still primarily refer to Israel's collective experience rather than to individual resurrection. But the preceding chapter includes a remarkable passage whose theology seems to anticipate Jesus' teaching in John 3:

> For I will take you out of the nations;
> I will gather you from all the countries
>   and bring you back into your own
>   land.
> I will *sprinkle clean water on you,*
>   and you will be clean;
> I will *cleanse you* from all your impurities
>   and from all your idols.
> I will give you a new heart
>   and *put a new spirit in you;*
> I will remove from you your heart of
>   stone
>   and give you a heart of flesh.
> And I will *put my Spirit in you*
>   and move you to follow my decrees
>   and be careful to keep my laws
>   (Ez 36:24–27).

Table 6.1
The Three Lifted-up Sayings in John's Gospel

In the dynamic, dramatic flow of John's Gospel, the following three lifted-up sayings progressively reveal to the reader the nature of Jesus' death:

1. "Just as Moses lifted up the snake in the desert, so the Son of Man must be lifted up, that everyone who believes in him may have eternal life" (3:14–15).
2. "When you have lifted up the Son of Man, then you will know that I am the one I claim to be" (8:28).
3. "'But I, when I am lifted up from the earth, will draw all people to myself.' He said this to show the kind of death he was going to die" (12:32).

Let's look at John 3 in light of this passage. First, we notice the parallelism between John 3:3 and 3:5. John 3:3 says, "I tell you the truth, no one can see the kingdom of God unless he is *born again*." John 3:5 has, "I tell you the truth, no one can enter the kingdom of God unless he is *born of water and the Spirit*." Two observations may be made. First, what does the Greek term *anōthen* (translated with "again" in the NIV in both 3:3 and 7) mean? Notably, in the only other three instances where the phrase occurs in John's Gospel, the NIV renders it with "from above" in both 3:31 and 19:11 (cf. Jas 1:17; 3:15, 17) and with "from top to bottom" (i.e., literally "from above") in 19:23 (=Mt 27:51/Mk 15:38; in Lk 1:3; Acts 26:5; and Gal 4:9 the term means "from the beginning"). Does *anōthen* then mean "again" or "from above" in the present passage? Nicodemus, of course, thought "again" was what the phrase meant; but as John indicates, he misunderstood Jesus' true message, which pointed to the rabbi's need to be born "from above," that is, born spiritually. The popular phrase "to be born again" is thus based on a misunderstanding. Second, we note that "born again [from above]" in verse 3 is further explained as "born of water and the Spirit" in verse 5. Some have suggested that "born of water" refers to water baptism. But would it have been meaningful for Jesus to inform Nicodemus that he must be baptized to go to heaven? Nothing in the context indicates that this is the case, and it is unlikely that Jesus would have expected Nicodemus already to have known this.

The above quoted passage from Ezekiel provides a more plausible backdrop. Here mention is made of "a new spirit" and "a new heart" God would give believers in the future, a reality that is also expressed in terms of "cleansing from all impurities" by "sprinkling with clean water." It appears therefore that "to be born by water and the Spirit" refers to a single event: spiritual rebirth, metaphorically expressed by the analogy of washing with clean water (cf. Ti 3:5: "He saved us through the washing of rebirth and renewal by the Holy Spirit"). Nicodemus may have been startled by this discovery of his need for spiritual rebirth; the per-

The landscape of Palestine is characterized by great variety. Here the Judean hill country provides vistas of fertile plains below.

ceptive reader of John's Gospel is already aware of this requirement. Consider the Prologue: "Yet to all who received him, to those who believed in his name, he gave the right to become children of God—children born not of natural descent, nor of human decision or a husband's will, but born of God" (1:12–13).

To this day, people's need for regeneration is not sufficiently recognized, and

---

Table 6.2

Jesus "Greater Than" Major Old Testament Figures

1. Greater than Jacob: "Are you greater than our father Jacob?"   4:12

2. Greater than Moses: "What will you do? Our forefathers ate the manna in the desert"   6:31*

3. Greater than Abraham: "Are you greater than our father Abraham?"   8:53

* Cf. 1:17; 5:39–40, 45–47; 9:28–29.

---

a good, moral life is upheld as God's sole expectation in many churches. But this neglect—and the ensuing nominalism—will prove fatal if not remedied. For what applies to Nicodemus applies to every person: "You must be born again."

Jesus does not stop his instruction of Nicodemus at this point, however. He proceeds to explain that "the Son of Man must be lifted up" just as Moses lifted up the serpent in the wilderness (3:14, referring to Nm 21:8–9). And just as every Israelite who had been bitten by a poisonous snake looked at the raised serpent and lived, so every person who "looks" at (that is, believes in) the "lifted up" Son of Man will have eternal life (3:15). This is one of three "lifted-up sayings" in John; at present, there is no indication Jesus is talking to Nicodemus about his *crucifixion*. In 8:28, the second such saying ("When you have lifted up the Son of Man, then you will know that I am the one I claim to be"), it is still not made explicit that the place where the Son of Man will be "lifted up" is the cross. But in the third instance, 12:32 ("But I, when I am lifted up from the earth, will draw all men to myself"), the veil is finally lifted. For as John editorializes, "He said this to show the kind of death he was going to die."

In John's theology, Jesus' cross is not a place of shame and humiliation; it is rather the place where Jesus is "glorified" (e.g., 12:28; 17:5). In distinctive Johannine terminology, the term "lifted up" has a double meaning: it means "being physically lifted up on the cross" (literal use) as well as "being exalted and honored" (figurative use). In this, John has significantly reworked the Synoptic tradition, where the focus is primarily on Jesus' humiliation at the cross. John also clusters the individual events of Jesus' crucifixion, burial, resurrection, ascension, and exaltation together as one single event, Jesus' "glorification." But more of this later when we discuss Jesus' last words to his disciples in the Upper Room.

With this instruction regarding the lifted-up Son of Man, Jesus and Nicodemus's conversation fades into the background, and, almost seamlessly, John the evangelist takes over (a similar transition between a character in the story and the evangelist may be detected later in the same chapter between 3:30 and 3:31ff.) and drives home the theological lesson for his readers (including us). "For God so loved the world,"

he says, "that he gave his one and only Son that whoever believes in him shall not perish but have eternal life" (3:16). It is a tribute to the profundity of John's thought that this sentence is one of the most well-known verses in the entire Bible (even in an age when biblical literacy is on the wane). John's statement makes clear that the "Son of Man" mentioned by Jesus is in fact God's one and only Son ("only begotten" = *monogenēs*, 3:16, 18), referred to already in the Prologue (1:14, 18).

The Testimony of John the Baptist (3:22–36)

By way of interlude between Jesus' conversation with Nicodemus and his encounter with the Samaritan woman (see introduction above), John returns to John the Baptist whom he had already mentioned in the Prologue (1:6–8, 15) and later in the opening chapter of his Gospel (1:19–37; see our treatment of John the Baptist in John's Gospel there). What we learn in the present passage is that John the Baptist had continued his practice of

At the time of Jesus' encounter with the Samaritan woman, the ancient city of Shechem was locatd in Samaritan territory near Mount Gerizim.

Jacob's well, one of the deepest wells in all of Palestine (over a hundred feet), was the setting for Jesus' conversation with the Samaritan woman.

baptism up to this point (information that is entirely consistent with that of the other Gospels), which raises the issue of the relationship between his ministry and that of Jesus. In a potent metaphor, John describes his role as that of "best man," as "friend of the bridegroom" (3:29), who rejoices with the groom (Jesus) without any sense of rivalry or competitiveness.

As the evangelist will make clear at the very end of his Gospel, this is a lesson all of Jesus' disciples need to learn (including the apostle Peter and John himself; 21:15–23).

Jesus and the Samaritan Woman (4:1–42)

Jesus' return trip from the Jerusalem Passover back to Galilee led him, by divine necessity (4:4), through Samaria. Samaritans occupied a middle position between Jews and Gentiles, considering themselves Jews but being viewed by Jews as Gentiles. This middle position required that the early church be a witness not just in Jerusalem and in all Judea, and then to the ends of the earth, but also in Samaria (Acts 1:8; cf. Acts 8). This sequence may also be reflected in the fact that in John Jesus first witnesses to the Jew Nicodemus (ch. 3), then to the Samaritan woman (ch. 4), and then hears of approaching Gentiles (12:20–22).

Only if we understand the acrimony and animosity between Jews and Samar-

Table 6.3 **The Unfolding Drama of Jesus and the Samaritan Woman (John 4)**	
1. Jesus engages in Samaritan mission	4:1–26
(Meanwhile, the disciples go to town to buy food)	4:8
2. Jesus instructs his disciples about mission	4:27–38
(Meanwhile, the woman goes back to town to get her townsmen)	4:28–30
3. Jesus reaps the mission harvest	4:39–42

Table 6.4
Jesus' "Work" in John's Gospel

The first and last references to Jesus' work *(ergon)* in John's Gospel, both in the singular, form an important *inclusio:*

"My food is to do the will of him who sent me and to finish his work" (4:34).
"I have brought you glory on earth by completing the work you gave me to do" (17:4).

Sometime in the fourth or fifth century B.C., the Samaritans erected their own sanctuary on Mount Gerizim. Razed by John Hyrcanus in 128 B.C., it continued to be a bone of contention between Jews and Samaritans in Jesus' day.

itans will we grasp the provocative nature of Jesus making a Samaritan (the "Good" Samaritan) the hero of one of his parables (Lk 10:25–37). Indeed, as John tells his readers, "Jews do not associate with Samaritans" (4:9). This is why the Samaritan woman is surprised when Jesus asks her for a drink, for he must have known that using a drinking vessel handled by a Samaritan would inevitably defile him, since Samaritans were considered "unclean" by Jews. But contemporary Jewish scruples of that sort were of no concern to Jesus (cf. Mk 7:19).

The setting for Jesus' encounter with the Samaritan woman is historic: Jacob's well. But their conversation has to bridge several major gulfs. First, an *ethnic* gulf: Samaritans and Jews had no dealings with one another, and their history was strained, to say the least. The Samaritans had built a temple on Mount Gerizim (cf. Dt 27:4–6) around 400 B.C., which was destroyed by the Jews in approximately 128 B.C., who claimed that proper worship must be conducted in the temple in Jerusalem. Second, there was a *religious* gulf: the Samaritans only acknowledged the Pentateuch, the Five Books of Moses, as Scripture; the Jews' canon also included the Writings and the Prophets. Then there is the *moral* gulf: Jesus, the Christ, the Son of God, and the Samaritan woman who has had five sexual partners and who is not married to her present companion (4:17–18).

In all of this, John highlights the amazing divine condescension that caused the preexistent Word to become flesh and to dwell among us. In the fullness of his humanity, Jesus is tired (4:6) and thirsty (4:7) and asks a Samaritan woman for a drink. Yet it is precisely this condescension that opens up opportunities for revelation: regarding Jesus' ability to grant eternal life ("living water," 4:10); regarding Jesus' supernatural knowledge (4:17–18; cf. 1:48); regarding the proper way of worship (in spirit and truth; 4:23–24); and regarding Jesus' true identity (he is the Christ; 4:25).

With Jesus' coming, the end-time spiritual harvest had begun: "Open your eyes and look at the fields! They are ripe for harvest."

In the end, the Samaritan woman goes to fetch some of her townsmen to come and see Jesus for themselves. Indeed, "many of the Samaritans from that town believed in him because of the woman's testimony" (3:39).

Thus the primary topic of this narrative is clear: mission. This is developed by the evangelist in the extended instruction section of 4:27–38. John had informed the reader earlier that Jesus' disciples had gone into the town to buy food (4:8). When the disciples return and are surprised to find Jesus talking with a woman, the Samaritan woman leaves to tell her townspeople about Jesus. This creates a window of opportunity for Jesus, which he promptly uses to instruct his disciples about their role in the messianic mission. As in the case of the woman, Jesus takes his point of departure from people's daily necessity for sustenance. In the case of the Samaritan woman, it was her need to come and draw water from the well; in the case of the disciples, it was the food they had bought nearby. But when dealing with the Samaritan, Jesus developed water symbolism in the direction of his ability to give eternal life (evangelism); in talking with his disci-

ples, Jesus talks about his mission and how they have entered it (discipleship): "My food is to do the will of him who sent me and to finish his work" (4:34; cf. 17:4).

In between these two references, John frequently refers to Jesus' "works" (*erga*) in the plural (5:20, 36; 7:3; 9:3, 4; 10:25, 32, 37, 38; 14:10, 11, 12; 15:24).

To illustrate his point, he uses two common sayings: "Four months more and then the harvest" (4:35); and "One sows and another reaps" (4:37). Regarding the first proverb, he claims that, to the contrary, spiritually speaking, the harvest is *now*; no waiting period is required. The harvest has arrived with Jesus' mission. The second maxim Jesus applies to himself and the disciples. He notes that they benefit from a long string of "others" who have sown and labored: divine spokesmen such as the prophets all the way up to John the Baptist, culminating in Jesus (4:38). The harvest is now, and the disciples are not merely called to follow Jesus, they are sent by him on a spiritual mission: "I sent you to reap" (4:38). (While translations usually render "sent" in the past tense, it can be argued that "send" would actually be a superior rendering;

if so, Jesus is here talking not about a sending in the past but about the disciples' mission in general.)[3]

Let's summarize what we've learned in our study of Jesus' encounter with the Samaritan woman. In an amazing act of condescension, Jesus bridges several major gulfs as he reaches out to this woman. What is more, he uses this experience to instruct his disciples regarding the mission of which they had become a part. With this, Jesus' first major ministry circuit has almost come to a close. The healing of the nobleman's son, labeled by John Jesus' "second sign" in Cana of Galilee, ties 4:43–54 in with 2:1–11, thus constituting 2:1–4:54 as the first major unit in John's narrative about Jesus.

The Third Sign: The Healing of the Nobleman's Son (4:43–54)

When Jesus returns to Galilee, he is "welcomed" there (4:45). But the welcome extended to Jesus turns out to be shallow and conditional: people are interested only in miracles (4:44, 45). As Jesus agonizes, "Unless you people see miraculous signs and wonders, you will never believe" (4:48). Tellingly, the only recorded sign performed by Jesus at this occasion involves "a certain royal official" (*basilikos*; 4:46), probably a (Gentile?) officer in Herod Antipas's service (Herod was

"Living Water"

The backdrop to Jesus' statements about "living water" is provided by two passages in the prophet Jeremiah:

This is what the LORD says: . . .
"My people have committed two sins:
They have forsaken me, the spring of living water,
and have dug their own cisterns,
broken cisterns that cannot hold water" (Jer 2:5, 13).

And again Jeremiah laments,

O LORD, the hope of Israel,
all who forsake you will be put to shame.
Those who turn away from you will be written in the dust
because they have forsaken the LORD,

the spring of living water (Jer 17:13).

At the same time, the psalmist would dream of a future day of renewed abundance in the Lord's presence:

They feast on the abundance of your house;
you give them drink from your river of delights.
For with you is the foundation of life;
in your light we see light (Ps 36:8–9).

And the prophet Isaiah envisions a time when all human thirst will again be quenched:

Come, all you who are thirsty,
come to the waters;
and you who have no money,
come, buy and eat!
Come, buy wine and milk

without money and without cost (Is 55:1).

In John 4, and in the revealing follow-up passage in 7:38–39, Jesus identifies himself plainly as the eschatological bringer of such abundant divine provision. He introduces himself as the one who can meet the longing of every human heart. Moreover, as John 7:38–39 reveals, "living water" is in fact an emblem of the Holy Spirit, who would be poured out in short order. With this the passage in Luke's Gospel coheres where Jesus is quoted as saying, "If you then . . . know how to give good gifts to your children, how much more will your Father in heaven give the Holy Spirit to those who ask him!" (Lk 11:13). God is indeed good, and this goodness is mediated through the gift of God's one and only son (Jn 3:16).

A harvester in the wheatfields of Samaria provides a suggestive backdrop for Jesus' instruction of his disciples regarding their mission.

tetrarch [not king] of Galilee from 4 B.C.–A.D. 39, but he was commonly regarded as king: cf., e.g., Mk 6:14; a similar designation is used for Blastus, "a trusted personal servant of the king" [Herod Agrippa I, Herod the Great's grandson] in Acts 12:20). The story resembles that of the Gentile centurion in Matthew 8:5–13 and Luke 7:2–10, but this is not the same incident.

As in the case of the wedding at Cana, Jesus condescends to meet the need of the hour, in the present instance, the well-being of the royal official's son. But rather than "coming down" to Capernaum where the child lay sick, Jesus heals the boy long-distance, another instance of John's emphasis on "hard" miracles of Jesus. Indeed, when the royal official learns from his servants that his son got better at the seventh hour (that is, about 1:00 P.M., counting from sunrise at 6:00 A.M.), he and his entire household believe (4:51–53). For this was the precise time Jesus had made the pronouncement that the official's son would live (4:53).

As in the case of the first sign in Cana of Galilee, no discourse accompanies the account of the healing of the royal official's son. Thus the evangelist refrains from drawing out any specific christo-

logical symbolism that may be reflected in Jesus' performance of this particular sign. We observe, however, that Jesus' working of signs in Galilee (similar to that in Jerusalem, see 2:23–25; 3:2) is unable to overcome the profound rejection he suffers from his own people (4:44). This rejection theme, already sounded in the Prologue (1:11), will reach an intermediate culmination point at the end of chapter 6 when many "disciples" (6:66) leave Jesus and climaxes in the pronouncement at the end of chapter 12 that "even after Jesus had done all these miraculous signs in their presence, they still would not believe in him."

What this makes clear is that signs by themselves are an insufficient basis for faith. Likewise, we should not think today that we will be able to reason anyone into the kingdom merely by skillful persuasion. This is not to discourage our evangelistic efforts; it rather challenges us to put our trust in God, not ourselves, as we seek to lead others to a saving knowledge of the Lord Jesus Christ. Rational argument and a presentation of the evidence for the historicity of Christ's resurrection, for example, have their place; but they will not succeed, unless faith is engendered by the work of the Holy Spirit. As

91

Study Questions

1. What were the social and spiritual dynamics underlying Jesus' conversation with Nicodemus?

2. What were the social and spiritual dynamics underlying Jesus' conversation with the Samaritan woman?

3. In what ways does Jesus use experiences in his own ministry to train his disciples for mission?

Paul indicates, even faith is ultimately a gracious gift of God (Eph 2:8–9), and accordingly, Paul's own preaching was carried out, not in reliance on sophisticated rhetoric or persuasive powers, but with spiritual conviction and a demonstration of the power of God (1 Cor 2:1–5).

With this, we have come to the end of the first major section of John's Gospel. We have traveled with Jesus from Cana in Galilee to Jerusalem, and back to Galilee via Samaria. We have witnessed his turning water into wine at the wedding at Cana; we have watched him confront rabbi Nicodemus with his need for spiritual regeneration; we have seen him lead a Samaritan woman to the realization that he knows her sinful heart and that she needs forgiveness and cleansing from Jesus, who is the Christ and the Savior of the world; and we have seen Jesus have mercy on the royal official from Capernaum by healing his son. Together with Jesus' disciples, we have seen a glimpse of Jesus' glory in his words and actions; and we have been instructed regarding the mission of Jesus which we, too, have entered. There is a harvest of Nicodemuses, Samaritan women, and royal officials to be reaped also in our day; and in our response to Jesus' call, we must be prepared to echo Isaiah's words: "Here am I. Send me!" (Is 6:8).

7 Escalating Conflict (Part 1): Signs ##4–5

John 5:1–6:71

For if Joshua had given them rest, God would not have spoken later about another day. There remains, then, a Sabbath-rest for the people of God; for anyone who enters God's rest also rests from his own work, just as God did from his.

—Hebrews 4:8–10

Supplemental Reading: Exodus 20:8–11; Deuteronomy 5:12–15; Exodus 16

Outline

- **The Fourth Sign: The Healing of the Lame Man (5:1–18)**
- **The Sabbath Controversy (5:19–47)**
- **The Fifth Sign: The Feeding of the Five Thousand (6:1–15)**
- **The Walking on the Water (6:16–21)**
- **The Bread of Life Discourse (6:22–59)**
- **Watershed: The Twelve Remain, Many Others Leave (6:60–71)**

Objectives

After reading this chapter, you should be able to

1. Explain the nature of the Sabbath controversy in John 5.
2. Relate the feeding of the five thousand to Jesus' discourse on the Bread of Life.
3. Describe the structural significance of the end of chapter 6 within the framework of the entire Gospel.

The twin pools of Bethesda, surrounded by five covered colonnades, witnessed Jesus' startling healing of an invalid.

After narrating Jesus' first ministry circuit from Cana of Galilee to Jerusalem and via Samaria back to Cana in chapters 2 through 4, John now embarks on a presentation of the remainder of Jesus' public ministry prior to his crucifixion. This presentation takes up chapters 5 through 12. As is clear also from the Synoptic Gospels, this phase of Jesus' ministry is characterized by escalating conflict. Once again, however, John is less concerned with being comprehensive than the Synoptic writers and more interested in selecting typical events and discourses in order to illustrate the response Jesus (the Christ) received from the Jewish people.

In the present volume, we will devote four entire chapters to this central portion of John's Gospel (chs. 7 through 10). The present chapter is devoted to a study of John 5 and 6 which feature two additional "signs" of Jesus: (1) his healing of a lame man (sign #4) which triggers the so-called Sabbath controversy (John 5) and (2) the feeding of the multitudes (sign #5) which is followed by Jesus' discourse on the "Bread of life" (Jn 6). The end of John 6 marks a watershed in Jesus' ministry, with many "disciples" (!) ceasing to

follow on account of Jesus' "hard teaching." Only the twelve, led by Peter, emerge as core group of Jesus' new messianic community.

What John 5 and 6 have in common, then, is that both chapters strike a note of conflict, be it between Jesus and his opposition or among the group of Jesus' followers. Let's see how this motif plays out in these two chapters as John's narrative of Jesus' messianic mission unfolds.

The Fourth Sign: The Healing of the Lame Man (5:1–18)

After an extended stay in Galilee, Jesus returns to Jerusalem in order to attend an unspecified Jewish feast. Since most of his readers are unfamiliar with Palestinian topography, John sets the stage by describing the scene of Jesus' next sign: the Pool of Bethesda, located near the Sheep Gate and surrounded by five covered colonnades. Every pilgrim attending one of the many religious festivals in Jerusalem would have seen the mass of

Table 7.1
Accusations Leveled Against Jesus by His Opponents in John's Gospel

Galilean, Nazarene	1:46; 7:41, 52; 18:5, 7; 19:19
Sabbath-breaker	5:16, 18; 9:16
Blasphemy	5:18; 8:59; 10:31, 33, 39; 19:7 (cf. Lv 24:16)
Deception of people	7:12, 47
Demon-possession	7:20; 8:48–52; 10:20–21
Illegitimate birth	8:41
Samaritan	8:48
A sinner	9:16, 24–25, 31
Madness	10:20
A criminal	18:30
Royal pretender, political threat	19:12; cf. 19:15, 21

needy individuals populating this site, especially during feast days.

As in the case of Nicodemus, the Samaritan woman, and the royal official, John shows Jesus' concern for a particular individual, in the present instance a man who has been invalid for thirty-eight years (v. 5; note that 6:2 mentions multiple "miraculous signs he [Jesus] had performed on the sick"). How did John obtain this information? In the verse that follows (v. 6), we are told how Jesus "learned that he [the lame man] had been in this condition for a long time." We may assume that in the actual encounter the man told Jesus about his prolonged period of suffering (that is, thirty-eight years) and that John recalled this piece of information as an eyewitness of the event.

Two things are significant about the way Jesus proceeds to heal the man. First, *Jesus asks him if he wants to get well* (5:6). Why does Jesus ask such an obvious question? *Of course* the man wants to get well! It seems that the point of Jesus' question is not to elicit the self-evident affirmative answer but to draw out the man's own perception of the obstacle that has kept him from getting well up to this point: the fact that he has no one to help him into the pool when the water is stirred (which, according to local superstition,

signaled the water's healing powers), so that by the time he has managed to drag himself into the pool, someone else has already gone in ahead of him (5:7)—and this cycle of futility has continued for thirty-eight years!

Second, Jesus heals the man *by his mere word* (5:8), totally apart from the pool's waters from which the man expected healing. And so the man is miraculously cured. Jesus has performed another "hard" miracle (cf. comments under 2:1–12 above).

If this were the Synoptic Gospels, the miracle itself would be sufficient to demonstrate Jesus' authority over sickness (cf. Mk 2:1–12) or his fulfillment of the messianic mission envisioned by Isaiah (cf. Mt 8:17; 12:18–21; Lk 4:18–19). In John, however, the miracle is transmuted into a "sign" (cf. 7:21–24), an act with inherent christological symbolism. In the present scenario, the clue to understanding this symbolism is provided by the fact that Jesus performs this healing *on a Sabbath* (esp. vv. 9–10, 16; cf. also ch. 9, esp. vv. 14, 16; for Sabbath healings in the Synoptics, see Mt 12:1–14 = Mk 2:23–3:6 = Lk 6:1–11; Mk 1:21–28 = Lk 4:31–37; Lk 13:10–17; Lk 14:1–6).

Notably, it is not the actual healing that is the Jews' primary concern. Rather, offense is taken at Jesus' telling the man *to pick up his mat and walk;* for oral tradition (though not the Old Testament itself) forbid the carrying of a mat on the Sabbath (v. 10). Imagine that—here a man is healed who had been lame for thirty-eight years, and all the Jews have to worry about is that the man violated the command to carry his mat in the process! When the Jews confront the lame man regarding this infraction of their Sabbath regulations, he simply shifts the blame to Jesus; for he had told him to do so. More precisely, John tells us that the man did not even know who Jesus was; for Jesus had slipped away into the crowd. Later Jesus met the man again at the temple and told him to stop sinning or something worse may happen to him. Yet the man goes away and tells the Jews that it was Jesus who healed him. (For an—unfavorable—comparison between this character and the man born blind in ch. 9, see the discussion there.)

The picture painted by John of Jewish sensibilities regarding oral traditions pertaining to the Law shows a religiously short-sighted people who had forgotten the true intent of the Law and, more important still, of the God who gave it to them in the first place. In this, John is en-

Tombstones on the Mount of Olives provided the backdrop for Jesus' prediction of the resurrection on the last day.

tirely consistent with the portrait provided also in the other Gospels. Matthew tells us how Jesus called the Pharisees "blind guides" who "strain out a gnat but swallow a camel" (Mt 24:24), an almost comical description of people who have lost sight of what is truly important in one's religious life. Those were the people who tithed even spices but neglected "the more important matters of the law—justice, mercy and faithfulness" (Mt 23:23). Even worse, the religious teachers used the multitude of religious regulations as sort of leverage over the common people in order to retain their own position of power and privilege: "They tie up heavy loads and put them on men's shoulders, but they themselves are not willing to lift a finger to move them" (Mt 24:4). Therefore Jesus regularly called the Pharisees "hypocrites," an expression derived from Greek actors who wore masks disguising the true face of the person underneath.

In the case of Jesus' healing of the lame man, the significance of who is Lord over the Sabbath dwarfs the particular miracle by comparison. Jesus' crucial statement is found in verse 17: "My Father is always at his work to this very day, and I, too, am working." As John himself

Tiberias, a city on the west side of the Sea of Galilee, was founded by Herod Antipas around A.D. 20 in honor of Tiberius, the Roman emperor. Gradually, the name of the city was transferred to the name of the lake.

points out in the following verse, Jesus was thus "calling God his own Father, making himself equal with God" (v. 18).

According to John, everything hinges on Jesus' unique relationship with God. Is he the only begotten (that is, the unique and eternal) Son of God, the "Son of the Father," or is he not? If so, all Jesus says and does attests to his messianic identity and provides revelation from God. This was the issue at stake in Jesus' confrontation with the Jewish authorities of his day; this is still the issue today; and this will be the issue in the future and for all eternity (see the Book of Revelation). It is a testimony to John's focus on the essentials and to his penetrating spiritual discernment that he centers his entire Gospel on the question of Jesus' identity. To borrow Jesus' question from Matthew's account: "Who do people say the Son of Man is? . . . But what about *you*? Who do *you* say I am?" (Mt 16:13, 15). In the end, people's answer to this question will be the only thing that matters; it alone will determine people's eternal destiny.

The Sabbath Controversy (5:19–47)

In the present section, Jesus develops further his statement of verse 17, "My Father is always at his work to this very day, and I, too, am working." In particular, Jesus defends himself against the following two charges: (1) he is a Sabbath-breaker; (2) he is blaspheming, because he claims a unique, equal relationship with God (v. 18). What is Jesus' line of defense?

Essentially, he elaborates on the nature of his relationship with God the Father. Jesus claims that everything he (the Son) does he is able to do only because he has seen the Father do it first. This "apprenticeship analogy" may well be rooted in Jesus' own earthly experience of learning the trade of carpentry from his adoptive father Joseph. ("Is this not Jesus, the son of Joseph, whose father and mother we know?" 6:42. In Mark 6:3, Jesus is called "the carpenter," while in Matthew 13:55 he is called "the carpenter's son.")

Jesus thus identifies his "work" with that of his Father, that is, God. God's work did not cease at creation, Jesus insists; he continues to be active; and Jesus himself co-labors with his Father (5:17). Doing God's work is Jesus' highest priority (4:34). But how does that relate to Jesus' healing of a man on a Sabbath? The answer is this: the one who created the Sabbath has authority over it; he determines its purpose, its use, and its limitations.

As Jesus would point out later, even the Jews made exceptions to the rule of refraining from work on the Sabbath, as in the case of circumcision (cf. *m. Sab* 18.3; 19.2–3). The Law mandated circumcision on the eighth day. If the eighth day fell on a Sabbath, the Jews faced a dilemma: should they keep the Sabbath and break the circumcision commandment or should they keep the circumcision commandment and break the Sabbath? Jewish experts in the Law had determined that in this case the circumcision commandment took precedence over the injunction to refrain from work on the Sabbath: a child must be circumcised. Jesus seizes upon this precedent: if it was deemed appropriate to override the Sabbath commandment in order to perform a circumcision, was it not equally permissible to heal an entire man on the Sabbath (7:23)? The Jewish legal experts were caught. In perfect rabbinic fashion, Jesus had appealed to a set precedent, which exposed Jewish objections to Jesus' healing of a man on the Sabbath as hypocritical and inconsistent.

In the present passage, however, Jesus talks about even "greater things" (5:20): the fact that he had been entrusted by the Father with the giving of eternal life and the rendering of eternal judgment (5:21–30). Of the purposes of Jesus' mission enumerated in John's Gospel, there is none that is more prominent than the giving of life (cf. 3:16–17; 6:33, 40, 44, 47, 50–58; 10:7–10; 17:2–3).[1] Jesus could be the life-giver, because "as the Father has life in himself, so he has granted the Son to have life in himself" (5:26). Like God, Jesus is an uncreated being; he already "was with God in the beginning" (1:2),

that is, prior to creation, and "in him was life" (1:4). Now just as God breathed life into the original creation, it has been granted to Jesus to award eternal life to those who believe in him. This may be called "rebirth" (Ti 3:5) or "new birth" (1 Pt 1:3 cf. v. 23); "birth from God" (Jn 1:13), "birth from above" (Jn 3:3, 7) or "birth from the Spirit" (Jn 3:5, 8); "adoption" (Rom 8:15, 23; Gal 4:5; Eph 1:5) or "new creation" (2 Cor 5:17; Gal 6:15). Whatever the specific terminology used, Jesus' words to Nicodemus retain their truthfulness: without such coming to life again people will remain in "death" (Jn 5:24), "darkness" (3:19), and under the wrath of God (3:36). And the only mediator and giver of this life is Jesus Christ.

We return to Jesus' fourth sign in John's Gospel, the healing of the lame man. For John, this miracle, amazing as it is in its own right, points beyond itself to who Jesus is: the eternal life-giver. And this is the tragedy John detects in those who opposed Jesus during his earthly ministry: in their concern for obedience to the Law, they missed the coming of the Lawgiver; in their concern for upholding the requirements for a religious life, they missed the one who is Life itself; in their concern for the study of the Scriptures, they missed the coming of the one of whom the Scriptures spoke (5:39–40, 45–47). The Jews' discipleship of Moses kept them from following their Messiah (9:28).

Many of Jesus' closest followers were Galilean fishermen.

In the end, John's Gospel serves the purpose of **theodicy** (the justification of the righteousness of God and of his actions). It is not that God did not provide adequate evidence that Jesus was the Christ—he did. The amazing, escalating signs of Jesus, carefully selected and captivatingly narrated in John's Gospel, prove that God unfailingly pursued rebellious humanity (including the Jews) with revelations of his power, mercy, and truth. It was the witnesses of such revelation who failed to respond to such manifestations of God with the only proper response: faith and obedience. As will be seen below, the theodicy of John's Gospel reaches its first major climax at the end of the first major portion of the Gospel (12:37–41) and ultimately culminates in Jesus' resurrection.

The Fifth Sign: The Feeding of the Five Thousand (6:1–15)

After signs ##1 and 3, both in Cana of Galilee, this is now Jesus' fifth sign recorded in John, again in Galilee (signs ##2 and 4 take place in Jerusalem). The pattern of narration is similar to chapter 5: Jesus' sign is followed by an extended discourse elaborating on the significance of what he had done. The scene is the eastern shore of the Sea of Galilee (called in 6:1 also "Sea of Tiberias," its later designation after the Roman emperor Tiberius who ruled from A.D. 14 to 37; cf. 21:1). The time is spring (see the reference to "plenty of grass" in 6:10) shortly before the Jewish Passover (v. 4). While Jesus had spent an earlier Passover in Jerusalem (cf. 2:13), he now reveals his true nature in his native Galilee (cf. 4:44). The mention of the Passover sets the context for what Jesus is about to do.

A comparison between John's account of the feeding of the five thousand and that of the Synoptics makes clear that John provides his own independent account. He mentions several details that are not found in any of the other Gospels, such as the crossing of the sea (v. 1); the approaching Passover (v. 4); the involvement

of Philip and Andrew (vv. 7–8); the fact that the five loaves contributed by the boy were loaves of *barley* (v. 9); and Jesus' command to his disciples to gather all the fragments so that nothing would be lost (v. 12). This is another instance of John's telling a story from his own eyewitness recollection (cf., e.g., 2:1–11). The fact that John is not dependent on the Synoptic Gospels in this instance (or in general) adds to the value of John's Gospel as independent apostolic eyewitness testimony.

One easily overlooked fact is that what is foremost in Jesus' mind here is his preparation and instruction of his disciples (6:5–9, 12–13, 16–21; cf., e.g., ch. 4). The purpose of Jesus' signs is not merely to reveal himself to the crowds; more important, Jesus uses these signs to deepen the faith of his disciples and to train them for ministry. Another little known (but highly significant) feature of John's account of the feeding of the multitude is the unmistakable allusion made to Elisha's miraculous feeding recounted in 2 Kings 4:42–44. Allusions can be verified by explicit verbal links between two passages; in the present case, the most obvious connection is provided by the word *paidarion*, "boy," used in the New Testament only here (6:9), but used several times in the Septuagint translation of the 2 Kings passage (there referring to Elisha's servant). Other links are the mention of barley and the overall mode of narration, including a question of disbelief, the command to distribute the loaves, and the fact that all ate with food left to spare.

Together with the link established between the present feeding and God's miraculous feeding of the Israelites in the wilderness in the days of Moses (6:31–32; see further below), John thus sets Jesus' ministry firmly in the context of salvation history, linking Jesus' signs with the two previous major periods of miraculous activity in the history of God's people: the ministries of Moses and of Elijah/Elisha. This does not necessarily mean that Jesus is presented by John as a new Moses or a new Elisha. Rather, it shows that John finds in Jesus certain characteristics that also marked the ministries of previous servants of God (albeit escalated). In particular, the account of the transfiguration comes to mind where Jesus is joined by

Moses and Elijah, speaking to them about his impending "exodus" (that is, the divine deliverance effected by his death on the cross; cf. Mk 9:2–8; Mt 17:1–8; Lk 9:28–36, esp. v. 31).

The feeding of the multitudes also conveys the image of Jesus presiding as a host over an abundant meal, a theme found already in the Prophets (e.g., Is 25:6) and picked up by Jesus in some of his parables (e.g., Mt 22:1–14; Lk 22:16, 29–30). A parallel between Jesus' first sign (at the wedding of Cana) and the feeding of the multitude may be detected: as in the previous case Jesus provided an abundance of wine, so he here provides an abundance of bread. Bread and wine, in turn, are symbolic of the eschatological messianic banquet.

Once again, John does not content himself with narrating a miracle Jesus performs; he shows how what Jesus *does* reveals who he *is:* in the present case, the Giver of eternal life. This is not understood by the people, who want to make Jesus king by force (6:15). But as Jesus tells Pilate later in the Gospel, his kingdom is not of this world (18:36). Owing to people's misunderstanding of his true (messianic) identity, Jesus therefore withdraws to be by himself (as was his regular practice; cf., e.g., Mk 1:35 = Lk 4:42; Mk 6:31–32 = Mt 14:13 = Lk 9:10), which sets the stage for the next event narrated in John's Gospel.

The Walking on the Water (6:16–21)

As in the other Gospels (except Luke), the feeding of the multitudes is followed by Jesus' walking on the water. The reason for this is not that John merely follows tradition. Rather, the placement of these events reflects the historical sequence in which they actually took place. In the context of his narrative, John probably includes the walking on the water for at least two reasons: one, because it provides a natural link between the feeding of the multitude and Jesus' Bread of Life discourse; and two, because it portrays Jesus' private revelation to his own disciples in form of a theophany (note the absolute "It is I" in 6:20; similarly, 8:58 and 18:5–6).

Mark and Matthew tell us that the disciples thought Jesus was a ghost (Mk 6:49; Mt 14:26). Mark also informs us that they had not understood about the loaves, for their hearts were hardened (Mk 6:52), while Matthew adds the episode with Peter and the response of worship when Jesus got into the boat (14:33). John's account is terser by comparison. The emphasis of his account lies on the calming effect of Jesus' presence on the disciples (v. 20). In short order, Jesus' followers had come from the mountaintop experience of the feeding of the multitudes (with

Jesus) to the terrifying experience of a mighty storm at sea (without Jesus). In case any of them had delusions of grandeur, this turn of events would have quickly brought them back down to earth.

Successes tend to breed overconfidence. In fact, sometimes successes are harder to deal with than defeats. And if we don't swell up with pride after a major achievement, we may suddenly feel depressed or at least deflated, as was Elijah's experience after his triumph over the prophets of Baal. Jesus' disciples went through many ups and downs. They knew the exhilarating sense of victory as well as the agony of defeat. Just think of Peter's three denials of Jesus and his threefold reinstitution to service by Jesus (Jn 18:15–18, 25–27; 21:15–19). Like the disciples, we must learn to weather the storms of life as well as to enjoy the sunshine while it lasts. Above all, we must learn to trust in Jesus' presence with us as we seek to follow him (Mt 28:20).

Meanwhile, the crowds, hungry for more, are in hot pursuit of Jesus (6:22–24, another passage reflecting the touch of eyewitness testimony).

The Bread of Life Discourse (6:22–59)

When the multitudes chase him down, Jesus has no illusion as to why they follow him: "I tell you the truth, you are looking for me, not because you saw miraculous signs but because you ate the loaves and had your fill" (v. 26). As in call-

ing his first disciples (1:35–51), his first Jerusalem appearance (2:24–25), and his conversations with Nicodemus and the Samaritan woman (chs. 3–4), Jesus discerns people's true motives. This, too, proves that he is the Son of God. Also, as in the case of previous conversations, Jesus does not merely answer questions addressed to him but rather responds with a challenge of his own: "Do not work for food that spoils, but for food that endures to eternal life" (v. 27; cf. 4:34).

When people ask him, "What must we do to do the works God requires?" (v. 28)—a question that shortly turns out to be less than perfectly sincere—Jesus replies, "The work of God is this: to believe in the one he has sent" (v. 29). Two things are remarkable about Jesus' response: first, that the work of God (that is, the work God requires) is not described in terms of acts of Law-keeping but as *believing in Jesus;* and second, that this work is really no human "work" at all: it is the work *of God.* Jesus' answer thus seeks to redirect people's focus from an introspective preoccupation with "works of the Law" (Paul's term) to trust in the God-sent Messiah, Jesus. But as at previous occasions, the Jews completely miss Jesus' point. Rather than having their eyes opened to God's reality in Jesus, they ask for a sign authenticating Jesus' authority (cf. 2:18). Once again, however, Jesus responds, not by acceding to people's request for a miraculous sign, but by pointing to the significance of the work *he has already performed,* in the present case, the feeding of the multitudes.

Unpredictable conditions on the Sea of Galilee could put the fear of God into even the most experienced fisherman among Jesus' disciples. The lake was the site of Jesus' miraculous walking on the water.

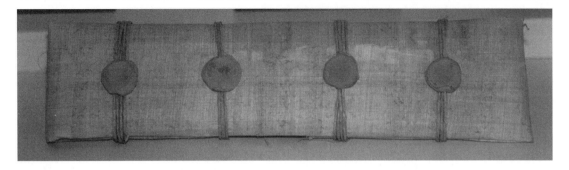

These clay seals found in Jerusalem illustrate the ancient practice of signing important documents.

A stone replica of the ark of the covenant was discovered in Capernaum, Jesus' head-quarters for most of his ministry.

The Jews had even suggested a possible sign for Jesus to duplicate: Moses' provision of manna in the wilderness (v. 31; cf. Nm 11:7–9; Ex 16; Neh 9:15; Pss 78:23–25; 105:40). Jesus counters that it was not *Moses* but *God* who had provided the manna (v. 32). And when the Jews, echoing the Samaritan woman's request for living water on an earlier occasion, plainly ask for Jesus to give them the same bread from heaven (v. 34), Jesus points to *himself* as the true Bread from Heaven. It is not so much that Jesus *gives* certain gifts—he himself *is* the gift (cf. 2 Cor 9:15)! Only he can satisfy people's hunger, only he can quench their thirst, not merely for material food and drink, but for spiritual sustenance (cf. Is 55:1–3; Rv 21:6). In a gripping passage, the prophet Isaiah had

exclaimed, "Oh, that you would rend the heavens and come down" (Is 64:1), similar to the theophany at the giving of the Law at Mount Sinai (Is 64:3). Acknowledging people's sinfulness, he pleads with God to remember that he is the Father of his people (64:8). We can do no better than quote the passage in full:

> Oh, that you would rend the heavens
> and come down,
> that the mountains would tremble
> before you!
> As when fire sets twigs ablaze
> and causes water to boil,
> come down to make your name known
> to your enemies
> and cause the nations to quake be-
> fore you!

This fourth-century A.D. synagogue in Capernaum was probably built on the foundations of the first-century synagogue where Jesus taught.

For when you did awesome things that
we did not expect,
you came down, and the mountains
trembled before you.
Since ancient times no one has heard,
no ear has perceived,
no eye has seen any God besides you,
who acts on behalf of those who
wait for him.

You come to the help of those who
gladly do right,
who remember your ways.
But when we continued to sin against
them,
you were angry.
How then can we be saved?
All of us have become like one who is
unclean,
and all our righteous acts are like
filthy rags;
we all shrivel up like a leaf,
and like the wind our sins sweep us
away.
No one calls on your name
or strives to lay hold of you;
for you have hidden your face from us
and made us waste away because
of our sins.
Yet, O LORD, you are our Father.
We are the clay, you are the potter;
we are all the work of your hand.
Do not be angry beyond measure, O
Lord;
do not remember our sins forever.
Oh, look upon us, we pray,
for we are all your people.
Your sacred cities have become a desert;
even Zion is a desert, Jerusalem a
desolation.
Our holy and glorious temple, where
our fathers praised you,
has been burned with fire,
and all that we treasured lies in
ruins.

The True Purpose of Scripture

Pure and simple, Jesus charged his opponents with what today might be called "bibliolatry," the worship of Scripture itself. Listen to what he says: "You diligently study the Scriptures because you think that by them you possess eternal life. These are the Scriptures that testify about me, yet you refuse to come to me to have life" (5:39–40). Is there something wrong with Bible study? Jesus suggests there is, if Bible study becomes an end in itself. As Jesus says in his follow-up statement, "Moses . . . wrote about *me*" (6:46). Do you and I find Jesus in the Old Testament? And do we engage in the study of Scripture as a means to encounter Jesus or are we caught up in the "minutiae of the Law" as the Pharisees were?

transsubstantia-tion

After all this, O LORD, will you hold
yourself back?
Will you keep silent and punish us
beyond measure? (Is 64:1–12).

Against this backdrop, the apostle John contends that *now,* with the coming of the Messiah, Isaiah's longing has been fulfilled: in Jesus, God *has* come down from heaven, and not merely to feed his people as he did in the wilderness, but to atone for their sins (cf. Is 52:13–53:12). However, God's gracious gift of salvation sets into even starker relief the tragedy of the present hour: the Jews have seen Jesus and still do not believe (v. 36), while those who look to the Son and believe will have eternal life (v. 40; cf. 1:11–13).

Ironically, Jesus' quite apparent humanity, which later became an obstacle for Gnostic heretics, here represents a major stumbling block for his contemporaries. Thus the Jews object to Jesus' lofty claims that they know Jesus' *earthly* family—how can he say that he came *down from heaven?* Like Nicodemus, the teacher of Israel, people do not understand "heavenly things," that is, spiritual truths (cf. 3:10–12). Some might view this intransigence to spiritual matters as an obstacle for God's purposes to be realized, but not Jesus: he sees in the Jews' opposition a confirmation of God's work in election and predestination: "No one can come to me unless the Father who sent me draws him" (v. 44), so that believing the one whom he has sent is "the work of *God*" (v. 29).

In what follows, Jesus explicitly claims to be the fulfillment of Isaiah's eschatological vision of a time when "they will all be taught by God" (v. 45; cf. Is 54:13). In fact, all will be taught by *Jesus*—for he alone is the bringer of direct revelation from God (v. 46). In this connection, it seems ironic that modern philosophy as well as postmodernism deny the very possibility of our access to ultimate reality. We can know only what we can see, it is argued; what is invisible or intangible can only be apprehended by religious instincts but not by human reason. Because all human knowledge is subjective, objective, absolute knowledge is an impossibility. Let everyone believe in what makes sense and works for them. To be sure, this would all be true, were it not for one important fact: that the preexistent Word has become flesh in Jesus, has dwelt among us, and has revealed God to us (1:14, 18). Because this is true, no one can come to the Father except through Jesus (14:6).

But back to the Bread of Life discourse: Jesus continues to make yet another important point ("from the lesser to the greater"): the Jews' ancestors who ate the manna in the wilderness died; but everyone who "eats the Bread from Heaven," that is, everyone who believes in Jesus, will live forever (vv. 49–51). Then Jesus carries the analogy one step further: the bread is his flesh which he gives for the life of the world (v. 51). On a literal level, Jesus' invitation for people to "eat his flesh" and "drink his blood" is, of course, deeply offensive to the Jews, who went to great lengths to avoid eating flesh containing blood.

John's later audience, on the other hand, will no doubt detect eucharistic overtones in Jesus' words, especially since John's is the only Gospel that does not include an account of the institution of the Lord's Supper. This does not mean that John espouses a version of what later came to be known as the Roman Catholic doctrine of **transsubstantiation,** which affirms that the communion elements are literally transformed from bread and wine into Jesus' flesh and blood during Mass. John's point is much more profound than metaphysical theories regarding the Lord's Supper: for him, Jesus' works reveal who Jesus essentially is, in

---

Table 7.2
The Seven "I Am" Sayings

1. "I am the bread of life"	6:35, 48, 51
2. "I am the light of the world"	8:12; 9:5
3. "I am the gate"	10:7, 9
4. "I am the good shepherd"	10:11, 14
5. "I am the resurrection and the life"	11:25
6. "I am the way and the truth and the life"	14:6
7. "I am the true vine"	15:1

1. Explain the issue at stake in the "Sabbath controversy."

2. Explore the relationship between the feeding of the multitude and Jesus' Bread of Life discourse.

3. Show the structural significance of the ending of chapter 6 in the context of the entire Gospel.

the present case, the source and giver of all true spiritual life.

But do the crowds, or even those who follow Jesus more closely at this critical juncture, understand the true significance of Jesus' words?

Watershed: The Twelve Remain, Many Others Leave (6:60–71)

As John informs us, on hearing Jesus' Bread of Life discourse, many even of his disciples said, "This is a hard teaching. Who can accept it?" (v. 60); and they turned back and no longer followed him (v. 66). One might expect that Jesus, in a state of panic that the very survival of his ministry was seriously jeopardized, at this point would have pleaded with his closest followers not to leave him as well. Not so. Jesus has confidence in God's plan for his life and in God's work in the core group of his new messianic community, the twelve (mentioned only here in 6:67, 70, 71; and 20:24; in the last two references, Judas Iscariot and Thomas respectively are referred to, almost incidentally, as "one of the twelve"). He is not disappointed: Simon Peter, as in the Synoptic Gospels the spokesman of the

disciples, responds to Jesus' challenge with a strong affirmation: "Lord, to whom shall we go? You have the words of eternal life. We believe and know that you are the Holy One of God" (vv. 68–69). To which Jesus replies: "Have I not chosen you, the Twelve? Yet one of you is a devil!" (v. 71, referring to Judas; cf. 12:4).

Structurally, this event marks a crucial watershed in Jesus' ministry. Halfway through the first major portion of John's Gospel (1:19–12:50), an important preliminary decision is made (cf. later 13:1–3). John shows that there is conflict and division not only between Jesus and his (Jewish) opposition but also among Jesus' followers. It is Jesus' words themselves which crystallize those among his followers who are "truly his disciples"—those who hold to his teaching (cf. 8:31). The first half of Jesus' public ministry narrated in John's Gospel thus closes on a note of failure: "from this time many of his disciples turned back and no longer followed him" (6:66), just as the second and final half concludes with the remark that "even after Jesus had done all these miraculous signs in their presence, they still would not believe in him" (12:37). To this is added the ominous reference to Judas, the one who, "though one of the Twelve, was later to betray him" (6:71). Yet there is a silver lining: the enduring commitment of the twelve (except for Judas: cf. 17:12) whom Jesus had chosen (6:70). Nevertheless, when the curtain reopens for the second act, the readers will witness that even Jesus' own brothers challenge him in doubt.

Key Words

Bread of Life discourse

theodicy

transsubstantiation

8 Escalating Conflict (Part 2)

John 7:1–8:59

Then the angel showed me the river of the water of life, as clear as crystal, flowing from the throne of God and of the Lamb.

—Revelation 22:1

Supplemental Reading: Leviticus 23:33–44; Numbers 29:12–40; Deuteronomy 16:13–17

Outline

- **The Unbelief of Jesus' Brothers (7:1–9)**
- **Jesus at the Feast of Tabernacles (7:10–52)**
- **Escalating Controversy: The Paternity Suit (8:12–59)**

Objectives

After reading this chapter, you should be able to

1. Elaborate on how Jesus fulfills the symbolism underlying the Feast of Tabernacles.
2. Sketch first-century Jewish messianic expectations in light of the representative questions featured in John's Gospel (especially ch. 7).
3. Explain the spiritual dynamics at work in the "paternity suit" between Jesus and the Jews in John 8.

The Feast of Tabernacles was celebrated in the fall (September/October), while the next festival mentioned in John's Gospel, the Feast of Dedication, fell in the winter (10:22), later followed by Jesus' final Passover (13:1). We thus enter the last half year of Jesus' public ministry. It is best to take chapters 7 and 8 (excluding the story of the adulterous woman, which almost certainly was not part of John's original Gospel)[1] as a narrative unit, followed by the account of the man born blind in chapter 9 (the sixth sign) and Jesus' **Good Shepherd discourse** in chapter 10. With the end of chapter 10, Jesus' public ministry nears its conclusion. Jesus returns to the place where John first baptized, hence where he started his own ministry (10:40), thus completing the circle. The pattern of escalating conflict with the Jews gives way to Jesus' climactic sign (ch. 11), his preparation for burial (ch. 12), and his final instruction of his inner circle (chs. 13–17).

The Unbelief of Jesus' Brothers (7:1–9)

In chapter 7, the pattern of escalated conflict continues. Jesus stays away from Judea, ministering in Galilee instead, because the Jews in Judea were waiting to take his life. Jesus' life thus evidences a keen sense of timing—something neither his mother (2:4) nor his brothers (7:6–8; cf. Mk 3:21, 31–35) understood. Thus the pattern of rejection is complete: Jesus is rejected not only in his native Galilee (4:44) and in Judea (7:1)—and thus by the Jewry as a whole (cf. 1:11)—but even by the members of his own family. Moreover, as we have seen in the previous chapter, John has already hinted that one of the twelve, Jesus' inner circle, will betray him (6:71).

Peter, the leader and spokesman of the disciples, will deny Jesus three times, despite pledges of loyalty (13:36–38). In fact, in keeping with Jesus' prediction, all of his followers "will be scattered, each to his own home. You will leave me all alone" (16:32). As John already indicated in the Prologue, "He was in the world,

and though the world was made through him, the world did not recognize him" (1:10). What a powerful portrait of the world's rejection of Jesus is painted here by John! But as the evangelist makes clear, the world's darkness only accentuates more fully the fact that Jesus is the light of the world (8:12; 9:5; cf. 1:5, 7–9). Which leads us to a discussion of Jesus' appearance at the Feast of Tabernacles.

Jesus at the Feast of Tabernacles (7:10–52)

Two important purposes guide John's presentation of this event: first, the way in which Jesus fulfills the symbolism inherent in this particular religious festival; and second, representative questions which are used by the fourth evangelist as a device to highlight people's thinking about Jesus' identity during the course of his earthly ministry as well as guiding the readers of John's Gospel in their thinking about Jesus. (For our purposes, we will not discuss the story of the adulterous woman in 7:53–8:11, because it is not found in the earliest manuscripts of John's Gospel and was almost certainly not part of the Gospel the way John wrote it. Once this account is purged from the Gospel, it becomes evident that 8:12 picks up where 7:52 left off, restoring the unity of 7:1–52 and 8:12–59, which will be dealt with here as one coherent section.)

The Feast of Tabernacles, celebrated, as mentioned, in the fall, was originally a harvest festival, recalling God's provision for his people during the wilderness wanderings (cf. Lv 23:42–43). Immensely popular, it was simply called "the Feast" by the Jews (e.g., 1 Kgs 8:2, 65; 12:32; 2 Chr 5:3; 7:8; Neh 8:14, 18; Ps 81:3; Ez 45:25).[2] The Jewish first-century historian Josephus calls it the holiest and greatest feast of the Jews (*Antiquities* 8.100). It followed shortly after the Day of Atonement and marked the conclusion of the annual cycle of religious festivals that began with Passover and Unleavened Bread six months earlier. The Feast of Tabernacles lasted seven days, culminating in an

Herod's temple, while outwardly a symbol of Jewish pride and national identity, had by Jesus' time become an empty shell of corrupt worship.

eighth day of special celebration and festive assembly. Owing to the daily solemn outpouring of water during the festival (cf. Nm 28:7; Is 12:3), the Feast of Tabernacles came to be associated with eschatological hopes (cf. Zec 14:16–19).

After his brothers have left for the Feast, Jesus goes also, not publicly, but in secret (v. 10). Not until halfway through the Feast does Jesus go up to the temple courts and begin to teach (v. 14). When the Jews express amazement at the profundity of Jesus' teaching in light of his lack of formal rabbinic training (v. 15), Jesus responds that he speaks not from himself, but from God (vv. 16–18). Again, he confronts the Jews regarding their hostility toward him (cf. 5:18), an antagonism which he ultimately roots in people's rebellion against God and his Law (v. 19). The crowds, in turn, charge him with being possessed by a demon, the most serious charge leveled against Jesus in the Gospel thus far (v. 20). Jesus' response reveals that the major issue is still his healing of the lame man on the Sabbath narrated in John 5 (vv. 21–24; for the specific argument, see already our discussion of ch. 5). From here on, John features a series of representative questions regarding Jesus' messiahship (see further below).

The entire narrative builds toward the climax of verse 37, where Jesus, on the last and greatest day of the Feast, stands up and proclaims in a loud voice,

> If anyone is thirsty,
>   let him come to me and drink.
> Whoever believes in me,
>   as the Scripture has said,
>   streams of living water will flow
>   from within him (vv. 37b–38).

As John explains, by this Jesus was referring to the Spirit who had not yet been given (v. 39). The image of streams of water flowing from a person's most innermost being may derive from Isaiah 58:11, which reads:

> You will be like a well-watered garden,
>   like a spring whose waters never fail.

This develops further the theme underlying the Feast of Tabernacles:

> With joy you will draw water
>   from the wells of salvation (Is 12:3).

But while Isaiah 12:3 talks about a person's salvation, Isaiah 58:11 speaks of the way in which believers will be a blessing to others. The point Jesus makes at this point in his ministry is therefore this: he

109

is the dispenser of the Holy Spirit, through whom those who come to him for salvation will be abundant blessings to others. The message is clear: Jesus fulfills the symbolism of the Feast of Tabernacles, conveyed by the waterpouring ceremonies that celebrated the abundance of God's blessings at harvest time in reminiscence of God's provision for his people in the wilderness.

Thus far we have focused on the first major purpose John pursues in recounting Jesus' appearance at the Feast of Tabernacles, his demonstration that Jesus fulfills the symbolism underlying this popular Jewish festival. We turn now to his second major purpose: by featuring representative questions regarding Jesus' messiahship, John seeks both to trace the development of popular sentiment regarding Jesus during his earthly ministry and to lead his contemporary readers along in their own decision making regarding Jesus, his identity, and his claims. These representative questions center around the question of whether Jesus is the Christ, highlighting difficulties Jesus' contemporaries had in squaring his claims with their own preconceived notions of who Messiah might be and serving also as a foil for dealing with potential objections John's readers might raise.[3]

Table 8.1
People's "Fear of the Jews"

1. The Jewish Populace: "But no one would say anything publicly about him *for fear of the Jews*" (7:13).
2. The Blind Man's Parents: "His parents said this because *they were afraid of the Jews*, for already the Jews had decided that anyone who acknowledged that Jesus was the Christ would be put out of the synagogue" (9:22).
3. Joseph of Arimathea: "Now Joseph was a disciple of Jesus, but secretly because *he feared the Jews*" (19:38).
4. Jesus' Disciples: "On the evening of that first day of the week . . . the disciple were together, with the doors locked *for fear of the Jews*" (20:19).

John 6:14–15 already made clear that people viewed the coming Messiah as a political figure restoring Israel to its former glory who would overthrow the Roman overlords. Concluding from the feeding miracle that Jesus is the Prophet predicted by Moses (Dt 18:18), they want to make him king. John dispels this notion of a primarily political Messiah in two ways: first, he shows how Jesus withdraws (6:15); second, he records Jesus' statement to Pilate later in the Gospel, "My kingdom is not of this world" (18:36). Thus it is clear that Jesus' kingship is not primarily political.

The next three messianic notions current in Jesus' day all surface in the present passage, John 7. "We know where *this man* is from; when *the Christ* comes, no one will know where *he* is from," the crowds mutter (7:27). This, of course, is an instance of Johannine irony: people think they know where Jesus comes from, that is, Galilee; but John's readers know better (see the Prologue). The second messianic expectation, then, was that the Messiah would be of mysterious origin. As John makes clear, Jesus does in fact fulfill this expectation: he is the mysterious Son of Man (cf. Dn 7:13), and he is the eternal Word-become-flesh.

Third, people expected the Messiah to perform an abundance of signs: "When the Christ comes, will he do more miraculous signs than this man?" (7:31). Every child knew about the signs and wonders Moses did at the exodus; the Messiah, it was conjectured, would perform even greater feats. Consider John 6:30–31: "What miraculous sign then will you give that we may see it and believe you? What will you do? Our forefathers ate the manna in the desert; as it is written: 'He gave them bread from heaven to eat.'" Once again, John demonstrates how Jesus fulfilled this expectation supremely. To this end, the evangelist selects seven striking signs, in many cases elaborating on their significance by way of extended discourses.

Fourth, people expected the Messiah to be born in Bethlehem in David's line. Matthew confirms this in 2:3–6: "When King Herod heard this he was disturbed, and all Jerusalem with him. When he had called together all the people's chief priests and teachers of the law, he asked them where the Christ was to be born. 'In Bethlehem in Judea,' they replied, 'for this is what the prophet has written:

> But you, Bethlehem, in the land of Judah,
> are by no means least among the
> rulers of Judah;
> for out of you will come a ruler
> who will be the shepherd of my
> people Israel.'"

In keeping with this sentiment, and in further development of the second objection outlined above, John records the objection of some, "How can the Christ come from Galilee? Does not the Scripture say that the Christ will come from David's family and from Bethlehem, the town where David lived?" (7:41–42). We encounter here yet another instance of Johannine irony. For as the readers of the Gospel well know (not from reading the Gospel itself, but from Christian tradition, another confirmation of John's assumption that his readers are familiar with the basic contours of the gospel message), Jesus was in fact born in Bethlehem, Galilee merely being the region where he was raised and headquartered. People were right about their expectation—they were simply deficient in their knowledge of Jesus' true origin, a motif that is part and parcel of the Johannine misunderstanding theme (cf. 7:52).

A fifth messianic expectation surfaces in 12:32–34. When Jesus speaks of his being "lifted up from the earth" (which John interprets as "showing the kind of death he was going to die"), the crowds object, "We have heard from the Law that the Christ will remain forever, so how can you say, 'The Son of Man must be lifted up?'" This highlights the major difficulty all four evangelists, and all early Christians, had to deal with: how could it be said that the Messiah had to die? Unless they provided a satisfactory answer to this question, they could not expect anyone to believe that Jesus, the Crucified, was the Messiah. Interestingly, Jesus does not attempt a full-fledged response (12:35–36). He merely reaffirms that he is the light, and that people should trust in the light, so that they might become sons of light.

The evangelist, however, provides a much more comprehensive answer to this crucial objection. Most important, he points out that people's unbelief in the Messiah itself actually fulfilled biblical prophecy. Just as they did not believe Isaiah's message, they did not accept the teaching of Jesus (12:38; cf. Is 53:1). What is more, people could not believe, because of God's judicial blinding of their eyes (12:39–40; cf. Is 6:10). This is expressed by John even more strongly than in the other Gospels, where people's blinding is cast as the *result* of God's work (cf. Mk 4:12 par.); for John, people's blinding was the very *purpose* God pursued in Jesus' work.

If it was God, then, who blinded people's eyes, it may be asked, how can they still be held responsible for not believing? Says Paul, dealing with this very issue in the Book of Romans,

> One of you will say to me: "Then why does God still blame us? For who resists his will?" But who are you, O man, to talk back to God? Shall what is formed say to him who formed it, "Why did you make me like this?" Does not the potter have the right to make out of the same lump of clay some pottery for noble purposes and some for common use?
>
> What if God, choosing to show his wrath and make his power known, bore with great patience the objects of his wrath—prepared for destruction? What if he did this to make the riches of his glory known to the objects of his mercy, whom he prepared in advance for glory—even us, whom he also called, not only from the Jews but also from the Gentiles? (Rom 9:19–24)

We may not understand how it can be "fair" for God to harden people and then to hold them responsible for hardening themselves. But if God is God, everything ultimately must be traced back to *his* action and will rather than to that of any one human being. If *people's* decisions can effectively thwart the purposes of *God*, then God is not fully the omnipotent God Scripture everywhere proclaims him to be. For even human evil ultimately serves the purposes of God. Joseph recognized this when he told his brothers, "*You* intended to harm me, but *God* intended it for good to accomplish what is now being done, the saving of many lives" (Gn 50:19). Pharaoh, Nebuchadnezzar, and Cyrus each in their

111

own day and way unwittingly served the purposes of God. So did Judas when he betrayed Jesus, and the Jewish high priest and Pontius Pilate when they condemned him to die.

This is also the unanimous testimony of the early church. As Peter told the Jews who had crucified Jesus in his sermon at Pentecost: "This man was handed over to you *by God's set purpose and foreknowledge;* and you, with the help of wicked men, put him to death by nailing him to the cross. *But God* raised him from the dead" (Acts 2:23–24). And again in Acts 3:13b, 18: "You handed him over to be killed . . . but *this is how God fulfilled what he had foretold through all the prophets,* saying that his Christ would suffer." Ultimately, the proof of Jesus' messiahship is the fact that God raised him from the dead. Thus John's seventh, climactic sign is Jesus' raising of Lazarus, which demon-

strates that Jesus is "the resurrection and the life" (11:25). And this sign is emblematic of Jesus' own resurrection (cf. already 10:17–18).

This brings us back to our point of departure, the question of how Jesus can predict his own death and still claim to be the Messiah. Here all four evangelists contend that this difficulty evaporates once it is realized that the Old Testament Scriptures predict just such a suffering Messiah, in particular Isaiah's "suffering Servant" in Isaiah 52:13–53:12.

> He was despised and rejected by men,
>   a man of sorrows, and familiar with suffering.
> Like one from whom men hide their faces
>   he was despised, and we esteemed him not.
> Surely he took up our infirmities
>   and carried our sorrows,

Knowing the Truth and Doing It

Two statements in John 7 and 8 highlight the importance of a person's commitment to *do* (not merely *know*) the truth. The first is found in John 7:17, where Jesus says: *"If anyone chooses to do God's will, he will find out whether my teaching comes from God or whether I speak on my own."* It is worth reflecting on this observation by Augustine who wrote, "Understanding is the reward of faith. . . . What is 'If any man be willing to do his will'? It is the same thing as to believe" (quoted in the *NIV Study Bible,* p. 1609). And, at another place, Augustine counseled, "Do not seek to understand in order to believe, but believe in order to understand." Both statements underscore the truth embodied in Jesus' teaching: we must be willing to take the "risk" of

stepping out in faith, or we will never experience the presence, assistance, and blessing of Christ.

The second statement, also made by Jesus, is found in John 8:31–32: "If you hold to my teaching, you are really my disciples. Then you will know the truth, and the truth will make you free." What is remarkable is that Jesus made this statement to "the Jews who had believed him." "Knowing the truth" is evidently more than a mere intellectual grasping of some concept, a philosophical contemplation of the nature of things or the like. Rather, truth is inextricably linked to Jesus Christ who *is* the truth (14:6) and who has provided access to God by dying for our sins. The basic human dilemma is not ignorance needing education; it is sinfulness needing redemption. John 8:44 provides a

telling commentary on Jesus' statement in 8:31–32: the devil did not "hold to the truth," preferring to carry out his own desires. His problem was not that he did not know the truth: he knew it, but chose not to act in accordance with it.

Perhaps James said it best: "Do not merely listen to the word, and so deceive yourselves. Do what it says. Anyone who listens to the word but does not do what it says is like a man who looks at his face in a mirror and, after looking at himself, goes away and immediately forgets what he looks like. But the man who looks intently into the perfect law that gives freedom, and continues to do this, not forgetting what he has heard, but doing it—he will be blessed in what he does" (Jas 1:22–25).

yet we considered him stricken by God,
　　smitten by him, and afflicted.
But he was pierced for our transgressions,
　　he was crushed for our iniquities;
the punishment that brought us peace
　　was upon him,
　　and by his wounds we are healed.

How could people have missed this crucial messianic passage? How could they pervert biblical teaching regarding the Messiah and conceive of him in merely political terms? And how can the Jewish people today miss the striking resemblance between Isaiah's Suffering Servant and the Lord Jesus Christ? This pivotal passage also answers the question why the Messiah had to die: he had to render atonement for the sins of his people. As the sinless Lamb of God (cf. 1:29, 36), Jesus laid down his life for his sheep (10:15). This is what theologians call the doctrine of substitutionary atonement, of Christ's vicarious sacrifice for us. Because of our sin, we deserved to die; but as Paul puts it, "God made him who had no sin to be sin for us, so that in him we might become the righteousness of God" (2 Cor 5:21).

We have come a long way in our examination of John's listing of representative questions concerning Jesus' messiahship. To sum up: John contends that the Messiah

1. is not merely a political figure restoring Israel to its former glory
2. is indeed of mysterious, eternal origin rather than a mere man (i.e., the Son of Man)
3. provides many striking signs of his messianic identity (the seven selected signs)
4. is born in Bethlehem in David's line
5. will live forever, but must be crucified in order to atone for people's sins; this is done in accordance with God's will and as predicted in the Scriptures; subsequent to the crucifixion, Jesus the Messiah was raised up from the dead

This concludes our study of John 7. We have seen how, according to John, Jesus fulfills the symbolism underlying the Jewish Feast of Tabernacles, and how people's representative questions regarding Jesus' background and identity can all be satisfactorily matched with what is known of Jesus' background and OT teaching regarding the Messiah. But we must read on; for we have not yet reached the climax in the drama John presents of the Jewish rejection of the Messiah and of his vindication by the God "who sent" him.

Escalating Controversy: The Paternity Suit (8:12–59)

John 8:12–59 covers the aftermath of Jesus' controversy with the Jewish leaders narrated in chapter 7, with 7:45–52 functioning as a transitional passage (regarding the omission of 7:53–8:11, see above). Chapter 7, in turn, further developed the controversy sparked already in chapter 5 with Jesus' healing of the lame man on a Sabbath (cf. 7:21). This shows how John skillfully develops as a major motif in the first part of his Gospel (esp. chs. 5–12) Jesus' escalating conflict with the Jews. In this regard, the Johannine witness theme plays a crucial role.[4] It appears that John has reversed the Synoptic portrayal of Jesus as on trial before the Romans and the Jews. According to John, it is really the world, including the Jews, who is on trial, and in keeping with this notion, John marshals a series of witnesses in defense of the truthfulness of Jesus' claims:

John the Baptist (chs. 1–3, 5; 1:7–8, 15, 32, 34; 3:32; 5:33)

Jesus himself (3:11; 13:21; 18:37) and his own works (5:36; 8:14, 18; 10:25, 32, 37–38)

the Father (chs. 5–8, 10, 12, 15, 17; e.g., 5:37; 8:18)

Moses and the Scriptures (chs. 5, 9; e.g., 5:39)

the Spirit (chs. 14–16; e.g., 15:26)

the disciples (chs. 1, 13, 15; e.g., 15:27)

the fourth evangelist (19:35; 21:24)

In the end, the verdict is this: "Light has come into the world, but men loved dark-

Owing to idolatrous worship, the Hinnom Valley near Jerusalem became synonymous with Gehenna or Hell in ancient Judaism.

ness instead of light because their deeds were evil" (3:19).

The Johannine motif of light and darkness, with which the present section opens (8:12), ties in several thematic strands in John's Gospel. First, one is reminded of the Word's participation in creation (1:3). Second, John uses the contrast between literal light and darkness to illustrate the *moral* contrast between spiritual life and spiritual death: "to walk in darkness" means to fail to see the moral implications of one's sin, while "to walk in the light" connotes life lived in full view of the reality of one's own sinfulness and need for salvation (cf. 12:35–36). Third, John uses the symbolism of the Feast of Tabernacles, in particular torch-lighting ceremonies, to point out how Jesus fulfills the essence of various Jewish festivals (8:12). Fourth, light symbolism provides continuity between Jesus' appearance at the Feast and his healing of the man born blind in chapter 9 (cf. esp. 9:4–5). The entire chapter becomes a parable of the Pharisees' spiritual blindness in contrast to the blind man's newfound vision. While he knew himself to be blind and in need of sight, to be given as a gracious gift from God, the Pharisees, although spiritually blind, claimed to be able to see, thus cutting themselves off

from God's mercy (cf. Mt 24:16–24, where Jesus repeatedly calls the Pharisees blind as well). We will return to this dynamic in greater detail shortly. Finally, the fourth evangelist returns to the light motif once more briefly in the context of the raising of Lazarus, reiterating that Jesus is the light of life (11:9–10) and then features light imagery prominently in Jesus' final discourse at the end of chapter 12.

We may make a few observations regarding John's use of the light motif: (1) the term "light" spans the entire first half of John's Gospel, from the Prologue (1:4, 5, 7, 8 [twice], 9) through the concluding section (12:35 [twice], 36 [three times], 46), in each of which it occurs six times; (2) notably, the phrase is entirely absent from the second major portion of John's Gospel, which indicates that it is part and parcel of John's presentation of Jesus' entrance into the world and ministry to the Jews in chapters 1–12; (3) the occurrences of the expression "light" are clustered in the following passages: 1:4–9; 3:19–21; 5:35; 8:12; 9:5; 11:9–10; 12:35–46; (4) the term "light" is linked with "life" most notably in 1:4 ("in him was life") and 8:12 ("the light of life"); this indicates that these two terms sustain a close relationship; a closer look indicates that John uses the term "life" even more frequently than "light," especially in the phrase "eternal life"; it appears therefore that "light" is occasionally used as a metaphor for eternal life in its spiritual, moral, and present-day implications.

For John, therefore, a life lived without Christ is a life lived in spiritual darkness. For Christ is the light that has come into the world; he is life itself. This would be a meaningful and powerful message to Jew and Gentile alike. To the Jew, it would resonate with the belief that God is the Creator, the Giver of light which makes life possible, the one who revealed to his people moral requirements he expected them to keep, but the observing of which was rendered difficult because of human sin ("darkness"). To the Gentile, the light/darkness metaphor would put Christ's coming in a basic, elementary context; it would also appeal to people's longing for significance and permanence of life beyond death. The same can be said for our culture: to the religious person, Jesus can be presented as the one who alone was sinless and who kept God's requirements perfectly in order to save us from our sin; to the nonreligious person,

Jesus can be presented as the one who alone is able to meet the deepest longings we are created for. Truly John is a master of contextualizing his faith in Jesus the Messiah to both religious and nonreligious audiences.

We can be brief about the specific details of the interchange narrated in 8:12–30, since this section in the main develops further points already made in chapter 7 (compare 8:12 with 7:37; 8:14 with 7:27–28; 8:15 with 7:24; 8:21–24 with 7:33). The parallelism between Jesus' statements in 7:37–38 and 8:12 is particularly pronounced:

If anyone is thirsty, let him come to me and drink.	I am the light of the world.
Whoever believes in me . . . streams of living water will flow from within him.	Whoever follows me will never walk in darkness, but will have the light of life.

The point made in both statements is the same: Jesus is the source of life.

But the Jews do not concede this. They (1) dispute the validity of Jesus' witness (8:13–18); and (2) challenge Jesus' identification with God the Father (8:19–30). As Jesus points out, this reveals their sinfulness (8:23–24) and lack of perspective (8:27–28). But he warns them solemnly that unless they perceive the connection between Jesus "the Son" and God "the Father" they will die in their sins (8:24).

John 8:31–59 elaborates further on the brewing "paternity suit" between the Pharisees and Jesus. Jesus is not fooled by the fact that many Jews put their faith in him (8:30). Rather, he emphasizes that it is those who *continue* to hold to his teaching who are truly his disciples (8:31). As will shortly become evident, this does not include these spurious believers. For their ethnic pride gets in the way. Claiming Abraham as their father, they deny their own sinfulness and need for salvation. It has become increasingly popular in recent years for scholars to assert that the Jewish people contemporary to Jesus knew themselves to be saved by grace and that keeping the requirements of the Law was merely understood in terms of "staying in" the covenant God had made with them at Sinai.[5] The present passage

---

Table 8.2
Some Factually Erroneous Statements Made by "the Jews" in John 7 and 8

1. *"Are you from Galilee, too? Look into it, and you will find that a prophet does not come out of Galilee" (7:52).* I have looked into it, and Jonah, for instance, did in fact come from Galilee. He was from Gath Hepher (2 Kgs 14:25) in Zebulun (Jos 19:10, 13), which was near Mount Tabor and west of the Sea of Galilee. Thus the Pharisees were wrong.

2. *"We are Abraham's descendants and have never been slaves of anyone" (8:33).* Never been slaves of anyone? What about Egypt? Assyria? The Babylonians, Persians, and Greeks? And what about the Romans? Apart from the brief interlude following the Maccabean revolt (165–63 B.C.), the Jews had, to the contrary, not been free from foreign overlords for a long time.

Study Questions

1. In what ways does Jesus fulfill the symbolism underlying the Feast of Tabernacles?

2. Trace representative questions regarding Jesus' messiahship through John's Gospel and show how John uses these to demonstrate that Jesus is the Christ.

3. Trace the Johannine motif of light and darkness through the first half of the Gospel.

seems to contradict this notion. For John's very point here is that the Jews' ethnic presumption blinded them regarding their need for a Savior.

In fact, some have contended that the Jews' statement, "We are not illegitimate children" (8:41), represents a thinly veiled allusion to the rumor of Jesus' birth out of wedlock. If this were Paul, he would deal with the Jews' appeal to Abraham as their father by pointing out that Abraham is the father of all those who believe, whether Jew or Gentile (referring to Gn 15:6; cf. Gal 3:6; Rom 4:3). But Jesus takes things one step further still: he charges that the Jews, contrary to their claim that *Abraham* is their father, in their sinfulness really have *the devil* as their spiritual father. For he is "a murderer from the beginning" (8:44), just as the Jews are out to kill the Son of God (5:18; 7:25, 30, 32, 44–52). And he is "the father of lies" (8:44), just as the Jews reject the one who has come to witness to the truth (cf. 18:37) and who himself is "the Way, the Truth, and the Life" (14:6). So why do the Jews reject their own Messiah? Jesus' analysis is

Key Word

Good Shepherd discourse

clear: "He who belongs to God hears what God says. The reason you do not hear is that you do not belong to God" (8:47).

Can civility of discourse deteriorate still further between the Jews and Jesus? It may seem hard to imagine that it can, but it does: after challenging even his earthly parentage, the Jews proceed to call Jesus "a Samaritan" (8:48) and "demon-possessed" (8:48, 52; cf. 7:20; 10:20–21: "demon-possessed and raving mad"). At this point the Synoptic Gospels provide corroborating evidence when they report the charge on part of Jesus' opponents, "He is possessed by Beelzebub [that is, Satan]. By the prince of demons he is driving out demons" (Mk 3:22 par.). According to Jesus, attributing the work of the Holy Spirit to Satan is an unpardonable sin that will never be forgiven (Mk 3:28–29). The Jews' calling Jesus "a Samaritan" shows their height of exasperation; they know full well that he is a Jew.

The present interchange makes one thing crystal-clear: people's opposition to the gospel is frequently not based on rational objections or intellectual argument but is at the root moral rebellion against God, a willful assertion of human autonomy and independence that prefers life without God over life with and under God. For sinful people resist conscious subjection of their wills to the will of God. In the case of the Jews, their primary problems likewise did not have to do with lack of information or logical argument. People wanted to fit God into their own system rather than submitting themselves to God's way of doing things.

In the end, Jesus' struggle with the Jews in chapter 8 remains completely unresolved. They claim Abraham as *their* father and acknowledge no spiritual need whatsoever; Jesus claims he alone knows God the Father—*his* Father—and that "before Abraham was born, I am!" (8:58). By the Jews' reaction—they pick up stones to stone him (8:59a)—it is clear that they understood the phrase "I am" to involve connotations of deity; for stoning was the punishment for blasphemy (cf. 10:33). But for now, Jesus eludes their grasp, hiding himself and slipping away from the temple grounds (8:59b).

9 Escalating Conflict (Part 3): Sign #6

John 9:1–10:42

> Whether he is a sinner or not, I don't know. One thing I do know. I was blind but now I see!
>
> —John 9:25

Supplemental Reading: Psalms 23, 100; Ezekiel 34; Zechariah 11:4–17; 13:7–9

Outline

- The Sixth Sign: The Healing of the Man Born Blind (ch. 9)
- The Good Shepherd Discourse (ch. 10)

Objectives

After reading this chapter, you should be able to

1. Elaborate on the dynamics operative in Jesus' sixth sign, the healing of the man born blind.
2. Discuss the biblical (including Jesus') perspective on the cause of suffering.
3. Illumine the Old Testament background of the Good Shepherd discourse.

The pool of Siloam (which means "sent") was the site of yet another amazing miracle performed by Jesus, the Sent One from the Father.

The Sixth Sign: The Healing of the Man Born Blind (ch. 9)

The healing of the man born blind constitutes the sixth sign chosen by John to demonstrate Jesus' messiahship. Like signs ##2 (the cleansing of the temple in ch. 2) and 4 (the healing of the lame man in ch. 5), it takes place in Jerusalem. The parallels between Jesus' healing of the lame man in chapter 5 and the healing of the man born blind in the present chapter are particularly pronounced. The site for the healing of the lame man is the pool of Bethesda (5:2); the healing of the man born blind takes place at the pool of Siloam (v. 7). In both cases, the healing is rendered difficult by the attending circumstances: the lame man had been in that condition *for thirty-eight years;* the blind man had been blind from birth.

In both instances, Jesus' chosen method of healing is unconventional. In the case of the lame man, he simply orders the man to walk, entirely sidestepping washing in the pool, and the invalid is cured that instant (5:8–9). In the case of the blind man, Jesus spits on the ground, makes

some mud with his saliva, and puts it on the man's eyes (cf. Mk 8:22–26). Then he tells the man to go and wash in the Pool of Siloam. The man does as told and comes home seeing (vv. 6–7). Moreover, both healings take place on a Sabbath (5:9; 9:14). However, while the lame man in chapter 5 reports Jesus to the authorities and then disappears from the scene, the healed blind man in chapter 9 turns out to be more loyal to the one who healed him. While his parents cower for fear of expulsion from the synagogue (v. 23), the man who had been blind stands his ground when interrogated by the Pharisees, and in the end is thrown out of the synagogue himself (v. 34).[1]

This is not the only healing of a blind man in the Gospels. Consider the following account of the healing of specific individuals:

Mk 8:22–26: healing of a blind man in Bethsaida

Mt 9:27–31: healing of two blind men

Mt 12:22–23: healing of demon-possessed man who had also been blind and mute

Mk 10:46–52 = Mt 20:29–34 = Lk 18:35–43: healing of two blind men near Jericho (including Bartimaeus).

What is even more important, both Matthew and Luke set Jesus' healing of the blind in the context of the ministry of Isaiah's Servant of the Lord (Lk 4:18–19; Mt 11:5 = Lk 7:21–22; Mt 15:30–31; 21:14; cf. Is 35:4–6; 61:1–2; see also Is 29:18; 42:7).

The significance of this larger witness of the Gospels for John's account is this: John's depiction of Jesus' healing of a blind man (in his case, the sixth sign) provides further proof that Jesus is in fact the Messiah. For John, too, patterns Jesus'

Table 9.1
The Unfolding Drama of Jesus and the Blind Man (Jn 9)

1. THE SETTING (9:1–5):
   The disciples: "Rabbi, who sinned, this man or his parents, that he was born blind?"
   Jesus: "This happened so that the work of God might be displayed in his life."

2. THE HEALING (9:6–7):
   Jesus to the blind man: "Go, wash in the Pool of Siloam."

3. THE NEIGHBORS' CHALLENGE (9:8–12):
   Neighbors: "Isn't this the same man who used to sit and beg? . . . How then were your eyes opened?"
   The man: "I am the man. . . . The man they call Jesus . . . told me to go to Siloam and wash. So I went and washed, and then I could see."

4. THE PHARISEES' INVESTIGATION (9:13–34):
   a. PHASE 1: Confronting the Man (9:13–17):
      Pharisees: "How did you receive your sight? And what do you have to say about him?"
      The man: "He put mud on my eyes, and I washed, and now I see. . . . He is a prophet."
   b. PHASE 2: Confronting the Man's Parents (9:18–23):
      Pharisees: "Is this your son?

   How is it that now he can see?"
   Parents: "We know he is our son, and we know he was born blind. But how he can see now, or who opened his eyes, we don't know. Ask him. He is of age; he will speak for himself."
   c. PHASE 3: Confronting the Man a Second Time (9:24–34):
      Pharisees: "What did he do to you? How did he open your eyes?"
      The man: "I have told you already and you did not listen . . . Do you want to become his disciples, too?" (Pharisees excommunicate the man.)

5. THE AFTERMATH (9:35–41):
   a. PHASE 1: Jesus and the Man (9:35–38):
      Jesus: "Do you believe in the Son of Man?"
      The man: "Lord, I believe."
   b. PHASE 2: Jesus and the Pharisees (9:39–41):
      Jesus: "For judgment I have come into this world, so that the blind will see and those who see will become blind."
      Pharisees: "What? Are we blind too?"
      Jesus: "If you were blind, you would not be guilty of sin; but now that you claim you can see, your guilt remains."

ministry to a significant extent after Isaiah's portrait of the Servant of the Lord (cf. esp. Jn 12:38–41).

In addition to this, John incorporates the healing of the blind man into the light–darkness symbolism he sustains through the entire first major section of his Gospel (see the discussion in the previous chapter). Just as Jesus turns out to be the Light of the world by fulfilling the symbolism underlying the Feast of Tabernacles (8:12), he proves to be the Light of the world by giving sight to the blind man (9:5). The world, and the Jews with it, lies in darkness (1:5, 10–11); whoever wants to walk in the light must come to Jesus (8:12b).

Now that we have investigated the intricate relationship John's account of the healing of the blind man sustains with the larger narrative and the remainder of the Gospel tradition, we may briefly explore the particulars of the event as recounted in John 9. John recalls how Jesus' disciples asked him at the outset of the healing whether it was the blind man who sinned or his parents so that the man was born blind (v. 2). This tight cause-and-effect relationship between sin and suffering was in accordance with contemporary Jewish beliefs (cf. 9:34: "steeped in sin at birth") and can be traced back as far as to the time of Job and his "comforters." Thus Eliphaz would ask, "Who, being innocent, has ever perished?" (Job 4:7). The implied answer: No one. And no matter how sincerely Job pleads his innocence, the conclusion his friends reach is clear: Job suffered, therefore he must have sinned.

Jesus disavows such clear-cut theories. "Neither this man nor his parents sinned" (to bring about the man's blindness), "but this happened so that the work of God might be displayed in his life" (v. 3). In an instance recorded only by Luke Jesus makes a similar point. As Luke tells us, some people approached Jesus regarding the Galileans whose blood Pilate had mixed with their sacrifices, which led Jesus to respond as follows:

> Do you think that these Galileans were worse sinners than all the other Galileans because they suffered this way?
> I tell you, no! But unless you repent, you too will all perish.

> Or those eighteen who died when the tower in Siloam fell on them—do you think they were more guilty than all the others living in Jerusalem?
> I tell you, no! But unless you repent, you too will all perish (Lk 13:1–5).

The application is evident: we may not always know the reason for someone's—including our own—suffering, and in the end this is not what is most important. Rather than wasting time by trying to figure out the root cause of suffering in a given instance, the important thing is to maintain a humble, repentant attitude, and, like Jesus, to see instances of suffering around us as opportunities for the work of God to be displayed in people's (or our) lives. To believe that good can come out of evil takes faith and defies the world's conventional wisdom that bad is bad no matter what. It takes faith in a Jesus who can—and does—work miracles and in a God who allowed Jesus (who was perfectly innocent) to die a cruel criminal's death on a cross in order to bring salvation and eternal life to us (who were perfectly guilty). Thank God that Jesus understood that he was dying not for his own sins but for ours; who knew that God would ultimately triumph over the evil perpetrated upon him, and who "entrusted himself to him who judges justly" (1 Pt 2:23). Let us do likewise and defy simplistic analyses of other people's—or our own—suffering, and see them as opportunities for God's glory to be revealed.

We have already recounted the way in which Jesus heals the man; we need not do so again. Indeed, *the way of healing* is what the Jews focus on (9:10; cf. 5:10); but this is not what is most important. The emphasis of John's narrative quickly turns to Jesus' identity. As the Pharisees conclude, "This man is not from God, for he does not keep the Sabbath" (v. 16; apparently, the Pharisees were once again concerned with the minutiae of oral Jewish tradition, in the present case objecting to Jesus' making of mud [!] in healing the blind man; vv. 6, 11; cf. 5:10–12). But others ask, "How can a sinner do such miraculous signs?" (v. 17). Unbelief seeks alternative explanations to manifest miracles: some believed the man whose

Table 9.2
References to Expulsion from the Synagogue in John's Gospel

1. "His parents said this because they were afraid of the Jews, for already the Jews had decided that anyone who acknowledged that Jesus was the Christ *would be put out of the synagogue*" (9:22).

2. "To this they replied, 'You were steeped in sin at birth; how dare you lecture us!' And *they threw him out*" (9:34; cf. 9:35).

3. "Yet at the same time many even among the leaders believed in him. But because of the Pharisees they would not confess their faith for fear *they would be put out of the synagogue*" (12:42).

4. "*They will put you out of the synagogue*; in fact, a time is coming when anyone who kills you will think he is offering a service to God" (16:2).

of John 9 is much like that of many Synoptic parables): "For judgment I have come into this world, so that the blind will see and those who see will become blind" (v. 39). The Pharisees, for their part, in yet another instance of Johannine irony, are completely unaware of their own spiritual blindness (v. 40), and thus their guilt remains (v. 41). The formerly blind man, on the other hand, walks home not only with his physical sight restored but also a spiritually changed man—a believer and worshiper of Jesus (v. 38).

And Jesus, who was the de facto person under investigation throughout the chapter, emerges in the end as the one who initiates encounters with both the formerly blind man and the Pharisees and who has the last word in a scathing pronouncement that leaves the Pharisees speechless and entirely exposed for their spiritual blindness. More than a mere miracle, this Johannine sign turns out to be a highly symbolic display of Jesus' ability to cure spiritual blindness. Conversely, as the present story makes clear, the only thing against which there is no remedy is spiritual pride that claims to see while being in fact blind.

blindness had been removed was not the one who used to sit at the Pool of Siloam and beg (v. 8); others disputed that the man had been blind in the first place (v. 18). But the man's parents confirm that this was indeed so (v. 20).

Most interesting is the development evident in the formerly blind man himself: first he calls Jesus a prophet (v. 17); then he counters the Pharisees' charge that Jesus is a sinner (on account of breaking the Sabbath) by the undeniable fact that he was blind but now he sees (v. 25); then he asks whether the Pharisees want to become Jesus' disciples, too (implying that he had already become one himself; v. 27); then he "lectures" them (the Pharisees' term; v. 34) by saying, "We know that God does not listen to sinners . . . If this man were not from God, he could do nothing" (v. 33). Finally, when Jesus tracks him down and asks him if he believes in him, he answers, "Lord, I believe," and worships him (v. 38).

For Jesus, this is in keeping with the reversal that has taken place through his ministry (here the underlying dynamic

The Good Shepherd Discourse (ch. 10)

Remarkably, chapter 10 proceeds without any transition from the previous chapter. This seems to indicate that the recipients of Jesus' Good Shepherd discourse are the same Pharisees who had been the target of Jesus' comments at the end of chapter 9. If so, this helps us understand the thrust of Jesus' words in chapter 10 even better. In the preceding chapter, Jesus' healing of the blind man had led to the man's excommunication from the local synagogue (9:34). Jesus saw in this provocative act an arrogant assertion of usurped authority that called for further comment. For the Pharisees were not only blind themselves (9:40–41); they also were "blind guides" (cf. Mt 23:16, 24), leading astray those entrusted to their care. They were the ones who spared no effort to win even a single proselyte, only to make him (in Jesus' terms) "twice as much a son of

Jesus presented himself as the "good shepherd" who, in contrast to the Jewish religious leaders of his day, cared for his followers in the tradition of Israel's first shepherd-king, David.

hell" as they were (Mt 23:15). These are strong words! As Jesus says in another place, "Things that cause people to sin are bound to come, but woe to that person through whom they come. It would be better for him to be thrown into the sea with a millstone tied around his neck than for him to cause one of these little ones to sin" (Lk 17:1–2).

The dark backdrop of Jesus' Good Shepherd discourse is therefore the blatant irresponsibility he perceives in the Jewish religious leadership. Sadly, the corruption characteristic of the Jewish leaders of Jesus' day was nothing new. As Zechariah puts it,

> Woe to the worthless shepherd,
> who deserts the flock!
> May the sword strike his arm and his
> right eye!
> May his arm be completely withered,
> his right eye totally blinded!
> (Zec 11:17).

But there is another shepherd, "the man who is close to me," whom the Lord will strike:

> "Awake, O sword, against my shepherd,
> against the man who is close to me!"
> declares the LORD Almighty.
> "Strike the shepherd,

> and the sheep will be scattered,
> and I will turn my hand against the
> little ones" (Zec 13:7).

Indeed,

> They will look on me,
> the one they have pierced,
> and they will mourn for him
> as one mourns for an only child,
> and grieve bitterly for him
> as one grieves for a firstborn son
> (Zec 12:10).

It is likely that John (and Jesus) has the contrasting images of the prophet Zechariah in mind as he pens the present discourse. On the one side is the worthless shepherd who deserts his flock; on the other is the shepherd who is stricken for the sake of his sheep, pierced publicly and eliciting great mourning and grief. The passage regarding "the one they have pierced" (Zec 12:10) is quoted by John in 19:37 with reference to Jesus' crucifixion and in Revelation 1:7 with reference to Jesus' glorious return. The passage "strike the shepherd and the sheep will be scattered" (Zec 13:7) is alluded to in John 16:32 (cf. Mt 26:31; Mk 14:27).

According to R. T. France's classic treatment *Jesus and the Old Testament*, "Zechariah 9–14 formed an important background both for Jesus' thought and words especially at the time of the passion, and also for the evangelists' presentation of the narrative."[2] As many as four figures in this section may be taken as messianic:

the king riding on a donkey (9:9–10; quoted in Jn 12:15; Mt 21:5)
the good shepherd (11:4–14)
the one "whom they have pierced" (12:10)
the smitten shepherd (13:7)

France argues that these four images should be seen as four aspects of a single messianic conception, "the Shepherd-King," presenting successive phases of his coming and the reaction of the people. According to France, this conception, in turn, represents a further reflection on the figure of the Servant of the Lord in Isaiah, therefore concentrating on the problem of the rejection, suffering, and death of the Messiah.[3]

To these two portraits, those of Isaiah and Zechariah, a third may be added, that of the exilic prophet Ezekiel. In chapter 34 of his book, Ezekiel reports an oracle he received from the Lord that must be quoted at some length to convey the full impact of this passage on our present subject of study, Jesus' "Good Shepherd Discourse" in John 10.

> Woe to the shepherds of Israel who only take care of themselves!
>   Should not shepherds take care of the flock?
> You eat the curds,
>   clothe yourselves with the wool
> and slaughter the choice animals,
>   but you do not take care of the flock.
> You have not strengthened the weak
>   or healed the sick
>   or bound up the injured.
> You have not brought back the strays
>   or searched for the lost.
> You have ruled them harshly and brutally.
> So they were scattered
>   because there was no shepherd . . .

After announcing divine judgment, the oracle turns to the promise of God's intervention through his Messiah.

> I myself will search for my sheep
>   and look after them.

> As a shepherd looks after his scattered flock when he is with them,
>   so will I look after my sheep.
> I will rescue them . . .
> I will bring them out from the nations and gather them . . .
> I will pasture them . . .
> I myself will tend my sheep and have them lie down . . .
> I will search for the lost . . .
> I will shepherd the flock with justice . . .
> I will save my flock . . .
> I will place over them one shepherd, my servant David,
> and he will tend them;
>   he will tend them and be their shepherd.
> I the LORD will be their God,
>   and my servant David will be prince among them.
> I the LORD have spoken.

After reading this extended quote from the prophet Ezekiel, it will be clear that Jesus placed himself squarely in the context of this messianic portrait (cf. also Jer 23:1–8). God's people, his "flock," had been led astray by irresponsible "shepherds," leaders who fed themselves rather than the people entrusted to them. The Pharisees contemporary to Jesus were just the latest representatives of this tradition of ungodly leadership in Israel (see also the Parable of the Wicked Tenants in Mk 12:1–12 par.). Jesus, for his part, knew himself to fulfill the messianic predictions surrounding the shepherd of the Lord, the "good shepherd" who could be trusted to protect and care for God's flock. Interestingly, the above passage proceeds upon a dual track: on the one hand, God says that *he himself* will tend his sheep; on the other, he will send *his servant David* to tend his sheep and be their shepherd. This is one of several instances in the Old Testament where a second figure on the same level as Yahweh (the Lord) emerges, preparing people, as it were, for the ministry of the God-sent Messiah who himself is God in the flesh, fulfilling his mission (cf. Mk 12:35–37 = Mt 22:41–46 = Lk 20:41–44).

The metaphor of the "flock," an everyday feature of Jewish life, pervades the Old Testament. God himself was called "the Shepherd of Israel" (Ps 80:1; cf. Ps 23; Is 40:10–11; Ez 34:11–16). Part of this imagery was also the notion of chief and undershepherds as well as that of hired hands. It was commonly known that in the case of danger to the flock hired hands were likely to abandon the flock entrusted to them to save their own skin while the actual shepherd of the flock would defend the safety of his sheep if necessary even at the risk of his own life. David, who was a shepherd before he became king, became a prototype of God's shepherd, even of the theme cluster surrounding the figure of a coming shepherd-king outlined above. As John 10 makes clear, Jesus saw himself as embodying the characteristics and expectations attached to this salvation-historical biblical figure. What is more, Jesus presented himself as "the" good shepherd par excellence. The contrast between the Jewish leaders of his day and Jesus himself only accentuated further the way in which the Jewish leadership had usurped the role God had given them on the one hand and Jesus' faithfulness to the God who had sent him on the other.

Throughout his ministry, Jesus varied in his approach to the following three groups. Toward the mass of "the people of the land" (Hebrew am-ha-aretz), the crowds, he felt compassion, as for a leaderless herd of sheep. They were "like sheep without a shepherd" (Mt 9:36; cf. 14:14; 15:32 = Mk 8:2; an allusion to Nm 27:17; cf. 1 Kgs 22:17; Ez 34:5–6; Zec 10:2). His own close followers, particularly the twelve, Jesus sought to protect from the false shepherds, the Jewish religious leadership, warning them against the all-pervasive "leaven of the Pharisees" (Mk 8:15

Did Jesus Come to Bring Judgment or Not?

In John 9:39, Jesus plainly asserts, "For judgment I have come into this world, so that the blind will see and those who see will become blind." The alert reader of John's Gospel will immediately notice the apparent contradiction between this statement and Jesus' earlier assertion (or John's earlier assertion regarding Jesus) in 3:17: "For God did not send his Son into the world to condemn the world, but to save the world through him." Later in the Gospel, Jesus clearly echoes the statement in 3:17, when he says in 12:47: "As for the person who hears my words but does not keep them, I do not judge him. For I did not come to judge the world, but to save it."

Did Jesus come to judge the world, or didn't he? In the above statements, he seems to affirm both. But how can both be true? At first glance,

this seems to be an impossibility. But as will be seen, a closer look reveals that, rightly understood, both affirmations are accurate.

In one sense, Jesus did not come to judge. The primary purpose of his first coming was to die on the cross for people's salvation from sin. Hence John's insistence that Jesus' came, not to judge, but to save (3:17). Anyone who rejects Jesus' offer of salvation is not so much judged by him as he brings judgment upon himself (12:47). God's wrath remains on him (3:36).

In another sense, Jesus' coming did indeed introduce an element of judgment. The sense in which "judgment" is here understood is that of division as that between light and darkness or truth and falsehood. Jesus, "the true light" (1:9), came into the world (8:12; 9:5), and "this is

the verdict [krisis = "judgment"]: Light has come into the world, but men loved darkness instead of light because their deeds were evil" (3:19). In that sense, it was inevitable that the Light's coming into the world exposed human sinfulness for what it was. Like moths to the light, people came to Jesus. Yet the closer they came, the more exposed became also their lying and evil hearts. Thus Jesus' parting challenge was for people to put their trust in the light while they had it, so they would become sons of light (12:35–36).

Thus while judgment was not the primary purpose for Jesus' coming into the world— that was salvation—it was inevitable that his coming resulted in judgment nonetheless. In those two different but related senses, Jesus both did and didn't come to bring judgment.

= Mt 16:6). For the third group, the Jewish leaders themselves, Jesus reserved his strongest language, pointing out how their judgment would be particularly severe (cf. esp. Mt 23). Interestingly, in his denunciation of the corruption of the Jewish religious leadership and the temple ritual, Jesus concurred with the Qumran sectaries, who had left Jerusalem for the wilderness near the Dead Sea, seeking to replace what they considered apostate worship with their own version of religious devotion. At the same time, Jesus radically differed from this radical Jewish sect by displaying the consciousness that he himself was the Messiah, something not even the founder of the Dead Sea community, the so-called Teacher of Righteousness, claimed for himself.

Against this backdrop, Jesus' Good Shepherd discourse is more readily understood. We will first trace the discourse in some detail, relating it to our preliminary discussion, and conclude by placing it in the context of John's narrative as a whole. The discourse bears a certain resemblance to Synoptic-style parables but is best classified as a "symbolic discourse," in which a given metaphor (in the present case, shepherding) provides the backdrop for extended reflection. In this sense, the present discourse has a certain affinity to allegories, yet with the important difference that allegories are construed on an abstract plane to convey general truths while symbolic discourses take their point of departure from features of everyday life and attach spiritual truths to the various aspects of the controlling metaphor. But the line should not be too sharply drawn; John himself simply calls the present discourse a "figure of speech" (Greek *paroimia*; cf. 16:25, 29), a rather broad term encompassing a variety of literary genres (cf., e.g., 2 Pt 2:22 where it is used for a string of proverbs or sayings).

In his discourse, Jesus presents himself as the legitimate shepherd of God's people, casting the Jewish religious leadership as illegitimate. In a case of mixed metaphors (both "I am sayings"), Jesus is both the door (or gate; vv. 7, 9) and the shepherd of the sheep (vv. 11, 14). The door represents salvation: "I am the gate; whoever enters through me will be saved" (v. 9). Anyone desiring abundant life (v. 10)

must enter the fold through Jesus (cf. 14:6). At the same time, Jesus is the good shepherd who lays down his life for the sheep (v. 11). The reference is plainly to Jesus' substitutionary atonement ("for" in vv. 11, 15 = Greek *hyper*; cf. 15:13).[4] By contrast, other would-be religious leaders are likened to thieves, robbers, and hired hands who desert the flock in times of danger (vv. 1, 8, 10, 12–13). In fact, Jesus asserts that "all who ever came before me were thieves and robbers" (v. 8). Jesus' vision of "one flock, one shepherd" (v. 16) alludes to prophetic passages in Ezekiel (34:23; 37:24) and Isaiah (56:8). Much can be said about the characteristics of sheep. In other places, they are portrayed as wayward (Is 53:6) or helpless (Mt 9:36). In the present case, however, sheep are used to convey a strongly positive image: the intimacy between the sheep and their legitimate shepherd. "I know my sheep and my sheep know me. . . . My sheep listen to my voice; I know them, and they follow me. I give them eternal life, and they shall never perish; no one can snatch them out of my hand" (vv. 14, 27–28).

The illegitimate Jewish religious leadership will not be permitted to disrupt the close relationship Jesus' followers enjoy with their master. In a striking phrase, Jesus, at the occasion of the Feast of Dedication, told the Jewish leadership that their unbelief proves that they do not belong to God's flock: "you do not believe because you are not my sheep" (v. 26). The Jews not part of God's flock? This must have seemed utterly absurd to Jesus' opponents, an unthinkable impossibility. But what Jesus' escalating controversy with the Jewish leadership of his day demonstrates very clearly is that the Jews' unbelief disqualified them from having any part in the future of God's people. Jesus' new messianic community would require faith in Jesus the Messiah (e.g. 3:16) and be built around a core group of followers who are now considered to be Jesus' "own" (compare 13:1 with 1:11).[5]

Jesus' conflict with the Jews has come full circle; it is "winter" (v. 22), and the Jews have grown dull to any evidence Jesus might supply regarding his messiahship. Pathetically, they challenge Jesus to tell them "plainly" if he is the Christ (v. 24)—this after numerous startling man-

Shema

ifestations of Jesus' messianic nature and power, including the turning of water into wine (2:1–11), the cleansing of the Temple (2:14–21), several other Jerusalem signs (2:23; 3:2; 6:2), the healing of the royal official's son (4:46–54) and of the lame man (5:1–15), the feeding of the multitudes (6:1–15), and the healing of the man born blind (ch. 9)—if these evidences did not convince the Jews, it may be asked, will they be convinced even if someone rises from the dead (cf. Lk 16:30–31)? As will soon become clear, they will not (chs. 11 and 21; cf. Acts). Thus the reader anticipates the conclusion reached in 12:37.

Not only this, a major charge on part of the Jews against Jesus also emerges with increasing clarity, that of blasphemy, of arrogating for himself the status of deity. This ran into inevitable conflict with Jewish monotheism, belief in the one true God. The **Shema** (from the Hebrew word "hear," the opening of Dt 6:4), was recited in every synagogue service: "Hear, O Israel: The LORD our God, the LORD is one." The people of Israel had not always heeded this truth. The golden calf incident, and the building of local shrines to a variety of deities after Solomon which led to the Assyrian and Babylonian exiles provide telling testimony of the Jews' idolatry and religious apostasy. But while the Jews continued to be vulnerable at many points, the exile had purged them once and for all from the error of idolatry. Hence Jesus' perceived attempt to make himself equal to God was considered to be the most serious religious offense possible.

This mounting charge of blasphemy builds steadily as John's narrative progresses. Consider what is at the heart of the Sabbath controversy in chapter 5: "For this reason the Jews tried all the harder to kill him; not only was he breaking the Sabbath, but he was even calling God his own Father, making himself equal to God" (5:18). Or contemplate the culmination of the "paternity suit" in chapter 8: "'I tell you the truth,' Jesus answered, 'before Abraham was, I am!' At this, they picked up stones to stone him, but Jesus hid himself, slipping away from the temple grounds" (8:58–59). Then note the climax of the "shepherd controversy" in the present chapter: Jesus said, "My Father, who has given them [his 'sheep'] to me, is greater than all . . . I and the Father are one." Again, the Jews picked up stones to stone him. And when challenged by Jesus, the Jews assert that it is not for any of Jesus' miracles that they seek to stone him "but for blasphemy, because you, a mere man, claim to be God" (vv. 30–31, 33).

It will remain for the rest of the present volume to trace the further outworking of this escalating rift between Jesus and "the Jews." The present chapter may conclude with a brief discussion of Jesus' own response to the charge of blasphemy in the immediate context (vv. 34–38). "Is it not written in your Law, 'I have said you are gods'?" Jesus replies. "If he called them 'gods,' to whom the word of God came—and the Scripture cannot be broken—what about the one whom the Father set apart as his very own and sent into the world? Why then do you accuse me of blasphemy because I said, 'I am God's Son'?" (vv. 34–36). With this, Jesus refers to Psalm 82:6, where Israel's judges (or other leaders and rulers) are called *elohim*, "gods," indicating that their tasks were divinely appointed. The argument is from the lesser to the greater (a common rabbinic device): if there is a sense in which even mere human beings can be called "gods" in Scripture, how much more is it appropriate to apply this designation to the one whom God set apart and sent!

As Jesus points out, his miracles provided ample evidence that the Father was "in" him, and he "in" the Father; in that sense, he and the Father are one (v. 38; cf.

Study Questions

1. Illustrate how the entire account of Jesus' healing of the blind man functions as a parable of the spiritual blindness of the Jewish religious leadership.

2. Set Jesus' Good Shepherd discourse in its Old Testament and contemporary context, with particular focus on the escalating controversy culminating in the charge of blasphemy.

ontological

v. 30; John's primary emphasis is on functional unity of mission and purpose rather than **ontological** unity; but it is clear that the Jews did not make this distinction; for them, Jesus infringed on the ontological

Key Words

Shema

ontological

uniqueness of God, even though they may not have phrased it in exactly those terms). With this, John, a skillful narrator, closes another narrative cycle, in the present case linking the end of this phase of Jesus' ministry with the early days of John the Baptist's ministry (vv. 40–41; for other, shorter ministry cycles of Jesus, see 1:29–2:1 and 2:1–4:54; see also Mk 4:35–5:43). Thus John reinforces the contrast between the ministries of Jesus and John the Baptist with which he had started his narrative immediately following the Prologue: John never performed a sign; yet John's witness concerning Jesus proved to be true (v. 41; cf. 1:6–9, 15, 19–36).

10 Escalating Conflict (Part 4): Sign #7

John 11:1–12:50

> I know that my Redeemer lives, and that in the end he will stand upon the earth. And after my skin has been destroyed, yet in my flesh I will see God.
>
> —Job 19:25–26

Supplemental Reading: Ezekiel 37:1–14; Daniel 12:1–3

Outline

- The Seventh Sign: The Raising of Lazarus (ch. 11)
- The Anointing at Bethany (12:1–11)
- The Triumphal Entry into Jerusalem (12:12–19)
- The Approaching of the Greeks (12:20–36a)
- The Unbelief of the Jews (12:36b–50)

Objectives

After reading this chapter, you should be able to

1. Highlight the structural significance of the raising of Lazarus in the context of John's entire narrative, and in particular chapters 1–12.
2. Discuss the issue of miracles, including the importance of Christ's resurrection for the Christian faith.
3. Show how the events narrated in John 11–12 culminate and round out John's presentation of Jesus' ministry in chapters 1–12.

The Seventh Sign: The Raising of Lazarus (ch. 11)

It may come as a surprise to you, but raisings of the dead are a very rare occurrence in the Gospels. In all four Gospels combined, there are only three such events:

the raising of Jairus's daughter (Mk 5:22–24, 38–42 = Mt 9:18–19, 23–25 = Lk 8:41–42, 49–56);

the raising of the widow's son at Nain (Lk 7:11–15);

the raising of Lazarus (Jn 11:1–44).

This brings into even sharper relief the stunning account of Jesus' raising of Lazarus from the dead in the present chapter. It is puzzling indeed why only John records this event (but see the Parable of the Rich Man and Lazarus in Lk 16:19–31). At the same time, we realize our indebtedness to John for his inclusion of material not found in the Synoptic Gospels.

Of the three raisings of the dead listed above, that of Lazarus is clearly the most spectacular. Both of the other raisings rate on a smaller scale and, when compared with the extensive account of the raising of Lazarus provided by John, appear to be of a much more private and personal nature than the highly public dimension attached to the raising of Lazarus.

The significance of the role of the raising of Lazarus in John's narrative as a whole cannot be exaggerated. Most important, the event constitutes the climactic, seventh sign selected by the evangelist in order to document Jesus' identity as "the resurrection and the life" (11:25). Moreover, the raising of Lazarus is the sign that most closely foreshadows Jesus' own resurrection (even though Jesus' resurrection also plays a role in the symbolism of the second sign recorded in John, the temple cleansing; see 2:20–22). Finally, the raising of Lazarus provides the focal point of Jesus' escalating conflict with the Jews, which we have tracked from the beginning of the Gospel (esp. in chs. 5–10). Historically, the event triggers the Jewish leadership's resolve to have Jesus arrested and tried for blasphemy (11:45–57). Structurally, the present chapter thus fulfills a crucial bridge function between the first ten chapters of John's Gospel (placing Jesus' ministry in relation to John the Baptist; 10:40–41) and the second half of the Gospel, in particular the Johannine passion narrative (chs. 18–20).

The preamble to the miracle occupies John 11:1–16. The evangelist first sets the scene and then provides added drama and suspense by the delay of Jesus' departure in order to help Lazarus (v. 6). Lazarus is known only from the present account (the speculation that the designation "the one you love" in v. 3 points to Lazarus as the "disciple Jesus loved," the author of John's Gospel, is entirely speculative); Mary and Martha, on the other hand, are also featured in the well-known episode recorded in Luke 10:38–42. There, at an earlier occasion, Mary is pictured sitting at Jesus' feet and listening to his instruction while her sister Martha is distracted by all the preparations that had to be made. When Martha asks Jesus to encourage Mary to help, he responds that Mary has chosen the better part, which will not be taken away from her. Two observations apply. First, it is evident once again how the different Gospels complement each other. Jesus' apparent close friendship with Lazarus and his sisters portrayed in John's Gospel presupposes earlier visits; Luke provides an account of one such occasion. Second, John seems to expect his readers to know either Luke's account or the tradition of Mary and Martha. This can be inferred from his designation of Bethany as "the village of Mary and her sister Martha" (v. 1; in v. 18, John adds for his readers unfamiliar with Palestine that Bethany was less than two miles from Jerusalem). John's explanation in the following verse that "this Mary was the same one who poured perfume on the Lord and wiped his feet with her hair" (v. 2) further confirms this, for the event is not actually narrated in John's Gospel until the following chapter (12:1–11).

When Jesus gets word that his friend is sick, his reaction is twofold: in a touch of divine omniscience, he affirms that Lazarus's sickness will not end in death

(v. 4; cf. v. 11); and he declares that the sickness provides an opportunity for God (and his Son) to be glorified (v. 4; cf. 9:3). As will become clear in due course, the raising of Lazarus will demonstrate that Jesus is the resurrection and the life. Yet mysteriously, Jesus stays where he is two more days (v. 6). Undaunted by his disciples' reminder of the Jews' hostility toward him (v. 8; cf. 10:31), and unmoved by Thomas's cynicism (v. 16), Jesus finally sets out for Bethany. Upon his arrival, he finds that Lazarus has already been in the tomb for four days, one day past the period of three days after which the Jews believed that a deceased person's spirit left his body. If Jesus had not delayed his coming, he would have arrived only two days after Lazarus's death; perhaps there would still have been time to work a miracle. But now it was too late, even for Jesus (or so it was thought). This, of course, only challenged people's faith (vv. 15, 25) while checking popular superstition (cf. 5:7); for as John makes clear throughout his Gospel, Jesus specializes in "hard" miracles, the present being the "hardest" of all.

John's account focuses initially on the two sisters, first Martha (vv. 20–27), then Mary (vv. 28–32). Both greet Jesus with identical words: "Lord, if you had been here, my brother would not have died" (vv. 21, 32). This makes clear that the sisters had enough faith in Jesus' ability to *keep* Lazarus *from dying*, but perhaps not enough faith to believe that Jesus could raise him from the dead. To be sure, Martha affirms her belief in the resurrection at the last day (v. 24), but she fails to see how, in Jesus, Resurrection and Life themselves have appeared (see the Synoptic phrase that the kingdom of God is near and in people's midst; cf. Mk 1:15; Lk 17:21). Still, Martha issues the most complete christological confession in the entire Gospel, remarkably similar to John's purpose statement at the end of the Gospel: "I believe that you are the Christ, the Son of God, who was to come into the world" (v. 27; cf. 20:31). Yet it is unclear to what extent she grasps the full significance of her words (similar to the initial confessions of Jesus' first followers in 1:35–51).

Gradually, the narrative shifts toward Jesus, and in particular toward the way in which Jesus is moved to compassion by the death of his friend. Jesus is "deeply moved in spirit and troubled" when he sees Mary weeping, as well as the Jews who accompanied her (v. 34), and when he is taken to the place where Lazarus has been laid, he bursts into tears (v. 35). What a beautiful display of Jesus' full humanity at the threshold of the most amazing display of his divinity in John's Gospel! Arriving at the tombsite, Jesus is once again deeply moved (v. 38). By now the spotlight is squarely on Jesus, and the eyes of all are fixed on him to see what he would do. He tersely commands for the stone to be taken away, Martha's protestations notwithstanding that Lazarus's corpse by that time exuded a strong odor. And after looking up and issuing a brief prayer for the benefit of those standing close to him, Jesus calls Lazarus to come out. Obedient to Jesus' command, the dead man appears, hands and feet still wrapped with strips of linen, a cloth around his face. Jesus orders bystanders to take off the man's grave clothes and to let him go.

What are we to say about this striking miracle? People today may choose not to believe in miracles because of antisupernaturalist presuppositions. They may dismiss the present account as mythical or legendary, claiming that people in Jesus' day were not sufficiently "enlightened" to understand that miracles don't happen. When Jesus walked on the water (if he did at all), perhaps he walked on rocks hidden slightly beneath the surface; when he fed the multitudes, he merely induced people to share their food with each other; and when he raised Lazarus, he merely resuscitated him rather than restoring life to a dead man. When Jesus himself rose from the dead, he either was not dead in the first place but merely appeared to be, or his followers psychologically imagined the appearances of the resurrected Jesus in form of hallucinations or visions.[1] Thus John Dominic Crossan, one of the founders of the Jesus Seminar, believes that Jesus' corpse has rotted away somewhere in Palestine and was eaten by worms.

It is clear that Christianity as a religion is based on the conviction that the resurrection of Jesus (and similarly, miracles such as the raising of Lazarus) are historical fact. This is demonstrable for both the early Christians and the apostle Paul. That Paul preached the resurrection as historical fact is nowhere clearer than in 1 Corinthians 15:3–5:

> For what I received I passed on to you as of first importance: That Christ died for our sins according to the Scriptures, that he was buried, and that he was raised on the third day according to the Scriptures, and that he appeared to Peter, and then to the Twelve.

But what if Christ has not in fact been raised? Listen to Paul's answer in 1 Corinthians 15:12–20:

> But if it is preached that Christ has been raised from the dead, how can some of you say that there is no resurrection of the dead? If there is no resurrection of the dead, then not even Christ has been raised. And if Christ has not been raised, our preaching is useless and so is your faith. More than that, we are then found to be false witnesses about God, for we have testified about God that he raised Christ from the dead. But he did not raise him if in fact the dead are not raised. For if the dead are not raised, then Christ has not been raised either. And if Christ has not been raised, your faith is futile; you are still in your sins. Then those also who have fallen asleep in Christ are lost. If only for this life we have hope in Christ, we are to be pitied more than all men. But Christ has indeed been raised from dead. . . .

Thus the significance of Jesus' raising of Lazarus is found to transcend the event itself. To be sure, Lazarus's life had been miraculously restored. But for John, what is even more important is that the raising of Lazarus constitutes a *sign*, that is, a demonstration of Jesus' true identity: he is the Christ, the Son of God. In particular, this, the seventh, climactic sign in John's Gospel, foreshadows Jesus' own resurrection. No more powerful sign could be given. Hence the period of Jesus' signs, confined to the first twelve chapters of John, comes to a close. In the ensuing meeting of the Sanhedrin, the high priest Caiaphas makes it perfectly clear that Jesus was to be sacrificed in order to salvage the Jews' relative political and religious autonomy in relation to the rul-

ing Romans. To him, it seemed politically expedient that one man, however innocent, should perish rather than that the whole nation be put in jeopardy. In this, he spoke better than he knew, for, as the evangelist tells us, as high priest that year he prophesied that Jesus would indeed die for the Jewish nation, and not for that nation only but also for the "scattered children of God" (that is, the Gentiles), to bring them together and to make them one (11:51–52; cf. 10:16; 12:20–33).

So, paradoxically, the Jews go ahead in their resolve to have Jesus executed, and in A.D. 70 the nation still perished when the Romans razed Jerusalem and the temple. The immediate consequence of the heightened hostility of the Jews is that Jesus no longer moved around publicly among the Jews but withdrew to a small village called Ephraim (perhaps a city also known as Ophrah, about fifteen miles north of Jerusalem). The chapter ends ominously with the information that the chief priests and Pharisees had already ordered Jesus' arrest at the upcoming Passover.

The Anointing at Bethany (12:1–11)

John concludes his presentation of Jesus' public ministry (with primary emphasis on the Jews) with accounts of the following events: Mary's anointing of Jesus at Bethany (vv. 1–11); Jesus' triumphal entry into Jerusalem (vv. 12–19); and the approaching of some Greeks to see Jesus (vv. 20–36a). This is followed by a summary indictment of Jewish unbelief (vv. 36b–50).

In the context of John's narrative, the anointing scene casts a long shadow forward to Jesus' imminent arrest, trial, condemnation, crucifixion, and burial. The only words recorded of Jesus at the anointing make this clear: "Leave her alone. It was intended that she should save this perfume for the day of my burial. You will always have the poor among you, but you will not always have me" (vv. 7–8). All four Gospels emphasize that Jesus foresaw his own violent, substitutionary death, underscoring that the condemning verdict did not take Jesus by surprise. At the heart of his Gospel, Mark records three passion predictions of Jesus (8:31–38; 9:30–37; 10:32–45); he is followed by the other Synoptic writers.

But it is John who stresses most explicitly that Jesus' death did not come as an accident but was fully willed and anticipated by our Lord. In a saying found only in John's Gospel, Jesus is recorded as saying, "The reason my Father loves me is that I lay down my life—only to take it up again. No one takes it from me, but I lay it down of my own accord. I have authority to lay it down and authority to take it up again" (10:17–18). At his own arrest, Jesus is shown to take the initiative, "knowing all that was going to happen to him" (18:4; cf. 13:1–3). And in another saying unique to John's Gospel, Jesus reminds Pilate, "You would have no power over me if it were not given to you from above" (19:11).

The evangelists' insistence that Jesus was not a tragic victim but in full control of the events surrounding his Passion is a crucial part of the gospel message. For it places the emphasis squarely on God's sovereignty and on his unfailing plan of the ages, culminating in Jesus' sacrifice on the cross, relativizing the evil perpetrated upon God's Suffering Servant by sinful people ultimately induced by Satan (cf. 13:2, 27). It is not as if in a dark hour evil took control and Jesus succumbed to it powerlessly. Rather, he chose to die freely for our sake. As Jesus told Peter who sought to defend him by drawing the sword and cutting off the servant's ear,

> Put you sword back in its place, for all who draw the sword will die by the sword. Do you think I cannot call on my Father, and he will at once put at my disposal more than twelve legions of angels? But how then would the Scriptures be fulfilled that say it must happen in this way? (Mt 26:52–54).

Part of this pattern where Jesus interprets events (especially toward the end of his life) in light of the anticipated end is his anointing for burial, to which we now turn. The account is closely linked with Jesus' raising of Lazarus. This ties in the present narrative unit with the preceding narrative. Theologically, the presence of Lazarus is shown to fuel further the Jews' hostility toward Jesus, for it serves as a constant reminder of the amazing miracle that had taken place. Consider the following strategic references, each of which contain a reference to Lazarus's raising from the dead:

The setting of the anointing: "Six days before the Passover, Jesus arrived at Bethany, *where Lazarus lived, whom Jesus had raised from the dead.* Here a dinner was given in Jesus' honor. Martha served, *while Lazarus was among those reclining at the table with him*" (vv. 1–2).

The conclusion of the anointing: "Meanwhile a large crowd of Jews found out that Jesus was there and came, not only because of him *but also to see Lazarus, whom he had raised from the dead.* So the chief priests made plans *to kill Lazarus as well, for on account of him many of the Jews were going over to Jesus and putting their faith in him*" (vv. 9–11).

The conclusion after the triumphal entry: "Now the crowd that was with him *when he called Lazarus from the tomb and raised him from the dead continued to spread the word.* Many people, because they had heard that he had given this miraculous sign, went out to meet him. So the Pharisees said to one another, 'See, this is getting us nowhere. Look how the whole world has gone after him!'" (vv. 17–19).

Nevertheless, the spotlight in the anointing narrative is not on Lazarus but on Mary his sister. Mary's lavish act toward Jesus made her a well–known figure in the early church. Expecting his readers to know her from oral or written tradition, John had already introduced her in the previous chapter with the following words: "This Mary, whose brother Lazarus now lay sick, was the same one who poured perfume on the Lord and wiped his feet with her hair" (11:2). Mark, followed by Matthew, records Jesus' saying, "I tell you the truth, wherever the gospel is preached throughout the world, what she has done will also be told, in memory of her" (Mk 14:9; Mt 26:13). As John 11:2 makes clear, Jesus' prediction had come true.

John's account of Mary's anointing of Jesus has the touch of eyewitness recollection: "Then Mary took about a pint of pure nard, an expensive perfume; she poured it on Jesus' feet and wiped his feet with her hair. *And the house was filled with the fragrance of the perfume"* (v. 3). Three striking facts render Mary's anointing of Jesus particularly remarkable. First, there is the value of the perfume. Only John and Mark tell us that the perfume was pure nard, extracted from a rare plant. It was valued at three hundred denarii, one denarius being a day's wages. In any other circumstance, it would therefore be hard to disagree with Judas that Mary's pouring out the entire flask of perfume on Jesus' feet constituted an inexcusable waste—allowing an entire year's wages to be dissolved in an instant of fleeting fragrance! But Mary did better than she knew: in her

---

Will the Exalted Christ Draw "All Things" or "All People" to Himself? (Jn 12:32)

"But I, when I am lifted up from the earth, will draw all people to myself" (John 12:32)—or is it "all things"? At least this is how several ancient manuscripts read, in particular the important papyrus p[66] [about A.D. 200] and the original hand of Codex Sinaiticus [4th cent. A.D.]. In the original Greek, the difference is just one letter:

"draw all people" reads *pantas helkusō*, while "draw all things" reads *panta helkusō*.

It is easy to see how a scribal error could have crept in.

Now on one level the opening question is misleading and the dilemma not as great as it might appear. For whichever reading of John 12:32 turns out to be original, *both* cosmic reconciliation through Christ ("all things") *and* a bona fide offer of salvation to all on the basis of Jesus' cross-work ("all people") are clearly taught in Scripture (cosmic: Rom 8:22; Col 1:15–20; personal: 2 Cor 5:11–21; Rom 5:1–11). The question is then primarily one of *Johannine* theology.

A look at the usage of the term "all" *(pas)* in John's Gospel suggests that while the evangelist uses *panta* several times in the neuter plural (e.g. 1:3; 3:35; 5:20; 13:3; 17:7), the instances of *pantes* in the masculine plural prevail (1:7, 16; 2:15; 3:26; 5:23, 28; 6:45; 7:21; 10:8; 11:48; 13:10, 11, 18; 13:35; 17:21). The pervading concern of John's Gospel is clearly, not so much that all *things* in the cosmos are drawn to God, but that all *people* be saved (if they believe; e.g. 1:12; 3:16; 20:30–31).

The reading "all people" is supported by substantial external evidence, including (in all likelihood) p[75] as well as Codices Alexandrinus and Vaticanus [4th/5th cent. A.D.]. So while it is possible that some scribes considered the reading "draw all things" too vague and added a final sigma *(s)* to an original *panta*, the preponderance of internal evidence (that is, Johannine theology) favors the reading "all people."

What, then, does Jesus mean here? The context is the coming of some Greeks to him toward the end of his ministry (12:20ff.). As it turns out, they never get to talk to Jesus.

Rather, the Lord responds to the Greeks' request (relayed by two of his disciples) by pointing to the need for him first to be crucified. *Then,* is the implication, the Greeks (that is, Gentiles at large) will be able to "see" him. After his crucifixion, is the thrust of the present passage, the exalted Jesus will draw *"all kinds of people"* to himself, including Gentiles like the Greeks who had just requested to see him. This is also confirmed by Jesus' earlier statement in 10:16 that he has "other sheep not in this sheep pen" [i.e. Judaism], which he "must bring also." For in keeping with salvation-historical distinctions, Jesus limited his earthly ministry (with certain individual exceptions) to the Jews. The bringing in of the Gentiles would be the task of the post-Pentecost church.

Note: For further study on the issue of the scope of Jesus' earthly ministry, see the forthcoming work by Andreas J. Köstenberger and Peter T. O'Brien, *Salvation to the Ends of the Earth: A Biblical Theology of Mission,* NSBT (Leicester, U.K.: IVP/Grand Rapids: Eerdmans).

devotion to Jesus, she may break etiquette and defy common sense, but, as Jesus points out, by doing so she anoints Jesus for the day of his burial. In due course, it would be Nicodemus and Joseph of Arimathea who fulfilled this task. As John tells us, "Nicodemus brought a mixture of myrrh and aloes, about seventy-five pounds. Taking Jesus' body, the two of them wrapped it, with the spices, in strips of linen. This was in accordance with Jewish burial customs" (19:39b–40). But by her prophetic act, Mary honors Jesus while still living, prior to the crucifixion.

There are two additional aspects of Mary's anointing that render this a highly unusual act. The anointing was unusual because Mary poured the oil on Jesus' feet (normally it was poured on the head) and because she used her hair to wipe them (it was considered improper for a woman to unbind her hair in public). Moreover, Mary's act displayed unusual humility, because it was a servant's task to care for the feet (cf. 1:27; 13:5).

However, this is not the end of the story (just as the Parable of the Prodigal Son does not end in Lk 15:24 but continues until v. 32). Remarkably, while one single verse is devoted to Mary's act of anointing Jesus, five full verses are given to Judas's taking offense and Jesus' rebuttal. This indicates that John pursues another important purpose in his narration of Jesus' anointing: he seeks to set the stage for Judas's imminent betrayal of Jesus. John had already hinted at this in 6:70–71: "Then Jesus replied, 'Have I not chosen you, the Twelve? Yet one of you is a devil!' (He meant Judas, the son of Simon Iscariot, *who, though one of the Twelve, was later to betray him*.)" That was the first ominous reference, strategically placed at the end of chapter 6, a time when many of Jesus' disciples leave him. Now, at the threshold of Jesus' final week, John develops the theme of Judas's apostasy more thoroughly.

John 12:4–6 elaborates on Judas's opposition in some detail: "But one of his disciples, Judas Iscariot, *who was later to betray him* [cf. 6:71], objected: 'Why wasn't this perfume sold and the money given to the poor? It was worth a year's wages.' He did not say this because he cared about the poor but because he was a thief; as keeper of the money bag, he used to help himself to what was put into it" (vv. 4–6). But Jesus rebuked Judas, in words already quoted above. A comparison with the parallel accounts by Mark and Matthew—Luke also records an anointing by a "sinful woman" (not Mary), but at an earlier occasion (at a Pharisee's house; 7:36–50)—underscores the degree to which John chooses to focus on Judas. Neither of the other two evangelists provides as much as the name of the person challenging the anointing, Mark obliquely referring to "some" (Mk 14:4), Matthew to "the disciples" (Mt 26:8). And only John adds the incriminating piece of information about Judas being a thief.

John's focus on Judas and his imminent betrayal of Jesus has the effect of zeroing in on Judas as the single individual who became the "point man" of Satan (cf. 13:2). As John narrates in the following chapter, "As soon as Judas took the bread [at the Last Supper], *Satan entered into him*" (13:27). With this, John provides a penetrating spiritual commentary on the forces behind Jesus' crucifixion: ultimately it was not the Jews or Pontius Pilate who were the chief protagonists of evil, but Satan himself. But in order for his readers not to be caught by surprise when one of Jesus' inner circle, the twelve, betrays Jesus, John prepares them in the present account. He reveals how Judas already demonstrated his antagonism toward God's work in Jesus' life prior to the actual betrayal. Keeper of the money bag was a responsibility that required trust—in Judas's case, this trust had been betrayed, foreshadowing his ultimate betrayal of Jesus. In the present instance, Judas expressed his dismay at how Jesus could allow such expensive perfume to go to waste; it was worth a year's wages. Overtly, he objects that the money could have been given to the poor. But John unmasks such pious posturing: Judas's true intentions were rather to keep the money for himself.

Ultimately, we must confess that we are not able to penetrate the inscrutable mystery of the origin of evil. Exactly how it happened that God's most glorious creature, Lucifer, the "bearer of light," fell, and demanded equal status with

God, later dragging humanity with him, will always remain a mystery, at least this side of heaven. The challenge is therefore not to explain evil but rather to accept its reality and to resist it wherever possible. Yet while there are many things we do not know about the origins of evil, we know of the existence of Satan and his demons. Satan, it must be remembered, is no match for God. He is not omnipresent; he can only be at one place at a time. He is not omnipotent; his power is limited by God. He is not omniscient; he does not know the future or the mind of God. Nevertheless, Satan is exceedingly intelligent (although his reason and will have been perverted). He fully realized that Jesus' death on the cross would provide a way for people to be saved, and as God's chief adversary, Satan sought to avert this substitutionary sacrifice of a sinless substitute at all cost. As John makes clear, at this pivotal moment in salvation history, Satan himself entered Judas to betray Jesus, not realizing that by doing so he only furthered ultimately the purposes of God: for Scripture must be fulfilled (e.g., 19:36; cf. Mt 26:54, 56).

To sum up. The account of the anointing is at the heart a tale of contrasts: on the one hand is Mary's lavish devotion to Jesus, on the other the looming prospect of Judas's betrayal of his master. In another contrast, the man whom Jesus had raised from the dead, Lazarus, takes part in the dinner, while Jesus himself is anointed for burial. This is the time for devotion or antagonism toward Jesus to come to the fore. The narrative enters a crucial phase.

The Triumphal Entry into Jerusalem (12:12–19)

At the triumphal entry into Jerusalem, Jesus displays the determination and resolve portrayed also by Luke: "Jesus resolutely set out for Jerusalem" (Lk 9:51). On a human level, the public acclaim for Jesus, which turns into a mob calling "Crucify him! Crucify him!" in a matter of days, highlights the treacherous nature of popularity. Theologically, the triumphal entry is shown to fulfill Old Testament prophecy. Both Old Testament passages featured in John convey the notion of Jesus' Davidic kingship. All four evangelists refer to Psalm 118:25–26: "Hosanna! Blessed is he who comes in the name of the Lord," to which John and Mark add references to "the King of Israel" (Jn 12:13d) or "the kingdom of our father David" (Mk 11:10). Jesus is here portrayed as the victor who has defeated the enemies; palm branches were commonly used to convey the celebration of victory.

John and Matthew also refer to Zechariah 9:9: "Shout, Daughter of Jerusalem! See, your king comes to you, . . . riding on . . . the foal of a donkey." We already considered the way in which John presents Jesus in light of Zechariah's messianic vision (see the discussion of messianic expectations in ch. 8). Riding on a donkey, a lowly animal, clearly conveyed the notion of humility, so characteristic of Jesus throughout his ministry (cf. Mt 11:29; 2 Cor 8:9; Phil 2:5–11). The donkey was also considered to be an animal of peace, in contrast to the war horse (cf. Zech 9:10). Interestingly, the Synoptics provide additional background information not given in John: Jesus' command to two of his disciples to go and get the colt in anticipation of his arrival in Jerusalem (Mk 11:2–3 = Mt 21:2–3 = Lk 19:29–31). John only mentions that "Jesus found a young donkey and sat upon it" without going into details (v. 14).

This highly public scene stands in marked contrast to the intimacy of Mary's anointing of Jesus preceding it. There is considerable narrative tension between Jesus being on the height of popularity and the looming betrayal and arrest of Jesus, already plotted by the Pharisees (11:57; 12:19). John has already completed his presentation of Jesus as the signs-working, God-sent Messiah. Now he supplies one further messianic portrait: that of the Davidic King of Israel who triumphs in humility. But this brief flickering up of popularity is not to be trusted. For Jesus knows that he must die, and that his death is imminent (vv. 32–33).

Especially at the time of major Jewish festivals, the area surrounding the temple would have provided Jesus with a large captive audience.

The Approaching of the Greeks (12:20–36a)

"Now there were some Greeks (*Hellēnes*) among those who went up to worship at the Feast" (v. 20). Who were those "Greeks"? In 7:35, the only other occurrence of the term in John's Gospel, reference is made to "Greeks" living in the Diaspora. A look at the remaining New Testament occurrences reveals that in virtually all instances the term is used in contrast with "Jews" (*Ioudaioi*; cf. Acts 14:1; 16:1; 18:4; 19:10, 17; 20:21; Rom 1:16; 2:9, 10; 3:9; 10:12; 1 Cor 1:22, 24; 10:32; 12:13; Gal 3:28; Col 3:11). This makes clear that the expression simply means "Gentile," whether literally Greek or of some other non-Jewish background. The term "Greek" was presumably used as an umbrella term for Gentile owing to the dominance of Greek culture and language in the Greco-Roman world at large (note that the term *Hellēnistēs* is used in Acts 6:1 and 9:29 for "Grecian [that is, Greek-speaking] Jews" [NIV]).

These "Greeks," that is, Gentiles, were in Jerusalem at the Passover "to worship at the Feast" (v. 20). Thus they were so-called God-fearers (cf., e.g., Acts 17:4: "God-fearing Greeks"), Gentiles who worshiped the God of Israel. These Gentiles approached Philip, one of Jesus' disciples, requesting "to see" Jesus (cf. 1:36, 39). Philip told Andrew, and both told Jesus. As John mentions in the opening chapter, both Philip and Andrew were from the Galilean town of Bethsaida (1:44). Both Philip and Andrew are also referred to in chapter 6 at the feeding of the multitude (6:5–9). This indicates that Philip and Andrew shared a close relationship and that they may have held a (minor?) leadership role among the disciples, albeit not comparable to Peter's. Perhaps the fact that Philip is a Greek name was a contributing factor to why these Gentiles approached this particular disciple.

As it turns out, these Gentiles never get to see Jesus. Jesus' response is cryptic and avoids direct reference to the "Greeks'" request. Rather than granting their wish or squarely turning it down, Jesus makes reference to his "hour": "The hour has come for the Son of Man to be glorified" (v. 23). This is remarkable; for throughout the Gospel up to this point, Jesus had reiterated that his hour had *not yet* come (cf. 2:4;

8:20). But now, startlingly for the reader of the Gospel, there is a sudden shift: Jesus' "hour" has come! And what is this "hour"? It is the hour of Jesus' *death:* "I tell you the truth, unless a kernel of wheat falls to the ground *and dies,* it remains only a single seed. But if it *dies,* it produces many seeds" (v. 24). The one who is about to die is the "Son of Man" (v. 23); it is he who will be "lifted up" from the earth, that is, exalted (both literally and figuratively) by crucifixion (vv. 32–33). John has already hinted at the "lifting up of the Son of Man" earlier in his Gospel (cf. 3:13–15; 8:28); now the time has come for the Son of Man (that is, Jesus) to be "glorified."

Again, John's choice of terms conveys his distinctive theological perspective. Unlike the Synoptic writers, who accentuate more keenly the shame endured and the pain suffered by Jesus as our sinless substitute at the cross, John presents the cross unequivocally as the place of Jesus' glorification. This is affirmed by the heavenly voice at the present occasion (v. 28), featured in John only here (the Synoptics also record instances at Jesus' baptism and transfiguration: Mk 1:11; 9:7 par.); by Jesus immediately after Judas's departure from the Upper Room (13:31–32); and in Jesus' final prayer (17:1, 5). The author of Hebrews, speaking of "Jesus . . . , who for the joy set before him endured the cross, scorning its shame, and sat down at the right hand of the throne of God" (Hb 12:2), holds these two perspectives in tension. Jesus first suffered, and then was exalted. Peter, in his first epistle, likewise speaks of "the sufferings of Christ and the glories that would follow" (1 Pt 1:11).

But John collapses these two perspectives. What is more, he allows Jesus' sufferings to be swallowed up in glory. According to John, Jesus is not glorified *despite* the cross, but *through* and *in* the cross. Why? Because it is at the cross that Jesus is revealed as the fully obedient, dependent Son of the Father who faithfully accomplished his mission. At the end of his earthly life, Jesus reports back to the Father, "I have brought you glory on earth by completing the work you gave me to do" (17:4). And at the cross he exclaims, "It is finished" (19:31). As we will see in the next chapter, the entire Upper Room discourse is cast plainly from the per-

spective of the exalted Jesus. His victory is never in doubt; his triumph is sure. Thus Jesus, incredibly, hours prior to his crucifixion, is not preoccupied with his imminent death, but with the disciples' modus operandi subsequent to his exaltation with the Father. To his own death, the Johannine Jesus refers, in almost unbelievable understatement, simply as his "going to the Father" (e.g., 13:1; 14:12; 16:28).

John's Gospel does not contain an account of Jesus' struggle in the Garden of Gethsemane, an account so dramatic in the Synoptics. The Johannine equivalent is simply this: "Now my heart is troubled, and what shall I say? 'Father, save me from this hour'? No, it was for this very reason I came to this hour. 'Father, glorify your name!'" (vv. 27–28a). But it is not only time for the glorification of the Son of Man; it is also the time for judgment on "this world" and "the prince [lit. "ruler," Grk. *archōn*] of this world" (that is, Satan; v. 31; cf. 14:30; 16:11; Eph 2:2). As John writes in his first epistle, "The reason the Son of God appeared was to destroy the devil's work" (1 Jn 3:8). As already mentioned in our discussion of John's treatment of Judas at the anointing of Jesus earlier in this chapter, John casts the cross as the final confrontation between Jesus and Satan. The cross is the place where Satan is destroyed, because, as John points out in the concluding section of the present chapter, the cross occurred in fulfillment of Scripture and in accordance with God's will (12:37–41). Those who choose to align themselves with Jesus by believing in him and following him therefore join in his spiritual victory and take part in proclaiming the good news of his triumph to others.

But the crowd does not hear the heavenly voice; some think it was thunder; some conjecture an angel had spoken to Jesus (12:29). And then the crowd voices the final messianic expectation (cast here as misunderstanding) in John's Gospel: "We have heard from the Law that the Christ will remain forever, so how can you say, 'The Son of Man must be lifted up'?" (v. 34). But as in the case of the Greeks, Jesus does not directly field this question. He merely counsels his interrogators to "put your trust in the light while you have it, so that you may become sons of light" (v. 36), and then leaves and hides himself from them.

How, then, are we to explain Jesus' response to the Gentiles' request in verse 20? It appears that, as in other instances, Jesus' change of subject indicates a gentle "no," or at least a "not yet." (Many of us are familiar with those kinds of answers to our prayers.) Thus when James and John (or really their mother) ask Jesus to let them sit at his right and left in his glory, Jesus responds that "to sit at my right or left is not for me to grant; these places belong to those for whom they have been prepared" (Mk 10:40 = Mt 20:23). Or when his disciples ask him, "Lord, are you at this time going to restore the kingdom of Israel?" Jesus responds, "It is not for you to know the times or dates the Father has set by his own authority. But you will receive power . . . and you will be my witnesses . . ." (Acts 1:6–8). Jesus did not say no, but he focused on the immediate task at hand.

In the present instance, Jesus' gentle yet evasive response should be interpreted similarly. The Gentiles may "see" Jesus, but not yet; this belongs to the time subsequent to Jesus' cross-death: "But I, *when I am lifted up from the earth*, will draw all men to myself" (12:32; "all men" does not mean literally all people, as if John were here espousing universalism, but "all *kinds of* people," that is, both Jews and Gentiles).[2] As Jesus told doubting Thomas,

"Because you have seen me, you have believed? Blessed are those who have not seen and yet have believed" (20:29). Thus, in a real sense, the first followers of Jesus have no advantage over later generations of believers. In both cases, faith takes precedence over physical seeing. As Paul puts it, "We live by faith, not by sight" (2 Cor 5:7). One day, the Gentiles who were at that occasion turned away by Jesus would be able to share in the blessing pronounced by Peter who wrote, "Though you have not seen him, you love him; and even though you do not see him now, you believe in him" (1 Pt 1:8).

Indeed, as Jesus said earlier in the Gospel, "I have other sheep that are not of this sheep pen. I must bring them also. They too will listen to my voice, and there shall be one flock and one shepherd" (10:16; cf. Paul in Eph 2:11–22; 4:3–6). But this will be the task of the exalted Jesus working through the disciples in the age of the Spirit (cf. the Book of Acts). First things first, and the first thing for Jesus now is to complete his mission to the Jews by dying, in keeping with Caiaphas's prophecy, "for the Jewish nation," and, as the evangelist is careful to point out, beyond this "also for the scattered children of God, to bring them together and make them one" (11:52). Others will be able to proclaim the message of salvation and forgiveness of sins in Jesus Christ to the world; Jesus alone is able to give his "flesh" "for the life of the world" (6:51) and to "lay down his life for the sheep" (10:11).

Study Questions

1. How does the raising of Lazarus relate to the rest of the Gospel?

2. What are the major purposes pursued by John in the account of the anointing of Jesus?

3. Who were the "Greeks" who approached Jesus at his last Passover? Did they get to see Jesus, and why or why not?

4. Explain John's use of Scripture in narrating the triumphal entry and the concluding section of chapter 12.

The Unbelief of the Jews (12:36b–50)

"Even after Jesus had done all these miraculous signs in their presence, they still would not believe in him" (v. 37). This is the final verdict pronounced by the evangelist on the Jewish people. John here engages in theodicy, the vindication of God and his righteous purposes (theodicy is also a major underlying purpose of the Books of Romans and Revelation). It is not that God has failed to provide adequate (even ample!) evidence of his power and reality in Jesus, John argues. Rather, he puts the blame squarely on the Jews and their failure to believe. In this, the Jews are no different than their ancestors in the days of Isaiah. As this prince of prophets lamented, "Lord, who has believed our message?" (v. 38 citing Is 53:1; cf. also Rom 10:16). The implied answer: no one. And what is the message referred to by Isaiah? It is the message of the suffering Servant of the Lord (cf. Is 52:13–53:12). Thus the Jewish nation in Jesus' day is no different from the Jews at the time of Isaiah: it is characterized by unbelief and a rejection of the message of God's spokesmen (cf. esp. the Parable of the Wicked Tenants in Mk 12:1–12 par. where the same point is made). In the case of Isaiah, the consequence was exile; in the case of Jesus, the result is even more severe: eternal condemnation.

But it is not as if Jewish unbelief succeeded in thwarting God's plan. To the contrary, it fulfilled it. Again, John draws on a quote from Isaiah:

> He has blinded their eyes
> and deadened their hearts,
> so they can neither see with their eyes,
> nor understand with their hearts,
> nor turn—and I would heal them
> (v. 40 citing Is 6:10).

This particular passage from Isaiah apparently constituted an important part of the early Christian apologetic for Jewish unbelief. It is quoted in every Gospel as well as in the Book of Acts, with the latter passage citing the apostle Paul (Mt 13:15; Mk 4:12; Lk 8:10; Ac 28:26–27).

But John drives home the point even more forcefully than the other evangelists. For he draws from the present passage the inference that "for this reason they [that is, the Jews] *could not* believe" (v. 39). This is reminiscent of Jesus' earlier saying to the Jews who opposed him, "you do not believe because *you are not my sheep*" (10:26). Or earlier still, "The reason you do not hear is that *you do not belong to God*" (8:47). This thread of passages underscores that for John human (Jewish) unbelief not only was unable to *resist* the plan of God but actually *fulfilled* it. While this may be difficult to understand intellectually, it is plainly required for God to be God, or human unbelief would in one sense be greater even than the will of God.[3]

According to John, Isaiah uttered the two statements cited (Is 53:1 and 6:10) because he saw Jesus' glory and spoke about *him* (v. 41). In a sense, of course, Isaiah saw primarily the glory of *God* (Is 6:1–4). In another sense, however, Isaiah foresaw the suffering and exaltation of Christ and thus spoke about him (cf. Is 52:13–53:12). In any case, God and Jesus are closely associated by John. In this he concurs with the early church at large, which applied the term "Lord" (Grk. *kyrios*)—which had in the Old Testament been used for God—freely to Jesus (cf., e.g., 1 Pt 1:25). In fact, "Jesus is Lord" (Grk. *Christos kyrios*) became the central confession of the early Christians (cf. Jn 13:13; Acts 2:36; Rom 10:9; Phil 2:11).

In his final indictment, Jesus cries out (a strong term; used for the Baptist in 1:15; for Jesus in 7:28, 37), "When a man believes in me, he does not believe in me only, but in the one who sent me" (v. 44). Conversely, no one can claim to believe in God and not believe in Jesus. For Jesus alone is the Sent One of God (cf. 9:7). Jesus' final words in chapter 12 echo the words of John's Prologue, providing the reader with a sense of closure. Thus Jesus' assertion, "I have come into the world as a light, so that no one who believes in me should stay in darkness" (v. 46) reiterates the Baptist's opening witness concerning the Light (1:7–9; cf. 1:4–5). But now it is Jesus himself who bears witness. And fittingly, the first major section of John's Gospel concludes with Jesus' assertion of his total dependence and obedience to the Father who sent him:

> I did not speak of my own accord,
> but the Father who sent me commanded me
> what to say and how to say it . . .
> (vv. 49–50).
> So whatever I say is just what the Father has told me to say.

And with this solemn closing assertion, the curtain closes on Act 1 in the Johannine drama of the Light's coming into the world. The scene will be very different when the curtain reopens in the following chapter.

Part

4

Encountering the Exalted Jesus: The Mission to the World

(John 13–20)

As the Father has sent me, I am sending you.

—John 20:21

11 Jesus' Farewell (Part 1)

John 13

A new command I give you: Love one another. As I have loved you, so you must love one another. By this all men will know that you are my disciples, if you love one another.

—John 13:34–35

Supplemental Reading: Psalm 41; Luke 7:36–50

Outline

- The Footwashing (13:1–20)
- The Betrayal (13:21–30)
- The New Commandment and Peter's Denials Foretold (13:31–38)

Objectives

After reading this chapter, you should be able to

1. Set out the framework and perspective from which the farewell discourse is presented.
2. Identify the major lessons taught in the footwashing.
3. Describe the relationship between John 13 and John 14–16.

Before we delve into our study of the so-called farewell discourse, a few general remarks may help to set this portion of John's Gospel into perspective. First, the material contained in chapters 13–17 is only found in John; if it were not for this Gospel, we would know comparatively little about Jesus' parting instructions to his followers. We would not know about the intensity of his concern for his disciples' love and unity or about his specific teaching on the role of the Spirit in believers' lives; and we would not have a record of his so-called **high priestly prayer** at the end of his earthly ministry.

Second, the underlying perspective of the farewell discourse is radically different from that prevailing in the first major section of John's Gospel. Chapters 1–12 deal with Jesus' ministry to the Jews, with his followers playing only a minor role, being featured simply as disciples of rabbi Jesus. The farewell discourse, on the other hand, presents Jesus' mission to the world, based, as it were, on his cross-death, and carried out in the power of the Spirit through his followers. The underlying assumption of John 13–17 is that Jesus has been exalted—as the exalted Lord, he will answer prayer offered in Jesus' name; as the exalted Lord, he will send his Spirit and direct the mission of his followers; as the exalted Lord, he takes his disciples into the life of the Trinity, which is characterized by mutual love and unity. The disciples thus have emerged from their status of lowly helpers in the first part of the Gospel to become partners in ministry. Consider the more endearing terms used for Jesus' followers in the second half of John's Gospel:

"his own" (*idioi*; 13:1; cf. 1:11)

"little children" (*teknia*; 13:33)

"friends" (*philoi*; 15:15)

"the men you gave me" (*tois anthrōpois hous edōkas moi*; 17:6)

"those who are mine" (*ta ema*; 17:10)

"my brothers" (*adelphoi mou*; 20:17)

"little children" (*paidia*; 21:4–5)[1]

Third, John's farewell discourse seems to be self-consciously patterned after Moses' farewell discourse in the Old Testament Book of Deuteronomy. This is supported by the extensive use of "covenant language" in John 13–16. Consider, for example, the preponderance of the five major verb themes of Exodus 33–34 and Deuteronomy, "love," "obey," "live," "know," and "see" in John 14:15–24:

> If you *love* me, you will *obey* what I command.
> And I will ask the Father, and he will give you another Counselor to be with you forever—the Spirit of truth.
> The world cannot accept him, because it neither *sees* him nor *knows* him.
> But you *know* him, for he *lives* with you and will be in you.
> I will not leave you as orphans; I will come to you.
> Before long, the world will not *see* me anymore, but you will *see* me.
> Because I *live*, you also will *live*.
> On that day you will realize that I am in the Father, and you are in me, and I am in you.
> Whoever has my commands and *obeys* them, he is the one who *loves* me.
> He who *loves* me will be *loved* by my Father,
> and I too will *love* him and show myself to him. . . .
> If anyone *loves* me, he will *obey* my teaching.
> My Father will *love* him, and we will come to him and make our home with him.
> He who does not *love* me will not *obey* my teaching.
> These words you hear are not my own; they belong to the Father who sent me.[2]

The important implication of this parallel language is that John casts Jesus as the new Moses who institutes a new covenant with his disciples (cf., e.g., the "new commandment" given to them in 13:34–35). Just as Moses was prevented by death from leading God's people into the Promised Land, Jesus will be—albeit only temporarily—separated from his followers. Yet in contrast to Moses, Jesus, as the new Joshua, entered heaven itself as our forerunner (cf. Hb 4:8, 14; 6:20; 12:2). Or, to use Johannine terminology, Jesus will go to prepare a place for his disciples (14:2–3) and be glorified in the Father's presence with the glory he had with him before the world began (17:5).

These three larger observations—the unique character of the farewell discourse recorded in John, the shift in perspective from the earthly to the exalted Jesus, and the patterning of the farewell discourse after Moses' farewell discourse recorded in Deuteronomy—will serve to set our study of John 13–17 into proper perspective. The entire section is controlled by one purpose: Jesus' preparation of his followers for the immediate future—that is, the trauma and loss resulting from his crucifixion and burial—and the time after his ascension. Let us now develop these observations in greater detail in our study of Jesus' farewell according to John.

The Footwashing (13:1–20)

Verse 1 sets the scene, not merely for the footwashing, but for the entire farewell discourse: "It was just before the Passover Feast. Jesus knew that the time had come for him to leave this world and go to the Father. Having loved his own who were in the world, he now showed them the full extent of his love" (13:1). The time marker "just before the Passover" continues the buildup to Jesus' last Passover (cf. "six days before the Passover" in 12:1; "the next day" in 12:12). "Jesus knew that his time had come" echoes Jesus' words in 12:23, "The hour has come for the Son of Man to be glorified." "To leave this world and go to the Father" is an euphemism for the cruel cross-death about to be suffered by the Messiah. "Having loved his own . . . , he now showed them the full extent of his love" signals love as the major theme of the farewell discourse and the Gospel as a whole (cf. 3:16). The contrast between Jesus' leaving "this world" and the disciples" being "in the world" indicates the occasion and purpose of the upcoming section: the gap left by Jesus' departure and the disciples' need for instruction on how to cope with life in this world once Jesus has left.

Verses 2–4, one long string of phrases in the original (all participles indicating preceding action), sets the scene for the immediate occasion, the footwashing. The main action narrated is found in verse 4: Jesus "got up." In verses 2 and 3, the evangelist provides the framework:

dinner had been served (v. 2; cf. 12:2; 21:20)

the devil (diabolos) had already cast it (ballō) into Judas's heart to betray Jesus (v. 2)

Jesus did what he was about to do fully aware that the Father had given all things into his hands and that he had come from God and was returning to God (v. 3)

Why does John stress these three preliminary observations with respect to the footwashing that is about to ensue? Saving the first and most mundane element for last, we will briefly comment on the second and third aspects of John's framework. The devil had already cast it into Judas's heart to betray Jesus. This statement is probably designed to draw attention to Jesus' patience, kindness, and love even of his enemies. Think of it: knowing that Judas was about to betray him, Jesus washed his disciples' feet—including Judas's! Jesus faced his imminent betrayal, arrest, and trial with open eyes, actively moving forward to bring about these events (cf., e.g., v. 27: "What you are about to do, do quickly").

Jesus did what he was about to do fully aware that the Father had given all things into his hands and that he had come from God and was returning to God. John here emphasizes that, at the outset of the footwashing, Jesus was fully assured of his status. He knew he was the Son of God; yet he lowered himself to the status of slave—what amazing condescension! No one said it better than Paul: Jesus, "being in very nature God, did not consider equality with God something to be grasped (or held onto)" (Phil 2:6). In this the footwashing becomes an acted parable of the theological significance of the incarnation itself.

Dinner had been served. By this time, people's feet should long have been cleaned. The practice of footwashing has a long Old Testament tradition (e.g., Gn 18:4; 19:2; 24:32; 43:24; 1 Sm 25:41). In the dry climate of Palestine, with the extensive walking necessary to get from place to place, usually in sandals (cf. 1:27), this was an essential act of hygiene, especially since people did not sit on separate chairs at a table but reclined side by side by leaning back in close proximity to one another (cf. 13:23). It was a matter of common hospitality, the breach of which constituted a serious affront (thus Jesus tells Simon the Pharisee in Lk 7:44: "I came into your house. You did not give me any water for my feet"). Usually, this task of footwashing was performed by slaves. In the present instance, however, the presumable absence of slaves may have led to a situation where this service had not been performed by anyone. Someone had to step into the role of servant.

But who? Rabbinic sources indicate that the task was considered by Jews to be too menial even for Jewish disciples to perform. Hence Jesus' followers were backed up by their own culture and religious tra-

dition. An understanding of this background makes Jesus' action even more remarkable. For here Jesus stoops to perform a task that was considered to be too menial *even for his disciples!* And he was their Lord! Surely all of the disciples' eyes were fixed on him (and once again the account seems to reflect eyewitness testimony) when he, presumably in stunned silence and with all conversation hushed, "got up from the meal, took off his outer clothing, and wrapped a towel around his waist" and "after that, poured water into a basin and began to wash his disciples' feet, dying them with the towel that was wrapped around him" (vv. 4–5).

Every act of Jesus, described here in excruciating detail, would have been like a dagger in the disciples' hearts, convicting them of their pride and refusal to lower themselves to the role of servant. The unthinkable nature of Jesus' condescension is highlighted by Peter's initial refusal to have his feet washed by his

The Chronology of the Passion Narrative in John and the Synoptics

The Synoptic Gospels clearly present the Last Supper observed by Jesus and the twelve as a Passover meal (Mk 14:12, 14, 16; Mt 26:17, 19; Lk 22:7–8, 15), celebrated during the early hours of 15 Nisan (Thursday night; that year, Passover ran from Thursday night to Friday night). While John does not explicitly refer to this last meal as a Passover meal, nothing in his Gospel precludes that according to John, too, Jesus' last supper with his disciples was in fact a Passover celebration (Jn 13:1, 27; 18:28; 19:14, 31, 36, 42). When reference is made to the Jews still looking forward to eating the Passover (18:28), this may use the term "Passover" to refer to the en-

tire Passover week including the Feast of Unleavened Bread. And when John (in 19:14) refers to the Day of Preparation of "the Passover" *(paraskeuē tou pascha),* he does not mean the day preceding the actual *Passover meal* but the day preceding the *Sabbath* following it (i.e., Friday), taking "Passover" again to refer to the entire week of festivities associated with the actual Passover meal (cf. Mk 15:42). This will be important when Jesus' body must be taken down from the cross by sundown in order not to defile the "special" Sabbath (during Passover week) about to begin (cf. 19:31–37). Thus John and the Synoptics concur in placing Jesus' death

on Friday (19:31; Nisan 15), with Jesus and his disciples having celebrated a Passover meal on Thursday evening.

Note: Regarding the time of Jesus' crucifixion in John and the Synoptics, see *Sidebar: References to Time in John's Gospel.* For a thorough exposition and defense of the above chronology, see D. A. Carson, *Gospel According to John* (Grand Rapids: Eerdmans, 1991), 455–58 and commentary on John 13:1, 27; 18:28; 19:14, 31, 36, and 42; and Craig L. Blomberg, *The Historical Reliability of the Gospels* (Leicester, U.K./Downers Grove: InterVarsity, 1987), 175–80, which also includes further helpful bibliographic references.

Master: "Lord, are *you* going to wash my feet?" (v. 6). And even after Jesus' reassuring words, "You do not realize now what I am doing, but later you will understand" (v. 7), Peter still insists, "You shall never wash my feet" (v. 8). However, when Jesus tells him that unless he allows Jesus to wash his feet, he has no part with him, Peter flip-flops, asking Jesus to wash, not just his feet, but also his hands and head (v. 9). Continuing to exploit the metaphoric possibilities of the event, Jesus explains that, just as a person who has had a bath needs only to wash his feet, Peter is clean (that is, cleansed, not from physical dirt but from the spiritual pollution of sin, presumably on account of his close association with Jesus and his faith in Jesus' word; cf. 6:68–69). As it were, he only needs a lesson on Christian service, not regeneration. The situation is different for Judas, as the evangelist reminds his readers once again (cf. 6:70–71; 12:4–6; 13:2).

Actions may speak louder than words, but explanations still help. So Jesus, when done washing his disciples' feet (of which only the encounter with Peter is recorded explicitly), puts on his clothes, returns to his place at the table, and explains to his— no doubt still stunned—followers the significance of what he has just done.

> Do you understand what I have done for you? . . . You call me "Teacher" and "Lord," and rightly so, for that is what I am. Now that I, your Lord and Teacher, have washed your feet, you also should wash one another's feet. I have set you an example that you should do as I have done for you. I tell you the truth, no servant is greater than his master, nor is a messenger greater than the one who sent him. Now that you know these things, you will be blessed if you do them (vv. 12b–17).

The lesson here taught fleshes out Jesus' verbal instruction at an earlier point in his ministry. Commenting on James's and John's desire to occupy the places of honor at Jesus' side, Jesus had called his disciples together and said,

> You know that those who are regarded as rulers of the Gentiles lord it over them, and their high officials exercise authority over them. Not so with you. Instead, whoever wants to become great among you must be your servant, and whoever wants to be first must be slave of all. For even the Son of Man did not come to be served, but to serve, and to give his life as a ransom for many (Mk 10:42–45).

Incredibly, Jesus' followers were not convinced by these words. As the account of the footwashing in John 13 makes clear, they needed more than mere verbal instruction—they needed an object lesson, a visual, practical demonstration of what Jesus' teaching looked like in action. Are they so different from many of us today?

The object lesson was not for the church to institute a sacrament of footwashing— this would be to institutionalize what was meant by Jesus only as an *example* of the kind of attitude he sought to promote. "Washing one another's feet" should be taken rather as an emblem of lowering oneself to meet another's need *whatever* that need happens to be at a particular moment. In the Upper Room, the need of the hour was clean feet. In your and my life, the need may take on a virtually limitless number of forms. We must be perceptive and caring in order to identify such needs and then meet them as we are able. As Paul wrote, "Carry each other's burdens, and in this way you will fulfill the law of Christ" (Gal 6:2). Or again, "Do nothing out of selfish ambition or vain conceit, but in humility consider others better than yourselves. Each of you should look not only to your own interests, but also to the interests of others" (Phil 2:3–4).

It is hard to think of an event that better encapsulates the attitude of Christ Jesus commended in the following verses by Paul than the footwashing:

> Your attitude should be the same as that of Christ Jesus:
> Who, being in very nature God,
> did not consider equality with God something to be grasped,
> but made himself nothing,
> taking the very nature of a servant,
> being made in human likeness.
> And being found in appearance as a man,
> he humbled himself

and became obedient to death—
even death on a cross! (Phil 2:6–8).

The footwashing is one of several instances where Jesus, the master-teacher, used, in good rabbinic fashion, the technique of visual demonstration as a teaching tool.[3] This highlights the importance of role modeling and of setting an example in our lives, be it in teaching, parenting, or other forms of relationships with believers or unbelievers. Christlike relationships can be an extremely powerful incentive for others to consider the faith. "See how they love one another," the surrounding world said about the early Christians. Can the world say the same thing about us?

Another lesson stands out powerfully from Jesus' example. It is our Lord's inner freedom to humble himself to a lower position that is due him for the purpose of meeting other people's needs. Importantly, his motives were not legalism, guilt, or a sense of religious obligation. Rather, he was induced by love (v. 1). Again, it is as if Paul had this act in mind when he wrote, "You, my brothers, were called to be free. But do not use your freedom to indulge the sinful nature; rather, serve one another in love" (Gal 5:13). This may involve the breaking of social convention, as in the present case or, earlier in John's Gospel, Jesus' dealings with the Samaritan woman (cf. esp. 4:27: "Just then his disciples returned and were surprised to find him talking with a woman"). Jesus was no slave to his social status, his pride, privilege, or position. He was truly free, and yet, he used this freedom not for himself, but to serve others. We ought to follow Jesus' example. As Jesus emphasized repeatedly, "No servant is greater than his master, nor is a messenger greater than the one who sent him" (v. 16; cf. v. 20; 15:20; Mt 10:24; Lk 6:40; cf. Mk 10:45; Lk 22:27).

By this Jesus does not become merely the inspiration for modern-day acts of charity removed from the Christian context in which the footwashing was performed. First of all, Jesus is here not talking about believers' relationships with the outside world; he is referring to their relationships *with each another*. Second, it is everywhere presupposed that people are already *Christians* who then are called to serve one another in love: "you are [already] clean" (v. 10). This presupposes that people are disciples, that they call Jesus their Lord and Master. Good works are not presented as a substitute for faith, or as a way to please God, but as an obligation for those who have already chosen to follow Jesus as their Lord. To sum up Paul's dictum: salvation is *by grace through faith for works* (cf. Eph 2:8–10); we must not put the cart before the horse. Moreover, Christians who act thus will by their actions furnish undeniable proof that they are indeed true followers of their Lord. "By this all

Table 11.1
Parallel Sayings of Jesus in John's Gospel and the Synoptics

Gospel of John	Synoptics
"Follow me" (1:32; 21:19)	Mk 1:17; 2:14; 10:21; Mt 4:19; 9:9; Lk 5:27; 9:59; 18:22
"A prophet is not without honor . . ." (4:44)	Mt 13:57; Lk 4:24
"The man who loves his life will lose it" (12:25)	Mk 8:34–35; Mt 16:24–25; Lk 9:23–24
"No servant is greater than his master" (13:16; 15:20)	Mt 10:24; Lk 6:40 (cf. 22:27)

Table 11.2
"The Greatest of These Is Love"

Occurrences of the "love" word group in John 1–12	12
Occurrences of the "love" word group in John 13–21	45

men will know that you are my disciples, if you love one another" (13:35).

Some have suggested that John's focus on intracommunity relations indicates that John's entire Gospel represents a sectarian document. Using a sociological grid, certain scholars have concluded that the so-called Johannine community, similar to the Qumran community, sustained a negative attitude toward the outside world, perhaps in response to experiencing social ostracism as a result of the faith of its members. But this overlooks one crucial fact: the strong mission theme running through the entire Gospel. "For God so loved the world," says the banner verse of John's Gospel, "that he gave his one and only Son, that whoever believes in him shall not perish but have eternal life" (3:16). Jesus' final prayer is pervaded by a desire "to let the world know that you sent me" (17:23), "so that the world may believe" (17:21). The mission theme climaxes in the commissioning scene in 20:21: "As the Father has sent me, I am sending you." These central verses in John's Gospel hardly support the notion that behind it stands a group that stood aloof to the surrounding world and had separated itself from it.[4]

Finally, modeling the themes of love and servanthood, Jesus does not sell out to a form of romantic idealism or a humanistic notion of the brotherhood of man and the universal Fatherhood of God. He remains keenly aware of the fact that in the shadow of the footwashing looms his betrayer: "I am not referring to all of you; I know those I have chosen. But this is to fulfill the scripture: 'He who shares my bread has lifted up his heel against me' [Ps 41:9]. I am telling you now

before it happens, so that when it does happen you will believe that I am he" (vv. 18–19). And with this, the transition is made from Jesus' sheer act of self-emptying love to Judas's imminent betrayal.

The Betrayal (13:21–30)

After this, Jesus was "troubled in spirit" (*tarassō*; v. 21). This is another instance where John provides us with a display of Jesus' humanity, including a full range of emotions. The present expression occurs with particular frequency in John's Gospel. It is used for water being "stirred" (5:7). It also serves to describe Jesus' reaction to Lazarus's death (11:33) and to his own imminent death (12:27). The two remaining references pertain to Jesus' counsel for his followers "not to be troubled" in light of Jesus' imminent death; he has given them his peace, and they must believe (14:1, 27). The expression also is chosen to depict the emotional turmoil suffered by Herod at reports of the birth of another king (Mt 2:3) and by the disciples at the occasion of Jesus' walking on the water (Mk 6:50 = Mt 14:26). Paul uses the term for those who would "stir up trouble" for the Galatians (Gal 1:7; 5:10). Often the term also conveys the notion of fear (e.g., 14:27; Lk 1:12; 1 Pt 3:14). In the present passage, Jesus' emotional state may best be captured as ragged, perturbed like the waters of a stormy sea, or agitated. His whole inner self convulsed at the thought of one of his closest followers betraying him to his enemies.

The disciples, for their part, respond to Jesus' announcement that one from their own midst would betray him with bewilderment and confusion. Their puzzlement may be compared to the women's perplexity who found the tomb empty after Jesus' resurrection (Lk 24:4). What to do? And is it I, Lord? Peter, always ingenious, motions to the disciple reclining next to him ("the disciple Jesus loved," v. 23), urging him to ask Jesus which one he meant. In the ensuing sequence of events, Judas—no surprise to the reader—emerges as the betrayer. Amazingly, the matter is still dealt with

Study Questions

1. Relate John 13 both to the first half of John's Gospel and to the rest of Jesus' farewell discourse.

2. Lay out the first-century Jewish cultural and religious background for Jesus' act of footwashing.

3. List at least three possible contemporary applications of Jesus' command arising from the footwashing.

in such a private and inconspicuous manner that the disciples do not pick up the cue, interpreting Jesus' parting words to Judas as perhaps an instruction to buy what is needed for the Feast or to give something to the poor (v. 29). As John tells it, the scene could hardly be more ominous: for as soon as Judas takes the bread, Satan enters into him (v. 27); and when Judas leaves the room, John remarks, in a phrase as terse as it is pregnant with meaning, "And it was night" (v. 30).

The New Commandment and Peter's Denials Foretold (13:31–38)

Jesus' reaction is characterized by almost visible relief. With Judas's departure, the new messianic community has been cleansed (cf. vv. 10–11). "Now is the Son of Man glorified and God is glorified in him" (v. 31). Now also is the time for Jesus' parting instructions to his disciples. Immediately, Jesus prepares his disciples (using the endearing term "little children") that he will be with them only a little while longer; where he is going, they cannot

come (v. 33). Then he issues his "new commandment": his followers ought to love each other the way he has loved them (v. 34; cf. 1 Jn 2:7–8). This way all people will recognize them as *Jesus'* disciples (v. 35). The commandment for people to love each other was, of course, not new (the Law already contained the injunction for people to love their neighbor as themselves: Lv 19:18); the commandment for believers in Jesus to love each other *the way Jesus loved them* (see the footwashing) was.

But perhaps tellingly, Peter picks up, not on the new commandment, but on an earlier part of Jesus' instruction: Jesus' saying "where I am going, you cannot come" (v. 36; cf. v. 33). Even though Jesus tells Peter that he will follow later, the apostle is not content with this—he wants to follow Jesus *now*. He is even willing to die for Jesus. Peter's undying pledge of loyalty will forever serve as a warning against an exaggerated confidence in one's own abilities. "Will you really lay down your life for me? I tell you the truth, before the rooster crows, you will disown me three times!" (13:38). As the rest of John's account will make clear, this, too, is a *fulfilled* prophecy of Jesus (cf. 18:15–18, 25–27). Moreover, as readers of the final chapter will learn, Peter *would* follow Jesus even in his manner of death (21:19; cf. the close verbal parallel with 12:33).[5] But now, after the new messianic community has been cleansed through the exposure and departure of Judas, the betrayer, and alerted to Peter's imminent denials, the stage is set for the in-depth instruction of Jesus' followers that is recorded in the next three chapters of John's Gospel.

Key Word

high priestly prayer

12 Jesus' Farewell (Part 2)

John 14–16

This is the victory that has overcome the world, even our faith.

—1 John 5:4

Supplemental Reading:
Deuteronomy 28–30

Outline

• **The Advantages of Jesus' Departure for His Disciples (14:1–31; 15:26–16:16)**

Preparing a Place (14:1–4)

Knowing the Way (14:5–7)

Greater Intimacy of Relationship (14:8–11)

Excursus: "In" Terminology in John's Gospel

Greater Works (14:12–14)

Another Divine Helping Presence (14:15–31; 15:26–16:16)

• **Jesus the True Vine (15:1–17)**

• **The World's Hatred (15:18–16:4a)**

• **The End Result of Jesus' Departure for His Disciples: Greater Joy (16:17–33)**

Objectives

After reading this chapter, you should be able to

1. Interpret Jesus' saying that he will go to "prepare a place" for his disciples.

2. Comment on the original as well as contemporary significance of Jesus' statement that he is "the way, the truth, and the life."

3. Identify the Old Testament antecedent theology of Johannine "in" terminology as well as the major theological message conveyed by it to the eleven, to John's first readers, and to us today.

4. Explain the significance of Jesus' promise of "greater works" to his followers.

5. Compare John's teaching on the Holy Spirit to that found in the Synoptic Gospels and discuss the two primary designations for the Spirit in John 14–16.

6. Explore the phenomenon of Christian suffering in light of John 15:18–25 and other New Testament passages on this topic.

While chapters 13 through 17 form a larger unit, chapter 13 may be considered a preamble (the cleansing of the messianic community) and chapter 17 a postlude (Jesus' high priestly prayer) to the actual farewell discourse in chapters 14 through 16. Now that the betrayer has left, the stage is set for Jesus to instruct the eleven regarding life after Jesus has departed from earth and gone back to heaven where he came from (see 13:1). During these crucial moments, Jesus reminds them that he is the Way to the Father (ch. 14); that they must remain in close relationship with him, just as branches derive their life from the vine to which they are organically related (ch. 15); that once he has left, the world's hatred will center on the disciples themselves (15:18–16:4a); that the Spirit will continue Jesus' work both in the world and with the disciples (16:4b–15; cf. 14:15–31); and that the disciples will shortly mourn Jesus' crucifixion yet that their sorrow will turn into joy when they see the resurrected Christ (16:16–33). Let's look at this exciting and unique portion of John's Gospel in greater detail.

The Advantages of Jesus' Departure for His Disciples (14:1–31; 15:26–16:16)

As mentioned earlier, the farewell discourse has one major purpose: the preparation of Jesus' followers for the time after his departure. Reading the present chapter thus requires a certain degree of historical empathy and imagination. What would it have been like to huddle around Jesus in this besieged, anxiety-laden moment? With the disciples' very existence on the line, many may have been tempted to second-guess their decision to follow Jesus in the first place. It seemed as if Jesus' entire mission—and the disciples' alongside his—had begun to unravel. This was a time of supreme testing of the disciples' faith and loyalty.

In this context, the primary need for Jesus' followers is for encouragement and reassurance. So Jesus tells them, "Do not let your hearts be troubled [the verb form in the original implies that the disciples were already worried and anxious; cf. v. 27]. Trust in God; trust also in me [or, alternatively: You trust in God; trust also in me]. In my Father's house are many rooms; if it were not so, I would have told you. I am going there to prepare a place for you. And if I go and prepare a place for you, I will come back and take you to be with me that you also may be where I am. You know the way to the place where I am going" (vv. 1–4).

Preparing a Place (14:1–4)

In this first piece of instruction, Jesus promises his followers that he will return (the "second coming," v. 3) and elaborates on one of the purposes for his going to the Father: he will prepare a place for his disciples in heaven (similar language is used in Mk 10:40; 1 Cor 2:9; Hb 11:16; 1 Pt 1:4). The Greek word for "rooms" is *monai* (from *monos*, "alone, single"), designating a single dwelling unit. Significantly, the only other reference of this word in the entire New Testament is found later in the same chapter when Jesus tells his disciples that he and the Father will come and "make their home" *(monē)* with anyone who obeys Jesus' teaching (v. 23).

In Jesus' day, many of these dwelling units were combined to form a mansion. It was customary for sons to add to their father's house once married, so that the entire estate grew into a large compound (called *insula*) centered around a communal courtyard. The image used by Jesus may also have conjured up notions of luxurious Greco-Roman villas, replete with numerous terraces and buildings, situated among shady gardens with an abundance of trees and flowing water. Jesus' listeners may have been familiar with this kind of setting from the Herodian palaces in Jerusalem, Tiberias, and Jericho (cf. Josephus, *Jewish War* 5.176–183).

This provision is in keeping with Jesus' response to Peter who had alerted his Lord to the sacrifice the twelve had made in following him: "I tell you the truth, no one who has left home or brothers or sisters or mother or father or children or fields for me and the gospel will fail to receive a hundred times as much in this present age (homes, brothers, sisters, mothers, children and fields—and with them, persecutions) and in the age to come, eternal life" (Mk 10:29–30 par.). The real cost in following Jesus is not to be denied—but the rewards will be out of this world.

Knowing the Way (14:5–7)

Jesus' statement, "You know the way to the place where I am going," provokes a series of queries from among his disciples, first by Thomas (who is known for his bluntness; v. 5; cf. 11:16; 20:24–29), then Philip (v. 8; cf. 1:43–48; 6:5–7; 12:21–22), then Judas (not Iscariot; surfacing only here; v. 22). Once again, John's account reflects firsthand experience, including the recollection of who asked questions at a particular time. Thomas is the first to speak up: "Lord, we don't know the way where you are going, so how can we know the way?" This remark, in turn, triggers the sixth "I am saying" featured in John's Gospel: "I am the way and the truth and the life. No one comes to the Father except through me" (v. 6).

It is hard to exhaust the multifaceted nature of Jesus' statement here. Thomas, of course, is looking for a literal road map, complete with specific directions that will enable him to know how to get where Jesus was going. But Jesus says that he himself is the way. Tellingly, the early Christians were initially called the followers of "the Way" (cf. Acts 9:2; 19:9, 23; 22:4; 24:14, 22). Jesus' claim of himself being the way (with the implication that no one can come to the Father but through him) is as timely today as it was when our Lord first uttered this statement. For we live in an age of religious pluralism, when Christianity's exclusive claims are considered inappropriately narrow, even intolerant, and when pluralism itself has, ironically, become the dogma by which all truth claims are judged.[1] It has been said that pluralism accepts no absolute truth claims other than its contention that there are no absolute truth claims.

Yet in a day when keeping the Law and scrupulous observance of religious customs were considered paramount (cf. 5:10; 6:28; 9:16), Jesus claimed that allegiance to himself was the Way. Jesus is the way; he is also the truth and the life (or perhaps better: truth and life; abstract nouns have the article in Greek, but not

necessarily in English). It is sometimes argued that way, truth, and life should be merged such as in "the true way of life," or the like. But a comparison with other instances in this Gospel where John links three terms with the conjunction "and" shows that the terms thus tied together remain distinct. In the phrase "cattle, sheep and doves" (2:14), "sheep and doves" is not further explicating the term "oxen." Likewise, in the expression "sin and righteousness and judgment" (16:8), "righteousness and judgment" is not further explicating "sin."

Nevertheless, of the three terms used in 14:6, "the Way" is the head term (cf. Thomas's question in v. 5, picking up on Jesus' comment in v. 4). Since he is the way, Jesus is also truth and life. What is more, he is "the" truth and "the" life, that is, truth and life par excellence. Both expressions hark back to the Prologue, where it is said that the Word-become-flesh was "full of grace and truth" and that "grace and truth came through Jesus Christ" (vv. 14, 17); and where it is also said that in that Word "was life, and that life was the light of men" (v. 4). To know the truth (8:32; 17:3) and to have life beyond the grave are the great aspirations of humankind. As John tells us, only in Jesus can these deepest of all human longings be fulfilled.

Greater Intimacy of Relationship (14:8–11)

The subject of the following interchange is one of the central themes of John's Gospel: the unity of God the Father and Jesus the Son (vv. 8–11). What is at stake here is nothing less than Jesus' ability to provide firsthand revelation of God. John has already made this clear in the conclusion of his Prologue: "No one has ever seen God, but God the One and Only, who is at the Father's side, has made him known" (1:18). In this, the revelation mediated by Jesus exceeds that provided through Moses in the Law (1:17; cf. 5:39–40, 45–47; 7:22–23).

The crucial issue of Jesus' unity with the Father pervades the entire Gospel and surfaces regularly in Jesus' confrontation with the Jewish religious leadership (e.g., 5:18; 10:30). John's manner of presentation clearly implies *ontological* unity (unity of being); but the emphasis lies on *functional* unity, that is, the way in which God is revealed in Jesus' words and works (called "signs" by John). Thus Jesus' audience is encouraged to "believe the miracles, that you may know and understand that the Father is in me, and I in the Father" (10:38).

As it turned out, the Jews at large rejected Jesus' claims and failed to believe (12:37–41). But now Jesus seeks to deepen the faith *of his followers*. As becomes apparent, even the Eleven have not fully grasped that anyone who has seen Jesus has seen the Father (v. 9). Any teacher will be able to testify how exasperating it can be when one's students still have not grasped a given lesson that the teacher has sought to impart to them for a long time. One can almost sense the frustration in Jesus' words: "Don't you know me, Philip, even after I have been among you such a long time? . . . How can you say, 'Show us the Father'? Don't you believe that I am in the Father, and that the Father is in me?" (vv. 9–10). Jesus even challenges this disciple in words almost identical to those used to exhort the unbelieving Jewish leadership: "Believe me when I say that I am in the Father and the Father is in me; or at least believe on the evidence of the miracles themselves" (v. 11; cf. 10:38).

At this final stage of his earthly ministry, Jesus is still confronting the root problem of his followers' relationship with him: their unbelief. This is confirmed by the other Gospels which reveal that building his disciples' faith was one of Jesus' key objectives (e.g., Mk 11:22–24; Mt 17:17–21). To this end, Jesus' vision is for a relationship with his disciples that is characterized by the kind of intimacy he himself enjoys with God the Father. As the following discussion will show, the fourth evangelist once again breaks new ground in his presentation of this vision.

Excursus: "In" Terminology in John's Gospel

Among the most frequent expressions used in John's Gospel to express Jesus' unity with the Father—as well as believers' unity with Jesus and the Father—is the terminology of being "in" one another. Thus Jesus is quoted as saying, "It is the Father, living in me, doing his work. Believe me when I say that I am *in* the Father and the Father is *in* me" (vv. 10–11).

Perhaps the first clear instance of such language in John's Gospel is Jesus' statement in 6:56, "Whoever eats my flesh and drinks my blood remains in me, and I in him." The next major reference is the already quoted passage in 10:38: "believe the miracles, that you may know and understand that the Father is in me, and I in the Father." But more often than not, "in" terminology in the first part of the Gospel is negative, such as in 8:44: "there is no truth in him [that is, Satan]." Only in the present passage do we find, for the first time, a more thorough development of "in" terminology:

> Don't you believe that I am in the Father,
>   and that the Father is in me?
> . . . it is the Father, living in me, who is
>   doing his work.
> Believe me when I say that I am in the
>   Father
>   and the Father is in me . . .
>   (vv. 10–11).

In 14:17, the emphasis shifts, significantly, from Jesus to the Spirit who will be "in" the disciples. "On that day," Jesus maintains, "you will realize that I am in my Father, and you are in me, and I am in you" (14:20). Thus believers will have come full circle: they will believe in Jesus' unity with the Father, and they will analogously be indwelt by the Spirit. The metaphorical possibilities of this theme are further explored in the allegory of the vine and the branches in chapter 15. The final passage featuring "in" terminology is found at the conclusion of Jesus' highpriestly prayer in chapter 17, where the Lord prays for believers:

> that all of them may be one, Father,
>   just as you are in me and I am in you.
> May they also be in us
>   so that the world may believe that
>   you have sent me.
> I have given them the glory that you
>   gave me,
>   that they may be one as we are one:
> I in them and you in me.
> May they be brought to complete unity
>   to let the world know that you sent
>   me . . . (vv. 21–23).

Thus "in" terminology culminates in Jesus' prayer for his disciples' unity, not as an end in itself, but for the sake of his followers' mission to the world. While the term "Trinity" is not yet used, the trinitarian framework is firmly in place: the Father, Jesus, and the Spirit are said to indwell the disciples, and the result is to be the disciples' unity (and love) among each other, in keeping with the unity (and love) characteristic of the persons of the Godhead.

John is not the only New Testament writer to stress believers' union with Christ. This theme is also very prominent in Paul, so prominent, in fact, that it has regularly been proposed as the central motif in Paul's theology.[2] Albeit less frequently, "in" terminology is also found in Peter's writings (cf. 1 Pt 5:14).

What, then, is the point stressed by John (and ultimately Jesus) in his use of "in" terminology? It is the intimacy of relationship desired by Jesus with believers, an intimacy even greater in the Spirit than the one possible when Jesus was still physically among his earthly followers. Again, the theme is already sounded in the Prologue: "The Word became flesh and made his dwelling among us. We have seen his glory, the glory of the One and Only, who came from the Father, full of grace and truth" (1:14). Thus, in the context of Jesus' parting words to his disciples, Jesus seeks to impress upon them the fact that his cross-death will result, not in lesser, but in greater intimacy between himself and his followers.

This development, in turn, marks the culmination of the progress of salvation history. For after the first man and his wife had been barred from God's immediate presence subsequent to the Fall, God had dwelt among his people in a variety of ways, including the tabernacle and later the temple, but never as permanently and irrevocably as he would subsequent to Jesus' death and exaltation. As Luke's account of the outpouring of the Holy Spirit at Pentecost makes clear, this is an event of major eschatological proportions: "In the last days, God says, I will pour out my Spirit on all people" (Acts 2:17 quoting Jl 2:28). In Old Testament times, no one lesser than King David pleaded with God, "Do not cast me from your presence or take your Holy Spirit from me" (Ps 51:11). We must not fear the same; for in these last days, God's Holy Spirit has come to dwell permanently with his people and in each believer.

"In" terminology thus is (new) covenant terminology. Consider the major Old Testament passage referring to the new covenant, Jeremiah 31:

> "I will put my law in their minds
>   and write it on their hearts.
> I will be their God
>   and they will be my people.
> No longer will a man teach his neighbor,
>   or a man his brother, saying, 'Know the LORD,'
> because they will all know me,
>   from the least of them to the greatest," declares the LORD (Jer 31:33–34).

Ezekiel concurs with this vision:

> "I will put my Spirit in you and you will live . . . ," declares the LORD . . .
> "They will be my people, and I will be their God.
> My servant David will be king over them. . . .
> I will put my sanctuary among them forever.
> My dwelling place will be with them;
> I will be their God, and they will be my people" (Ez 37:14, 23–24, 26–27).

In a very real sense, the covenant phrase "I will be their God and they will be my people" has now been expanded to the formulation "I in them and you in me" (17:23). Indeed, John is "the evangelist of the covenant people."[3]

Greater Works (14:12–14)

From our exploration of "in" terminology, it is only a small step to the next affirmation of Jesus that we must consider in some detail, his promise that believers will do the things he has been doing, and that they will do "even greater things than these" (v. 12). We have already seen how Jesus' entire purpose in the farewell discourse is to encourage his disciples that, contrary to their expectations, it would actually be better for Jesus to move on to the next stage of salvation history. For the Spirit could only be given subsequent to Jesus' "exaltation" at the cross and his return to the Father. This, then, is the reason why believers will be able to do greater works than even Jesus: "because I am going to the Father" (v. 12c). For once Jesus is exalted in his Father's presence, believers will be able to pray to the Father *in Jesus' name*, and Jesus himself will answer these prayers (vv. 13–14).

This does not refer primarily (or even secondarily) to believers' ability to work miracles like Jesus did. (In any case, it is hard to imagine greater miracles than Jesus' raising of Lazarus.) After all, only Jesus' works are termed "signs" in John's Gospel. Rather, what is envisioned here are works of a more general nature, works performed at a stage in salvation history where Jesus' cross-work has been completed and the Spirit energizes believers' ministry in a way unprecedented in previous times. Clearly the Eleven would have been greatly encouraged to hear (whether they believed it at that time, of course, is another question) that their works after Jesus' exaltation would exceed the scope of even Jesus' own works during his earthly ministry.

As mentioned in the introduction, understanding the impact of Jesus' words to his original audience requires historical imagination. For what was a novel vision for Jesus' first followers has become an everyday reality for us today: to be indwelt by the Spirit and to pray—and receive answers to prayer—in Jesus' name.

In the following section, we consider Jesus' teaching on the ministry of the Holy Spirit in believers' lives in greater detail, grouping together both major blocks within the farewell discourse where this topic is addressed.

Another Divine Helping Presence (14:15–31; 15:26–16:16)

Continuing to encourage his disciples, Jesus proceeds to elaborate on another major advantage of his "going to the Father"—the giving of the Spirit. As John has made clear earlier in his Gospel, this giving of the Spirit was possible only subsequent to Jesus' glorification (7:39). With this glorification now imminent (cf. 12:23; 13:1), Jesus spends much of his time in the Upper Room preparing his followers for life in the age of the Spirit.

Here John's Gospel fills in a major gap in the Synoptic accounts. For as a survey of these writings shows, references to the Spirit are limited almost exclusively to his role in Jesus' earthly ministry: he conceives Jesus in Mary's womb resulting in the virgin birth (Mt 1:18, 20; Lk 1:35); descends on Jesus at his baptism (Mk 1:10) and leads him into the wilderness at the temptation (Mk 1:12); rests on Jesus throughout his ministry, designating him as Isaiah's Servant of the Lord (Lk 4:18 citing Is 61:1; Lk 10:21; cf. Mt 12:18 citing Is 42:1); and the blasphemy against the Holy Spirit (that is, attributing God's work through Jesus to Satan) cannot be forgiven (Mk 3:29 par.). The only instances transcending the role of the Spirit in Jesus' own ministry are the Baptist's designation of Jesus as the one who will "baptize with the Holy Spirit" (Mk 1:8 par.); Luke's reference to God's giving of the Holy Spirit to those who ask (Lk 11:13); and Jesus' promise to his followers that the Holy Spirit will speak for them in times of persecution (Mk 13:11 = Lk 12:12).

In the first half of his Gospel, John's treatment of the Spirit largely resembles that of the Synoptics. Thus he also includes the Baptist's designation of Jesus as the one who will baptize with the Holy Spirit (1:32–33; cf. Mk 1:8 par.) and emphasizes that the Spirit in all his fullness rested on Jesus during his earthly ministry (1:32; 3:34; cf. Lk 4:18). Moreover, John stresses the Spirit's role in regeneration (3:5, 6, 8; cf. 1:12–13), worship (4:23–24), and the giving of life (6:63). But as in John's presentation of Jesus' followers (see ch. 11 above), his adoption of a postexaltation vantage point regarding Jesus leads to a vastly different portrayal in the second half of his Gospel, most notably in the farewell discourse. In this unique body of teaching, the Spirit is featured primarily by the use of two characteristic designations: "the *paraklētos*" (14:16, 26; 15:26; 16:7; elsewhere in the New Testament only in 1 John 2:1, there with reference to Jesus "our Advocate" with God the Father), and "the Spirit of truth" (14:17; 15:26; 16:13). The fact that both expressions are used side by side in 15:26 makes it clear that they are closely related.

We will first deal with the designation "Spirit of truth," since it is the more straightforward and noncontroversial of these terms. In the context of the present chapter, Jesus has just been characterized as "the truth" (14:6), in keeping with statements already made in the Prologue (1:14, 17). The concept of truth in John's Gospel encompasses several aspects:

1. truthfulness as opposed to falsehood: "to speak the truth" means to make a true rather than false statement, that is, to represent the facts as they actually are (cf. 8:40, 45, 46; 16:7; "to witness to the truth": 5:33; 18:37);
2. truth in its finality as compared to previous, preliminary expressions: this is its *eschatological* dimension (cf. esp. 1:17: "the law was given through Moses; grace and truth came through Jesus Christ");
3. truth is an identifiable body of knowledge with actual propositional content (e.g., 8:32: "you will know the truth"; 16:13: "he will guide you into all truth");
4. truth is a sphere of operation, be it for worship (4:23–24) or sanctification (17:17, 19).[4]

The Spirit is involved in all four aspects: he accurately represents the truth regarding Jesus; he is the eschatological gift of God; he imparts true knowledge of God; and he is operative in both worship and sanctification.

We turn to a discussion of the second major designation of the Spirit in John, that of *paraklētos*. The translation of this term has proved particularly difficult, since there does not seem to be an exact equivalent in the English language. None of the expressions chosen in various English translations seems fully adequate: "the Counselor" (NIV) smacks too much of contemporary notions of counseling, focusing primarily on emotional or psychological aspects (though the legal term Counselor is more appropriate); "the Helper" (NASB, ISV) is more neutral but lacks the legal connotation possibly present; the fact that some translations give several alternative renderings in footnotes also suggests that any one English rendering may be inadequate (cf., e.g., NLT: "the Counselor; or Comforter, or Encourager, or Advocate"). Some make reference to the root meaning of the word, "one called alongside to help," but it is unclear whether first-century users of this expression consciously drew on this background. There is evidence that the phrase was used in a legal setting, but it is less clear that the meaning should be restricted to "Advocate" or the like.[5] Perhaps "helping Presence" captures the import of the term better than any other, for the following reasons: (1) this is what Jesus was while with the disciples; (2) this encompasses the various functions laid out for the Spirit in John 14–16; (3) this transcends (but may include) the legal context of the term (see esp. 16:7–11).

Significantly, the first reference to the Spirit in John 14 refers to him as "another" *paraklētos*. This indicates that the Spirit's presence with the disciples will replace Jesus' presence with them while on earth. According to John, then, the primary role of the Spirit is that of substitute presence for Jesus: "he lives with you and will be in you" (14:17). When the Spirit comes to dwell in believers, it is as if Jesus himself takes up residence in them. "The Spirit is the divine presence when Jesus' physical presence is taken away from his followers."[6] Thus Jesus is able to refer to the coming of the Spirit by saying, "I will come to you" (14:18). This relieves a primary concern for Jesus' first followers in the original setting of the Farewell Discourse: Jesus' departure will not leave them as orphans (cf. v. 18); just as God was present with them through Jesus, he will continue to be present with them through his Spirit.

The Spirit's role thus ensures the continuity between Jesus' pre- and postglorification ministry. What is more, the coming of the Spirit will actually constitute an advance in God's operations with and through the disciples: "But I tell you the truth: It is for your good that I am going away. Unless I go away, the Counselor will not come to you; but if I go, I will send him to you" (16:7; cf. 14:12).

As Jesus' substitute presence, the Spirit will have a variety of functions in believers' lives:

he will bring to remembrance all that Jesus taught his disciples (14:26);
he will testify regarding Jesus together with his followers (15:26);

Spirit take center stage while the cross of Christ is barely ever preached demonstrably departs from the New Testament teaching on the person and role of the Holy Spirit. For the Spirit's role is not to exalt himself; it is to exalt Christ. As the eminent theologian Donald Guthrie maintains, "any movement claiming the possession of the Spirit . . . which glorifies the Spirit instead of Christ . . . [is] alien to the teaching of Jesus about the Spirit."[7]

In concluding our discussion of this section of John's Gospel, we draw attention to the fact that certain aspects of Jesus' teaching in John 14–16, while crucial for the Eleven, have no direct relevance for later believers. This must be kept in mind when dealing with Judas's question in verse 22, and again in the section on the "little while" in 16:17–33. We will take up this issue further in our discussion of the latter passage.

Jesus used vineyard imagery to portray the closeness of relationship he desired between himself and his followers following his ascension.

he will convict the world of sin, (un)righteousness, and judgment (16:8–11); and he will guide Jesus' disciples into all truth and disclose what is to come (16:13).

Historically, this included the formation of the New Testament canon (esp. the Gospels but also the Epistles and Revelation) as apostolic testimony to Jesus. While initially focused on the Eleven (cf. 15:27: "for you have been with me from the beginning"), the Spirit, in a secondary sense, fulfills similar roles in believers today. He illumines the spiritual meaning of Jesus' words and works both to believers and, through believers, also to the unbelieving world.

In all of these functions, the ministry of the Spirit remains closely linked with the person of Jesus. Just as Jesus is everywhere in John's Gospel portrayed as the Sent One who is fully dependent on and obedient to the Father, the Spirit is said to be "sent" by both the Father and Jesus (14:26; 15:26) and to focus his teaching on the illumination of the spiritual significance of God's work in Jesus (14:26; 15:26; 16:9). This is where certain Christian groups have gone astray in recent years: in an effort to recover biblical teaching on the Spirit, people have lost sight of the fact that it is Jesus, not the Spirit, who remains central in the teaching of the New Testament. A church where miraculous manifestations of the

Jesus the True Vine (15:1–17)

Chapter 14 concludes with the statement, "Come now; let us leave" (v. 31). Chapter 15 opens with Jesus' allegory of the vine. It is possible that Jesus and the Eleven have left the Upper Room and are passing through scenery illustrating Jesus' teaching. The next geographical piece of information is found in 18:1, where the group is said to cross the Kidron Valley east of Jerusalem and to enter an olive grove on the other side.

A vineyard setting would indeed be a highly suggestive environment for Jesus' teaching, especially since "God's vineyard" is a frequent Old Testament designation for Israel (cf. Is 5:1–7; 27:2–6; Jer 2:21; Ez 15; 19:10–14; Hos 10:1; Ps 80:9–16). Most famous is the Song of the Vineyard in Isaiah 5:

> I will sing for the one I love
> a song about his vineyard:
> My loved one had a vineyard
> on a fertile hillside.
> He dug it up and cleared it of stones
> and planted it with the choicest vines.
> He built a watchtower in it
> and cut out a winepress as well.

Then he looked for a crop of good
grapes,
but it yielded only bad fruit (vv. 1–2).

The prophetic message centered on Israel as God's vineyard in the Old Testament is therefore this: God carefully cultivated his vineyard and in due time expected to collect fruit from it, but Israel has yielded only bad fruit; hence God will replace Israel with a more fruitful nation. This point is driven home in Jesus' Parable of the Wicked Tenants (Mk 12:1–12 par.):

> A man planted a vineyard. He put a wall around it, dug a pit for the winepress and built a watchtower. Then he rented the vineyard to some farmers and went away on a journey. At harvest time he sent a servant to the tenants to collect from them some of the fruit of the vineyard. But they seized him, beat him and sent him away empty-handed. Then he sent another servant to them; they struck this man on the head and treated him shamefully. He sent still another, and that one they killed. He sent many others; some of them they beat, others they killed. He had one left to send, a son, whom he loved. He sent him last of all, saying, "They will respect him." But the tenants said to one another, "This is the heir. Come, let's kill him, and the inheritance will be ours." So they took him and killed him, and threw him out of the vineyard. What then will the owner of the vineyard do? He will come and kill those tenants and give the vineyard to others.

Nevertheless, John does not teach a **replacement theology** whereby the church takes the place of Israel. As a closer look at John 15 indicates, it is not believers in Jesus who are depicted as the vine. Rather, the vine is Jesus. Jesus himself is therefore the replacement for Israel, just as he has already been portrayed as the replacement of the temple and the fulfillment of the symbolism of various Jewish feasts. Jesus thus embodies and fulfills God's true intentions for Israel; he is the paradigmatic vine, the channel through whom God's blessings flow and who bears much fruit. Indeed, by dying Jesus will prove exceedingly fruitful: "I tell you the truth, unless a kernel of wheat falls to

the ground and dies, it remains only a single seed. But if it dies, it produces many seeds" (12:23–24). The parallel between the fruitfulness of Jesus and that of his disciples, depicted in the present allegory as branches of the vine, is obvious: "This is to my Father's glory, that you bear much fruit, showing yourselves to be my disciples. . . . I chose you and appointed you to go and bear fruit—fruit that will last" (15:8, 16).

Theologically, then, John's point is that Jesus now replaces Israel as the focus of God's plan of salvation, with the implication that faith in Jesus becomes the decisive characteristic for membership among the people of God. Israel, ethnically constrained as God's chosen people, has been transmuted into the new messianic community, made up of believing Jews and Gentiles, united by their faith in Jesus the Messiah. This does not mean that there no longer remains a place for Jews in the family of God. What it does mean, however, is that Jews must come to God on *his* terms, not theirs. A paradigm shift has taken place in which faith in Jesus has superseded keeping the Law as the primary religious point of reference. As Paul writes, "Christ is the end [*telos*] of the law" (Rom 10:4): he is its fulfillment and thus replacement (literally, its "end").

Does this mean that Israel as an ethnic group has ceased to be a factor in God's salvific purposes? This appears to be the implication in certain parts of the New Testament. Thus Paul can call *the church* "the Israel of God" (Gal 6:16), and Peter is able to apply Old Testament designations of Israel freely to his predominantly Gentile audience (see esp. 1 Pt 1:1; 2:4–10). Yet Paul's discussion in Romans 9–11 makes clear that God still has a purpose for ethnic Israel. At the present time, his focus has shifted to bringing in the Gentiles, but at the end of salvation history his attention will once again be directed to the Jewish nation. At last, at Christ's return, the Jews will recognize their Messiah, and "so all Israel [not necessarily every single Jew alive at that time, but the nation as a whole as represented by its leadership] will be saved" (Rom 11:26). This excludes all ethnic or religious pride and exalts only the glorious grace of God. For it is faith that constitutes the grounds for salvation, not human merit or ethnic origin.

What does this mean for John's original audience? If we are correct in inferring that many of John's first intended readers were Diaspora Jews and proselytes, the message is clear:

A reversal has taken place that requires a rethinking of categories. The issue is no longer one of others joining *Jews* in *their* special and privileged position with God, but one of *Jews* being invited to join the universal Messianic community that had been inaugurated by the mission of the Messiah, the Son of God, viz. *Jesus*. "The Jews," i.e., the Jewish nation represented by the religious and political leadership, had rejected the Messiah, but God had raised him from the dead. The effects of Jesus'

The Eternal Subordination of the Son

"I and the Father are one" (10:30). "The Father is greater than I" (14:28). How are we to reconcile these apparently contradictory statements? Let's take one statement at a time.

"I and the Father are one." Here it is important to note that the Greek numeral underlying "one" is neuter, not masculine, in gender. Hence Jesus does not say that he and the Father are one person. Rather, they are one entity (yet two persons). This refers to functional as well as ontological unity. Jesus and the Father are one in purpose (functional unity). Yet they are also one in essence (ontological unity). Thus Jesus preexisted with the Father from eternity (1:1–2; cf. 17:5, 24), co-created the world (1:3), and has life in himself as does the Father (5:26). The very fact that the Jews seek to stone Jesus for blasphemy proves that they understood Jesus' claim to deity very well indeed (even though they rejected it). The truth of Jesus' equality with God must, however, be balanced with his filial subordination to the Father, which is taught just as clearly in John's Gospel.

"The Father is greater than I." (See also 10:29: "My Father . . . is greater than all.") Let's look at the context of Jesus' statement. In his Farewell Discourse, it is Jesus' major burden to convince his followers that his impending "departure" (an euphemism for his crucifixion) is actually advantageous for all parties concerned. It is better for the disciples, for Jesus will send "another helping presence," that is, the Spirit (14:16). And it is—now we have arrived at the context of the statement we are here considering— even better for Jesus himself, for "the Father is greater than I." In other words, Jesus will have it better in heaven in the Father's presence than he had it on earth while confined to human "flesh" (1:14). In the end, John—or Jesus—makes no explicit effort to reconcile the truths that Jesus is one with the Father and that the Father is at the same time greater than Jesus. Moreover, the eternal subordination of the Son is also clearly taught in other parts of Scripture such as 1 Corinthians 15:28.

Does the fact that we struggle with this apparent paradox reveal more about us than it does about the alleged contradictory nature of the issue itself? Many have seen in Jesus' equality with the Father accompanied by his voluntary submission to the Father a paradigm for the husband and wife relationship (cf. esp. 1 Cor 11:3). For here, too, Scripture teaches at the same time that husband and wife are fellow-heirs in Christ (1 Pt 3:7) and that wives are to submit to their husbands (Eph 5:22, 24; Col 3:18; 1 Pt 3:1, 5–6). Those who prefer to conceive of the contemporary husband and wife relationship therefore in exclusively egalitarian terms must dispute the analogy between Christ's relationship with the Father and the husband and wife relationship or deny the eternal subordination of the Son altogether. Yet if Scripture teaches that none other than Christ sustains a relationship with God that is characterized by both equality and submission, there is no reason why the same should not be true for husbands and wives as well. Indeed, according to 1 Corinthians 11:3, Christ has modeled both the husband's loving "headship" and the wife's voluntary "submission" in his own respective relationships with the church and with the Father.

death extend to the world, *through the disciples*, who are sent into the world to do greater works than even Jesus did during his earthly ministry, in the power of his Spirit. The eschatological time of harvest has dawned.[8]

While Jesus is the vine, and his followers are the branches, it is the Father who is the gardener. As such, he prunes the branches in order to make them even more fruitful (v. 2). The disciples have already been cleansed; now they must simply remain in Jesus (v. 3; cf. 13:10). For just as branches cannot bear fruit once severed from the vine, so believers cannot be fruitful apart from Jesus (v. 5). Anyone who does not remain in Jesus is like a branch that is thrown away and withers; such branches are picked up, thrown into the fire, and burned (v. 6). This does not necessarily refer to apostate believers. The more immediate reference may be to Judas, who, though one of the Twelve, did not remain with Jesus (note esp. the close verbal parallel between 15:3 and 13:10–11). But what does "remain in Jesus" mean?

Initially, "remaining with Jesus" simply meant for Jesus' first followers to spend the night in Jesus' apartment (1:38–39). But already in 6:56, Jesus uses this term with a strongly spiritual connotation: "Whoever eats my flesh and drinks my blood remains in me, and I in him." Thus "remaining 'in' Jesus" (see our discussion of "in" terminology above) entails appropriating his sacrifice at the cross and living in existential identification with him. A new dimension of "remaining in Jesus" is added by the reference in 8:31: "If you hold to my teaching [lit. "remain in my word"], you are really my disciples." "Remaining in Jesus" thus also involves holding to his teaching and "remaining in his word." Another aspect of "remaining in Jesus" comes to the fore in Jesus' promise to his disciples that the Spirit will "remain" (that is, take up residence) in them (14:17; cf. 14:10: "the Father remaining in me does his works"). "Remaining in Jesus" is synonymous with being indwelt with the Spirit and producing corresponding spiritual fruit.

Strikingly, the vast majority of theologically significant instances of the term "remain" (Grk. *menō*) occur in chapters 14 and 15, with ten references in 15:4–10 alone. The disciples are to remain in Jesus; in particular, they are to remain *in his love* by obeying his commandments (15:9–10; love continues to be the major theme in vv. 11–17). The vine metaphor thus becomes an illustration of the close-knit, organic relationship Jesus desired with his disciples. This is expressed here even more profoundly than in the related shepherd/sheep metaphor in chapter 10. Jesus' "sheep" hear his voice and follow him; through the Spirit, and sustained by obedience to his commandments, Jesus' followers are to draw their life blood from their exalted Lord just as branches draw their vitality from the vine. This may seem unremarkable to those of us who have practiced and experienced this kind of lifestyle for years. For the disciples, at this stage of salvation history, Jesus' words were, perhaps cryptic, but certainly of vital importance.

The World's Hatred (15:18–16:4a)

Just as Jesus' "new commandment" for his disciples to love one another dominated the end of the previous section (15:9–17, elaborating on 13:34–35), the world's hatred of the disciples provides the dark backdrop to Jesus' words in the present unit. Instruction on the world's hatred of the disciples is necessary, for during Jesus' earthly ministry it was he, not his followers, who bore the major brunt of the world's (including "the Jews'") persecution. But once Jesus has been removed from the scene, the world's hatred will inevitably turn toward them. James of Zebedee, John's brother, would be martyred by Herod Agrippa I in A.D. 42, and Peter almost followed suit. Their close identification with Jesus will mean that people's response toward them will mirror their response toward Jesus: "If they persecuted me, they will persecute you also. If they obeyed my teaching, they will obey yours also" (v. 20). People's response to Jesus, in turn, mirrors people's response to God: "He who hates me hates my Father as well" (v. 23). Thus it is impossible for anyone to claim he loves while hating Jesus or his followers.

Moreover, Jesus stresses that people persisted in their unbelief despite overwhelming evidence: "If I had not done among them what no one else did, they would not be guilty of sin. But now they have seen these miracles, and yet they have hated both me and my Father" (v. 24). Thus it is clear that at the root of people's unbelief is not lack of information but sinful rebellion against God. Nevertheless, despite people's certain opposition, the disciples must testify to what they have seen and heard (v. 27). As John writes in his first epistle,

That which was from the beginning,
  which we have heard,
  which we have seen with our eyes,
  which we have looked at
  and our hands have touched —
this we proclaim concerning the Word
  of life.
The life appeared;
  we have seen it and testify to it,
  and we proclaim to you the eternal
  life,
  which was with the Father
  and has appeared to us.
We proclaim to you
  what we have seen and heard,
  so that you also may have fellowship with us.
  And our fellowship is with the Father
  and with his Son, Jesus Christ (1 Jn
  1:1–3).

Notably, Jesus' words in the present passage are addressed primarily to the Eleven, the future *leaders* of the Christian movement. As Peter and John replied when the Jewish Sanhedrin tried to intimidate them and keep them from witnessing, "Judge for yourselves whether it is right in God's sight to obey you rather than God. For we cannot help speaking about what we have seen and heard" (Acts 4:20). Does that "holy compulsion" characterize your and my attitude toward the world? Are we like Paul who exclaimed, "Woe to me if I don't preach the gospel" (1 Cor 9:16)? To be sure, "everyone who wants to live a godly life in Christ Jesus will be persecuted" (2 Tim 3:12), but that does not absolve Christians from their responsibility to witness to the

truth they have come to know and experience. This is the truth to which the apostle Peter solemnly testified in his first epistle (cf. esp. 1 Pt 2:13–3:22).

The most stirring assessment of the role of apostle in the early church may come from the apostle Paul who wrote to the Corinthians,

For it seems to me that God has put us apostles on display at the end of the procession, like men condemned to die in the arena. We have been made a spectacle to the whole universe, to angels as well as to men. We are fools for Christ, but you are so wise in Christ! We are weak, but you are strong! You are honored, we are dishonored! To this very hour we go hungry and thirsty, we are in rags, we are brutally treated, we are homeless. We work hard with our own hands. When we are cursed, we bless; when we are persecuted, we endure it; when we are slandered, we answer kindly. Up to this moment we have become the scum of the earth, the refuse of the world (1 Cor 4:9–13).

What in the case of the blind man in chapter 9 was still a local phenomenon (cf. v. 22), and what kept some in Jesus' day from openly confessing their faith (12:42), would soon be the norm: "they will put you out of the synagogue" (16:2). In fact, people will try to kill Christians on account of their faith. This is not the time for dreaming of being carried to heaven on "flowery beds of ease"; as throughout his ministry, Jesus is perfectly clear about the cost of following him. The history of the early church furnishes abundant proof of the accuracy of Jesus' predictions. This is clear from both biblical (the Book of Acts, the New Testament Epistles, and Revelation 2–3) and extrabiblical sources. Consider this report about unspeakable suffering inflicted on early believers, provided by a Roman historian who himself was hostile to the Christian faith:

But all human efforts, all the lavish gifts of the emperor, and the propitiations of the gods did not banish the sinister belief that the conflagration [the fire of Rome in A.D. 64] was the result of an order. Consequently, to get rid of the report, Nero fastened the guilt and inflicted the most exquisite tortures on a class hated for their abominations, called Christians by the populace. Christus, from whom the name had its origin, suffered the extreme penalty during the reign of Tiberius at the hands of one of our procurators, Pontius Pilatus, and a most mischievous superstition thus checked for the moment, again broke out not only in Judaea, the first source of the evil, but even in Rome, where all things hideous and shameful from every part of the world find their centre and become popular.

Accordingly, an arrest was first made of all who pleaded guilty; then, upon their information, an immense multitude was convicted, not so much of the crime of firing the city, as of hatred against mankind. Mockery of every sort was added to their deaths. Covered with the skins of beasts, they were torn by dogs and perished, or were nailed to crosses, or were doomed to the flames and burnt, to serve as a nightly illumination when daylight had expired. Nero offered his gardens for the spectacle, and was exhibiting a show in the circus, while he mingled with the people in the dress of a charioteer or stood aloft on a car. Hence, even for criminals who deserve extreme and exemplary punishment, there arose a feeling of compassion; for it was not, as it seemed, for the public good, but to glut one man's cruelty, that they were being destroyed.[9]

Many of our Christian brothers and sisters in other parts of the world suffer persecution today. In our own country, suffering for the faith is still not so overt as to be an issue of primary concern. Still, we may sometimes wonder if the reason why Christians in the United States do not suffer more is because they do not clearly and openly identify with Christ. Evangelical Christianity has developed into an almost self-contained, self-sustaining subculture, complete with Christian bookstores, TV and radio stations,

---

"Trust in God; Trust Also in Me"? (Jn 14:1b)

The Greek word for "trust" used twice in John 14:1b can be either an indicative ("You trust") or an imperative ("trust!"). We are thus left with four possible renderings of this phrase:

1. "You trust in God; you trust also in me" (two indicatives)
2. "You trust in God; trust also in me" (indicative/imperative)
3. "Trust in God; you trust also in me" (imperative/indicative)
4. "Trust in God; trust also in me" (two imperatives)

Reading #1 can immediately be ruled out because of the preceding context where Jesus exhorts his disciples not to let their hearts be troubled (14:1a), with the implication that they were indeed anxious (as the present imperative form of the word for "do not let be troubled," *tarassesthō*, makes clear). Thus what follows must clearly be a command to trust. For this reason reading #3 likewise makes no sense.

Which leaves us with readings ##2 and 4. Is Jesus saying "You trust in God; trust also in me," or, "Trust in God; trust also in me"? Both statements exhort Jesus' disciples to trust in him. The question is simply whether Jesus also exhorts them to trust in God or whether he invokes their existing trust in God to exhort them equally to trust in him. The decision of the NIV seems entirely sensible here: reading #4 is put in the text as the most probable ("Trust in God; trust also in me"), while a footnote indicates the possibility of reading #2: "You trust in God; trust also in me."

Jesus, then, is issuing a double command to his disciples. "Trust in God," he says. "And trust also in me." Just as they now can pray, not only to God, but also to Jesus (14:13–14; 16:23–24), and just as it is not only the Father who loves them, but also Jesus (14:21, 23; 16:26–27), they are enjoined to trust in both God and Jesus at the same time. For to trust in God means to trust in Jesus. The same is true for us today.

Christian celebrities, be it pastors of mega-churches or best-selling authors, and the list could go on and on. Just look a recent issue of *Christianity Today!* Or look at the *Shepherd's Guide*, a listing of Christians in business. Many Christians live in a co-coon that enables them to go through life almost completely insulated, without ever having to deal with non-Christians. Yet as a result, we frequently fail to fulfill the function of salt and light in our culture (cf. Mt 5:13–16). We must remember Jesus' warning that salt, once it has lost its saltiness, is no longer good for anything, except to be thrown out and trampled by men (Mt 5:13).

In our highly pluralistic, postmodern culture, it will be increasingly unpopular to proclaim the biblical message that "there is no other name under heaven given to men by which we must be saved" but Jesus (the message of Peter and John in Acts 4:12). We will be labeled as intolerant, mocked as narrow-minded religious bigots, or even suffer social or economic ostracism. Are we willing to suffer socially, economically, or otherwise for our faith? This does not mean that we must invite suffering like the church father Polycarp, bishop of Smyrna, who deterred his friends from rescuing him from martyrdom in order to increase his heavenly reward. But we must be faithful and courageous and have our priorities straight. As Jesus said, "You cannot serve both God and Money" (Mt 6:24). Our Christian faith must be the core commitment at the center of our lives rather than

an addendum. Like Abel, we must give God our very best rather than bring a token offering like Cain (Hb 11:4). If this involves a decisive break with our past, so be it.

We conclude with this stirring testimony by the apostle Paul: "But whatever was to my profit I now consider loss for the sake of Christ. What is more, I consider everything a loss compared to the surpassing greatness of knowing Christ Jesus my Lord, for whose sake I have lost all things. I consider them rubbish, that I may gain Christ and be found in him" (Phil 3:7–9a).

The End Result of Jesus' Departure for His Disciples: Greater Joy (16:17–33)

Jesus' statement at the end of his instructions about the Holy Spirit provides the point of departure for the closing section of the farewell discourse: "In a little while you will see me no more, and then after a little while you will see me" (16:16). This is not the first time people are portrayed in John's Gospel as puzzled by a reference to Jesus' departure. Compare 7:33–36: "Jesus said, 'I am with you for only a short time, and then I go to the one who sent me. You will look for me, but you will not find me; and where I am, you cannot come.' The Jews said to one another, 'Where does this man intend to go that we cannot find him? Will he go where our people live scattered among the Greeks, and teach the Greeks? What did he mean when he said, 'You will look for me, but you will not find me,' and 'Where I am, you cannot come'?" Or note Jesus' words to his followers at the outset of the farewell discourse, "My children, I will be with you only a little longer. You will look for me, and just as I told the Jews, so I tell you now: Where I am going, you cannot come" (13:33), a comment that ensued in Peter's question and Jesus' prediction of this disciple's denials.

Study Questions

1. What are some of the advantages of Jesus' departure for his followers?

2. What is the most plausible English rendering of the term *paraklētos*, and why?

3. What are the roles of the Spirit in believers' lives and in the world according to John 14–16?

4. What is the background and import of John's "in" terminology?

Jesus' consciousness that the days of his earthly ministry were limited surfaces repeatedly in John's Gospel, including in 9:4–5 ("As long as it is day, we must do the work of him who sent me. Night is coming, when no one can work. While I am in the world, I am the light of the world") and 12:35–36 ("You are going to have the light just a little while longer. Walk while you have the light, before darkness overtakes you. . . . Put your trust in the light while you have it, so that you may become sons of light"). By this John seeks to stress the importance of people making a decision regarding Jesus while it is still time. This sense of urgency must be conveyed today just as it was expressed by the fourth evangelist in his day. For no one knows the day or the hour of his death, and then it will be too late to make a decision regarding Christ. Moreover, not making a decision is a decision as well. As John makes clear, the human condition is not one of neutrality; we are sinful and the objects of God's wrath (3:36).

The regularity with which people fail to understand Jesus' references to his imminent departure underscores human inability to comprehend spiritual truth. As Jesus tells Nicodemus, "I have spoken to you of earthly things and you do not believe; how then will you believe if I speak of heavenly things?" (3:12). But as John makes clear, the disciples are no better: even they understand only subsequent to Jesus' resurrection (cf. 2:22; 12:16). At pres-

ent, Jesus prepares his followers for the period of mourning at the occasion of his crucifixion, which will be followed by rejoicing shortly thereafter at his resurrection. Jesus likens these emotional states to a woman's experience in childbirth. Prior to the birth, the pain is intense and real; but as soon as the birth has taken place, all pain is forgotten for joy that a child has been brought into the world. Once again, Jesus seeks to encourage his followers and to build their faith. Rather than being preoccupied with his own imminent painful suffering, our Lord is primarily concerned with the trauma his death will temporarily cause his disciples. They should be encouraged that their time of mourning will be comparatively brief and that it will be followed by a period of great rejoicing. The author of Hebrews speaks to this issue when he writes, "Let us fix our eyes on Jesus, the author and perfecter of our faith, who *for the joy set before* him endured the cross" (Hb 12:2).

His disciples finally appear to understand, maintaining, "Now you are speaking clearly and without figures of speech. Now we can see that you know all things and that you do not even need to have anyone ask you questions. This makes us believe that you came from God" (16:29–30). But Jesus' response is telling: "You believe at last? A time is coming when you will be scattered, each to his own home. You will leave me all alone" (16:31–32). Jesus died alone, bearing our sins on the cross. This illustrates the gap that forever exists between the Savior and the beneficiaries of his redemptive work. And with this, Jesus' farewell discourse concludes, ending with some final words of encouragement: "I have told you these things, so that in me you may have peace. In this world you will have trouble. But take heart! I have overcome the world" (16:33).

Key Word

replacement theology

13 Jesus' Farewell (Part 3)

John 17

Then I heard the voice of the Lord saying,
"Whom shall I send? And who will go for
us?" And I said, "Here I am. Send me!"

—Isaiah 6:8

**Supplemental Reading: John 6:11;
11:41–42; 12:27–28; Matthew 11:25–26;
Luke 22:42; 23:34**

Outline

- **Jesus' Parting Prayer (ch. 17)**
  Jesus Prays for Himself (17:1–5)
  Jesus Prays for His Followers (17:6–19)
  Jesus Prays for Later Believers
    (17:20–26)

Objectives

**After reading this chapter, you should
be able to**

1. List the characteristics of Jesus as the
   Sent Son presented in John's Gospel.
2. Name Jesus' major concerns for his
   disciples.
3. Show the relationship between Jesus'
   prayer in chapter 17 and the rest of
   John's Gospel.

Jesus' Parting Prayer (ch. 17)

Like the material in chapters 14 through 16 (the farewell discourse), Jesus' prayer in chapter 17 is unique to John's Gospel. It is by far the longest prayer of Jesus recorded in any Gospel and comes at a strategic point in Jesus' ministry, sandwiched between his final instructions to his closest followers and his passion. Jesus' "high-priestly prayer," as it is sometimes called, affords us a rare glimpse into Jesus' consciousness and perspective on his imminent suffering. Once the prayer is ended, the final events of Jesus' earthly life ensue in rapid succession: the arrest (18:1–11); the Jewish and Roman trials (18:12–19:16); the crucifixion (19:17–37); the burial (19:38–42); the empty tomb and Jesus' resurrection appearances (chs. 20–21). But for one last time, Jesus pauses to take inventory of his earthly ministry, giving his final account to the Father and, by praying, expressing his complete dependence on the Father even in this crucial hour.

Jesus Prays for Himself (17:1–5)

We cannot be certain about the exact circumstances or even location of Jesus' prayer. Immediately before the prayer, Jesus is instructing his disciples. Immediately after the prayer, Jesus is leaving with his followers to cross the Kidron Valley. It is therefore a reasonable assumption that Jesus uttered the prayer recorded in the present chapter within the hearing of at least some of his disciples. Yet the focus of John's account of Jesus' prayer is on Jesus alone. He lifts his eyes toward heaven, the

customary attitude in prayer (11:41; cf. Mk 7:34; Mt 18:13; Ps 123:1), and prays, first for himself, then for his disciples, and finally for those who would come to faith through his disciples' testimony.

Jesus' address for God is simply "Father" (v. 1). This is even more intimate than the address used in the so-called Lord's Prayer, "Our Father in heaven" (Mt 6:9). Even the infamous Jesus Seminar, notorious for its skepticism regarding the authenticity of the Gospel materials, acknowledges that Jesus did in fact address God as his Father. "The time has come" (v. 1): John has used the expression "the time" (or "hour") of Jesus as a dramatic device throughout his Gospel ("not yet come": 2:4; 7:30; 8:20; "has come": 12:23; 13:1), building toward the climax of the "glorification of the Son," John's shorthand for the cluster of events comprising Jesus' crucifixion, burial, resurrection, ascension, and exaltation with God the Father.

"Glorify your Son, that your Son may glorify you" (v. 1). Jesus here commits his imminent death into God's hands (cf. 12:23–24, 32–33). Jesus' supreme concern is that this death glorify God (cf. 12:28; 21:19). He does not ask God to "save him from this hour" (12:27) but to sustain him through this trying experience so that glory be accrued to God. Years later, the apostle Peter, in meditation on the portrayal of the Suffering Servant in Isaiah 53, was able to hold up Jesus as an example in his suffering (1 Pt 2:21–24):

> To this you were called, because Christ suffered for you, leaving you an example, that you should follow in his steps.
>
> "He committed no sin, and no deceit was found in his mouth" (Is 53:9).
>
> When they hurled their insults at him, he did not retaliate; when he suffered, he made no threats. Instead, he entrusted himself to him who judges justly. He himself bore our sins in his body on the tree, so that we might die to sins and live for righteousness; by his wounds you have been healed (Is 53:5).

John's account makes clear how Jesus was able to meet his hour of death with

Table 13.1

How Jesus Addresses God in Prayer (Jn 17)

"Father"	17:1, 5, 21, 24
"Holy Father"	17:11
"Righteous Father"	17:25

such a remarkable attitude: he was given strength and perspective through times of extended prayer to God.

In the context of John's Gospel, Jesus' final prayer in chapter 17 culminates the evangelist's portrayal of Jesus as the obedient, dependent Son of the Father. This aspect of Jesus' earthly ministry is an integral part of Jesus' ability to accomplish his mission. Importantly, as the obedient, dependent Son of the Father, Jesus is presented as the model for the mission of his followers. This comes to the fore in the present prayer (17:18) and climaxes in the commissioning narrative toward the end of John's Gospel (20:21). I have elsewhere explored this crucial intersection of motifs in greater detail.[1] Here we may simply summarize John's teaching regarding Jesus as the sent Son as follows. The sent one is to:

1. bring glory and honor to the sender (5:23; 7:18);
2. do the sender's will (4:34; 5:30, 38; 6:38–39) and works (5:36; 9:4);
3. speak the sender's words (3:34; 7:16; 12:49; 14:10b, 24);
4. be accountable to the sender (ch. 17);
5. bear witness to the sender (5:36; 7:28 = 8:26);
6. represent the sender accurately (12:44–45; 13:20; 15:18–25);
7. exercise delegated authority (5:21–22, 27; 13:3; 17:2; 20:23);
8. know the sender intimately (7:29; cf. 15:21; 17:8, 25);
9. live in a close relationship with the sender (8:16, 18, 29; 16:32);
10. follow the sender's example (13:16).

In all these things, Jesus the sent Son serves as the example. Believers, as his representatives, are to walk in his footsteps (17:18; 20:21).

"For you granted him authority over all people that he might give eternal life to all those you have given him" (v. 2). Three interrelated aspects of this statement require comment: (1) the authority given to Jesus; (2) the bestowal of eternal life; and (3) that Jesus gives this life to those God has given to him. Concerning Jesus' authority, John has already noted that God has entrusted to him the authority to judge (5:27). Also, Jesus has the

authority to lay down his life and to take it up again (10:18). Matthew makes clear that all authority in heaven and on earth has been given to Jesus (Mt 28:18). Jesus, the Son of Man who is about to be glorified and thus fulfill his earthly mission, here anticipates his exalted, authoritative position subsequent to his crucifixion and resurrection. This authority enables him to bestow eternal life on all those God has given to him.

The phrase "eternal life," while found in the Synoptics (Mk 10:17 = Mt 19:16 = Lk 18:18; Mk 10:30 = Mt 19:29 = Lk 18:30; Mt 25:46; Lk 10:25), is a trademark of John's Gospel, functioning as the Johannine equivalent to the Synoptic motif of the "kingdom of God" (see ch. 3 above). The expression pervades chapters 3 through 12 (3:15, 16, 36; 4:14, 36; 5:24, 39; 6:27, 40, 47, 54, 68; 10:28; 12:25, 50) and culminates in the present chapter (17:2, 3). The following simple affirmation that believing in Jesus is the only prerequisite for receiving the gift of eternal life runs throughout the entire Gospel: "Whoever believes in the Son has eternal life, but whoever rejects the Son will not see life, for God's wrath remains on him" (3:36); "I tell you the truth, he who believes has everlasting life" (6:47). Only Jesus has "words of eternal life" (6:68), and the essence of eternal life is to know the only true God and Jesus Christ whom he has sent (17:3).

As John emphasizes, the possession of eternal life is not relegated to some time subsequent to death; people can have eternal life already in the here and now: "I tell you the truth, whoever hears my word and believes him who sent me *has eternal life* and will not be condemned; he *has crossed over from death to life*" (5:24). In this emphasis on the present possession of eternal life (his "inaugurated eschatology"), John differs from the perspective conveyed by the Synoptics who, in keeping with the Jewish attitude prevalent at the time of Christ, view eternal life primarily as a possession to be attained in "the age to come." But in John, the distinction between "the present age" and "the age to come" is collapsed; with Jesus, eternity has entered into human existence already in the here and now.[2] This realization is rooted in the knowledge that

God is life itself, and that Jesus is the Son of God (cf. 1:4; 5:26; 20:31).

But Jesus has authority to bestow eternal life only on those the Father has given him. This underscores once again the subordination of the Son to the Father: "the Father is greater than I" (14:28—see sidebar, p. 160). As the Son, Jesus voluntarily submits to the Father. The doctrine of the eternal subordination of the Son has recently come under attack by some who seek to limit the Son's subordination to his temporary earthly state of existence. These proponents affirm that the three persons of the Trinity are eternally equal, not merely in personhood, but also in role. The major driving force behind this challenge of the traditional viewpoint of the eternal subordination of the Son appears to be frequently the contemporary notion of egalitarian role relationships between men and women. For Jesus' voluntary submission to the Father has traditionally been cited as the perfect paradigm for complementarian male-female relationships in that it combines the notion of equality in personhood with differences in role.[3]

However, it must be maintained that the eternal subordination of the Son is clearly taught in Scripture. As Paul writes, "When he has done this [that is, destroyed the last enemy], then *the Son himself will be made subject to him who put everything under him*, so that God may be all in all" (1 Cor 15:28). Moreover, "the head of every man is Christ, and the head of the woman is man, and *the head of Christ is God*" (1 Cor 11:3). This passage also makes clear that Christ functions as example both for the husband's authority and the woman's submission in his exercise of authority over the man ("the head of every man is Christ") and his submission to God ("the head of Christ is God"). Thus John and Paul concur in teaching the eternal subordination of the Son to the Father, a notion that pervades Jesus' final prayer in John 17. Jesus is the Father's agent, as in creation, so also in redemption; he gives eternal life to all those the Father has given him.

"Now this is eternal life: that they may know you, the only true God, and Jesus Christ, whom you have sent" (v. 3). "To know" God does not merely refer to cognitive knowledge; it involves a personal

relationship. This is in keeping with the Hebrew use of the term "to know," which encompasses even the most intimate human relationship, sexual intercourse. Thus Genesis 4:1 tells us that Adam "knew" (LXX: *ginōskō*) his wife Eve, and she became pregnant and gave birth to her son. Likewise, knowing God means entering into a growing personal relationship with him through Jesus Christ. God is the "only true God"; this is affirmed supremely in the Hebrew *Shema:* "Hear, O Israel: The LORD our God, the LORD is one" (Deut 6:4). ". . . and Jesus Christ whom you sent": Jesus, in turn, is the exclusive agent, the sole authorized representative of this one true God. He is the God-sent Messiah (Hebrew term), God's Anointed One, the Christ (Greek term). Just as there is only one true God, there is only one way to the Father. This way is Jesus Christ (here and in 1:17; this reveals hindsight: "Christ" has now become Jesus' last name).

"I have brought you glory on earth by finishing the work you gave me to do" (v. 4). Jesus is ready to die; he has completed the work God gave him to do. In his classic *Tyranny of the Urgent*, Charles E. Hummel comments on this verse as follows:

> How could Jesus use the word "finished"? His three-year ministry seemed all too short. A prostitute at Simon's banquet had found forgiveness and a new life, but many others still walked the street without forgiveness and a new life. For every ten withered muscles that had flexed into health, a hundred remained impotent. Yet on that last night, with many useful tasks undone and urgent human needs unmet, the Lord had peace; He knew He had finished God's work . . .
>
> We may wonder why our Lord's ministry was so short, why it could not have lasted another five or ten years, why so many wretched sufferers were left in their misery. Scripture gives no answer to these questions, and we leave them in the mystery of God's purposes. But we do know that Jesus' prayerful waiting for God's instructions freed Him from the tyranny of the urgent. It gave Him a sense of direction, set a steady pace, and enabled Him to do every task *God* assigned. And on the

Revealer

last night He could say, "I have finished the work which thou gavest me to do."[4]

In the framework of John's Gospel, Jesus' report to the Father that he has completed the work he has given him to do in 17:4 mirrors the statement at the beginning of Jesus' ministry recorded in 4:34 where Jesus tells his disciples, "My food is to do the will of him who sent me and to finish his work." In context, Jesus made clear that meeting people's spiritual needs (in that case, the Samaritan woman's) was more important to him even than eating. An anecdote recounted in Mark's Gospel confirms this: "Then Jesus entered a house, and again a crowd gathered, so that he and his disciples were not even able to eat. When his family heard about this, they went to take charge of him, for they said, 'He is out of his mind'" (Mk 3:20–21). We, too, must be prepared to forego material conveniences for the sake of meeting the spiritual needs of others.

At the same time, Jesus was resolved to "finish his work" and to "complete *the work you have given me to do.*" This, too, constitutes the major challenge for each one of us: determining which are the tasks God has called us to perform, and then performing them. Paul confirms this, when he writes that "we are God's workmanship, created in Christ Jesus to do good works, *which God prepared in advance for us to do*" (Eph 2:10). In Jesus' case, the work God gave him to do centered on the cross (e.g., 12:23–24). When Jesus utters his final prayer, the cross still lies before him. But by faith, he already considers even the cross-work to have been accomplished. The agonizing hours of Jesus' arrest, trials, and events surrounding the crucifixion still await our Lord. But soon he will be able to utter his last word from the cross: "It is finished" (19:30).

"And now, Father, glorify me in your presence with the glory I had with you before the world began" (v. 5). This verse alludes to Jesus' preexistence prior to the incarnation, a reality already expressed in John's Prologue and reaffirmed throughout the Gospel in passages such as Jesus' statement to the Jews, "Before Abraham was, I am" (8:58). Of all the Gospels, John's most clearly affirms the preexistence of Jesus Christ. In the present passage, Jesus looks beyond his imminent suffering at the cross to the glory awaiting him in the Father's presence. In this, too, he becomes an example worth emulating. For we, too, must look past any trials in this world to the eternal glory prepared for us in heaven in the Father's presence. Yet there remains an important difference: we have not yet seen what lies ahead for us; Christ had been in God's glorious, eternal presence and chosen to take on human flesh for the purpose of redemption. When he prayed his final prayer, he knew exactly what awaited him.

Jesus Prays for His Followers (17:6–19)

Jesus describes his ministry to his disciples in terms of revealing God's name to them. This echoes the affirmation in the Prologue that Jesus "narrated" (i.e., explained) the Father. The fact that John can subsume Jesus' entire ministry under the category of revelation has caused some to postulate that John knows Jesus exclusively as the **Revealer** in keeping with the Gnostic revealer myth. According to this myth, the Revealer comes to earth in order to impart to human beings the knowledge that they have a divine spark within them. This knowledge in effect amounts to salvation.

However, it is unlikely that John's portrait of Jesus is indebted to Gnosticism, for at least two reasons: first, the "revealer myth" described above almost certainly did not arise until the second century A.D., thus postdating John's Gospel; and second, John demonstrably does not teach, as Gnosticism did, that knowledge is salvation; rather, he presents Jesus not merely as the Revealer but also as the Redeemer. Jesus is the Lamb of God who takes away the sin of the world (1:29, 36); the Savior of the World (4:42); the Bread of Life who gives his flesh and blood for the life of the world (6:51); the Good Shepherd who gives his life for the sheep (10:15, 17–18).

All of these images express one great truth: that Jesus made substitutionary atonement for sin, dying as a vicarious sacrifice for the forgiveness of sins and the salvation of sinners. The dichotomy "revelation or redemption" is therefore a false one; as John's Gospel makes clear,

171

Jesus provided both. Moreover, these two aspects of Jesus' work are shown in John to be intertwined. For at the cross where Jesus provided redemption God's love for mankind is revealed (3:16). Thus according to John, revelation itself (and knowledge thereof) is not redemption, but redemption is also the revelation of God's love. Consequently, John is not a proto-Gnostic; instead, later Gnosticism distorts the message of John's Gospel.[5]

What is Jesus' report to the Father regarding his disciples? Consider the following list from verses 6–9:

they obeyed the Father's word (v. 6);

they know that everything the Father has given Jesus comes from him (v. 7);

they have accepted the words the Father has given Jesus (v. 8);

they believed that the Father has sent Jesus (v. 9).

In the above list, the first characteristic parallels the third, while the second is analogous to the fourth. Thus it is possible to reduce the results of Jesus' mission to two: (1) imparting the conviction that Jesus is the Sent One from the Father; and (2) engendering acceptance of and obedience to God's word as proclaimed by Jesus.

What, then, does Jesus pray for his followers? In light of his imminent departure, his key concern is for God's protection of them while they are still in the world (v. 11). While Jesus was with them, he protected them. None has been lost except Judas; and he was lost only so that

Scripture would be fulfilled (v. 12). Jesus' prayer is not for God to take his followers *out of* the world but to protect them as long as they are in the world, particularly from the evil one (vv. 14–15). How will this protection be realized? Jesus' prayer focuses on two aspects of God's work: believers' unity (v. 11; cf. vv. 21–23) and their sanctification in the truth, which is God's Word (v. 17).

Jesus Prays for Later Believers (17:20–26)

Jesus' vision transcends the present; his reach goes beyond his immediate followers to those who will believe through their message (v. 20). Again, his prayer is for their unity. For it is Jesus' desire that through the unity of his followers the world may come to realize that the Father sent him. Look how Jesus' desire for the unity of his followers pervades this entire section and how their unity is to be rooted in Jesus' own unity with the Father:

> I pray . . . that all of them may be one,
> Father,
> just as you are in me and I am in you.
> May they also be in us
> so that the world may believe that
> you have sent me.
> I have given them the glory that you
> gave me,
> that they may be one as we are one:
> I in them and you in me.
> May they be brought to complete unity
> to let the world know that you sent
> me and have loved them
> even as you have loved me.

Unity (together with love) constitutes an essential prerequisite for evangelism.[6] Outreach to unbelievers is rooted in the community of believers as a whole rather than being the isolated enterprise of individuals who have the gift of evangelism. This realization has come to the fore once again in the present postmodern climate, which accentuates the subjective nature of knowledge and truth. In such an atmosphere, it is very difficult to reason someone into the kingdom by mere rational argument. Rather, the unbeliever must first be brought into the community of believers where he or she can experience unified and loving relationships among Christians. This experience, in

Study Questions

1. How is the subordination of the Son to the Father evident in John 17?

2. What are Jesus' primary prayer concerns for his disciples?

3. Explain the relationship among the following: Jesus relationship with the Father; believers' relationships with one another; and their mission to the world.

turn, will prepare the unbeliever to hear the gospel message.

Jesus has one more request: he wants his followers to see the preexistent glory the Father has given him (v. 25). This echoes his words to the disciples that he is going to prepare a place for them (14:1–4). As he concludes his prayer, Jesus reiterates his conviction that his disciples have truly come to know the Father in him (v. 26). With this assurance, the Johannine Jesus is prepared to die. For he has ensured that subsequent to his departure there remains a circle of his followers who are able to proclaim the true knowledge of God to yet others. As chapters 13 through 17 make clear, focusing the major part of his three years of public ministry on the training of the Twelve has been the centerpiece of his mission.[7] Now his death and resurrection will give them the message they must proclaim to the world.

Key Word

Revealer myth

14 The Passion, Resurrection, and Commissioning

John 18–20

"The Jews insisted, 'We have a law, and according to that law he must die, because he claimed to be the Son of God.'"

—John 19:7

Supplemental Reading: Mark 14:43–15:47

Outline

- **The Betrayal and Arrest of Jesus (18:1–11)**
- **Jesus Questioned by the High Priest, Denied by Peter (18:12–27)**
- **Jesus before Pilate (18:28–19:16a)**
- **Jesus' Crucifixion and Burial (19:16b–41)**
- **Jesus' Resurrection and Appearances (ch. 20)**

Objectives

After reading this chapter, you should be able to

1. Narrate the sequence of events from Jesus' arrest to his burial.
2. Explain why, according to John 18–19, Jesus was crucified, illumining the political and religious dynamics at work for both Jews and Romans.
3. Describe the perspective from which John chooses to narrate the final events of Jesus' life.

After his high priestly prayer, Jesus crossed the Kidron Valley with his disciples on his way to the Garden of Gethsemane.

The major theme of John's Passion narrative is the otherworldly kingship of Jesus (hence his policy of nonretaliation). The evangelist shows that the case against Jesus is groundless: three times Pilate repeats that he finds no basis for a charge against Jesus (18:38; 19:4, 6). Pilate is cast as a cowardly and superstitious political opportunist who is easily manipulated and intimidated by the Jewish leaders, while the Jews charge Jesus with blasphemy, contending they have no king but Caesar (19:15). Thus, ironically, Barabbas, the "son of the father," a convicted insurrectionist, is released rather than Jesus, the "Son of the Father," whom Pilate finds innocent of any criminal charges. But in the end all of this fulfills scriptural predictions regarding the Jewish Messiah (19:24, 28–29, 36–37).

The Betrayal and Arrest of Jesus (18:1–11)

A close reading of the Passion narrative reveals once again eyewitness testimony (cf. esp. 19:35). Only this Gospel

mentions the name of the servant whose ear was cut off as Malchus and identifies Simon Peter as the one who drew the sword (18:10); features the informal hearing before Annas, Caiaphas's father-in-law (18:12–14, 19–24); and provides the information that Nicodemus accompanied Joseph of Arimathea at the occasion of Jesus' burial (19:39).

In keeping with the introduction to the second half of John's Gospel (cf. 13:1, 3), Jesus' arrest is portrayed from the vantage point of God's sovereign plan: Jesus, "knowing all that was going to happen to him" (18:4), is shown to take the initiative throughout the entire arrest proceedings. "Who is it you want?" Jesus asks the motley crowd that has come with torches, lanterns, and weapons to arrest him (18:3–4). "Jesus of Nazareth," they reply, and when Jesus identifies himself, they draw back and fall to the ground as if struck by a theophany (an appearance of God; 18:6). Disdainfully, John (the evangelist) adds that Judas "the traitor" was standing there with them (i.e., Jesus' enemies).

The scene repeats itself, and Jesus all but encourages those who had come for his arrest to proceed (cf. 13:27) in order to protect his disciples. As the evangelist notes,

Table 14.1
Illegalities in Jesus' Trial Surfacing in John

1. Jewish trial:
   a. before Annas:
      The high priest questions Jesus about his disciples and his teaching (18:19): but first witnesses must be produced to establish an accused person's guilt.
      Jesus struck in the face (18:22): Jesus challenges his accusers to furnish actual testimony of wrongdoing (18:23).
   b. before Caiaphas:
      John provides *no details* here (cf. 18:24, 28), so no illegalities can be determined from his account alone.
2. Roman trial:
   c. before Pilate:
      no charges are brought against Jesus (18:29); the Jews merely call him a criminal they want to have executed (18:30–31); Pilate reiterates three times that he finds no basis for a charge against Jesus (18:37; 19:4, 6; similarly, Lk 23:4, 14, 22);
      no witnesses are ever produced;
      Jesus never actually stands trial;
      the verdict is clearly based on political expediency, not evidence.

this took place so that Jesus' words would be fulfilled: "I have not lost one of those you gave me" (18:8; cf. 6:39; 10:28–29; 17:12). Notably, it is once again Simon Peter who seeks to resist the will of God in bringing about Jesus' crucifixion by seeking to take things into his own hands (18:10–11; cf. Mt 16:22–23). Jesus counsels Peter to put his sword away; his methods are not those of the Zealots. Rather, Jesus is determined to "drink the cup *the Father* has given" him (18:11); he knows that God is in total control of events.

Jesus Questioned by the High Priest, Denied by Peter (18:12–27)

The present section oscillates between Jesus' informal hearing before Annas (18:12–14, 19–24) and Peter's denials of Jesus (18:15–18, 19–24). By providing an account of Jesus' appearance before Annas, John again fills an important gap, since the Synoptics do not record this event, focusing exclusively on the formal Jewish trial before Caiaphas. By way of background, Annas was deposed by the Romans in A.D. 15; his son-in-law Caiaphas held the high priesthood from A.D.

The Garden of Gethsemane, an olive grove, was one of Jesus' favorite meeting places with his disciples. Here Jesus was arrested after agonizing times of prayer.

177

Jesus often taught on the steps leading up to the temple.

18 to 36 ("the high priest that year" in v. 13 means "the high priest at that time").

Apparently, in deference to Annas's continuing power and stature, Jesus was first brought to him. The absence of witnesses suggests that this hearing was merely informal. When questioned about his disciples and his teaching, Jesus merely states that these were a matter of public record (18:20–21). At this, one of the bystanders strikes Jesus in the face; but Jesus is not intimidated: "If I said something wrong," he retorts, "testify as to what is wrong. But if I spoke the truth, why did you strike me?" (18:23; cf. 18:34). Thus the hearing before Annas remains entirely inconclusive, and Jesus is sent to Caiaphas.

Christian tradition identifies Herod's Antonia fortress with the Praetorium where Jesus was tried and sentenced to be crucified.

Peter, meanwhile, has denied his Lord three times, in keeping with Jesus' prediction (cf. 13:38). The "other disciple" who secures Peter access to the courtyard of the high priest is probably the apostle John (who also is the writer of this Gospel). This is suggested by the use of the designation "other disciple" with reference to the "disciple Jesus loved" (i.e., the apostle John; 13:23) in 20:1–9 (cf. esp. 20:2: "the other disciple, the one Jesus loved"). As in the Upper Room, the evangelist is shown to have superior access to Jesus (cf. 13:23–25).

While warming himself by a fire in that cold night, Peter denies three times that he is one of Jesus' disciples: to a slave girl

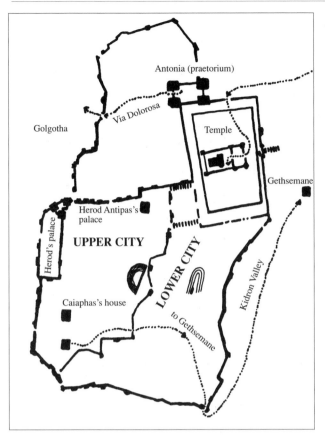

Map 14.1: Jerusalem at the Time of Jesus

Passover season (the whole festival of Passover and Unleavened Bread lasted seven days). The Jews present Jesus to Pilate as a common criminal they need executed. Since the Sanhedrin did not have authority to impose the death penalty, it needed the Romans to provide the legal sanctions. John again knows better: this happened so that Jesus' words regarding his manner of death (i.e., "lifting up," crucifixion) might be fulfilled (18:32).

Throughout the proceedings, Pilate displays the customary reluctance of Roman officials to get involved in internal Jewish religious affairs (cf. Acts 19:35–41; 23:23–26:32). The governor is therefore primarily interested in possible political ramifications. Although Jesus was presented to him by the Jews as a common criminal (without specifying charges, which shows that they were not interested in a fair Roman trial; 18:30), Pilate immediately addresses Jesus as a "king": "Are you the king of the Jews?" (18:33). Jesus responds with a counter–question: Is that Pilate's own idea or did others talk to him about Jesus? "Am I a Jew?" Pilate asks rhetorically, indicating his disinterest in Jewish religious matters. "What is it you have done?"

at the door (18:16–18); to a group standing with him at the fire (18:25); and to one of the high priest's servants, a relative of the man whose ear Peter had cut off (18:26–27). Mark notes that it was at that time that Peter remembered Jesus' prediction and broke down and wept (Mk 14:72); John does not deem it necessary to supply this information. He immediately moves on to Jesus' encounter with Pilate.

In 1961 a team of Italian archaeologists excavated in Caesarea the only known inscription bearing the name of Pontius Pilate from his lifetime.

Jesus before Pilate (18:28–19:16a)

By now it is early morning. Mark seems to indicate that the chief priests held a second meeting of the Sanhedrin to give their actions the appearance of legality (Mk 15:1). After this the Jews lead Jesus from Caiaphas to the palace of the Roman governor. Amazingly, while about to have their Messiah crucified, the Jews are scrupulously concerned about avoiding ceremonial uncleanness during

With this, Jesus points to the nonpolitical nature of his kingship (18:36). Pilate correctly infers that, whether of this world or not, Jesus still claims to be a king. Which Jesus concedes: "You are right in saying I am a king . . . I came into the world to testify to the truth. Everyone on the side of truth listens to me" (18:37). Does that include Pilate? Apparently not. For he merely shrugs off Jesus' remark with another rhetorical question: "What is truth?" (18:38), unaware that the one before him is himself the Truth (14:6). With this Pilate goes out to the Jews and reports that he finds no basis for a charge against Jesus. Hoping to gain Jesus' release by compromise, Pilate offers to set him free as part of the customary goodwill gesture of the governor's release of a prisoner at Passover. But the Jews prefer Barabbas (Aramaic: "son of the father").

Then Jesus is flogged (19:1). A crown of thorns is put on his head and a purple robe on his shoulders (19:2). The Roman soldiers ridicule Jesus for his alleged kingship, paying mock homage to him and striking him in the face (19:3). Once more Pilate maintains that he finds no charge against Jesus, presenting him to the people with the famous statement, "Here is the man!" (Latin: *ecce homo*; 19:5). But the chief priests call for Jesus' crucifixion (19:6). Pilate desperately seeks to avoid incurring guilt by condemning an innocent man, but the Jews are relentless: "We have a law, and according to that law he must die," they insist, "because he claimed to be the Son of God" (19:7; this may refer to Lv 24:16: "Anyone who blasphemes the name of the LORD must be put to death").

When Pilate therefore inquires of Jesus regarding his origin, Jesus gives no answer. It was he who had told his disciples not to give what is sacred to dogs nor to throw pearls before pigs (Mt 7:6). Pilate is puzzled by Jesus' refusal to seize the opportunity to extricate himself from the situation: "Don't you realize I have power either to free you or to crucify you?" (19:10). But Jesus merely replies that the Jews who handed him over to

---

Table 14.2

The Unfolding Drama of Jesus' Trial Before Pilate: Behind the Scenes and Before "the Jews"

Behind the Scenes	Before "the Jews"
	1. Pilate to the Jews: "What charges are you bringing against this man?" (18:29–32)
2. Pilate to Jesus: "Are you the king of the Jews?" (18:33–38a)	
	3. Pilate to the Jews: "I find no basis for a charge against him" (18:38b–40).
4. Pilate has Jesus flogged. The soldiers mock him: "Hail, King of the Jews!" (19:1–3)	
	5. Pilate to the Jews: "I find no basis for a charge against him." He brings Jesus out and says: "Here is the man!" But the Jews shout, "Crucify! Crucify!" (19:4–7).
6. Pilate to Jesus: "Where do you come from?" No answer. Pilate tries to set Jesus free but the Jews are adamant (19:8–12).	
	7. Pilate brings Jesus out, sits down on the bēma (judgment seat) and hands Jesus over to be crucified (19:13–16).

While probably not the actual site of Jesus' burial and resurrection, the Garden Tomb provides a plausible scenario for these events.

Pilate have greater guilt and that even Pilate would have no authority over him unless it had been given him from above (19:11).

Desperately torn between his own best judgment and his need to placate the Jews, Pilate still seeks for ways to release Jesus, but the Jews know how to bring him to his knees: "If you let this man go, you are no friend of Caesar [i.e., the Roman Emperor who had appointed him]. Anyone who claims to be a king opposes Caesar" (19:12). "Shall I crucify your king?" Pilate asks. To which the chief priests reply, in the ultimate betrayal of their religious heritage: "We have no king but Caesar" (19:15). And with this Pilate hands Jesus over to them to be crucified (19:16).

Jesus' Crucifixion and Burial (19:16b–41)

John's account of Jesus' crucifixion is somber and restrained. Jesus carried his own cross. He went to the Place of the Skull (called Golgotha in Aramaic; the Latin term is Calvary). He was crucified with two others, one on his left and the other on his right. Pilate had prepared a sign that read, in Greek, Latin, and Ara-

maic respectively, JESUS OF NAZARETH, THE KING OF THE JEWS. When the chief priests protested that this was only what Jesus *claimed* to be, not what he really was, Pilate let the wording of the sign stand. When Jesus was readied for crucifixion, the soldiers divided his clothes. But when they came to his seamless robe, they decided to cast lots for it, thus fulfilling Scripture (19:24; cf. Ps 22:8).

Near the cross stood a group of women, including Jesus' mother and Mary Magdalene. In Jesus' first of three words from the cross recorded by John, Jesus gave the "disciple he loved" charge of his mother, perhaps because his own brothers still did not believe in him (19:26–27). Later Jesus uttered the second word from the cross, "I am thirsty," in order that Scripture might be fulfilled (19:28; cf. Ps 69:21). He was given a sponge soaked in wine vinegar and drank from it. With this, he said, thirdly, "It is finished," bowed his head, and gave up his spirit (19:30). When the Roman soldiers came to take down the corpses and saw Jesus was already dead, they did not break his bones but merely pierced his side with a spear. This, too, fulfilled Scripture (Ps 34:20; Zec 12:10).

Thereafter, Joseph of Arimathea, a member of the Sanhedrin and secret disciple of Jesus, asked Pilate for Jesus' body in order to bury him. Accompanied by

Nicodemus, Joseph ensured that Jesus received a proper burial and laid him in a new garden tomb. According to Isaiah's prophecy, Jesus was "with the rich in his death" (Is 53:9).

Jesus' Resurrection and Appearances (ch. 20)

Chapter 20 opens on the third day after Jesus' crucifixion and burial, early "on the first day of the week" (i.e., Sunday). Mary Magdalene, one of Jesus' most committed female followers (cf. 19:25), went to the tomb when it was still dark and found that the stone had been removed from the entrance. She immediately reports this to Peter and John ("the other disciple, the one Jesus loved," v. 2), and the two men set out to the tomb without delay. John, presumably being the younger, outran Peter, but, out of deference to the head apostle, waited for Peter, who entered the tomb. He saw the strips of linen as well as the burial cloth that had been around Jesus' head. But curiously, the cloth was folded up by it-

When Mary Magdalene arrived at Jesus' tomb early Sunday morning, the large stone sealing it had already been removed.

self, separate from the linen. Then the other disciple (John) also went inside, saw, and believed (Peter's response is not recorded). Still, he did not understand from Scripture that Jesus had to rise from the dead.

One can sense the puzzlement and excitement that Jesus' followers felt at this point. After three dark days of discouragement and fear, there was a bright ray of hope. Jesus' body was no longer in the tomb—what had happened? Had someone removed the stone and stolen the body, as the Jews would later allege? But had not Roman guards been posted at the entrance of the tomb at the Jews' request? And if the body had in fact been stolen, where was it now? And who had stolen it, and why? Perhaps it was at that time that the disciples began to remember Jesus' prediction that he would see them again "in a little while" (16:17–22). True, they all had been scattered at the arrest (16:32); but now they had banded together again, united by their common experience with Jesus and the sense that Jesus' death may not be the end of the story. But where *was* Jesus' body?

Peter and John went back home, but Mary stayed at the tomb, standing outside

Table 14.3

Jesus' Resurrection Appearances to His Disciples in John's Gospel

1. "On the evening of that first day of the week"
   Focus: the commissioning
   20:19–23

2. "A week later"
   Focus: Thomas's unbelief
   20:26–29

3. "Afterward Jesus appeared again to his disciples"
   Focus: the reinstitution of Peter
   21:1–14 (21:14: "the third time")

crying. At this point, she spotted two angels in white, sitting in the tomb where Jesus' body had lain. Engaged in conversation with the angels, Mary suddenly turns and sees Jesus, without realizing that it was him. Jesus' question is the same as the angels': "Woman, why are you crying?" (v. 15; cf. v. 13). In a comical touch, Mary, mistaking Jesus for the gardener, presses him to tell her what he had done with Jesus' body if he had in fact taken it. One word from Jesus suffices to open Mary's eyes: "Mary" (v. 16). She exclaims "Rabbouni" (which means "teacher" in Aramaic) and embraces him. But Jesus tells her rather to go to his "brothers" about what she has seen. And this is what Mary does, proclaiming to the disciples the joyful news: "I have seen the Lord!" (v. 18).

The first person to see the risen Lord—a woman, and one with a checkered past at that (cf. Lk 8:2)? In an age and culture in which women were not considered legitimate legal witnesses, this is in fact highly significant. Some have elevated this instance as proof that the New Testament teaches an egalitarian model of male–female relationships in the church. While this seems precarious in light of explicit didactic passages such as 1 Timothy 2:11–15 later in the New Testament canon, it breaks down rigid traditionalism in the way men's and women's roles in the church are conceived. Women as well as men are called to bear witness to the Good

News they have received—this is the clear implication of Jesus' command issued to Mary Magdalene in the present passage.

Scene 2 starts in 20:19, "on the evening of that first day of the week." The disciples had huddled together behind locked doors out of fear for the Jews, when Jesus suddenly stood in their midst. After issuing the traditional Jewish greeting, "Peace" (*shalom*; v. 19), Jesus identified himself to his followers by showing them his nail-pierced hands and the wound in his side (v. 20), proceeding to issue his commission. Some, especially Peter, may initially have been apprehensive to see Jesus in light of their less-than-perfect performance surrounding Jesus' crucifixion. But joy prevails, and Jesus shows no sign of ill-will but rather attends to the business at hand (v. 20).

The first startling fact about the appearance of the risen Lord among his disciples is his ability to walk through closed doors. This indicates that resurrected bodies are no longer subject to the same limitations that apply to our present earthly bodies. At other occasions, Jesus is able to vanish from sight at an instant (Lk 24:31). His followers may mistake him for a ghost (Lk 24:39) or initially fail to recognize him (Lk 24:16; Jn 20:14; 21:4). But while Jesus' glorified body is able to walk through closed doors and to appear or disappear apparently at will, it is still the *glorified* body of the same Jesus who was crucified only a short time prior to his resurrection appearances. As Paul wrote,

> The body that is sown is perishable,
> it is raised imperishable;
> it is sown in dishonor,
> it is raised in glory;
> it is sown in weakness,
> it is raised in power;
> it is sown a natural body,
> it is raised a spiritual body
> (1 Cor 15:42b–44).

The apostle continues,

> For the perishable must clothe itself
> with the imperishable,
> and the mortal with immortality.
> When the perishable has been clothed
> with the imperishable,
> and the mortal with immortality,

then the saying that is written will come true:

"Death has been swallowed up in victory."

"Where, O death, is your victory?
Where, O death, is your sting?" . . .

But thanks be to God! He gives us the victory

through our Lord Jesus Christ
(1 Cor 15:53–57).

Theologically, Christ's resurrection cannot be separated from his crucifixion. For what the crucifixion accomplished, that is, Christ's substitutionary sacrifice for our sin, is sealed and accepted by God's raising Jesus from the dead. Christ's resurrection is also his divine vindication. At the same time, through the resurrection, Satan and the evil world powers behind Christ's crucifixion stand judged and condemned. Moreover, all those who are identified with Christ through faith, Jesus' first followers as well as those of us who have not seen and yet have believed, have, spiritually speaking, already shared in both Jesus' crucifixion and his resurrection.

This union, identification, and participation with Christ is given expression in Christian baptism. As Paul explains, "All of us who were baptized into Christ Jesus were baptized into his death. We were therefore buried with him through baptism into death in order that, just as Christ was raised from the dead through the glory of the Father, we too may live a new life" (Rom 6:4). Paul continues, "If we have been united with him like this in his death, we will certainly also be united with him in his resurrection" (Rom 6:5). The implication for this present life for us is that we should consider our old sinful selves as dead, yielding the members of

our body to God as instruments of righteousness (Rom 6:6–14).

Of course, the Ten (the Eleven minus Thomas, see v. 24) had not yet had time to think through these implications in detail. This will take place in the age of the Spirit under the theological leadership of the apostle Paul. In the present passage, the Ten, both personally and as representatives of the church at large, receive Jesus' commission (20:21–23). This is one of three commissioning passages in the Gospels (to which one may add the commission in Acts 1:7–8). The shorter—and almost certainly authentic—version of Mark's Gospel does not contain a commissioning; Matthew and Luke both add such accounts. How is John's version distinct? It is so primarily in that it is firmly based on the paradigm of Jesus as the Sent One from the Father, bringing into play everything that has been said in the entire Gospel up to this point about Jesus' fulfillment of his role as the Sent Son (see ch. 13, above).

Now Jesus appears in a new role. No longer is he the sent one. Rather, he is the one who sends: "I am sending you" (v. 21b). How does he send his followers? "As the Father sent me" (v. 21a). This pledges his disciples to the same obedient and dependent relationship Jesus had sustained during the course of his earthly ministry. As the Farewell Discourse made clear, Jesus will not disappear from the scene subsequent to his departure. He will continue to head up the disciples' mission as their exalted Lord, operating through his substitute presence, the *paraklētos* and Spirit of truth. As Luke explains, the history of the early church is simply the account of what the exalted Jesus *continued to do* through his disciples under the guidance of the Holy Spirit (cf. Acts 1:1).

Verse 22 may suggest that the disciples received the Spirit at that occasion ("Receive the Holy Spirit"). But a closer look indicates that this conclusion, which would be at odds with Luke's report that the Spirit was not given until Pentecost (Acts 1–2), would be premature. This is already suggested by the verb form used by John to depict Jesus' action: "he breathed on them." A rare word, it does not refer to the actual impartation of the Spirit (as in "breathed into") but merely

Table 14.4
"The Christ, the Son of God, Is Jesus" (Jn 20:31)

Jesus as the "Christ": 1:41; 4:25, 29; 7:26, 27, 31, 41, 42; 9:22; 10:24; 11:27; 12:34; 20:31

Jesus as the "Son of God": 1:39, 49; 3:18; 5:25; 10:36; 11:4, 27; 19:7; 20:31

to a symbolic gesture connoting Jesus' creation of his new covenant community in analogy to the creation of man, where God "breathed into the man's nostrils the breath of life, and the man became a living being" (Gn 2:7).[1]

Rather than receiving the Spirit at this point, the present commissioning marks the formal establishment of the new messianic community that will go forward in the power of the Spirit, proclaiming the Good News of the forgiveness of sins in Jesus' name (cf. Lk 24:47). Regarding this

pronounced forgiveness, the believing community has declarative rather than originating power: it is merely authorized to apply the forgiveness made available through Jesus' work on the cross on the basis of faith (v. 23; cf. Mt 16:19; 18:18; Is 22:22; Rv 3:7). It is therefore not possible to enter into a true relationship with God in Christ apart from genuine repentance and faith.

In the context of Jesus' original audience, this applies particularly to people such as the Pharisees, who refused to ac-

The Sanhedrin's Role in Jesus' Crucifixion

The origins of the Jewish ruling council, the "Sanhedrin" (from the Greek *synedrion*, gathering, assembly), lie in the intertestamental period. Initially, the Council was made up of priests and elders who functioned under the direction of the high priest. The Sanhedrin consisted mostly of Sadducees until Salome (76–67 B.C.) appointed Pharisees as well. In New Testament times, the Sanhedrin was comprised of chief priests, elders, and scribes. When in A.D. 6 Judea became a Roman province, the Sanhedrin attained significant autonomy in handling internal Jewish affairs. After the fall of Jerusalem in A.D. 70 the Sanhedrin ceased to exist, as did the party of the Sadducees.

John's Gospel makes clear, as do the Synoptics, that the Sanhedrin was the legal Jewish body that bore ultimate responsibility for Jesus' death. As John traces the plot to take Jesus' life throughout his Gospel, the Sanhedrin

occupies the central role. At the same time, John makes it clear that the Sanhedrin was not united in its opposition against Jesus.

Nicodemus, the "Teacher of Israel" (3:10) and "a member of the Jewish ruling council" (3:1), is portrayed as sincerely interested in Jesus' message (3:1–2, 4, 9), openly admonishing his fellow-council members to fairness (7:50–52) and even (together with another "secret follower" of Jesus, Joseph of Arimathea) assuming responsibility for Jesus' burial (19:38–42), a duty customarily fulfilled by a Jewish rabbi's disciples.

At the heart of the Sanhedrin's case against Jesus was the charge of "blasphemy" (5:18). When Jesus "broke" the Sabbath by healing a man and telling him to pick up his mat—a violation of Jewish, though not biblical, law—and then cast his action in continuity with God the Father's continuing work (5:17), "the Jews tried all

the harder to kill him; not only was he breaking the Sabbath, but he was even calling God his own Father, making himself equal with God" (5:18). The Sanhedrin's rising antagonism toward Jesus supplies the Johannine narrative with its major element of drama and suspense (e.g. 7:1, 27, 30, 32), although for the reader it is an open secret what will happen to Jesus.

Intermittently, Sanhedrin meetings are called (7:45–52; 11:47–53), yet God is shown supernaturally to protect Jesus until his "time" has come (e.g., 7:30). The inexorable drive toward Jesus' crucifixion climaxes in the Jewish and Roman trials that make up the Johannine passion narrative (18:1–19:16a). In it the Sanhedrin is shown cynically to manipulate both the Roman procurator (simply called "Pilate" in John's Gospel; esp. 19:12, 15) and the masses (19:6, 15) to achieve their sinister ends.

knowledge their own spiritual blindness (9:39–41; cf. 8:33) and who would thus die in their sin unless they believed in Jesus (8:21, 23–24). This was equally true for John's first readers and remains applicable today. We live in a nation that is still nominally Christian. Our coins read "In God We Trust," and the founders of our nation appealed to divine providence and guidance. But shallow traditionalism does not save. Neither does church attendance nor membership. As Keith Green used to say, "Going to church doesn't make you a Christian, just as going to McDonald's doesn't make you a hamburger." As Jesus told Nicodemus, "You must be born from above" (3:3). This, in turn, requires hum-

bling oneself before God, confession of one's need for a Savior, and repentance as well as faith in Christ.

The commissioning scene is doubtless the focal point of the present chapter. But there remains some follow-up. Thomas, one of the Eleven, was not with the disciples at that occasion. Moreover, when the other disciples told him that they had seen the Lord, Thomas responded, with skepticism that has earned him the nickname "Doubting Thomas" ever since, "Unless I see the nail marks in his hands and put my finger where the nails were, and put my hand into his side, I will not believe it" (vv. 24–25). In modern terms, Thomas was an evidentialist. "Show me,"

The So-called Johannine Pentecost (Jn 20:22)

In the Johannine commissioning narrative, we find this puzzling statement: "And with that he breathed on them and said, 'Receive the Holy Spirit. If you forgive anyone his sins, they are forgiven; if you do not forgive them, they are not forgiven'" (20:22–23). What is puzzling about this statement is that none of the other Gospels record such a giving of the Spirit to Jesus' disciples prior to Pentecost (cf. Acts 2). Is the present passage the Johannine equivalent to the Lucan Pentecost? The problem with this view, of course, is that it implicates John with altering historical fact in order to accommodate his particular theological bent. And while this is serious enough an offense for you and me, it is infinitely more serious for a writer of sacred, inspired Scripture. Is there an alternative to this conclusion?

In fact, there is. First of all, one notices that the Greek says "he breathed on," not necessarily "breathed into." Thus Jesus may not actually have imparted his Spirit on his disciples at that point but rather have engaged merely in a visual demonstration in order to make a theological point. But what is that point?

As we look for Old Testament parallels of the rare term *emphysaō*, we note that the exact same term is found in Genesis 2:7 *(enephysēsen)*. There God is shown to breathe his Spirit into Adam at creation, which constitutes Adam as a "living being." The message of John 20:22 thus becomes clear. By self-consciously employing creation symbolism at this important historical juncture of the disciples' commissioning, the risen Lord seeks to convey to his followers—and the evangelist to his later readers—that this commissioning consti-

tutes them as the new messianic community. Just as God breathed his Spirit on Adam at creation (which constituted him as a "living being"), Jesus breathes his Spirit on his gathered followers (which constitutes them as the new messianic community). This is therefore not the Johannine *substitute*, but the anticipatory theological *explication* of the events at Pentecost.

Thus the alleged discrepancy disappears. What emerges instead is yet another instance where John grounds his narrative in the soil of the creation chapters of Genesis. This should not surprise us in a book that opens with the same words as Genesis ("in the beginning") and develops systematically motifs such as "life" and "light" which are prominently featured in the opening chapters of that book.

he said. Now there is nothing wrong with wanting one's faith to be based on reality rather than make-believe. At the same time, God does not welcome a demanding attitude that places conditions on him.

A week later Jesus' disciples were in the house again, doors locked, but this time Thomas was with them. Once again, Jesus suddenly stood among his followers, issuing his customary greeting. Displaying divine omniscience (he had not physically been with the disciples when Thomas registered his doubts), he singles Thomas out and challenges him, "Put

The Purpose of John's Gospel (Jn 20:30–31)

John is the only evangelist who provides his readers with a clear purpose statement: "I have written these things in order that you might believe" (20:31). Yet, somewhat ironically, interpreters are divided as to how this phrase should be taken. Is John here talking about engendering first-time faith, or is he seeking to strengthen the (already existing) faith of a believing community?

The problem is complicated by the textual variant pertaining to the word "believe" in the original Greek. Some manuscripts, including Codex Alexandrinus [fifth century A.D.], have the aorist subjunctive form *pisteusēte*, while others, such as (apparently) p[66] [ca. A.D. 200] as well as Codices Sinaiticus and Vaticanus [fourth century A.D.] have the present subjunctive *pisteuēte*.

It has been alleged that the aorist reading would support the notion that John wrote to engender first-time faith, while the present variant would suggest that the people to whom he wrote were already believers. However, it has become increasingly clear that such a distinction, while convenient, does not do justice to the way the

Greek subjunctive actually functions. Thus the simple equation:

present subjunctive = written to strengthen the faith of believers
aorist subjunctive = written to encourage first-time faith

does not hold. This may be for the better, since it is hard to determine, on mere textual grounds, whether *pisteusēte* or *pisteuēte* is original (but note that in the case of the identical phrase in 19:35, the vast majority of manuscripts has the aorist subjunctive).

This is one time when a knowledge of Greek (including textual criticism) does not solve all our problems. We are therefore thrust on the venerable Reformation principle of determining which of the two possible renderings is the more natural. Would an unencumbered reader have understood John more likely to say, "I have written these things in order that you may believe," that is, *for the first time*, in the sense of placing one's trust in Jesus? Or would he have taken John to mean "I have written these things in order that you might *continue* to be-

lieve," in the sense of strengthening already existing faith?

I must confess my sympathies lie decidedly with the former alternative. For John's evident concern throughout the entire Gospel is to bring people to (first-time) faith in Christ. That does not mean that John's Gospel was written *directly* to unbelievers; it is certainly possible (even probable) that John wrote his Gospel to equip believers to evangelize. Yet whether directly or indirectly, the thrust of John's Gospel is clearly evangelistic. This, then, is how John probably meant the phrase "in order that you might believe" to be understood.

Note: For further study, see esp. Richard Bauckham, *The Gospels for All Christians: Rethinking the Gospel Audiences* (Grand Rapids: Eerdmans, 1997); and D. A. Carson, "The Purpose of the Fourth Gospel: Jn 20:31 Reconsidered," *Journal of Biblical Literature* 106 (1987): 639–51. For a use of John's Gospel as it was intended (i.e., for evangelism), see Roy D. Clements, *Introducing Jesus* (Eastbourne: Kingsway, 1988).

your finger here; see my hands. Reach out your hand and put it into my side. Stop doubting and believe" (v. 27). Suddenly, Thomas feels no more need for further verification. Rather than examining the evidence, he responds in worship: "My Lord and my God!" (v. 28). Notably, at the time John wrote his Gospel, the same designation (Latin *dominus et deus*) was applied to the Roman emperor Domitian (A.D. 81–96). The counter-cultural message of John's Gospel is clear: Jesus, not the Roman emperor, is Lord and God, and he alone must be worshiped.

There is one other reason why the scene surrounding Thomas has important implications for John's readers. Unlike Jesus' first followers, they were dependent on others' testimony. Rather than being able to see and hear for themselves, they had to base their faith on the apostolic word, including John's written Gospel. Was this an inferior form of faith? By no means! As Jesus says, "Because you have *seen* me, you have believed? Blessed are those who have *not* seen and *yet* have believed" (v. 29). Thus, paradoxically, it turns out that believing without seeing, far from being *inferior*, is actually *superior*. For it involves taking God at his word. Listen to the definition of faith according to the Epistle of Hebrews: "Now faith is being sure of what we hope for and certain of what we *do not see*" (Hb 11:1). The situation is the same today: God calls us to trust in Christ on the basis of the apostolic word.

Study Questions

1. How is Scripture fulfilled through the events surrounding Jesus' crucifixion?

2. What is the basic sequence of events making up John's passion narrative?

3. What do we learn about the nature of our resurrection body from Jesus' resurrection appearances?

John 20:30–31 contains the clearest purpose statement found in any of the Gospels: "Jesus did many other miraculous signs in the presence of his disciples, which are not recorded in this book. But these are written that you may believe that Jesus is the Christ, the Son of God, and that by believing you may have life in his name." We may look back to our study of John's Gospel. All the major themes were covered: certain selected signs of Jesus; the necessity of believing that the Christ, the Son of God, is in fact Jesus, even if that involved adjusting one's messianic expectations; and the promise of present (not merely future) possession of eternal life. The twin foci of John's message are these: Jesus is the sent Son of God the Father; and the time for believing is now.

If the Gospel concluded at this point, the purpose statement of 20:30–31 would provide sufficient closure. In fact, it has been conjectured that John originally planned to finish his Gospel at this point and only later appended an additional chapter. Alternatively, the suggestion has been made that someone other than John, perhaps some of his disciples, added chapter 21 after the apostle's death. However, the presence of an epilogue seems required by the opening Prologue in order to preserve balance and symmetry of structure. The Prologue, in turn, is tied in so closely with the remainder of the Gospel that its composition cannot be relegated to a later follower of John. Also, there is no textual evidence that the Gospel ever circulated in any form other than the present, canonical one. Finally, ending the Gospel at 20:30–31 might have seemed a bit abrupt moments after the encounter between Jesus and Thomas.

For this reason we maintain that the epilogue constitutes an integral part of John's Gospel. It is part of John's overall literary plan and provides the culmination of various strands carefully woven earlier in the Gospel. It remains for the next chapter to develop these observations in greater detail.

Part
5

Encountering the One
Who Calls Us to Follow

John 21

You must follow me.
—John 21:22c

15 What It Means to Follow Jesus

John 21

If anyone would come after me,
  he must deny himself and take up his cross and follow me.
For whoever wants to save his life will lose it,
  but whoever loses his life for me and for the gospel will save it.
What good is it for a man to gain the whole world, yet forfeit his soul?
  Or what can a man give in exchange for his soul?
If anyone is ashamed of me and my words in this adulterous and sinful generation,
  the Son of Man will be ashamed of him when he comes in the Father's glory with the holy angels.

—Mark 8:34–38

Supplemental Reading: Luke 5:1–11; Matthew 16:15–19; Mark 16:7

Outline

- **Jesus Appears to Seven Disciples (21:1–14)**
- **Jesus and Peter (21:15–19)**
- **Jesus and the Disciple Jesus Loved (21:20–25)**

Objectives

After reading this chapter, you should be able to

1. Summarize the significance of Jesus' three resurrection appearances to his disciples.
2. Explain how John 21 supports the notion of Johannine authorship of the Gospel.
3. Relate Peter's commissioning to the remainder of the Gospel.

In the interim between Jesus' burial and his final resurrection appearances, the disciples briefly returned to their original vocation of fishing.

Jesus Appears to Seven Disciples (21:1–14)

Chapter 20 has already chronicled two of Jesus' resurrection appearances to his disciples (apart from the encounter with Mary Magdalene in 20:10–18): (1) the initial appearance to the Eleven minus Thomas, including Jesus' commissioning of his disciples (20:19–23); and (2) the follow-up scene with Thomas (20:24–29). The present chapter adds the third and final appearance featured in John's Gospel (21:1–14; v. 14: "This was now the third time Jesus appeared to his disciples after he was raised from the dead")—to seven of Jesus' followers by the Sea of Tiberias (v. 1; an alternative designation for the Sea of Galilee: cf. 6:1). This appearance, in turn, culminates in Jesus' special commissioning of Peter which is witnessed by the "disciple Jesus loved" (21:15–23). Notably, the featuring of Peter and the "disciple Jesus loved" in the final chapter of John's Gospel climaxes their parallel casting throughout the entire narrative (cf. esp. 13:23–25; 18:15–18; 20:2–10; 21:1–24).[1]

The seven disciples mentioned in verse 2 include: Simon Peter (the customary designation for Peter in this Gospel: 1:40; 6:8, 68; 13:6, 9, 24, 36; 18:10, 15, 25; 20:2, 6; 21:3, 7, 11); Thomas ("called Didymus" = "twin"; cf. 11:16; 20:24); Nathanael ("from Cana of Galilee;" tying in this portion with the opening chapter of the Gospel; cf. 1:44–51); the sons of Zebedee (John and James; e.g. Mk 1:19–20); and two other unnamed disciples. As developed in the opening chapter, the important implication for the authorship of John's Gospel is that, since the "disciple Jesus loved" is identified as the author in 21:24 (cf. 21:20), and since the "disciple Jesus loved" is one of the seven (21:7), the author of John's Gospel likewise must be one of the seven mentioned in 21:2. Thus it is eminently plausible that the author is John, one of the two sons of Zebedee.

But back to the story. "I'm going out to fish," Simon Peter says to his friends in a characteristic display of leadership and initiative. Unsurprisingly, his six associates decide to come along. It appears that despite the commissioning in 20:21–23, Peter has (however temporarily) returned to his old occupation. This is yet another argument against reading 20:21 as indicating an actual impartation of the Spirit at that point. For this would make it almost inexplicable why Peter would have gone back to fishing shortly after this event. In a familiar scene, the disciples

Septuagint | fish all night but catch nothing (cf. Lk 5:1–11). Early in the morning, with Peter and his friends probably both tired and hungry, a man calls them from the shore, asking, "Friends, haven't you any fish?"

The man is Jesus, but his disciples do not realize this yet. Jesus tells them to throw out the net on the right side of the boat, which they do. The resulting very large catch probably evokes the memory of similar experiences with Jesus earlier in his ministry. At least it does in the mind of the "disciple Jesus loved," for he cries out to Peter, "It is the Lord!" ("the Lord," Grk. *kyrios*, used for God in the **Septuagint** translation of the Old Testament, had become the standard designation for Jesus in the early church; cf. 20:18, 25). Peter, in his characteristic impetuousness, jumped into the water, while the other disciples followed in the boat, the net full of fish in tow. When the fish were counted, their number turned out to be 153 (some have sought to find an inherent symbolism in the number, but this is doubtful).

What followed was a breakfast with their risen Lord, a breakfast none of the disciples was soon to forget.

Jesus and Peter (21:15–19)

After breakfast, Jesus takes Peter aside to commission him for service. In the context of John's Gospel, Peter's threefold affirmation of his love for Jesus mirrors, and offsets, his threefold denial of Jesus preceding the crucifixion (cf. 18:15–18, 25–27). Some have drawn significance from the pattern of usage of two Greek words for "love" in verses 15–17:

Jesus	Peter
Simon son of John, do you love *(agapaō)* me more than these?	Yes, Lord, you know that I love *(phileō)* you.
Simon son of John, do you love *(agapaō)* me?	Yes, Lord, you know that I love *(phileō)* you.
Simon son of John, do you love *(phileō)* me?	Lord, you know all things; you know that I love *(phileō)* you.

Thus Jesus uses *agapaō* the first two times and switches to *phileō* the third time, while Peter responds by using the word *phileō* in all three instances. This has been taken to imply that Jesus lowered his standard of love from *agapaō* (divine type of love) to *phileō* (human type of love). However, such a distinction between two kinds of love, a divine and a human one, is not borne out by the Gospel as a whole. Thus in 3:19 it is said that "men *loved* darkness instead of light because their deeds were evil." But the word used here is *agapaō*! Divine love? Certainly not. Likewise, in 12:43 we read that the Jewish religious leaders *loved* praise from men more than praise from God. Again, the word used, *agapaō*, most definitely does not refer to a divine kind of love.

Conversely, in 5:20 we read that "the Father loves the Son" *(phileō)*, while in 16:27 it is said that the Father loves the disciples; again, the word used for the love exercised by God the Father is, not *agapaō*, but *phileō*. The fact that *agapaō*, allegedly reserved for divine love, is used by John with reference to human love, and the fact that *phileō*, supposedly denoting human love, is used by John to refer to divine love, surely confounds the above stated theory. It seems that John could use both terms to refer to both human and divine love. Probably he did not use these two words for love with this distinction in mind at all, rather employing them for the purpose of stylistic variation. The synonymous nature of the terms is made clear by the fact that the expression "the disciple Jesus loved" occurs in John's Gospel both with *agapaō* (13:23; 19:26; 21:7, 20) and *phileō* (20:2). Note also that slightly different terms are used for the task to which Peter is called: "feed my lambs" (v. 15); "take care of my sheep" (v. 16); and "feed my sheep" (v. 17). Finally, the words for "know" are also varied without apparent difference in meaning:

21:15: "Lord, you know *(oida)* that I love you."

193

21:16: "Lord, you know (*oida*) that I love you."

21:17: "Lord, you know (*oida*) all things; you know (*ginōskō*) that I love you."

It is apparent that in all these instances the use of similar expressions clearly serves the purpose of stylistic variation.

We conclude that the variation of verbs for love in the present passage is not significant for understanding John's message. More important may be the question of what is meant by "these" in Jesus' question to Peter, "Simon son of John, do you love me more than *these*?" (v. 15). Does Jesus mean "these *men*," pointing to the other disciples? Does he refer to "these *fish*," implying that Peter must love Jesus more than his natural profession? Or does Jesus ask Peter if he loves him *more than these men do?* Recourse to the original language does not solve the difficulty here. We are left to infer the answer from the surrounding context. Perhaps it is not necessary to choose. In the end, all three requirements apply. Jesus wants Peter to love him more than he loves other people (Mt 10:37; Lk 14:26); he wants Peter to love him more than he loves his natural profession (Mk 1:16–18; Lk 5:1–11); and he wants Peter to love him more than these other men do, excelling in loyalty and willingness to sacrifice for his master (Jn 6:67–69; 13:36–38).

Supreme love and loyalty to Jesus is the prerequisite for significant service to our Lord. This is made clear by Jesus immediately following Peter's threefold pledge of loyalty. "I tell you the truth, when you were younger you dressed yourself and went where you wanted; but when you are old you will stretch out your hands, and someone else will dress you and lead you where you do not want to go" (v. 18). As the evangelist explains, this was to indicate by which kind of death Peter would glorify God, that is, martyrdom (v. 19; cf. the close verbal parallel with 12:33). According to tradition, Jesus' prophecy came true; Peter was crucified upside down, refusing to suffer the same kind of death as his Lord.

Jesus and the Disciple Jesus Loved (21:20–25)

Peter, not content to know the nature and end of his own ministry calling, was curious about the fate that would befall John, his close associate (called "the disciple Jesus loved" in John 13–21; note the reference to 13:23 in 21:20). "Lord, what about him?" (v. 21). Throughout the course of Jesus' ministry, his disciples had compared themselves with one another, seeking to secure places of honor for themselves. One memorable instance involves the mother of James and John (the sons of Zebedee) requesting Jesus to reserve the places on his left and on his right in glory for her two sons, which predictably elicited the remaining disciples' indignation, presumably at least in part because they didn't have the idea first (cf. Mk 10:35–45).

Jesus, however, refuses to satisfy Peter's curiosity: "If I want him to remain alive until I return, what is that to you? You must follow me" (v. 22). Not surprisingly, this statement led to the rumor that John would not die until Jesus' return. But as he points out, that is *not* what Jesus said (v. 23). (Interestingly, part of Matthew's final chapter is likewise devoted to dispelling a false rumor, in his case that Jesus' disciples had stolen Jesus' body: Mt 28:11–15; cf. 27:62–66.) It is possible that these final verses were written by John's disciples after his death in an attempt to counter the notion that Jesus' prediction that John would not die until he returned had been proven erroneous by John's

Study Questions

1. What are the circumstances surrounding Jesus' three resurrection appearances to his disciples?

2. What is the primary purpose for Jesus' commissioning of Peter?

3. How does the final chapter of John's Gospel support the notion that the apostle John wrote the Gospel of John?

death. Alternatively, John himself, still alive, may have sought to dispel the rumor that Christ had promised to return during his own lifetime.

With this we have arrived at the final conclusion of John's Gospel. "This is the disciple who testifies to these things and who wrote them down. We know that his testimony is true" (v. 24). The phrase resembles the statement in 19:35, "The man who saw it has given testimony, and his testimony is true. He knows that he tells the truth, and he testifies so that you also may believe." Since it is clear that the affirmation in 19:35 must refer to an eyewitness of Jesus' crucifixion, the same arguably pertains to the author of the Gospel who is referred to in 21:24. The phrase "this is the disciple who testifies to these things and who wrote them down" in 21:24 refers back to "the disciple Jesus loved" in 21:20, thus identifying the author of John's Gospel with the disciple who sat beside Jesus in the Upper Room according to 13:23 and thus was one of the Twelve and in all likelihood the apostle John.

Many scholars believe that the expression "we know that his testimony is true" reflects the vantage point of followers of John who added this statement (or the entire chapter) after the apostle's death. This is possible. But it is equally possible that John himself wrote this phrase, using an apostolic "we" as in 1:14 (cf. also the rhetorical uses of "we" by Nicodemus and Jesus in 3:2 and 11). This is rendered likely by the expression "I suppose" in verse 25, which reverts back to the first person and is unlikely to have come from a group of John's followers after his death. It is therefore best to view the entire Gospel as the product of the apostle John, the son of Zebedee, eyewitness of Jesus' earthly ministry and closest human confidant of our Lord among his first followers.

In his final sentence, John points out once again that his account is merely selective rather than exhaustive (cf. 20:30). "Jesus did many other things as well. If every one of them were written down, I suppose that even the whole world would not have room for the books that would be written" (v. 25). This is readily apparent from a comparison with the other three Gospels, which contain numerous events not included in John's Gospel. But John's statement reminds us that even those Gospels had to be selective and include only a fraction of events even during Jesus' three-year ministry. Yet while we do not have an exhaustive account of Jesus' life and ministry, John has marshalled more than sufficient evidence (i.e., Jesus' "signs") for his readers to be persuaded that Jesus is in fact the Christ, the Son of God, so that by believing they will have eternal life already in the here and now. It remains for us to appropriate John's message for ourselves and to convey it to others who yet have to believe that Jesus is the One God promised, God's Son.

Key Word

Septuagint

---

16 Epilogue: John in the Context of Scripture

In the beginning God created the heavens and the earth.

—Genesis 1:1

In the beginning was the Word ... The Word became flesh and dwelt among us.

—John 1:1, 14

Outline

- **John and the Synoptic Gospels**
- **John and the Old Testament**
- **John and the Rest of the Johannine Corpus**
    John's Gospel and the Epistles
    John's Gospel and the Book of Revelation
- **John and the Rest of the New Testament**
    John and Paul
    John and Hebrews, Peter
- **Conclusion**

Objectives

After reading this chapter, you should be able to

1. Identify the unique characteristics of John's Gospel in relation to the Synoptic Gospels.
2. Demonstrate how John's theology is firmly rooted in the Old Testament.
3. Relate John's Gospel to the other Johannine writings and the rest of the New Testament.

John and the Synoptic Gospels

We have already looked at the differences and similarities between John's Gospel and the Synoptics in general terms at the outset of our study (see ch. 3). We have noted that John's Gospel does not feature many of the significant components found in the other Gospels, such as narrative parables, Jesus' teaching on the kingdom of God, the eschatological discourse, the Sermon on the Mount including the Lord's Prayer, and many others. In fact, while Matthew and Luke share over 90 percent of Mark's material, only 8 percent of John's content is paralleled in the Synoptics (e.g., the feeding of the five thousand in 6:1–14); 92 percent of John's Gospel is unique.[1]

Thus John's Gospel alone features Jesus' farewell discourse or selected works of Jesus termed "signs." In our effort to account for these remarkable differences in perspective, we concluded that John wrote his own story, without conscious and constant reference to his Synoptic counterparts. At the same time, John generally seems to assume his readers' familiarity with the Synoptic tradition, and, like the other evangelists, writes a Gospel, that is, an account of the events surrounding the life, death, and resurrection of Jesus. In the history of recent scholarship, this led P. Gardner-Smith to conclude that John wrote his account independently from the Synoptics. This thesis was further developed by C. H. Dodd and, along somewhat different lines, by J. A. T. Robinson, who contended that John's Gospel constitutes a primary historical witness.[2]

In the present chapter, which seeks to explore connections between John's Gospel and other biblical literature, we may build on the ground already covered by mapping the four stories that have come down to us as the fourfold Gospel according to Matthew, Mark, Luke, and John in relation to each other. Assuming **Markan priority** (i.e., the notion that Mark's Gospel was the first to be written), we will start with Mark's Gospel, then survey the Gospels written by Matthew and Luke, and conclude with a brief sketch of the literary plan underlying the Gospel of John.

All three Synoptic Gospels present Jesus' ministry in two phases: first, his ministry in Galilee (Mk 1:16–8:26; Mt 4:12–18:35; Lk 4:14–9:50); then, his journey to and ministry in Jerusalem (Mk 8:27–16:8; Mt 19:1–28:20; Lk 9:51–24:53). Mark—essentially followed by Matthew and Luke—further structures his Gospel by dividing both phases of Jesus' ministry into three parts, that in Galilee (Mk 1:16–3:12; 3:13–5:43; 6:1–8:26) as well as that in Judea and Jerusalem (Mk 8:27–10:52; 11:1–13:37; 14:1–16:8). The central section of Mark (8:27–10:52; par. Mt, Lk) features a total of three Passion predictions on the part of Jesus, which is in each case followed by a reference to discipleship failure and Jesus' teaching on the cost of discipleship (8:31–38; 9:30–37; 10:32–45). The watershed event in all three Gospels constitutes Peter's confession of Jesus as the Christ in Caesarea Philippi (Mk 8:27–30; Mt 16:13–16; Lk 9:18–20). The two major parables featured by Mark (to which Matthew and Luke add many more) are those of the four soils and of the wicked tenants, strategically placed in chapters 4 and 12.

Matthew, while essentially following Mark's outline, expands his material in several ways. First, he begins his Gospel with a genealogy of Jesus, followed by a birth narrative (interestingly, Luke does the same thing, but in reverse order). Second, he groups Jesus' teaching into five major discourses which he interjects between narrative portions, resulting in a sequential pattern of narrative—discourse—narrative—discourse, etc. This is indicated by virtually identical transitional phrases ("when Jesus had finished saying these things": cf. 7:28; 11:1; 13:53; 19:1; 26:1) as well as occasional summary statements (e.g., 4:23–25; 9:35–38). The five major discourses, reminiscent of the five books of Moses, are:

the Sermon on the Mount (chs. 5–7);

Jesus' instruction of the Twelve (ch. 10);

two chapters on the Parables of the Kingdom (chs. 13 and 18); and the seven woes, the eschatological discourse, and more kingdom parables (chs. 23–25).

Third, Matthew, writing to Jews, features a significant number of **fulfillment quotations** of the Old Testament, showing that all the major events in Jesus' ministry were in keeping with predictions found already in the Hebrew Scriptures (e.g., 1:22–23; 2:5–6, 15, 18, 23). Moreover, Matthew occasionally adds further information on topics of particular interest to him and his readers (e.g., on the temple tax in 17:24–27; Judas's suicide in 27:1–10; the rumor that Jesus' disciples had stolen his body in 27:62–66; 28:11–15; and the Great Commission in 28:16–20). As a result, Matthew leaves Mark's basic outline intact, but slows Mark's rapid pace by Jesus' extended discourses. This includes in particular more extensive ethical instruction and further material on Jesus' teaching on the kingdom of God.

Luke, in all likelihood also following Mark's blueprint while working independently from Matthew (though they may have shared sources other than Mark, be it written or oral; cf. Lk 1:1–14), adds a literary preface and, similar to Matthew, a birth narrative and a genealogy. Unlike Matthew, however, Luke traces Jesus' genealogy all the way back to Adam. This is explained by the fact that Luke wrote to Gentiles, thus stressing Jesus' humanity, while Matthew, who traced Jesus' ancestry back to Abraham and David, wrote primarily to Jews. Luke also includes most of the material featured in Matthew's Sermon on the Mount, but only some of it in one single section (Lk 6:17–49) while leaving the rest scattered throughout his Gospel. The most unique feature of Luke's Gospel is the extended "travel narrative" bridging Jesus' Galilean and Judean ministries (Lk 9:51–19:27). Luke's interest in a wide variety of people has led him to feature characters such as the Good Samaritan (10:25–37), the Prodigal Son (15:11–32), or Zacchaeus (19:11–27).

While Matthew and Luke thus have expanded and further developed the material already found in Mark in significant ways, producing accounts that reflect significant theological emphases in their own right, the so-called Synoptic Gospels remain closely aligned in many ways. Most important, they all culminate in a Passion narrative centered around Jesus' crucifixion, burial, and resurrection (Mk 11:1–16:8; Mt 21:1–28:20; Lk 19:24–24:53).

John, too, writes a Gospel. He, too, devotes a large amount of space to an account of Jesus' Passion (18:1–20:31). But this is where the similarities end. Rather than following the Synoptic geographical pattern of dividing Jesus' ministry into two parts, the first one in Galilee, the second one in Judea, John organizes his account of Jesus' ministry around Jesus' attendance of major Jewish feasts in Jerusalem, which has Jesus headquartered in Galilee with periodic visits to Judea. Interestingly, John, too, divides his book into two major parts, albeit using not a geographical, but a theological criterion: in the first major section, he presents Jesus' mission to the Jews; in the second half of his Gospel, he narrates Jesus' mission to the world. And rather than recounting a variety of Jesus' miracles as do the Synoptics, John eliminates certain kinds of miracles altogether, such as demon exorcisms, and selects just seven particularly striking feats. These he calls, not "works of power" (*dynameis;* thus the Synoptics), but "signs" (*sēmeia*), and discusses them with regard to their christological symbolism.

He also includes a large section, the farewell discourse (chs. 13–17), not found in the Synoptics at all, writing from a decidedly postglorification perspective (see also the Prologue and the portrayal of the cross as the place where Jesus is "lifted up") while respecting the distinction between people's understanding prior and subsequent to the cross (the Johannine "misunderstanding" theme), and centers his entire message around the identity of Christ and people's need to make a decision regarding him: Is he the Christ, or isn't he? If he is, will they believe or not? This is the question to which John's entire Gospel inexorably leads.

As such, John's Gospel is more overtly theological than the Synoptics, more deliberately synthetic, more christologically focused and evangelistically oriented. John still cares about history. He still sees Christ as the climax of salvation history and views his calling of twelve disciples as the establishment of a new covenant community in further development of God's dealings with his people in the history of Israel. But all this is now set in a universal perspective. Faith has entirely replaced ethnicity as the identifying mark of the member of God's messianic community (3:16). A Christian is one who recognizes God's glory *in Jesus,* including the cross.

As it is, John's entire Gospel is as much a commentary on the significance of Jesus' life, a demonstration of the display of God's sovereignty in every aspect of Jesus' ministry, as it is a simple record of what Jesus said and did. It is that—for John highly prizes the importance of accurate witness—but it is much more. Thus John's Gospel towers over the Synoptics as the theological pinnacle of the Gospel tradition and establishes John's place as the first-century church's foremost theologian together with Paul.[3]

"No one has ever seen God; God the One and Only, who is at the side of the Father, he has made him known" (1:18)—this is John's bedrock conviction, and if this is so, then the question becomes, What are you and I going to do with this final, definitive revelation of God in Christ? As the writer of Hebrews said, how shall we escape if we neglect so great a salvation (Hb 2:3)? There remains nothing but the prospect of divine judgment: "It is a dreadful thing to fall into the hands of the living God" (Hb 10:31). John is one whose life has forever been changed by his encounter with Jesus. And in faithful obedience to Jesus' commission, John writes his Gospel, seeking to persuade as many as would listen that Jesus is the Christ, the Son of God.

John and the Old Testament

Apart from Jesus' teaching itself, the Old Testament is John's primary sourcebook.[4] Explicit quotations reveal this only imperfectly. For John's Gospel is replete with allusions to Old Testament symbolism and patterns even where no specific Old Testament passage is quoted.[5] The importance of the Old Testament for John's theology is already revealed in the opening words of the Gospel, "In the beginning was the Word," a clear allusion to the first words of the Old Testament canon in the Book of Genesis. In the Prologue alone, reference is made to God's giving of the Law through Moses (1:17); the "dwelling" (lit., "tenting") of the Word among God's people through Jesus (1:14); and God's dealings with Israel in the wilderness (1:14–18; cf. Ex 33–34). This sets the theme for John's presentation of Jesus as the final revelation of God.

The body of John's Gospel features a total of fourteen explicit Old Testament quotations, nine in Part One (1:19–12:50) and five in Part Two (13–21). To this may be added four passages with a citation formula but no explicit quotation (7:38, 42; 17:12; 19:28). The two most significant clusters of quotations are found in the concluding section of Part One (12:38, 40) and in the Passion narrative (19:24, 36, 37). Most remarkable is John's inclusion of several fulfillment quotations in Part Two of his Gospel, which represents a commonality with Matthew's account (13:18; 15:25; 19:24, 36, 37). The distribution of John's fourteen Old Testament quotations among Old Testament books is in line with the New Testament as a whole (with the Psalms, the Book of Isaiah, and the Pentateuch being the three most frequently quoted OT books). Seven citations are from the Psalms (22:18; 35:19/69:9; 41:9; 69:4; 78:24; 82:6; 118:25–26); four from Isaiah (6:10; 40:3; 53:1; 54:13); two from Zechariah (9:9; 12:10); and one from the Pentateuch (Ex 12:46/Nm 9:12). Six quotations stem from the fourth evangelist himself (12:15, 38, 40; 19:24, 36, 37); four quotations are attributed to Jesus (6:45; 10:34; 13:18; 15:25); and one each to John the Baptist (1:23), Jesus' disciples (2:17), Jesus' Jewish interrogators (6:31), and the crowds (12:13).

Table 16.1 features a list of quotations in chronological order.

In the following discussion, we will cover both explicit Old Testament quotations and the most significant allusions to the Old Testament in John. The initial quotation relates to John the Baptist, who identifies himself as the one of whom Isaiah spoke: "I am the voice of one calling in the desert, 'Make straight the way for the Lord'" (1:23; cf. Is 40:3). Here the fourth evangelist coheres closely with the Synoptic writers, who also portray John's ministry of preparing God's people for the Messiah in this way (Mk 1:3; Mt 3:3; Lk 3:4). In this context it should be noted that the Baptist calls Jesus "the Lamb of God" in the immediate context, which also may be indebted to language used by Isaiah (1:29, 36; cf. 53:7: "led like a lamb to the slaughter").

The second quotation is found in 2:17 in conjunction with Jesus' cleansing of the temple. There the evangelist points out that this powerful act evoked in Jesus' disciples the memory of the figure depicted in Psalm 69:9: "Zeal for your house will consume me." A psalm of David, this portion speaks of a righteous sufferer:

> For I endure scorn for your sake,
>   and shame covers my face.
> I am a stranger to my brothers,
>   an alien to my own mother's sons;
> for zeal for your house consumes me,
>   and the insults of those who insult
>   you fall on me (Ps 69:7–9).

Table 16.1: OT Quotations in the Gospel of John

John	OT Quotation
1:23	Is 40:3
2:17	Ps 69:9
6:31	Ps 78:24
6:45	Is 54:13
10:34	Ps 82:6
12:13	Ps 118:25–26
12:15	Zec 9:9
12:38	Is 53:1
12:40	Is 6:10
13:18	Ps 41:9
15:25	Ps 35:19/69:4
19:24	Ps 22:18
19:36	Ex 12:46/Nm 9:12
19:37	Zec 12:10

The phrase "those who hate me without reason" in verse 4 of this psalm (cf. Ps 35:19) is quoted in 15:25. The original reference to "God's house" pertains to the temple which David ordered rebuilt by his son Solomon. Now the Son of David again displays zeal for God's house, the Jerusalem temple, by driving out the merchants who had dared to turn Jesus' Father's house into a market (2:16). But Jesus would not have the physical structure of the temple restored; this project had already been carried out by Herod (cf. 2:20). Rather, he predicted that this temple would be destroyed as a sign of God's judgment on Israel (Mk 13:2 par.). In fact, the new center of worship for God's people will no longer be a physical building at all (4:23–24). Worship will rather focus on the resurrected body of Jesus (2:21–22).

Jesus' teaching on the necessity of a new birth "of water and spirit" in his encounter with Nicodemus also reflects Old Testament teaching (3:5). For it is clear that Jesus expects Nicodemus to understand these things as the "Teacher of Israel" (3:10). And how could he understand unless the Old Testament already instructed God's people about their need for a spiritual rebirth? Jesus probably thought of passages such as Ezekiel 36:24–27:

> For I will take you out of the nations;
>   I will gather you from all the countries
>   and bring you back into your own
>   land.
> I will sprinkle clean water on you, and
>   you will be clean;
>   I will cleanse you from all your im-
>   purities and from all your idols.
> I will give you a new heart
>   and put a new spirit in you;
> I will remove from you your heart of
>   stone
>   and give you a heart of flesh.
> And I will put my Spirit in you
>   and move you to follow my decrees
>   and be careful to keep my laws.

As the above passage makes clear, spiritual cleansing is depicted as a consequence of God's impartation of his Spirit into the hearts of his people. Regeneration and cleansing from sin go hand in hand. Thus it is best to interpret Jesus' teaching on the necessity of a new birth "of water and spirit" as referring to *one* spiritual birth that will have a cleansing and renewing effect.[6]

Another Old Testament allusion forms part of Jesus' instruction to Nicodemus, that of the bronze serpent in the wilderness. Just as people's lives were spared who, having been bitten by snakes in the wilderness, looked at the serpent raised on a pole by Moses, those looking in faith at the raised body of Jesus will live (3:14–15). This shows that Jesus detected in this event depicted in the Old Testament a typological element that pointed beyond itself to an aspect of his own life, in this case his manner of death and its saving effect on those who "looked" at him in faith.

The third explicit Old Testament quotation in John's Gospel is found in 6:31 where the crowds refer to Psalm 78:24: "He gave them bread from heaven to eat" (cf. Ps 105:40). This, of course, refers to God's provision of food for Israel during the wilderness wanderings. Apparently, people expected the Messiah to perform a similar, if not greater, feat (cf. 6:30–31). In the context of chapter 6, Jesus had already performed a startling miracle, feeding the multitude. But people, not recognizing that this already marked out Jesus as God's Messiah, ask for another sign (6:30). This, in turn, gives Jesus (and John) an opportunity to explain that Jesus' miracles, great as they are, are "signs" pointing to something greater still: Jesus himself. For in Old Testament times, God had miraculously rained bread from heaven to feed his people. But now, in Jesus, the Bread from Heaven itself had come down. What God has graciously done through Moses is now superseded by his work in and through Jesus Christ (6:32–33; cf. 1:17).

In this context we find the fourth explicit Old Testament reference: "they will all be taught by God" (6:45; cf. Is 54:13). By this Jesus makes clear that in his teaching Isaiah's prophecy is fulfilled. He is the Teacher sent from God, the only one who has seen the Father and who has come to bear witness (6:46; cf. 1:18; 18:36). Will people listen and recognize that in Jesus the hour of eschatological fulfillment has dawned?

Perhaps the most difficult Old Testament reference in John's Gospel is 7:38:

"just as the Scripture says, 'rivers of living water will flow out of his belly.'" As pointed out earlier, the occasion at which Jesus uttered this statement is the final, the "greatest" day of the Feast of Tabernacles (7:37), which abounded in torch-lighting and water-pouring ceremonies symbolizing God's various provisions for his people. However, no clear Old Testament passage comes to mind. Perhaps the present reference is reminiscent of the celebration of the same feast in Nehemiah's day, where God's people recalled God's provision of water from the rock and his giving of his good Spirit (cf. Neh 9, esp. v. 20).

Jesus' assertion in 8:12, repeated in 9:5, that he is the "Light of the World," recalls the second Servant Song in Isaiah where it is said that the Messiah will be a "light for the Gentiles." John's portrayal of Jesus as the "Good Shepherd" conjures up contrasts with Israel's "faithless shepherds" according to Ezekiel 34 and Zechariah 9–13. Jesus' statement in 10:16 that he must bring other sheep also so that there will be one flock and one shepherd combines prophetic passages in Isaiah 56:8 ("I will gather still others to them besides those already gathered") and Ezekiel 34:23 ("I will place over them one shepherd, my servant David"; similarly cf. Ez 37:24). In a similar vein, John 15 later elaborates on the imagery of Israel as God's vineyard, found most prominently in Isaiah 5.

The fifth explicit Old Testament quotation in John's Gospel is found in 10:34. Referring to Psalm 82:6, Jesus points out to his Jewish opponents that in that passage even those to whom the Word of God came were called "gods" (conveying that they were divinely appointed). If this designation can in one sense be appropriate even for human beings (i.e., human judges or rulers), Jesus argues in a from-the-lesser-to-the-greater argument, "What about the one whom the Father set apart as his very own and sent into the world"? (10:36). The present instance shows Jesus as thoroughly conversant with contemporary rabbinic styles of argumentation such as the *Qal wahomer* ("light and heavy") argument. For it was commonly recognized that what applies in a less important case will certainly apply in a more important case.[7] Moreover, Jesus here affirms the unshakable authority of God's

Word when he asserts that "Scripture cannot be broken" (10:35).

Scripture quotations six and seven are conjoined at the occasion of Jesus' triumphal entry. Combining Psalm 118:25–26 and Zechariah 9:9, John, in keeping with Synoptic tradition, presents Jesus as the humble Davidic king.

Quotations eight and nine close out the first half of John's Gospel. Both are found in Isaiah and draw an analogy between Jewish unbelief in the prophet's day and as encountered by Jesus (12:38, 40 citing Is 53:1; 6:10). Again, John here reflects common Old Testament usage of the early church; the words from Isaiah 6:10 are quoted by Jesus (Mt 13:14–15; Mk 4:12; Lk 8:10) and Paul (Acts 28:26–27) and found in all four Gospels as well as Acts; Isaiah 53:1 is also quoted by Paul in Romans 10:16. In the present context, John's reference to the Old Testament serves the purpose of theodicy (the "justification of God"). It was not that God failed to provide adequate testimony in support of Jesus' messiahship. Rather, it was the Jews' stubborn unbelief that resisted even the most striking manifestations of Jesus' divine nature and mission. Things haven't changed all that much from Isaiah's day until the days of Jesus; God's people have always resisted the message of his spokesmen (12:38). What is more, this unbelief, rather than thwarting God's plan, was in fact actively brought about by God (12:40).

As mentioned, Part Two of John's Gospel features several fulfillment quotations. In 13:18, Jesus emphasizes that Judas's betrayal did not catch him by surprise. Rather, this was "to fulfill the scripture: 'He who shares my bread has lifted up his heel against me.'" The same reference is found in Matthew 26:23. Later in the Farewell Discourse, Jesus points out to his followers that even the world's hatred "is to fulfill what is written in their Law: 'They hated me without reason'" (Pss 35:19; 69:4).

The final three Old Testament quotations all relate to Jesus' crucifixion. According to John, the following events constitute fulfillments of Scripture:

the soldiers' dividing Jesus' garments among them (19:24; cf. Ps 22:18; Mk 15:24; Lk 23:34);

the soldiers' refraining from breaking Jesus' legs (19:36; Ex 12:46; Nm 9:12); and

one of the soldiers' piercing Jesus' side with a spear (19:37; Zec 12:10).

Notably, only John mentions the second and third instances. This may be explained by the fact that he was a close eyewitness of these events (19:35).

Overall, it may be observed that John's use of the Old Testament does not differ significantly from that of the Synoptic writers. Occasionally, John, providing his own, independent account, supplements the Synoptic records, but by and large he stays safely within the confines of the portraits provided by Mark, Matthew, and Luke. John's primary contribution in his use of the Old Testament does not lie with his explicit quotations but with his elaboration on Jesus' fulfillment of Old Testament symbolism. This includes extended sections such as the discourse on the Bread of Life, the Good Shepherd, and the Vine and the Branches. John's structural placement of an Old Testament allusion at the beginning of his Gospel and two quotations from Isaiah at the end of the first major portion of his Gospel highlight the deliberate nature of his Old Testament usage.

John and the Rest of the Johannine Corpus[8]

John's Gospel and the Epistles

John's Epistles were probably penned a few years after his Gospel to congregations familiar with the Gospel. This seems to be the implication of repeated references to "what you have had from the beginning" (i.e., the gospel) in John's first two Epistles (e.g. 1 Jn 1:1; 2:7, 24; 3:11; 2 Jn 5, 6). Apparently, the congregations under John's jurisdiction had been infiltrated by proto-Gnostic teachers who had shaken the confidence of believers by denying the reality of sin (1 Jn 1:8, 10) and maintaining the necessity of special "inside information" (this is the implication of 1 Jn 2:20, 27). John's first Epistle, written shortly after those teachers had left the congregation (1 Jn 2:19), is designed to reassure the still shaken-up believers (see esp. 1 Jn 5:13; see also 2:20, 27; 3:24; 4:13). John's second and third Epistles deal with particular local problems involving the issue of extending hospitality to itinerant teachers.

The striking similarity in style and numerous verbal and conceptual parallels all but assure common authorship. John "the elder," so-called in the second and third Epistles (2 Jn 1; 3 Jn 1), is therefore none other than the apostle who penned the Gospel. "Elder" may refer to John's towering spiritual stature among his congregations as well as to the apostle's advanced age at the time of writing. Here are some of the most important parallels between John's Gospel and his Epistles:

the contrast between light and darkness (Jn 1:4–9; 3:9–21; 12:35–36; 1 Jn 1:5–7; 2:8–11);

the negative characterization of "the world" (Jn 1:10; 3:19–21; 1 Jn 2:15–17) which must be "overcome" (Jn 16:33; 1 Jn 5:4–5; cf. 2:13–14; 4:4); the notion that Jesus is the Light of the world (8:12; 9:5) also implies that the world is a dark place, as does the fact that the world needs salvation (3:16; 4:42);

the use of the term *Paraclete* (for the Spirit in Jn 14:16, 26; 16:26; 16:7; for Jesus in 1 Jn 2:1); and the term "S/spirit of truth" (Jn 14:17; 15:26; 16:13; 1 Jn 4:6; 5:6);

the Spirit's ministry of teaching believers (Jn 14:26; 1 Jn 2:20, 27);

references to the "new commandment" of love (Jn 13:34–35; 1 Jn 2:7–8; 4:21);

the emphasis on truth (Jn 1:14, 17; 3:21; 4:24, 25; 5:33; etc.; 1 Jn 1:6, 8; 2:4, 21; etc.);

"eternal life" terminology (Jn 3:15–16, 36; 4:14, 36; etc.; 1 Jn 1:2; 2:25; 3:15; 5:11, 13, 20);

"witness" terminology (Jn 1:7, 8, 15, 32, 34; etc.; 1 Jn 1:2; 4:14; 5:6–11);

the importance of "believing" (almost one hundred times in John; 1 Jn 3:23; 4:1, 16; 5:1, 5, 10, 13);

the address of believers as "little children" (Jn 13:33; 21:5; 1 Jn 2:1, 12, 14, 18, 28; 3:7, 18; 4:4; 5:21);

the assurance of answered prayer (Jn 14:13–14; 15:7, 16; 16:23–24; 1 Jn 3:22; 5:14–15);

the importance of being "in" Jesus (Jn 6:56; 10:38; 14:10–11, 20; 15:4–10; 17:21–23; 1 Jn 3:24; 5:20);

the designation *diabolos* for the devil, and the contrast between the children of God and the children of the devil (Jn 6:70; 8:44; 13:2; 1 Jn 3:1–2, 8, 10);

references to believers' having already passed from death into life (Jn 5:24 = 1 Jn 3:14);

the characterization of Jesus as the Christ, the Son of God (Jn 20:30–31; 1 Jn 2:22; 4:15; 5:1, 5);

the insistence that no one has ever seen God (Jn 1:18: *theon oudeis heōraken pōpote*; 1 Jn 4:12: *theon oudeis pōpote tetheatai*);

God's sending of his "only begotten" Son into the world in order that those who believe in him may have life (Jn 3:16–17; 1 Jn 4:7);

the use of the term "perfected" (Jn 13:1; 19:28, 30; 1 Jn 2:5; 4:12, 17, 18);

the centrality of forgiveness of sins (Jn 20:23; 1 Jn 2:12);

the frequent use of substantival participles ("the one who"; e.g. Jn 14:12; 1 Jn 2:17, 29; 3:4, 7, 8), "just as" comparisons (Jn 17:18; 20:21; 1 Jn 4:17), and of simple terms central to the book's message, such as:

know (1 Jn 2:3, 4, 5, 13, 14, 18, 29; etc.);

keep the commandments (Jn 14:15, 21; 15:10; 1 Jn 2:3, 4; 3:22; 5:2, 3);

remain (e.g. Jn 15:4–10; 1 Jn 2:6, 10, 14, 17, 19, 24, 27, 28; etc.);

love (Jn 3:16; 13:1, 34–35; etc.; 1 Jn 2:5, 10, 15; 3:1, 10–11, 14, 16–18, 23, 24; etc.);

born of God (Jn 1:13; 3:3–8; 1 Jn 2:29; 3:9; 4:7; 5:1, 4, 18); and

children of God (Jn 1:12; 11:52; 1 Jn 3:1, 2; 5:2).

In light of these striking terminological and conceptual similarities, common authorship seems assured. Nevertheless, there are differences occasioned by the different genres and occasions for writing of the Gospel on the one hand and the Epistles on the other. For example, one notes the glaring absence of any Old Testament references in the epistles. This sets these writings apart from the Gospel which, as noted, is based on the substructure of Old Testament theology. The reason for this difference may be that John's Gospel is an account of the life and ministry of Jesus both to the Jews and ultimately to the world, while the Epistles deal with an early Gnostic threat to already established Christian communities. In the latter context, the need of the hour was to safeguard the original gospel message against distortions by reaffirming the basic Christian confession of Jesus as God come in the flesh who rendered atonement for sin.

John's Gospel and the Book of Revelation

Somewhat different is the third major component of the Johannine writings in the New Testament canon, the Book of Revelation. This apocalyptic, highly symbolic work records four visions given to John the seer while in exile on the island of Patmos off the coast of Greece (1:10–3:22; 4–16; 17:1–21:8; 21:9–22:21 based on the phrase "in the Spirit," which only occurs in 1:10; 4:2; 17:3; and 21:10). The entire book is framed in form of an epistle directed toward seven churches in Asia Minor (cf. chs. 2–3), the area also traditionally associated with the genesis of John's Gospel and epistles. The Book of Revelation is written primarily to strengthen believers in the face of suffering at the end of the first century when the Roman emperor cult forced Christians to choose between allegiance to Jesus Christ or Caesar.

Commonalities between John's Gospel and the Apocalypse include:

the christological titles "Lamb" (Jn 1:29, 36; twenty-eight times in Rv) and "Logos" (Jn 1:1, 14; Rv 19:13);

the eschatological images of shepherding (Jn 10:1–16; 21:15–17; Rv 2:27; 7:17; 12:5; 19:15) and living water (Jn 4:14; 6:35; 7:37–38; Rv 7:17; 21:6; 22:1, 17);

statements regarding God's dwelling with people (Jn 1:14; Rv 7:15; 21:3) and the absence of the temple (Jn 2:19, 21; 4:20–26; Rv 21:22);

the importance assigned to the number 7 (Jn: signs, I am sayings; Rv: seals, trumpets, bowls);

the characterization of Satan as the archenemy of Jesus (Jn 6:70; 8:44; 13:2, 27; Rv 2:9–10, 13, 24; 3:9; 12:9, 12; 20:2, 7, 10);

the contrast between believers and the world in John and between those with God's seal and those with the mark of the beast in Revelation;

the quotation of Zechariah 12:10 in John 19:36–37 and Revelation 1:7;

"witness" and "glory" terminologies; and

a stress on the necessity of perseverance as well as the sovereignty and predestinatory counsel of God.

It appears that differences in genre and occasion for writing account adequately for the different orientation of John's Gospel on the one hand and the Apocalypse on the other. In keeping with the different genres of John's Gospel, Epistles, and the Book of Revelation, John respectively functions as apostle (Gospel), elder (epistles), and seer (Revelation). This shows John's versatility. In different circumstances, he could write an evangelistic account of Jesus' life, reassure believers in light of proto-Gnostic heresies, or encourage believers to persevere in light of mounting persecution. All three functions attest to John's status as one of the "pillars" of the early church (Gal 2:9), even more so in the period after A.D. 70 when both Peter and Paul had been martyred.

John and the Rest of the New Testament

John and Paul

John and Paul ministered in Ephesus, and it is likely that John reaped some of the fruit of Paul's labors there. Because John wrote his Gospel several years after Paul, it used to be widely assumed that John's Gospel is based on Pauline Christianity. But common theological interests may be expressed in quite different ways. Thus one searches John's Gospel in vain for the characteristic Pauline dichotomy between flesh *(sarx)* and Spirit *(pneuma)* or between the Law *(nomos)* and the "law-free" gospel *(euangelion;* the expression is from Rom 3:21). Likewise, Paul's favorite christological term "Lord" *(kyrios)* is rare in John, to name but a few of several obvious differences.

Nevertheless, these divergences in perspective notwithstanding, there are several points of contact between John's Gospel and the writings of Paul. Both emphasize love (Jn 13:13–14, 34–35; 1 Cor 13), consider the world to be in darkness and its wisdom futile (Jn 1:5, 10; 3:19; 1 Cor 1:18–2:16), and use the phrase "in Christ" or "in him" (Jn 6:56; 10:38; 14:10–11, 20; 15:4–10; 17:21–23; Rom 6:11; 8:1; 12:5; etc.). Both know God as Father, John stressing his role in conception ("born of God," 1:13), Paul in adoption (Rom 8:23; Gal 4:4–7). Both center the gospel on Jesus Christ crucified, buried, and risen (Jn 18–20; 1 Cor 15:1–3) and depict Israel's destiny by the use of similar imagery, branches of a vine in John's case (Jn 15), an olive tree in Paul's (Rom 11:17–24). Both also include strong predestinarian teaching as part of their emphasis on God's sovereignty and in the service of theodicy (Jn 12:37–40; Rom 9–11).

These points of contact make clear that John and Paul preached the same gospel and that their theological core commitments were ultimately based on the same foundation, the Messiah predicted and foreshadowed in the Old Testament, who had appeared in the person of Jesus Christ. However, these areas of overlap are not to minimize the differences in perspective between these two towering theologians of the early church. Thus unlike Paul, John nowhere elaborates on the relationship between sin and the Law. Consequently, he also lacks an equivalent to the Pauline antithesis between works and faith. Likewise, John has no explicit doctrine of justification, just as he does not feature the Pauline corollaries to justification, such as reconciliation, calling, election, adoption into sonship, and sanctification. This suggests that John must be understood in his own right rather than merely be subsumed under the Pauline presentation of the gospel.

John and Hebrews, Peter

There are several rather striking similarities between the Book of Hebrews and John's Gospel. John shares with Hebrews a high Christology. Points of contact can already be detected in the respective prologues (Jn 1:1–18; Hb 1:1–4). Both stress that Jesus is the locus of God's final revelation (Jn 1:18; Hb 1:2), and both set God's redemptive work through Christ in conscious parallel to creation (Jn 1:1; Hb 1:3). Both also emphasize that Jesus is the last in a long series of divine emissaries and harbingers of revelation (Jn 4:34; Hb 1:2). Both also share a major emphasis on faith (John throughout; Hb 11) and portray Jesus as exalted subsequent to his suffering. Nevertheless, there are important differences in perspective as well. Thus Hebrews accentuates hope while John focuses on the believer's present possession of eternal life; Johannine "in" Christ language is absent from Hebrews; and Hebrews views the Christian life more in terms of struggle on account of believers' weariness and reluctance to suffer.

John and Peter were close associates in ministry (cf. Acts 3–4; 8:14–25; Gal 2:9; cf. Lk 5:8–10). One might therefore expect to find a certain degree of similarity between their respective writings. Indeed, John and Peter share the following commonalities: the presentation of Jesus as both

Study Questions

1. Trace the story lines of each of the three Synoptic Gospels and relate these to that of John's Gospel.

2. Comment on each of the fourteen explicit Old Testament quotations in John's Gospel, considering also the book's most significant Old Testament allusions.

3. Discuss the points of contact between John's Gospel and the other Johannine writings as well as similarities and differences between John and Paul, Hebrews, or Peter.

Lamb and shepherd (Jn 1:29, 36; 10:12; 21:15–19; 1 Pt 1:19; 2:25; 5:24); the designation of believers as those who are "in Christ" (1 Jn 2:5–6; 1 Pt 5:14) and as those who believe in Jesus although they do not now see him (Jn 20:29; 1 Pt 1:8); their challenge of believers to joyful suffering for Christ (Jn 1:18, 25; 1 Pt 2:13–4:2); and their emphasis on brotherly love (Jn 13:34; 15:9, 12, 17; 17:26; 1 Pt 1:22; 2:17; 4:8). Moreover, neither John nor Peter discusses the role of the Law or the formal organization of the church.

Conclusion

Apart from these points of contact, John sustains a close community of spirit with several other New Testament writings. Against those who in recent years have sought to marginalize John's Gospel by attributing it to a sectarian fringe group beyond the pale of mainstream first-century Christianity, it must be maintained that, with all its distinctness, John's Gospel is part and parcel of canonical biblical revelation and must be restored to its rightful place in contemporary schol-arship and the life of the church. The New Testament writings show John ministering alongside Peter (Acts 3–4), Peter ministering with the help of Mark (1 Pt 5:13), Mark aiding Paul (Col 4:10; 2 Tim 4:11), Paul being helped by Luke (see esp. the "we" passages in Acts), Luke using other documents as his sources (Lk 1:1–4), and the list goes on and on. The early church thus constituted a closely integrated network, including its leadership.[9] May John's remarkable theological achievement which is the Gospel of John not cloud the fact that, with all his unusual spiritual perceptiveness, John was still very much a team player who found himself thoroughly at home in the bosom of the first-century apostolic church.

Key Words

Markan priority
fulfillment quotations

Appendix 1

The History of the Interpretation of John's Gospel

Outline

- **The Early Church and the Fathers**
- **The Following Centuries**
- **The Recent Interpretation of John's Gospel**
  - Nineteenth and Early Twentieth Centuries
  - The Rehabilitation of John's Gospel in Recent Scholarship
  - The "New Look" on the Fourth Gospel and the "Johannine Community Hypothesis"
  - The Contemporary Scene and Conclusion

Objectives

After reading this chapter, you should be able to

1. Characterize the reception of John's Gospel by the early Fathers and the Gnostics.
2. Trace the decline in regard for John's reliability in nineteenth- and early-twentieth-century scholarship.
3. List the factors in recent scholarship that have led to a remarkable rehabilitation of John's integrity in the past few decades.

Diatessaron

The Early Church and the Fathers

In the first chapter, we have already reviewed the evidence for the authorship of John's Gospel. We found little reason to disagree with the church father Irenaeus's contention who wrote soon after A.D. 180 that, "Lastly, John, the Lord's disciple, who also reclined on his breast, himself produced the Gospel when he was staying in Ephesus in Asia."[1] This, we found, was after all not only asserted by Irenaeus (a disciple of Polycarp, who in turn had been a disciple of the apostle John), it is also supported by the Gospel's internal evidence. In the present chapter, we need not go over the same territory. Rather, we will briefly survey the history of interpretation of John's Gospel, mindful that we stand in an illustrious tradition of interpreters from whom we have much to learn in our efforts to apprehend John's message for today.[2]

We may begin with the remarkable fact that, around A.D. 170, Tatian in Rome, the pupil of Justin Martyr, already used the basic outline of John's Gospel, including its chronology, as the basis for his synopsis of the four canonical Gospels (called **"Diatessaron,"** Grk. for "four"). Interestingly, the Nag Hammadi finds, a Gnostic library dating from the second or third century A.D. which was discovered shortly after World War II in Egypt, provide ample evidence that John's Gospel was a favorite (see particularly the Gospel of Truth and the Gospel of Philip).[3] In fact, the first commentary on John's Gospel was written by the Gnostic Heracleon. The New Testament apocryphal books Apocryphon of John and Acts of John, both of which are built around the author of John's Gospel, also attest to John's stature in the second-century church, as does the influence of the Fourth Gospel on a number of apocryphal Gospels, including the Gospel of Peter, possibly the Gospel of Thomas, and also the Gospel fragment contained in the Egerton Papyrus. In the first half of the third century A.D., Origen calls the Fourth Gospel "the choice one of the Gospels," distinguishing sharply between the four canonical Gospels and the others.[4]

The Following Centuries

In the following centuries, the church looked to John's Gospel to combat distorted teachings on the nature of Christ, in particular by Arius, who accentuated Jesus' humanity to the extent that his deity seemed compromised (such as Athanasius at the Council of Nicea in A.D. 325).[5] As Burge notes, the "high respect [for John's Gospel] continued through Medieval Christendom. From Augustine (354–430) to Aquinas (1224–1274) and beyond, John provided the portrait of a Jesus who directly revealed the Father. Mysticism and sacramentalism likewise found in John the language and symbolic images they enjoyed. Commentaries from this period abound."[6] During the Reformation period, Calvin considered John's Gospel to be "a key to open the door to understanding the others [i.e., the other Gospels]."[7]

The Recent Interpretation of John's Gospel

Nineteenth and Early Twentieth Centuries

In more recent history, Friedrich Schleiermacher, the father of modern biblical interpretation, still maintained (in lectures delivered in 1832) that John was an eyewitness whose Gospel was historically trustworthy. Yet others, such as Karl Gottlieb Bretschneider (1820), expressed skepticism regarding John's reliability.[8] David Friedrich Strauss, writing in 1835, claimed that all four Gospels, but especially John, should be classified, not as accurate historical narratives, but as myths and legends. Moreover, similar to Bretschneider, Strauss believed that the Synoptics and John contained irreconcilable differences, so that one had to choose between one or the other gospel tradition—and Strauss, for his part, preferred the Synoptics. Still later, Ferdinand Christian Baur, the head of the "Tübingen school," attributed John's Gospel to a Hellenistic community and dated it between A.D. 150 and 170.

But this frontal assault on the reliability of John did not go unchallenged. The British scholar B. F. Westcott defended the apostolic authorship of John's Gospel in a commentary published in 1882. In Germany, the task of rehabilitating John fell largely to the Tübingen scholar Adolf Schlatter in works written in 1902 and 1930.[9] Nevertheless, even today many still follow the skeptical arguments advanced against the trustworthiness of John's Gospel in the nineteenth century, further developed in this century by scholars such as Rudolf Bultmann (1884–1972) whose hugely influential commentary appeared in 1941 (ET 1971).[10] During this period, two stereotypes developed and became deeply ingrained in the fabric of Johannine scholarship: first, that the Synoptic Gospels were interested in history while John, as "the spiritual Gospel" (Clement of Alexandria's term), favored theology; and second, that John was a product of Hellenistic Christianity while at least some of the Synoptic Gospels, in particular Matthew, came from a Jewish milieu.[11]

The writings of the Qumran sect show a certain affinity to the language (though not necessarily theology) of John's Gospel. Depicted is Cave 4, where many of the most famous scrolls were found.

The Rehabilitation of John's Gospel in Recent Scholarship

In recent years, the pendulum has swung decisively the other way. Several factors combined to rehabilitate John's Gospel in a truly remarkable fashion. First, archaeological evidence has come to light in form of the **John Rylands papyrus** (p[52]), an Egyptian fragment containing John 18:31–33 and 37–38 which is dated around A.D. 125.[12] Allowing for time for John's original manuscript to be copied and to make its way from Ephesus in Asia Minor to Egypt, this pushes the date of writing of John's Gospel back to the late first century. So much for Baur's hypothesis that the Gospel was not published until after A.D. 150!

Second, the stunning discovery of a sectarian library at Qumran near the Dead Sea (popularly known as the Dead Sea Scrolls) indicates that the language of John's Gospel, rather than reflecting Hellenistic traits, is closely paralleled in this particular brand of Judaism.[13] This effectively overturned the thesis that the Fourth Gospel is a product of a Greek community, a remarkable rehabilitation of those who, like Adolf Schlatter, had de-

Study Questions

1. List at least five scholars who have had an important role in the history of interpretation of John's Gospel and identify their contribution.

2. Name three factors that led to a rehabilitation of John's Gospel in recent decades.

fended the Gospel's Jewish provenance all along.

Third, scholars from Leon Morris to John Pryor have shown conclusively that the writer of John's Gospel was thoroughly familiar with Palestinian topography and that his theology is thoroughly rooted in Old Testament conceptualities.[14] This further confirms John's grounding in a Jewish milieu and his basic conceptual framework of viewing the Christian community in continuity with the history of God's people in the Old Testament.

Fourth, further support came from an unexpected direction. In chapter 16, we have already referred to the highly influential work by P. Gardner-Smith, who in 1938 advocated the thesis that John wrote his Gospel independently from the Synoptics. According to Gardner-Smith, the issue is not merely whether John knew the Synoptics but if he depended on them in writing his account. Viewed from this perspective, it seems precarious to argue for dependence in light of the fact that John contains only about 8 percent of the Synoptic material. But—and here is the important implication for the historical value of the Fourth Gospel—if John wrote independently, then his historical witness should be considered of primary significance.

The "New Look" on the Fourth Gospel and the "Johannine Community Hypothesis"

Of the chroniclers of these trends, none is better known than J. A. T. Robinson (1919–83). In a famous essay entitled "The New Look on the Fourth Gospel," which first appeared in 1959, he described the "old look" that had dominated Johannine scholarship until recently as follows: (1) John depends on sources, particularly the Synoptics; (2) John's background is not Jewish, but Greek, and is influenced by Gnostic ideas; (3) John cannot be taken seriously as a historical witness; (4) John's theology, and in particular his Christology, reflects late-first-century thought; (5) the author of John's Gospel is not an eyewitness, much less the apostle John.[15] But the "new look" refuted these claims, concluding that (1) there is continuity between historical traditions about Jesus and the material included in the Fourth Gospel; (2) the setting of John's Gospel is early-first-century Jewish Christianity, so that (3) questions regarding the Gospel's authorship, date, and other introductory matters must be reopened.

Thus John's Gospel was rehabilitated in two important ways: first, it was found that the Fourth Gospel provides an independent historical witness to Jesus; and second, the conclusion gained ground that John's Gospel is rooted in Jewish rather than Greek life and thought. Despite these positive contributions, however, and the appearance of conservatism, Robinson's presentation still left the door wide open for a departure from the notion of apostolic authorship. For all the "new look" required was a vague affirmation of continuity between authentic "Johannine tradition" and the material included in the Fourth Gospel. But this contention does little to strengthen confidence in the apostolic eyewitness character of John's Gospel; it merely encourages some kind of connection—which may be more or less remote—between the events narrated in the Fourth Gospel and those who witnessed them.

That the "new look" marked no complete return to the traditional view is confirmed by the latest challenge to the apostolic character of John's Gospel subsequent to Robinson's seminal essay. This challenge can be summarized under the umbrella term "Johannine community hypothesis." Popularized by J. Louis Martyn and his colleague Raymond E. Brown, this view holds that the Fourth Gospel was actually authored by a group that traced its origins to John the apostle and that used the gospel story to work through conflicts

birkath-ha-minim

it experienced in its own day.[16] It was conjectured that the members of this "Johannine community" had been expelled from their Jewish mother synagogue in the aftermath of the curses on the Christians *(birkath-ha-minim)* allegedly imposed on Christians around A.D. 90 and that the Fourth Gospel represents an attempt either to recover from this traumatic event or to evangelize some of the members of this mother synagogue. For a while this view, though virtually unsupported by direct evidence, rose to astonishing prominence, achieving almost paradigmatic status.[17] But recently scholars such as Martin Hengel and Richard Bauckham have decisively shown that there is no historic evidence even for the existence of such a "Johannine community" and that John's Gospel represents, not a sectarian document, but rather an apostolic Gospel aimed at a universal readership.[18]

The Contemporary Scene and Conclusion

The current scene in Johannine scholarship is characterized by increasing confusion, even chaos. Attenders of the Johannine section of the Society of Biblical Literature, a major professional society meeting annually for the purpose of scholarly exchange, are treated to a smorgasbord of lectures that are for the most part experimental and speculative, and concerned primarily with the impact of John's Gospel on the contemporary reader. In these kinds of settings, the underlying assumption has largely become that John's Gospel does not have a determinate meaning controlled by authorial intent, so that the conventional kinds of questions of authorship or date are irrelevant. Rather, the text of John's Gospel

becomes material for academic experimentation. Thus paper titles at the 1998 Annual Meeting include: "A King is Bound in the Tresses: Allusions to the Song of Songs in the Fourth Gospel" and "Transcending Alterity: The Proverbial Strange Woman Meets the Johannine Samaritan Woman."

As a result, it is notions of political correctness, not authorial intent, that increasingly controls biblical interpretation. This may be a negative way to end this discussion, but perhaps it injects a dose of realism into the idealistic world of some of us who may surmise that the fare served in the present work is representative of contemporary Johannine scholarship at large. It is not. Nevertheless, there continues to be a presence of sane responsible interpretation of John's Gospel epitomized by recent works such as the commentaries of D. A. Carson or Herman Ridderbos. It is to these works that the serious student of John's Gospel may turn in an age that is characterized by a dizzying array of methods while the plain message of John's Gospel often completely vanishes from sight. May not one of us permit our study of John's Gospel to degenerate into some kind of intellectual game.

Key Words

New look

Diatessaron

John Rylands papyrus

birkath-ha-minim

Appendix 2

John's Gospel and the Study of the Historical Jesus

Outline

- Jesus and the Logic of History
- The Study of the Historical Jesus: John's Portrayal of Jesus as a Jewish Rabbi
- The Jesus Seminar and the Historical Value of John's Gospel

Objectives

After reading this chapter, you should be able to

1. Appreciate the value of John's Gospel in the recent discussion of the "historical Jesus."
2. Defend the Jewishness of Jesus over against the hypotheses of the Jesus Seminar.

Jesus and the Logic of History

Paul Barnett, in his compelling recent work entitled *Jesus and the Logic of History*, points out that there is only one plausible explanation for the explosive growth of the early Christian movement: that Jesus was in fact who he claimed to be, the Messiah and the Son of God. This not only coheres precisely with John's purpose statement, it also is an eminently historical matter. Few people dispute that Jesus is a historical figure. And those who do do so arguably out of ignorance or in disregard of powerful evidence, foremost of all that provided by Roman historians who were adamantly opposed to Christianity, but who, as historians, presupposed the fact of his historical existence.[1]

The contributors to a recent compendium on Jesus scholarship titled *Jesus Under Fire* as well as Gregory Boyd in his powerful work *Cynic Sage or Son of God? Recovering the Real Jesus in an Age of Revisionist Replies* have likewise shown that we have every reason to be confident in the Gospels' portrait of Jesus' life and ministry.[2] There is no need here to reproduce the arguments of these books in the present volume. These and other works furnish more than adequate proof that we have every reason to believe both in the full humanity and deity of Christ as well as in the historical fact of his resurrection, to name but some of the most crucial claims advanced with regard to Jesus in the canonical Gospels.[3]

The Study of the Historical Jesus: John's Portrayal of Jesus as a Jewish Rabbi

But does John's Gospel provide reliable information regarding the so-called historical Jesus, or do we have to content ourselves exclusively with the Synoptics in this regard? This seems to be the inevitable conclusion, for even conservative scholars, in their defense of the trustworthiness of the Gospels' portrait of Jesus, rely almost exclusively on data found in the Synoptic Gospels and Acts. But this conclusion would be both premature and erroneous. For it does not follow that, merely because John is particularly interested in drawing out the theological implications of Jesus' ministry, he is therefore disinterested in or even falsifies history. Indeed, the truthfulness of his theology arguably hinges on the historicity of the events on which it is based.

Indeed, as I have argued in a recent scholarly article, John's Gospel is a very valuable historical source indeed.[4] To give but one example, the Fourth Gospel shows, in some ways even more clearly than the Synoptic Gospels, how Jesus was approached by his contemporaries primarily as a rabbi, a Jewish religious teacher. For while the Synoptic writers (esp. Luke) generally use the Greek equivalent for "teacher," *didaskalos,* John frequently provides also the Hebrew/Aramaic term *rabbi* (cf. 1:38, 49; 3:2; 4:31; 6:25; 9:2; 11:8; 20:16). Thus the conclusion is warranted that "John is unmatched both in the range of individuals referring to Jesus as *rabbi* and the consistency with which *rabbi* is the chosen address of Jesus."[5]

This, of course, does not imply that Jesus was nothing but a rabbi—but it allows us a fascinating glimpse on the way in which Jesus was primarily perceived, not just by his immediate followers, but also by the general populace of his day. To be sure, John maintains that, beside being a teacher, Jesus is also the preexistent Word-become-flesh as well as the Son of God. But John makes clear that Jesus adopted a certain cultural identity appropriate for his day and environment—that of a Jewish rabbi. Moreover, what is even more important in light of our present concern, it is John who emerges as the most important source for our knowledge of this particular aspect of Jesus' ministry.

The Jesus Seminar and the Historical Value of John's Gospel

This brings us to the most highly publicized recent effort to come to terms with the so-called historical Jesus, the Jesus Seminar. It is apparent that the above conclusion flies in the face of contentions recently popularized by members of the Jesus Seminar that Jesus was an itinerant

Jewish sage or the like.[6] For while there may be certain surface similarities—Jesus' modest lifestyle, his denunciation of materialism, his traveling ministry—there is little (if any) evidence that Cynic philosophy had even a presence in first-century Galilee. And why would Jesus, who was so eminently Jewish, use the identity of a Cynic Greek philosopher when that of a Jewish rabbi lay much closer at hand? This strains credulity.

Space does not permit a fuller discussion of the value of John's Gospel in the study of the "historical Jesus." We conclude with the following observations. It is an observable fact that contemporary discussions of the "historical Jesus" regularly adduce evidence from the Synoptic Gospels and Acts while John's Gospel is all but ignored, even by conservative interpreters. However, if, as has been argued in the present volume, John's Gospel provides an accurate, trustworthy account of Jesus' life, not merely in terms of theology, but also with regard to history, contemporary scholarship must begin to take the Fourth Gospel seriously once again. May this little book make a small contribution to the renewed appreciation of John's Gospel in terms of history, literature, and theology, and our efforts will have been amply rewarded.

Study Questions

1. Provide reasons why the explosive growth of the early Christian movement is explained adequately only by the accuracy of Jesus' claims.

2. Illustrate the importance of John's Gospel as a historical witness by discussing the Fourth Gospel's references to Jesus as a Jewish rabbi.

3. Discuss the inadequacy of the conclusions of the "Jesus Seminar" regarding the identity of the "historical Jesus."

Notes

Chapter 1: History: How John's Gospel Came to Be

1. See D. A. Carson, D. J. Moo, and L. L. Morris, *An Introduction to the New Testament* (Grand Rapids: Zondervan, 1992), 142.

2. "Diaspora Jews" here refers to the Jews living in dispersion over the Greco-Roman world in the days of the early church. "Proselytes" refers to Gentiles who joined Jewish monotheism, synagogue worship, food laws, Sabbath-keeping, and circumcision.

3. Richard Bauckham, ed., *The Gospels for All Christians: Rethinking the Gospel Audiences* (Grand Rapids: Eerdmans, 1997), esp. Bauckham, "For Whom Were Gospels Written?" 9–48.

4. See esp. the essays in *Jews and Christians: The Parting of the Ways* A.D. 70 to 135, ed. James D. G. Dunn (Tübingen: J. C. B. Mohr [Paul Siebeck], 1992), esp. Philip S. Alexander, "'The Parting of the Ways' from the Perspective of Rabbinic Judaism," 1–25; and Martin Goodman, "Diaspora Reactions to the Destruction of the Temple," 27–38.

5. See Bauckham, *Gospels for All Christians.*

Chapter 2: Literature: Mapping John's Story

1. On postmodernism, see D. A. Carson, *The Gagging of God: Christianity Confronts Pluralism* (Grand Rapids: Zondervan, 1996). On the role of the author in interpretation, see E. D. Hirsch Jr., *Validity in Interpretation* (New Haven, Conn., and London: Yale University Press, 1967).

2. See ch. 3 in Hirsch, *Validity in Interpretation.*

3. See Martin Hengel, "The Titles of the Gospels and the Gospel of Mark," in *Studies in the Gospel of Mark* (Philadelphia: Fortress, 1985), 64–84.

4. D. A. Carson, D. J. Moo, and L. Morris, *An Introduction to the New Testament* (Grand Rapids: Zondervan, 1992), 48.

5. Willard M. Swartley, *Israel's Scripture Traditions and the Synoptic Gospels: Story Shaping Story* (Peabody, Mass.: Hendrickson, 1994).

Chapter 3: Theology: John's Major Themes

1. Aphoristic sayings are short, often catchy or memorable, pronouncements such as Jesus' statement, "For the Son of Man came to seek and to save what was lost" (Lk 19:10).

2. Samuel Sandmel, "Parallelomania," *Journal of Biblical Literature* 81 (1962): 1–13.

3. Cf. John W. Pryor, *John: Evangelist of the Covenant People: The Narrative and Themes of the Fourth Gospel* (Downers Grove: InterVarsity, 1992), 55, 64, 89, 119–20, 126, 130–31, 158, 160, 166.

4. Richard Bauckham, ed., *The Gospels for All Christians: Rethinking the Gospel Audiences* (Grand Rapids: Eerdmans, 1997).

5. Cf. C. S. Lewis, *Mere Christianity* (New York: Macmillan, 1960), 56.

6. Cf. Anthony E. Harvey, "Christ as Agent," in *The Glory of Christ in the New Testament: Studies in Christology in Memory of George Bradford Caird*, ed. L. D. Hurst and N. T. Wright (Oxford: Clarendon, 1987), 239–50.

7. On the humanity of Jesus in John's Gospel, see esp. Marianne Meye Thompson, *The Humanity of Jesus in the Fourth Gospel* (Philadelphia: Fortress, 1988).

8. See J. Terence Forestell, *The Word of the Cross: Salvation as Revelation in the Fourth Gospel*, AnBib 57 (Rome: Biblical Institute Press, 1974).

9. Cf. D. A. Carson, *The Gospel according to John* (Grand Rapids: Eerdmans, 1991), 153.

10. George E. Ladd, *A Theology of the New Testament*, 2nd ed. (Grand Rapids: Eerdmans, 1993), 295.

Chapter 4: The Incarnation of the Word

1. Zeno, *Fragments* in J. von Arnim, *Stoicorum Veterum Fragmenta*, I (1964), 175, quoted in C. K. Barrett, *The New Testament Background: Selected Documents*, rev. and exp. ed. (San Francisco: Harper & Row, 1989), 66.

2. Zeno, *Fragments* 162, cited in Barrett, *New Testament Background*, 67.

3. Samuel Sandmel, "Parallelomania," *Journal of Biblical Literature* 81 (1962): 1–13.

4. This chart is adapted from Scott R. Swain, "Truth in the Gospel of John" (Th.M. thesis, Wake Forest, N.C., 1998), 30.

5. See already the discussion above.

6. Some have suggested that the Jews' statement as part of their "paternity dispute" with Jesus, "We are not illegitimate children" (8:41), constitutes a veiled allusion to the virgin birth.

7. See Larry W. Hurtado, *One God, One Lord: Early Christian Devotion and Ancient Jewish Monotheism* (Philadelphia: Fortress, 1988).

Chapter 5: Jesus' Early Ministry (Part 1): From John the Baptist to the Temple Cleansing (Signs ## 1–2)

1. The term "inclusio" designates the literary device current in John's day of an author's conscious placement of a term at the beginning and the end of a section in order to highlight a parallelism and to bind together the material included between the first and second instances of the term.

2. I have sought to demonstrate this in "Jesus as Rabbi in the Fourth Gospel," *Bulletin of Biblical Research* 8 (1998): 97–128.

3. Augustine, quoted in Lyman Abott, *An Illustrated Commentary on the Gospel according to St. John* (New York and Chicago: A. S. Barnes, 1879), 32.

4. For a detailed discussion of the prophetic symbolism entailed by Jesus' cleansing of the temple and the argument that this event should be considered the second sign recorded in John's Gospel, see my "The Seventh Johannine Sign: A Study in John's Christology," *Bulletin of Biblical Research* 5 (1995): 87–103.

5. The term is used by C. K. Barrett, "The House of Prayer and

the Den of Thieves," in *Jesus und Paulus,* ed. E. Earle Ellis and Erich Gräßer (Göttingen: Vandenhoeck & Ruprecht, 1975), 13–20.

6. See Harold W. Hoehner, *Chronological Aspects of the Life of Christ* (Grand Rapids: Zondervan, 1977), 38–43.

Chapter 6: Jesus' Early Ministry (Part 2): Ministering to Nicodemus, the Samaritan Woman, and the Nobleman's Son (Sign #3)

1. This assumes that we have here a fairly full account of Nicodemus's actual interchange with Jesus. It further assumes that we possess a reliable representation of what Jesus and Nicodemus actually said during their encounter. I think that these are eminently defensible conclusions; at this point it seems sufficient to merely acknowledge that these are presuppositions underlying the above analysis.

2. See the comparison chart between kingdom and eternal life in ch. 3 above.

3. On 4:34–38 see my *Missions of Jesus and the Disciples according to the Fourth Gospel* (Grand Rapids: Eerdmans, 1998), 180–84.

Chapter 7: Escalating Conflict (Part 1): The Sabbath Controversy, Feeding the Multitude, Major Defections (Signs ##4–5)

1. See my *Missions of Jesus and the Disciples according to the Fourth Gospel* (Grand Rapids: Eerdmans, 1998), 75–76.

Chapter 8: Escalating Conflict (Part 2): Confronting Unbelief at Home and in Jerusalem; Jesus at the Feast of Tabernacles

1. See the discussion in Bruce M. Metzger, *A Textual Commentary to the New Testament,* rev. ed. (New York: UBS, 1994), 187–89.

2. See Str-B 2:774.

3. For a survey of John's presentation of "the Coming One," see my *Missions of Jesus and the Disciples according to the Fourth Gospel* (Grand Rapids: Eerdmans, 1998), 94–96.

4. Cf. J. Daryl Charles, "'Will the Court Please Call in the Prime Witness?' John 1:29–34 and the 'Witness'-Motif," *Trinity Journal* 10 NS (1989): 71–83.

5. This has been called "the new

perspective on Paul," pioneered by E. P. Sanders in his watershed work *Paul and Palestinian Judaism* (Minneapolis: Fortress, 1977).

Chapter 9: Escalating Conflict (Part 3): Opening the Blind Man's Eyes, Shepherding God's Flock (Sign #6)

1. For this reason we must part company with David R. Beck, *The Discipleship Paradigm: Readers & Anonymous Characters in the Fourth Gospel* (Leiden: Brill, 1997), who contends that both the lame man in ch. 5 and the blind man in ch. 9 are positive characters in John's Gospel.

2. London: Tyndale, 1971. See also my *Missions of Jesus and the Disciples according to the Fourth Gospel* (Grand Rapids: Eerdmans, 1998), 133–38.

3. France, *Jesus and the OT,* 104.

4. On the nature of Jesus' work according to the Fourth Gospel, see the section with this title in my *Missions of Jesus and the Disciples according to the Fourth Gospel,* 74–81.

5. For a list of ways in which John appropriates old covenant language to designate Jesus' new messianic community, see my *Missions of Jesus and the Disciples,* 162, in adaptation of John W. Pryor, *John: Evangelist of the Covenant People* (Downers Grove: InterVarsity, 1992).

Chapter 10: Escalating Conflict (Part 4): Raising Lazarus, the Anointing, the Triumphal Entry, and Jewish Unbelief (Sign #7)

1. For a thorough discussion of various substitute theories for the historicity and reality of Christ's resurrection, see Adolf Schlatter, *The History of the Christ,* trans. Andreas J. Köstenberger (Grand Rapids: Baker, 1997), 375–83.

2. This conclusively settles the knotty textual problem in 12:32 whether the original reading is "all men" (*pantas*) or "all things" (*panta*) in favor of "all [kinds of] men" (*pantas*). See *Sidebar: Will the Exalted Christ Draw "All Things" or "All People" to Himself? (John 12:32).*

3. On this topic, see esp. D. A. Carson, *Divine Sovereignty & Human Responsibility: Biblical Perspectives in Tension* (Atlanta: John Knox, 1981), esp. 125–98.

Chapter 11: Jesus' Farewell (Part 1)

1. On this widening of the term "disciple" in John's Gospel, see my *Missions of Jesus and the Disciples according to the Fourth Gospel* (Grand Rapids: Eerdmans, 1998), 149–53.

2. See esp. Aelred Lacomara, "Deuteronomy and the Farewell Discourse (Jn. 13:31–16:33)," *Catholic Biblical Quarterly* 36 (1974): 65–84; and John W. Pryor, *John: Evangelist of the Covenant People* (Downers Grove: InterVarsity, 1992), esp. 160, 166, and 216, n. 8, referring also to Edward Malatesta, *Interiority and Covenant,* AnBib 69 (Rome: Biblical Institute Press, 1978), 42–77.

3. See here my "Jesus as Rabbi in the Fourth Gospel," *Bulletin of Biblical Research* 8 (1998): 97–128.

4. For a full exploration of the mission theme in John, including a critique of the "Johannine community hypothesis," see my *Missions of Jesus and the Disciples.*

5. On this parallelism, see my *Missions of Jesus and the Disciples,* 154–61, esp. 158–59.

Chapter 12: Jesus' Farewell (Part 2)

1. For a comprehensive treatment and critique of religious pluralism within the larger framework of postmodernism, see esp. D. A. Carson, *The Gagging of God* (Grand Rapids: Zondervan, 1996).

2. For a helpful survey, see the first chapter in N. T. Wright, *What Saint Paul Really Said* (Grand Rapids: Eerdmans, 1997).

3. The phrase is John Pryor's: see his book with this title (Downers Grove: InterVarsity, 1992).

4. I am indebted for some of these observations to the unpublished Th.M. thesis of my student Scott R. Swain, "Truth in the Gospel of John" (Wake Forest, N.C., 1998).

5. Standard Greek reference works cite the following meanings: Liddell and Scott: one called to one's aid, legal assistant, advocate, summoned, intercessor; TDNT: legal advisor, helper, advocate in court. For a helpful survey, see Rudolf Schnackenburg, *The Gospel According to St. John,* Vol. 3 (New York: Crossroad, 1990), 144–50.

6. Leon Morris, *Jesus Is the Christ* (Grand Rapids: Eerdmans, 1989), 159.

7. Donald Guthrie, *New Testament Theology* (Downers Grove:

InterVarsity, 1981), 531; quoted in Morris, *Jesus Is the Christ,* 158.

8. Cf. Andreas J. Köstenberger, *The Missions of Jesus and the Disciples according to the Fourth Gospel* (Grand Rapids: Eerdmans, 1998), 166–67.

9. Tacitus, *Annals* xv. 44, quoted in C. K. Barrett, *The New Testament Background: Selected Documents,* rev. ed. (San Francisco: Harper & Row, 1989), 15–16.

Chapter 13: Jesus' Farewell (Part 3)

1. See my *Missions of Jesus and the Disciples according to the Fourth Gospel* (Grand Rapids: Eerdmans, 1998), 96–121, esp. 107–11.

2. See George Eldon Ladd, *A Theology of the New Testament,* rev. ed. (Grand Rapids: Eerdmans, 1993), 290–95.

3. For a detailed study of the most important New Testament passage concerning the roles of women and men in the church, see Andreas J. Köstenberger, Thomas R. Schreiner, and H. Scott Baldwin, eds., *Women in the Church: A Fresh Analysis of 1 Timothy 2:8–15* (Grand Rapids: Baker, 1995). A summary of the argument of this work by the present author is "'The Crux of the Matter': Paul's Pastoral Pronouncements Regarding Women's Roles in 1 Timothy 2:9–15," *Faith & Mission* 14 (1996): 24–48.

4. Charles E. Hummel, *Tyranny of the Urgent* (Downers Grove: InterVarsity, 1967), 6–9.

5. For a more detailed discussion of this issue, see my *Missions of Jesus and the Disciples,* 74–81.

6. See on this topic my *Missions of Jesus and the Disciples,* 189–90.

7. Cf. A. B. Bruce, *The Training of the Twelve* (Grand Rapids: Kregel, 1971 [1894]); Robert E. Coleman, *The Master Plan of Evangelism* (Old Tappan, N.J.: Revell, 1963); idem, *The Mind of the Master* (Old Tappan, N.J.: Revell, 1977).

Chapter 14: Jesus' Passion, Resurrection, and Commissioning of His Followers

1. See further Sidebar: The So-called "Johannine Pentecost" (John 20:22).

Chapter 15: What It Means to Follow Jesus

1. See my *Missions of Jesus and the Disciples according to the Fourth*

Gospel (Grand Rapids: Eerdmans, 1998), 154–61.

Chapter 16: Conclusion: John in the Context of Scripture

1. Cf. Gary Burge, *Interpreting the Gospel of John* (Grand Rapids: Baker, 1992), 23.

2. Cf. C. H. Dodd, *The Interpretation of the Fourth Gospel* (Cambridge: Cambridge University Press, 1953) and *Historical Tradition in the Fourth Gospel* (Cambridge: Cambridge University Press, 1963); and John A. T. Robinson, *Redating the New Testament* (Philadelphia: Westminster, 1976) and *The Priority of John* (London: SCM, 1985). On the "new look on the Fourth Gospel" spawned by Robinson, see further Appendix 1 below.

3. Thus Rudolf Bultmann centers his highly influential *Theology of the New Testament,* 2 vols., trans. Kendrick Grobel (New York: Charles Scribner's Sons, 1951 and 1955) on the theological contributions made by Paul (Vol. 1) and John (Vol. 2).

4. This is where John differs from Paul, whose primary source-book is the Old Testament, not Jesus. Contra David Wenham, *Paul: Follower of Jesus or Founder of Christianity?* (Grand Rapids: Eerdmans, 1995), which I reviewed in *Trinity Journal* 16 (1995): 259–62.

5. For a helpful survey of John's use of the Old Testament, see especially D. A. Carson, "John and the Johannine Epistles," in *It Is Written: Scripture Citing Scripture,* ed. D. A. Carson and H. G. M. Williamson (Cambridge: Cambridge University Press, 1988), 245–64.

6. For this interpretation see Linda Belleville, *Trinity Journal* 1 (1980): 125–41, followed by D. A. Carson, *The Gospel According to John* (Grand Rapids: Eerdmans, 1991), 191–96.

7. See Richard N. Longenecker, *Biblical Exegesis in the Apostolic Period* (Grand Rapids: Eerdmans, 1975), 34.

8. The following discussion is adapted from my entry, "John, Gospel of," in the forthcoming *New Dictionary of Biblical Theology,* ed. Desmond Alexander and Brian Rosner (Leicester, U.K.: InterVarsity).

9. See here the remarkable recent work edited by Richard Bauckham, *The Gospels for All Christians: Rethinking the Gospel Audiences* (Grand Rapids: Eerdmans, 1997).

Appendix 1: The History of the Interpretation of John's Gospel

1. *Adv. Haer.* 3.1.1. = Eusebius, *H.E.* 5.8.4. See also Martin Hengel, *The Johannine Question,* trans. John Bowden (Philadelphia: Trinity Press International, 1989), 1–23.

2. For a helpful similar (but more detailed) survey, including references to further literature, see Gary M. Burge, *Interpreting the Gospel of John* (Grand Rapids: Baker, 1992), 15–35.

3. See C. K. Barrett, "The Theological Vocabulary of the Fourth Gospel and of the Gospel of Truth," in *Essays on John* (Philadelphia: Westminster, 1982), 50–64.

4. Cf. Christoph Ernst Luthardt, *St. John the Author of the Fourth Gospel,* trans. Caspar René Gregory (Edinburgh: T. & T. Clark, 1875), 38.

5. Cf. Maurice Wiles, *The Spiritual Gospel: The Interpretation of the Fourth Gospel in the Early Church* (Cambridge: Cambridge University Press, 1960).

6. See Burge, *Interpreting the Gospel of John,* 17.

7. John Calvin, *The Gospel According to St. John,* Vol. 1, trans. T. H. L. Parker (Grand Rapids: Eerdmans, 1959), 6.

8. For a survey of Johannine scholarship prior to Bretschneider, see my "Frühe Zweifel an der johanneischen Verfasserschaft des vierten Evangeliums in der modernen Interpretationsgeschichte," *European Journal of Theology* 5 (1996): 37–46.

9. Cf. B. F. Westcott, *The Gospel According to St. John,* repr. ed. (Grand Rapids: Eerdmans, 1975); Adolf Schlatter, *Die Sprache und Heimat des vierten Evangelisten [The Language and Provenance of the Fourth Evangelist]* (Stuttgart: Calwer, 1902); idem, *Der Evangelist Johannes: Wie er spricht, denkt und glaubt [John the Evangelist: How He Speaks, Thinks, and Believes]* (Stuttgart: Calwer, 1930).

10. See Rudolf Bultmann, *The Gospel of John,* trans. G. R. Beasley-

Murray (Philadelphia: Westminster, 1971). Even though Bultmann was firmly committed to antisupernaturalism, his commentary has been so influential that John Ashton, in his work *Understanding the Fourth Gospel* (Oxford: Clarendon, 1991), 3–117, can divide the history of scholarship on John in three simple categories: Before Bultmann; Bultmann; and After Bultmann.

11. On the tension between history and theology in New Testament theology in general and the evaluation of John's Gospel in particular, see Stephen Neill and Tom Wright, *The Interpretation of the New Testament 1861–1986*, 2nd ed. (Oxford/New York: Oxford University Press, 1988), 430–39.

12. The John Rylands papyrus is the oldest extant exemplar of any portion of the New Testament in existence today. See Bruce Manning Metzger, *The Text of the New Testament: Its Transmission, Corruption, and Restoration*, 2nd ed. (New York/Oxford: Oxford University Press, 1968), 38–39.

13. Cf. James H. Charlesworth, ed., *John and the Dead Sea Scrolls* (New York: Crossroad, 1990).

14. See Leon Morris, *Studies in the Fourth Gospel* (Grand Rapids: Eerdmans, 1969); John W. Pryor, *John: Evangelist of the Covenant People: The Narrative and Themes of the Fourth Gospel* (Downers Grove: InterVarsity, 1992).

15. Robinson's essay is most accessible in John A. T. Robinson, *Twelve New Testament Studies*, SBT 34 (London: SCM, 1962), 94–106.

16. See J. Louis Martyn, *History and Theology in the Fourth Gospel*, rev. ed. (Nashville: Abingdon, 1979); Raymond E. Brown, *The Community of the Beloved Disciple* (New York: Paulist, 1979).

17. See D. Moody Smith, "The Contribution of J. Louis Martyn to the Understanding of the Gospel of John," in *The Conversation Continues. Studies in Paul and John. In Honor of J. Louis Martyn*, ed. Robert T. Fortna and Beverly R. Gaventa (Nashville: Abingdon, 1990), 275–94.

18. Martin Hengel, *Die johanneische Frage*, WUNT 67 (Tübingen: J.C.B. Mohr [Paul Siebeck], 1993), a significantly expanded version of *The Johannine Question;* and Richard Bauckham, ed., *The Gospels for All Christians: Rethinking the Gospel Audiences* (Grand Rapids: Eerdmans, 1998).

Appendix 2: John's Gospel and the Study of the Historical Jesus

1. For relevant background information, see esp. C. K. Barrett, *The New Testament Background: Selected Documents*, rev. ed. (San Francisco: Harper, 1987). See also Murray J. Harris, *Three Crucial Questions about Jesus* (Grand Rapids: Baker, 1994), esp. 13–29; and Edwin Yamauchi, "Jesus Outside the New Testament: What Is the Evidence?" in *Jesus Under Fire: Modern Scholarship Reinvents the Historical Jesus*, ed. Michael J. Wilkins and J. P. Moreland (Grand Rapids: Zondervan, 1995), 207–29.

2. See Wilkins and Moreland, eds., *Jesus Under Fire;* and Gregory A. Boyd, *Cynic Sage or Son of God?* (Wheaton, Ill.: Victor, 1995).

3. Helpful works include further Craig L. Blomberg, *The Historical Reliability of the Gospels* (Downers Grove: InterVarsity, 1987), and the classic by F. F. Bruce, *The New Testament Documents: Are They Reliable?*, 5th ed. (Downers Grove: InterVarsity, 1960).

4. Andreas J. Köstenberger, "Jesus as Rabbi in the Fourth Gospel," *Bulletin of Biblical Research* 8 (1998): 97–128.

5. Köstenberger, "Jesus as Rabbi," 110–11.

6. For a resounding critique of the contentions of the Jesus Seminar and related scholars, see, apart from the already cited *Jesus Under Fire,* esp. Boyd, *Cynic Sage or Son of God?* and N. T. Wright, *Who Was Jesus?* (Grand Rapids: Eerdmans, 1992).

Glossary

Aphorism: concise, memorable saying (e.g., "The Son of Man came to seek and save sinners")

Apocalyptic: symbolic depiction of eschatological (i.e., end-time) material

Apocrypha: without further qualification, refers to specific books included in the Old Testament canon by Roman Catholics but rejected by Protestants (e.g., Jubilees, Tobit, or 2 Maccabees)

Aqedah: Abraham's offering up of Isaac according to Genesis 22

Aretalogy: stories of the miraculous deeds of a godlike hero

Asides: instances where the evangelist seeks to clarify a given issue or undertakes to provide additional information to make an aspect of his narrative intelligible to his readers (e.g., 1:38: "rabbi" [which means Teacher]; or 1:41: "the Messiah" [i.e., the Christ]).

Birkath-ha-Minim: the "curses on the Christians" (the "minim" or heretics) imposed around A.D. 90 which are alleged by some proponents to constitute the primary background of John's Gospel; according to this view, the Gospel represents an attempt by the members of a "Johannine community" who had been expelled from their mother synagogue in the aftermath of these curses to recover from this traumatic event or to evangelize some of the members of this mother synagogue; see also "Johannine community hypothesis"

Bread of Life Discourse: Jesus' discourse expanding on the significance of his feeding of the multitude culminating in his claim to be the "the Bread of Life" in escalation of God's giving of manna to wilderness Israel (cf. 6:22–59)

Diaspora: the Jews living in "dispersion" subsequent to the Babylonian and Assyrian exiles in pre–New Testament times

Diatessaron: first extant synopsis of the four Gospels compiled by Tatian (*diatessaron* = Greek "four"), the pupil of Justin Martyr, around A.D. 170 in Rome; notably,

it uses the outline and chronology of John's Gospel as its basis

Dominus et Deus: Latin "Lord and God," designation applied to Roman emperors such as Domitian (A.D. 81–96); the Greek equivalent is used by Thomas in John 20:28 with reference to Jesus

Doublet: an instance where a certain type of event occurred more than once during Jesus' ministry (e.g., feedings of a multitude)

Ecce homo: Latin "Here is the man," Pilate's famous statement regarding Jesus recorded in John 19:5

Ecclesiology: biblical teaching on the church

Eschatology: biblical teaching on the end times

External evidence: data derived from sources other than the document under consideration

Farewell Discourse: also called Upper Room Discourse; this refers primarily to the unique material narrated in John 14–16, although sometimes the term is used to refer to the entire section of John 13–17, with chapter 13 as a preamble and chapter 17 as a postlude to the actual discourse narrated in chapters 14–16

Fulfillment quotations: introductory formulas to quotations of Hebrew Scripture, such as: "this happened in order that the word spoken by the prophet Isaiah might be fulfilled" (cf. Jn 13:18; 15:25; 19:24, 36, 37)

Genre: kind of literature represented by a given work, such as novel, science fiction, romance, biography, or historical narrative

Gnosticism: the first major Christian heresy that denied, on the basis of a matter–spirit dualism, the reality of Jesus' incarnation, human sinfulness and need for atonement, and Christ's bodily resurrection

God-fearers: Gentiles worshiping the God of Israel (but without subjecting themselves to Jewish customs more fully as did proselytes; see below)

Good Shepherd Discourse: Jesus' portrayal of himself as the "Good Shepherd" in John 10

High Priestly Prayer: Jesus' prayer recorded in John 17

Historical-critical method: umbrella term for various interpretive tools aimed at discerning the historicity of certain biblical events, including source and redaction criticism; unfortunately, this approach has historically been wedded to a skeptical stance toward the reliability of Scripture; see also Redaction criticism, Source criticism

I am sayings: statements of Jesus unique to John by which Jesus identifies himself in continuity with God's self-designation to Moses as "I am" (cf. Ex 3:14; e.g., "I am the Bread of Life")

Incarnation: Jesus' assumption of humanity for the purpose of redemption (Jn 1:14: "the Word became flesh")

Inclusio: literary device by which a certain term is used at the beginning and at the end of a section, tying it together as a literary unit (e.g., "first sign" and "second sign" in Cana of Galilee in Jn 2:11 and 4:54)

Internal evidence: data derived from the document under consideration itself

Johannine circle: see Johannine community hypothesis

Johannine community hypothesis: theory that behind John's Gospel stands a community that traces its origins to the apostle John; according to this view, the Gospel presents the history of the "Johannine community" (or "school" or "circle") under the guise of the events of Jesus' earthly ministry

Johannine school: see Johannine community hypothesis

John Rylands papyrus: abbreviated p[52], this papyrus fragment found in Egypt constitutes the earliest extant manuscript of John's Gospel (or any portion of the New Testament, for that matter); it contains John 18:31–33 and 37–38 and is dated around A.D. 125

Lifted-up sayings: three Johannine sayings referring to the necessity of the "lifting up" of the Son of Man, whereby "lifting up" refers both to Jesus' crucifixion (his physical "lifting up") and his exaltation (figurative use) accomplished thereby (Jn 3:14; 8:28; 12:32)

Logos: portrayal of Jesus as the preexistent "Word" (cf. Jn 1:1, 14)

Markan priority: the notion that Mark's Gospel was the first to be written

Midrash: legendary expansions of historical narrative

Misunderstandings: instances in John where the evangelist emphasizes people's inability to understand the significance of Jesus' words or deeds prior to Jesus' "glorification" and the giving of the Spirit (e.g., the Jews' thinking in 2:20 that Jesus was speaking about literally rebuilding the temple in three days)

New look: expression derived from a famous article entitled "The New Look on the Fourth Gospel" published by John A. T. Robinson in 1959, in which the author sought to rehabilitate the independent nature and thus historical reliability of John's Gospel; Robinson also noted the consensus that the setting of John's Gospel is first-century Jewish Christianity

Omniscience: knowing everything

Ontological: related to being

Parallelomania: injudicious use of alleged parallels to establish literary dependence

Paraclete: unique Johannine designation of the Holy Spirit (Grk. *paraklētos*) best translated as "Helping Presence" or "Advocate"

Proselytes: Gentiles who joined Jewish monotheism, synagogue worship, food laws, Sabbath-keeping, and circumcision

Rabbi: Aramaic term for "teacher" (Grk. *didaskalos*) commonly applied to Jesus by his disciples in keeping with the designation of first-century Jewish religious teachers in Palestine

Redaction criticism: historical-critical tool designed to uncover particular emphases of the persons ultimately responsible for the publication of the Gospels (i.e., the evangelists); see also Historical-critical method

Replacement theme: recurring Johannine motif presenting Jesus as the substitute for various institutions in the life of Israel, such as some of the major feasts (including the Passover) or the temple

Replacement theology: teaching that the church replaces Israel in God's plan of salvation (arguably not taught in John)

Revealer myth: second-century Gnostic theological construct regarding the coming to earth of a divine messenger for the purpose of imparting to human beings the knowledge that they have a divine spark within them; this knowledge, the Gnostics contended, constituted salvation

Sabbath controversy: dispute between Jesus and the Jewish leaders (led by the Pharisees) that ensued after Jesus healed a man on the Jewish Sabbath (recorded in Jn 5)

Second Temple: the rebuilt Solomonic temple after the Babylonian exile

Septuagint: the Greek translation of the Hebrew Scriptures (abbreviated LXX for Greek "seventy," according to the legendary belief that the translation was prepared in seventy days)

Shema: from the Hebrew word "hear," the opening of Dt 6:4, the following affirmation was recited in every synagogue service: "Hear, O Israel: The LORD our God, the LORD is one"

Source criticism: historical-critical tool aimed at studying the use of sources by a later writer; in Gospel studies applied particularly to the so-called Synoptic problem, that is, the relationship among the Gospels of Matthew, Mark, and Luke

Stoicism: Greek philosophy according to which impersonal Reason governs the universe; alleged by some to constitute the background for John's Logos doctrine

Substitutionary atonement: Jesus' dying on the cross for our sins

Symbolic discourse: genre in which a given metaphor (e.g., shepherding) provides the backdrop for extended reflection (e.g., the "Good Shepherd Discourse" in Jn 10)

Synoptics: the Gospels of Matthew, Mark, and Luke (Grk. *syn* = together, *opsis* = view)

Theodicy: the justification of the righteousness of God and of his actions (*theos* = God; *dikaios* = righteous)

Transsubstantiation: Roman Catholic doctrine affirming that the Communion elements are literally transformed from bread and wine into Jesus' flesh and blood during Mass

Select Annotated Bibliography

1. Commentaries

Barrett, C. K. *The Gospel According to St. John.* 2nd ed. Philadelphia: Westminster, 1978. One of the best commentaries on John, but now superseded by Carson.

Beasley-Murray, George R. *John.* Word Biblical Commentary 36. Waco, Tex.: Word, 1987. Always worth consulting.

Brown, Raymond E. *The Gospel According to John.* 2 vols. Anchor Bible Commentary 29A–B. New York: Doubleday, 1966, 1970. Critical, yet very extensive, including helpful excursuses on major Johannine themes.

Carson, D. A. *The Gospel According to John.* Grand Rapids: Eerdmans, 1991. One of the best evangelical commentaries on John now available, especially on difficult exegetical issues.

Moloney, Francis J. *The Gospel of John.* Sacra Pagina 4. Collegeville, Minn.: Liturgical, 1998. The most recent thorough exegetical commentary, including helpful up-to-date bibliographies (pp. 24–31).

Morris, Leon. *The Gospel According to John.* New International Commentary on the New Testament. Rev. ed. Grand Rapids: Eerdmans, 1995. Consistently helpful.

Ridderbos, Herman. *The Gospel of John: A Theological Commentary.* Translated by John Vriend. Grand Rapids: Eerdmans, 1997. The new standard on theological synthesis. Less detailed than Carson, but more overtly theological in orientation.

Schnackenburg, Rudolf. *The Gospel According to St. John.* Herder's Theological Commentary on the New Testament. 3 vols. Translated by Kevin Smyth et al. New York: Crossroads, 1990 (1965, 1971, 1975). Very thorough (similar to Brown), moderately critical, always worth consulting.

2. Other Significant Works

Ashton, John, ed. *The Interpretation of John.* 2nd ed. Edinburgh: T. & T. Clark, 1997. Useful anthology of influential work on John, now in its second edition.

Bauckham, Richard, ed. *The Gospels for All Christians: Rethinking the Gospel Audiences.* Grand Rapids: Eerdmans, 1997. A seminal work on the universal orientation of the Gospels. Powerful refutation of the "Johannine community hypothesis."

Beasley-Murray, George R. *Gospel of Life: Theology in the Fourth Gospel.* Peabody, Mass.: Hendrickson, 1991. Interesting essays on selected themes in Johannine theology, including the mission of Jesus, the lifting up of the Son of Man, the ministry of the Holy Spirit, and the sacraments.

Burge, Gary M. *Interpreting the Gospel of John.* Baker Exegetical Guides to the New Testament. Grand Rapids: Baker, 1992. A very useful introduction to studying John's Gospel. The book is part of the Baker Exegetical Guides to the New Testament, all of which come highly recommended.

Carson, D. A., Douglas J. Moo, and Leon Morris. *An Introduction to the New Testament.* Grand Rapids: Zondervan, 1991, pp. 135–79. A helpful survey of the relevant introductory matters relating to John's Gospel.

Carson, D. A. "John and the Johannine Epistles." In *It Is Written: Scripture Citing Scripture,* ed. D. A. Carson and H. G. M. Williamson. Cambridge: Cambridge University Press, 1988, pp. 246–64. A good starting point for studying John's use of the Old Testament.

———. *Divine Sovereignty and Human Responsibility. Biblical Perspectives in Tension.* Repr. ed. Grand Rapids: Baker, 1997 (1981). A revised version of Carson's dissertation under B. Lindars at the University of Cambridge. His study of the divine sovereignty/human responsibility matrix culminates in an investigation of the teaching of John's Gospel on this topic. A carefully nuanced proposal of a "compatibilist" position.

Charlesworth, James H., ed. *John and the Dead Sea Scrolls.* New York: Crossroad, 1991. A helpful introduction to the relevance of Dead Sea Scrolls research for Johannine studies.

Culpepper, R. Alan. *The Anatomy of the Fourth Gospel: A Study in Literary Design.* Philadelphia: Fortress, 1983. A highly influential (though controversial) study on the literary design of John's Gospel. Unfortunately, however, Culpepper entirely eliminates historical concerns from consideration.

Culpepper, R. Alan, and C. Clifton Black, ed. *Exploring the Gospel of John. In Honor of D. Moody Smith.* Louisville, Ky.: Westminster/John Knox, 1996. A recent collection of essays that replaces more dated anthologies in relevance. Contributors include Thompson, Davies, Charlesworth, Borgen, Martyn, Barrett, Culpepper, Smalley, Dunn, and Meeks.

Harris, Murray J. *Jesus as God. The New Testament Use of Theos in Reference to Jesus.* Grand Rapids: Baker, 1992. While encompassing the entire New Testament, Harris's study is particularly important for students of John's

Gospel, since several references to Jesus as God are found in John.

Köstenberger, Andreas J. *The Missions of Jesus and the Disciples According to the Fourth Gospel.* Grand Rapids: Eerdmans, 1998. A recent study of the heretofore largely neglected "mission" theme in John. Note esp. ch. 3 on Jesus and ch. 4 on the disciples in John's Gospel.

Ladd, George Eldon. *A Theology of the New Testament.* 2nd ed. Grand Rapids: Eerdmans, 1994, pp. 249–344. This is one of the finest New Testament theologies written by an American in the twentieth century. Ladd uses a biblical-theological approach in an effort to appreciate the distinct teachings of the various New Testament writings, including John's Gospel. A bit dated, but still worth consulting.

Martyn, J. Louis. *History and Theology in the Fourth Gospel.* New York: Harper & Row, 1968. Rev. ed. Nashville: Abingdon, 1979. Another highly influential study that also sparked Raymond Brown's similar *Community of the Beloved Disciple* (New York: Paulist, 1979). Martyn is an outspoken advocate of the "Johannine community hypothesis." The word "history" in the title of his book refers to the history of the "Johannine community," which Martyn sees reflected in the Johannine narrative. Controversial but important reading.

Morris, Leon L. *Jesus Is the Christ: Studies in the Theology of John.* Grand Rapids: Eerdmans, 1989. Originally developed for a classroom setting, this volume (now unfortunately out of print) contains helpful chapters on many of the most significant themes found in John's Gospel, including the relation between signs and discourses, Jesus the Christ, Jesus the Son of God, God the Father, the Holy Spirit, believe, and life.

———. *Studies in the Fourth Gospel.* Grand Rapids: Eerdmans, 1969. Out of print, but well worth hunting down at a used bookstore. Detailed essays on such crucial themes as John's relationship to the Synoptics, history and theology in the Fourth Gospel, and the authorship of John's Gospel.

Pryor, John W. *John: Evangelist of the Covenant People. The Narrative and Themes of the Fourth Gospel.* Downers Grove: InterVarsity, 1992. Countering the recent trend in Johannine studies toward a marginalization of the Gospel of John, Pryor shows convincingly that the substructure of John's narrative is salvation-historical, linking Jesus' new covenant community systematically with Old Testament antecedents. A very significant work.

Robinson, John A. T. *The Priority of John,* ed. J. F. Coakley. London: SCM, 1985. Robinson, a highly controversial writer, argues that John is a Gospel with independent historical value. Hence it can be dated early. Worth consulting for its fresh, provocative approach.

Smalley, Stephen S. *John: Evangelist and Interpreter. History and Interpretation in the Fourth Gospel.* Greenwood, S.C.: Attic, 1978. An older but still helpful survey of the major issues and themes of John's Gospel.

Smith, D. Moody. *The Theology of the Gospel of John.* Cambridge: Cambridge University Press, 1994. A critical survey of Johannine theology. Unfortunately, this is one of the few such surveys available. What is needed is an evangelical equivalent.

———. *John among the Gospels: The Relationship in Twentieth-Century Research.* Minneapolis: Fortress, 1992. Helpful survey of John's relationship to the Synoptic Gospels in recent research.

Taylor, Michael J. *A Companion to John. Readings in Johannine Theology (John's Gospel and Epistles).* New York: Alba, 1977. Older but still helpful anthology of significant studies on selected Johaninne themes, including the Logos motif, the Johannine signs, the "I am" passages, sacraments, and ecclesiology.

Thompson, Marianne Meye. *The Humanity of Jesus in the Fourth Gospel.* Philadelphia: Fortress, 1988. A successful rebuttal of the notion that John's Gospel unilaterally focuses on Jesus' divinity while downplaying his humanity.

Tools for Study

I. Proper Names in John's Gospel

A. Named individuals and groups

1. Abraham (*Abraam*; 11/73)
   - 8:33 We are A.'s descendants
   - 8:37 I know you are A.'s descendants
   - 8:39 A. is our father
   - 8:39 If you were A.'s children
   - 8:39 you would do the things A. did
   - 8:40 A. did not do such things
   - 8:52 A. died and so did the prophets
   - 8:53 Are you greater than our father A.
   - 8:56 Your father A. rejoiced
   - 8:57 and you have seen A.
   - 8:58 before A. was born, I am

2. Andreas (*Andreas*; 5/13)
   - 1:40 A., Simon Peter's brother
   - 1:44 Philip, like A. and Peter
   - 6:8 A., Simon Peter's brother
   - 12:22 Philip went to tell A.
   - 12:22 A. and Philip in turn told Jesus

3. Annas (*Annas*; 2/4)
   - 18:13 brought him first to A.
   - 18:24 Then A. sent him, still bound

4. Barabbas (*Barabbas*; 2/11)
   - 18:40 Give us B.
   - 18:40 Now B. had taken part in a rebellion

5. Caiaphas (*Kaiaphas*; 5/9)
   - 11:49 C., who was high priest that year
   - 18:13 who was the father-in-law of C.
   - 18:14 C. was the one who had advised

18:28 Then the Jews led Jesus from C.

6. Clopas (*Klōpas*; 1/1)
   - 19:25 Mary the wife of C.

7. David (*Dauid*; 2/59)
   - 7:42 Christ will come from D.'s family
   - 7:42 Bethlehem, the town where D. lived

8. Didymus (*Didymos*; 3/3; see also Thomas)
   - 11:16 Then Thomas (called D.) said
   - 20:24 Now Thomas (called D.), one of the
   - 21:2 Simon Peter, Thomas (called D.)

9. Elijah (*Elias*; 2/29)
   - 1:21 Are you E.?
   - 1:25 not the Christ, nor E.

10. Isaiah (*Ēsaias*; 4/22)
    - 1:23 John replied in the words of I.
    - 12:38 This was to fulfill the word of I.
    - 12:39 as I. says elsewhere
    - 12:41 I. said this because he saw Jesus'

11. Iscariot (*Iskariōtēs*; 5/8; see also Judas)
    - 6:71 He meant Judas, the son of Simon I.
    - 12:4 Judas I., who was later to betray
    - 13:2 prompted Judas I., son of Simon
    - 13:26 gave it to Judas I., son of Simon
    - 14:22 Then Judas (not Judas I.) said

12. Jacob (*Iakōb*; 3/27)
    - 4:5 a ground J. had given to his son
    - 4:6 J.'s well was there

4:12 Are you greater than our father J.

13. Jesus (*Iēsous*; 237/898)
    - 1:17 truth came through J. Christ
    - 1:29 John saw J. coming toward him
    - 1:36 When he saw J. passing by he
    - 1:37 they followed J.
    - 1:38 J. saw them following
    - 1:42 And he brought him to J.
    - 1:42 J. looked at him and said
    - 1:43 The next day J. decided to
    - 1:45 J. of Nazareth, the son of
    - 1:47 When J. saw Nathanael
    - 1:48 J. answered, "I saw you while
    - 1:50 J. said, "You believe because
    - 2:1 J.' mother was there
    - 2:2 and J. and his disciples
    - 2:3 J.' mother said to him
    - 2:4 involve me?" J. replied
    - 2:7 J. said to the servants
    - 2:11 J. performed at Cana in
    - 2:13 J. went up to Jerusalem
    - 2:19 J. answered them, "Destroy
    - 2:22 words that J. had spoken
    - 2:24 But J. would not entrust
    - 3:3 In reply J. declared
    - 3:5 J. answered, "I tell you
    - 3:10 Israel's teacher," said J.
    - 3:22 After this, J. and his
    - 4:1 heard that J. was gaining
    - 4:2 in fact it was not J. who
    - 4:3 When the Lord [J.] learned
    - 4:6 and J., tired as he was
    - 4:7 J. said to her, "Will you
    - 4:10 J. answered her, "If you knew
    - 4:13 J. answered, "Everyone who
    - 4:17 J. said to her, "You are right
    - 4:21 J. declared, "Believe me
    - 4:26 Then J. declared, "I who
    - 4:34 "My food," said Jesus
    - 4:44 Now J. himself had pointed out
    - 4:47 When this man heard that J.
    - 4:48 signs and wonders," J. told
    - 4:50 J. replied, "You may go

227

4:50 The man took J. at his word

4:53 exact time at which J. had

4:54 second miraculous sign that J.

5:1 Some time later, J. went up

5:6 When J. saw him lying there

5:8 Then J. said to him, "Get up

5:13 for J. had slipped away into

5:14 Later J. found him at the

5:15 told the Jews that it was J.

5:16 So, because J. was doing these

5:17 J. said to them, "My Father

5:19 J. gave them this answer: "I

6:1 Some time after this, J.

6:3 Then J. went up on a mountainside

6:5 When J. looked up and saw a great

6:10 J. said, "Have the people sit

6:11 J. then took the loaves, gave

6:15 J., knowing that they intended

6:17 and J. had not yet joined them

6:19 they saw J. approaching the boat

6:22 and that J. had not entered it

6:24 that neither J. nor his disciples

6:24 to Capernaum in search of J.

6:26 J. answered, "I tell you the

6:29 J. answered, "The work of God

6:32 J. said to them, "I tell you

6:35 Then J. declared, "I am the

6:42 Is this not Jesus, the son of

6:43 among yourselves," J. answered

6:53 J. said to them, "I tell you

6:61 J. said to them, "Does this

6:64 For J. had known from the

6:67 do you?" J. asked the Twelve

6:70 Then J. replied, "Have I not

7:1 After this, J. went around in

7:6 Therefore J. told them, "The

7:14 did J. go up to the temple

7:16 J. answered, "My teaching is

7:21 J. said to them, "I did one

7:28 Then J., still teaching in

7:33 J. said, "I am with you for

7:37 J. stood and said in a loud

7:39 J. had not yet been glorified

8:12 When J. spoke again to the

8:14 J. answered, "Even if I

8:19 J. replied. "If you knew me

8:25 claiming all along," J. replied

8:28 So J. said, "When you have

8:31 To the J. who had believed him

8:34 J. replied, "I tell you the

8:39 Abraham's children," said J.

8:42 J. said to them, "If God were

8:49 by a demon," said J., "but I

8:54 J. replied, "If I glorify

8:58 J. answered, "before Abraham

8:59 but J. hid himself, slipping

9:3 said J., "but this happened

9:11 The man they call Jesus made

9:14 Now the day on which J. had

9:35 J. heard that they had thrown

9:37 J. said, "You have now seen

9:39 J. said, "For judgment I have

9:41 J. said, "If you were blind

10:6 J. used this figure of speech

10:7 Therefore J. said again, "I

10:23 and J. was in the temple area

10:25 J. answered, "I did tell you

10:34 J. answered them, "Is it not

11:4 When he heard this, J. said

11:5 J. loved Martha and her sister

11:9 J. answered, "Are there not

11:13 J. had been speaking of his

11:14 So then he [J.] told them

11:17 On his arrival, J. found that

11:20 When Martha heard that J. was

11:21 "Lord," Martha said to J.

11:23 J. said to her, "Your brother

11:25 J. said to her, "I am the

11:30 Now J. had not yet entered

11:32 the place where J. was and

11:33 When J. saw her weeping,

11:35 J. wept

11:38 J., once more deeply moved

11:39 away the stone," he [J.] said

11:40 Then J. said, "Did I not tell

11:41 Then J. looked up and said

11:44 J. said to them, "Take off

11:46 told them what J. had done

11:51 prophesied that J. would die

11:54 Therefore J. no longer moved

11:56 They kept looking for J.

12:1 J. arrived at Bethany, where

12:1 Lazarus lived, whom J. had

12:3 she poured it on J.' feet

12:7 "Leave her alone," J. replied

12:9 found out that J. was there

12:11 Jews were going over to J.

12:12 J. was on his way to Jerusalem

12:14 J. found a young donkey and

12:16 Only after J. was glorified

12:21 we would like to see J.

12:22 and Philip in turn told J.

12:23 J. replied, "The hour has

12:30 J. said, "This voice was for

12:35 Then J. told them, "You are

12:36 J. left and hid himself from

12:44 Then J. cried out, "When a

13:1 J. knew that the time had come

13:7 J. replied, "You do not

13:8 J. answered, "Unless I wash

13:10 J. answered, "A person who

13:21 J. was troubled in spirit and

13:23 the disciple whom J. loved

13:23 was reclining next to him [J.]

13:25 Leaning back against J., he

13:26 J. answered, "It is the one

13:27 do quickly," J. told him

13:29 some thought J. was telling

13:31 When he was gone, J. said

13:36 J. replied, "Where I am going

13:38 Then J. answered, "Will you

14:6 J. answered, "I am the way

14:9 J. answered, "Don't you know

14:23 J. replied, "If anyone loves

16:19 J. saw that they wanted to ask

16:31 believe at last!" J. answered

17:1 After J. said this, he looked

17:3 the only true God, and J. Christ

18:1 finished praying, J. left with

18:2 because J. had often met there

18:4 J., knowing all that was going

18:5 "J. of Nazareth," they replied

18:7 And they said, "J. of Nazareth"

18:8 that I am he," J. answered

18:11 J. commanded Peter, "Put your

18:12 arrested J. They bound him

18:15 disciple were following J.

18:15 he went with J. into the high

18:19 the high priest questioned J.

18:20 to the world," J. replied

18:22 When J. said this, one of the

18:23 J. replied, "testify as to

18:28 Then the Jews led J. from

18:32 so that the words J. had spoken

18:33 summoned J. and asked him

18:34 "Is that your idea," J. asked

18:36 J. said, "My kingdom is not

18:37 J. answered, "You are right

19:1 Then Pilate took J. and had him

19:5 When J. came out wearing the

19:9 do you come from?" he asked J.

19:9 but J. gave him no answer

19:11 J. answered, "You would have no

19:13 he brought J. out and sat down

19:16 the soldiers took charge of J.

19:18 and J. in the middle

19:19 J. OF NAZARETH, THE KING

19:20 the place where J. was crucified

19:23 When the soldiers crucified J.

19:25 Near the cross of J. stood his

19:26 When J. saw his mother there

19:28 J. said, "I am thirsty"

19:30 J. said, "It is finished"

19:33 But when they came to J. and

19:38 Pilate for the body of J.

19:38 Now Joseph was a disciple of J.

19:40 Taking J.' body, the two of

19:42 nearby, they laid J. there

20:2 disciple, the one Jesus loved

20:12 seated where J.' body had been

20:14 and saw J. standing there, but

20:14 did not realize that it was J.

20:15 "Woman," he [J.] said

20:16 J. said to her, "Mary"

20:17 J. said, "Do not hold on to me

20:19 J. came and stood among them and

20:24 with the disciples when J. came

20:26 J. came and stood among them

20:29 Then J. told him, "Because you

20:30 J. did many other miraculous

20:31 believe that J. is the Christ

21:1 Afterward J. appeared again

21:4 Early in the morning, J. stood

21:4 did not realize that it was J.

21:5 He [J.] called out to them

21:7 Then the disciple whom J. loved

21:10 J. said to them, "Bring some

21:12 J. said to them, "Come and have

21:13 J. came, took the bread and gave

21:14 This was now the third time J.

21:15 When they had finished eating, J.

21:20 the disciple whom J. loved was

21:21 When Peter saw him, he asked [J.]

21:22 J. answered, "If I want him to

21:23 But J. did not say that he would

21:25 J. did many other things as well

14. John (*Iōannēs;* 22/135)

1:6 sent from God; his name was J.

1:15 J. testifies concerning him

1:19 Now this was J.'s testimony

1:26 "I baptize with water," J.

1:28 Jordan, where J. was baptizing

1:32 Then J. gave this testimony:

1:35 The next day J. was there again

1:40 two who heard what J. had said

1:42 You are Simon son of J.

3:23 Now J. also was baptizing

3:24 This was before J. was put in

3:25 some of J.'s disciples and a

3:26 They came to J. and said to

3:27 To this J. replied, "A man

5:33 You have sent to J. and he has

5:36 weightier than that of J.

10:40 where J. had been baptizing

10:41 J. never performed a miraculous

10:41 all that J. said about this man

21:15 Simon son of J., do you truly

21:16 Simon son of J., do you truly

21:17 Simon son of J., do you love

15. Joseph (*Jōsēph*; 4/35)

1:45 Jesus of Nazareth, son of J.

4:5 Jacob had given to his son J.

6:42 Is this not Jesus, the son of J.

19:38 Later, J. of Arimathea asked

16. Judas (*Ioudas*; 9/44)

6:71 He meant J., the son of Simon

12:4 J. Iscariot, who was later to betray

13:2 prompted J. Iscariot, son of Simon

13:26 gave it to J. Iscariot, son of Simon

13:29 Since J. had charge of the money

14:22 Then Judas (not J. Iscariot) said

18:2 Now J., who betrayed him

18:3 So J. came to the grove

18:5 And J. the traitor was standing

17. Lazarus (*Lazaros*; 11/15)

11:1 Now a man named L. was sick

11:2 This Mary, whose brother L.

11:5 Jesus loved . . . L.

11:11 Our friend L. has fallen asleep

11:14 Lazarus is dead

11:43 L., come out

12:1 Bethany, where L. lived

12:2 L. was among those reclining

12:9 to see L., whom he had raised

12:10 made plans to kill L. as well

12:17 when he called L. from the tomb

18. Magdalene (*Magdalēnē*; 3/12)

19:25 and Mary M.

20:1 Mary M. went to the tomb

20:18 Mary M. went to the disciples

19. Malchus (*Malchos*; 1/1)

18:10 The servant's name was Malchus

20. Martha (*Martha*; 9/13)

11:1 village of Mary and her sister M.

11:5 Jesus loved M. and her sister

11:19 many Jews had come to M. and Mary

11:20 When M. heard that Jesus was coming

11:21 "Lord," M. said to Jesus

11:24 M. answered, "I know that

11:30 the place where M. had met him

11:39 said M., the sister of the dead man

12:2 M. served, while Lazarus was among

21. Mary (*Maria[m]*; 15/54)

11:1 village of M. and her sister Martha

11:2 This M., whose brother Lazarus

11:19 many Jews had come to Martha and M.

11:20 but M. stayed at home

11:28 went back and called her sister M.

11:31 who had been with M. in the house

11:32 When M. reached the place where

11:45 Jews who had come to visit M.

12:3 Then M. took about a pint of pure

19:25 M. the wife of Clopas

19:25 M. Magdalene

20:1 M. Magdalene went to the tomb

20:11 M. stood outside the tomb crying

20:16 Jesus said to her, "Mary"

20:18 M. Magdalene went to the disciples

22. Moses (*Mōusēs*; 12/79)

1:17 For the law was given through M.

1:45 We have found the one M. wrote

3:14 Just as M. lifted up the snake

5:45 Your accuser is M., on whom

5:46 If you believed M., you would

6:32 it is not M. who has given you

7:19 Has not M. given you the law?

7:22 because M. gave you circumcision

7:22 not come from M. but from

9:28 We are disciples of M.

9:29 We know that God spoke to M.

23. Nathanael (*Nathanaēl*; 6/6)

1:45 Philip found N. and told him

1:46 come from there?" N. asked

1:47 When Jesus saw N. approaching

1:48 "How do you know me?" N. asked

1:49 Then N. declared, "Rabbi, you

21:2 N. from Cana in Galilee

24. Nicodemus (*Nikodēmos*; 5/5)

3:1 a man of the Pharisees named N.

3:4 when he is old?" N. asked

3:9 "How can this be?" N. asked

7:50 N., who had gone to Jesus earlier

19:39 He was accompanied by N., the man

25. Peter (*Petros*; 34/156; see also Simon)

1:40 Andrew, Simon P.'s brother, was

1:42 which, when translated, is P.

1:44 Philip, like Andrew and P., was

6:8 Andrew, Simon P.'s brother, spoke

6:68 Simon P. answered him, "Lord

13:6 He came to Simon P., who said to

13:8 "No," said P., "you shall never

13:9 "Then, Lord," Simon P. replied

13:24 Simon P. motioned to this disciple

13:36 Simon P. asked him, "Lord, where

13:37 P. asked, "Lord, why can't I

18:10 Then Simon P., who had a sword

18:11 Jesus commanded P., "Put your

18:15 Simon P. and another disciple

18:16 but P. had to wait outside the

18:16 and brought P. in

18:17 the girl at the door asked P.

18:18 P. also was standing with them

18:25 As Simon P. stood warming himself

18:26 the man whose ear P. had cut off

18:27 Again P. denied it, and at that

20:2 So she came running to Simon P.

20:3 So P. and the other disciple

20:4 the other disciple outran P.

20:6 Then Simon P., who was behind him

21:2 Simon P.

21:3 out to fish," Simon P. told them

21:7 whom Jesus loved said to P.

21:7 As soon as Simon P. heard him say

21:11 Simon P. climbed aboard

21:15 eating, Jesus said to Simon P.

21:17 P. was hurt because Jesus asked

21:20 P. turned and saw that the

21:21 When P. saw him, he asked, "Lord

26. Pharisees (*Pharisaioi*; 19/97)

1:24 Now some P. who had been sent

3:1 man of the P. named Nicodemus

4:1 The P. heard that Jesus was

7:32 The P. heard the crowd

7:32 chief priests and the P. sent

7:45 the chief priests and the P.

7:47 deceived you also?" the P.

7:48 rulers or of the P. believed

8:13 The P. challenged him, "Here

9:13 They brought to the P. the man

9:15 the P. also asked him how he

9:16 Some of the P. said, "This man

9:40 Some P. who were with him heard

11:46 But some of them went to the P.

11:47 the chief priests and the P.

11:57 the chief priests and the P.

12:19 So the P. said to one another

12:42 But because of the P. they

18:3 the chief priests and P.

27. Philip (*Philippos*; 12/36)

1:43 Finding P., he said to him

1:44 P., like Andrew and Peter

1:45 P. found Nathanael

1:46 "Come and see," said P.

1:48 fig tree before P. called you

6:5 he said to P., "Where shall

6:7 P. answered him, "Eight months'

12:21 P., who was from Bethsaida

12:22 P. went to tell Andrew

12:22 Andrew and P. in turn told

14:8 P. said, "Lord, show us the

14:9 Don't you know me, P., even

28. Pilate (*Pilatos*; 20/55)

18:29 So P. came out to them and

18:31 P. said, "Take him yourselves

18:33 P. then went back inside the

18:35 "Am I a Jew?" P. replied

18:37 "You are a king, then!" said P.

18:38 "What is truth?" P. asked

19:1 Then P. took Jesus and had him

19:4 Once more P. came out and said

19:6 But P. answered, "You take

19:8 When P. heard this, he was

19:10 refuse to speak to me?" P. said

19:12 From then on, P. tried to set

19:13 When P. heard this, he brought

19:15 crucify your king?" P. asked

19:19 P. had a notice prepared and

19:21 Jews protested to P., "Do not

19:22 P. answered, "What I have

19:31 they asked P. to have the legs

19:38 asked P. for the body of Jesus

19:38 With P.'s permission, he came

29. Satan (*Satanas*; 1/34; see also devil, *diabolos* [3/37]: 6:70; 8:44; 13:2)

13:27 the bread, Satan entered into him

30. Simon (*Simōn*; 25/75; see also Peter, Judas)

1:40 Andrew, S. Peter's brother

1:41 find his brother S. and tell him

1:42 You are S. son of John

6:8 Andrew, S. Peter's brother

6:68 S. Peter answered him, "Lord

6:71 Judas, the son of S. Iscariot

13:2 Judas Iscariot, son of S.

13:6 He came to S. Peter, who said

13:9 "Then, Lord," S. Peter replied

13:24 S. Peter motioned to this

13:26 Judas Iscariot, son of S.

13:36 S. Peter asked him, "Lord

18:10 Then S. Peter, who had a sword

18:15 S. Peter and another disciple

18:25 As S. Peter stood warming himself

20:2 So she came running to S. Peter

20:6 Then S. Peter, who was behind him

21:2 S. Peter

21:3 out to fish," S. Peter told them

21:7 As soon as S. Peter heard him say

21:11 S. Peter climbed aboard and

21:15 eating, Jesus said to S. Peter

21:15 S. son of John, do you truly

21:16 S. son of John, do you truly

21:17 S. son of John, do you love

31. Thomas (*Thōmas*; 7/11)

11:16 Then T. (called Didymus) said

14:5 T. said to him, "Lord, we

20:24 Now T. (called Didymus), one of them

20:26 and T. was with them

20:27 Then he said to T., "Put your

20:28 T. said to him, "My Lord and my God

21:2 Simon Peter, T. (called Didymus)

32. Zebedee (*Zebedaios*; 1/12)

21:2 the sons of Z.

B. Ethnically or Geographically Constrained Designations

1. Galileans (*Galilaioi*; 1/11)

4:45 the G. welcomed him

2. Greeks (*Hellēnes*; 3/25)

7:35 live scattered among the G.

7:35 and teach the G.

12:20 Now there were some G.

3. Israel (*Israēl*; 4/68)

1:31 that he might be revealed to I.

1:49 you are the king of I.

3:10 You are I.'s teacher

12:13 Blessed is the King of I.

4. Israelite (*Israelitēs*; 1/9)

1:47 Here is a true I.

5. Jerusalemites (*Hierosolymitai*; 1/2)

7:25 some of the people of Jerusalem

6. Jew(s) (*Ioudaios/Ioudaioi*; 71/195)

1:19 J. of Jerusalem sent priests

2:6 the kind used by the J. for

2:13 the Jewish Passover [P. of the J.]

2:18 Then the J. demanded of him

2:20 The J. replied, "It has taken

3:1 member of the Jewish ruling council

3:22 out into the Judean countryside

3:25 John's disciples and a certain Jew

4:9 You are a Jew and I am a Samaritan

4:9 For J. do not associate with

4:22 for salvation is from the J.

5:1 Jerusalem for a feast of the J.

5:10 so the J. said to the man who

5:15 told the J. that it was Jesus

5:16 the Sabbath, the J. persecuted

5:18 the J. tried all the harder to

6:4 The Jewish Passover Feast was

6:41 At this the J. began to grumble

6:52 Then the J. began to argue

7:1 because the J. there were waiting

7:2 But when the Jewish Feast of

7:11 Now at the Feast the J. were

7:13 about him for fear of the J.

7:15 The J. were amazed and asked

7:35 The J. said to one another

8:22 This made the J. ask, "Will he

8:31 To the J. who had believed him

8:48 The J. answered him, "Aren't

8:52 At this the J. exclaimed

8:57 50 years old," the J. said

9:18 The J. still did not believe

9:22 they were afraid of the J.

9:22 already the J. had decided

10:19 At these words the J. were

10:24 The J. gathered around him

10:31 Again the J. picked up stones

10:33 the J., "but for blasphemy

11:8 the J. tried to stone you

11:19 many J. had come to Martha

11:31 When the J. who had been

11:33 and the J. who had come

11:36 Then the J. said, "See how

11:45 J. who had come to visit Mary

11:54 about publicly among the J.

11:55 time for the Jewish Passover

12:9 large crowd of J. found out

12:11 many of the J. were going

13:33 and just as I told the J.

18:12 and the Jewish officials

18:14 one who had advised the J.

18:20 where all the J. come together

18:31 anyone," the J. objected

18:33 Are you the king of the J.?

18:35 Am I a Jew?

18:36 prevent my arrest by the J.

18:39 release "the king of the J."?

19:3 Hail, king of the J.!

19:7 The J. insisted, "We have a

19:12 but the J. kept shouting

19:14 Pilate said to the J.

19:19 THE KING OF THE J.

19:20 Many of the J. read this sign

19:21 The chief priests of the J.

19:21 not write, "The King of the J.

19:21 claimed to be king of the J.

19:31 Because the J. did not want

19:38 because he feared the J.

19:40 with Jewish burial customs

19:42 Jewish day of Preparation

20:19 locked for fear of the J.

7. Nazarene (*Nazōraios*; 3/13; see also Nazareth)

18:5 "Jesus of N.," they replied

18:7 And they said, "Jesus of N."

19:19 It read: JESUS OF N., THE KING

8. Romans (*Rhōmaios*; 1/12)

11:48 and then the Romans will come

9. Samaritan(s) (*Samaritēs*; 4/9; see also Samaria)

4:9 For Jews do not associate with S.

4:39 Many of the S. from that town

4:40 So when the S. came to him

8:48 you are a S. and demon-possessed

10. Samaritan woman (*Samaritis*; 2/2; see also Samaria)

4:9 The S. woman said to him, "You

4:9 You are a Jew and I am a S. woman

II. Place Names in John's Gospel

1. Aenon (*Ainōn*; 1/1)

3:23 John also was baptizing at A. near Salim

2. Arimathea (*Arimatheia*; 1/4)

19:38 Later, Joseph of A. asked Pilate

3. Bethany (*Bethania*; 4/12)

1:28 at B. on the other side of the Jordan

11:1 Lazarus was sick. He was from B.

11:18 B. was less than 2 miles from Jerusalem

12:1 before the Passover Jesus arrived at B.

4. Bethesda (*Bēthesda/Bēthzatha*; 1/1)

5:2 which in Aramaic is called B.

5. Bethlehem (*Bēthleem*; 1/8)

7:42 will come from David's family and from B.

6. Bethsaida (*Bēthsaida*; 2/7)

1:44 Philip . . . was from the town of B.

12:21 Philip, who was from B. in Galilee

7. Cana (*Kana*; 4/4)

2:1 a wedding took place at C. in Galilee

2:11 Jesus performed at C. in Galilee

4:46 Once more he visited C. in Galilee

21:2 Nathanael from C. in Galilee

8. Capernaum (*Kapharnaoum*; 5/16)

2:12 After this he went down to C.

4:46 whose son lay sick at C.

6:17 set off across the lake for C.

6:24 went to C. in search of Jesus

6:59 teaching in the synagogue in C.

9. Ephraim (*Ephraim*; 1/1)

11:54 desert, to a village called E.

10. Gabbatha (*Gabbatha*; 1/1; see Stone Pavement)

19:13 which in Aramaic is G.

11. Galilee (*Galilaia*; 17/61)

1:43 Jesus decided to leave for G.

2:1 wedding took place at Cana in G.

2:11 Jesus performed at Cana in G.

4:3 and went back once more to G.

4:43 after two days he left for G.

4:45 When he arrived in G., the

4:46 Once more he visited Cana in G.

4:47 Jesus had arrived in G. from

4:54 having come from Judea to G.

6:1 far shore of the Sea of G.

7:1 Jesus went around in G.

7:9 Having said this, he stayed in G.

7:41 How can the Christ come from G.?

7:52 prophet does not come out of G.

12:21 who was from Bethsaida in G.

21:2 Nathanael from Cana in G.

12. Golgotha (*Golgotha*; 1/3; see Place of the Skull)

19:17 Skull (which in Aramaic is called G.)

13. Jerusalem (*Hierosolyma*; 11/62)

1:19 the Jews of J. sent priests and

2:13 Passover, Jesus went up to J.

2:23 while he was in J. at the Passover

4:20 where we must worship is in J.

4:21 neither on this mountain nor in J.

4:45 he had done in J. at the Passover

5:1 Jesus went up to J. for a feast

5:2 Now there is in J. near the Sheep

10:22 came the Feast of Dedication at J.

11:18 was less than two miles from J.

11:55 went up from the country to J.

14. Jordan (*Jordanēs*; 3/15)

1:28 Bethany on the other side of the J.

3:26 with you on the other side of the J.

10:40 Then Jesus went back across the J.

15. Judea (*Ioudaia*; 6/43)

4:3 learned of this, he left J. and

4:47 Jesus had arrived in Galilee from J.

4:54 having come from J. to Galilee

7:1 purposely staying away from J.

7:3 You ought to leave here and go to J.

11:7 Let us go back to J.

16. Kidron (*Kedrōn*; 1/1)

18:1 and crossed the Kidron Valley

17. Nazareth (*Nazaret*; 2/4; see also Nazarene)

1:45 Jesus of N., the son of Joseph

1:46 N.! Can anything good come from

18. Place of the Skull (*Kranion*; 1/4; Aram. *Golgotha*)

19:17 the place of the S. (which in

19. Praetorium (*Praitōrion*; 4/8)

18:28 palace of the Roman governor

18:28 Jews did not enter the palace

18:33 went back inside the palace

19:9 he went back inside the palace

20. Salim (*Saleim*; 1/1)

3:23 was baptizing at Aenon near S.

21. Samaria (*Samareia*; 3/11)

4:4 Now he had to go through S.

4:5 So he came to a town in S.

4:7 When a Samaritan woman came

22. Siloam (*Silōam*; 2/3)

9:7 wash in the pool of S.

9:11 told me to go to S. and wash

23. Solomon's Colonnade (*Stoa tou Solomōnos*; 1/3; cf. Acts 3:11; 5:12)

10:23 temple area walking in Sol.'s C.

24. Stone Pavement (*Lithostrōtos*; 1/1; Aram. Gabbatha)

19:13 known as the S. P. (which in

25. Sychar (*Sychar*; 1/1)

4:5 a town in Samaria called S.

26. Tiberias (*Tiberias*; 3/3)

6:1 that is, the Sea of T.

6:23 Then some boats from T. landed

21:1 by the Sea of T.

III. Important Theological Terms in John's Gospel

A. Christ

1. Christ (*Christos*; 19/527)

1:17 truth came through Jesus C.

1:20 I am not the C.

1:25 if you are not the C.

1:41 Messiah (that is, the C.)

3:28 I am not the C.

4:25 the Messiah (called C.)

4:29 Could this be the C.?

7:26 concluded that he is the C.?

7:27 when the C. comes, no one will

7:31 When the C. comes, will he do

7:41 Other said, "He is the C."

7:41 How can the C. come from

7:42 say that the C. will come

9:22 that Jesus was the C. would

10:24 If you are the C., tell us

11:27 I believe that you are the C.

12:34 from the Law that the C. will

17:3 only true God, and Jesus C.

20:31 believe that Jesus is the C.

B. Darkness/Night

1. dark (*skotos*; 1/31)

3:19 men loved darkness instead of

2. darkness (*skotia*; 8/16)

1:5 The light shines in the d.

1:5 but the d. has not understood

6:17 By now it was d., and Jesus

8:12 me will never walk in d., but

12:35 before d. overtakes you

12:35 The man who walks in the dark

12:46 in me should stay in d.

20:1 while it was still dark

3. night (*nyx*; 6/61)

3:2 He came to Jesus at n.

9:4 N. is coming, when no one

11:10 It is when he walks by n.

13:30 he went out. And it was n.

19:39 had visited Jesus at n.

21:3 but that n. they caught

C. Death (and related terms)

1. dead (*nekros*; 8/128)

2:22 he was raised from the d.

5:21 as the Father raises the d.

5:25 come when the d. will hear

12:1 Jesus had raised from the d.

12:9 he had raised from the d.

12:17 raised him from the d.

20:9 Jesus had to rise from the d.

21:14 after he was raised from the d.

2. dead (*thnēskō*; 2/9)

11:44 The d. man came out

19:33 found that he was already d.

3. death (*thanatos*; 8/120)

5:24 crossed over from d. to life

8:51 he will never see d.

8:52 he will never taste d.

11:4 sickness will not end in d.

11:13 been speaking of his d., but

12:33 to show the kind of d. he

18:32 indicating the kind of d. he

21:19 to indicate the kind of d.

4. destruction (*apōleia*; 1/18)

17:12 except the one doomed to d.

5. to die (*apothnemskom*; 28/111)

4:47 son, who was close to death

4:49 come down before my child dies

6:49 in the desert, but they died

6:50 a man may eat and not die

6:58 forefathers ate manna and died

8:21 and you will d. in your sins

8:24 that you would d. in your sins

8:24 you will indeed d. in your sins

8:52 he will never taste death

8:53 father Abraham? He died, and

8:53 so did [died] the prophets

11:14 Lazarus is dead

11:16 go, that we may d. with him

11:21 brother would not have died

11:25 live, even though he dies

11:26 believes in me will never d.

11:32 brother would not have died

11:37 have kept this man from dying

11:50 better for you that one man d.

11:51 prophesied that Jesus would d.

12:24 falls to the ground and dies

12:24 But if it dies, it produces

12:33 of death he was going to d.

18:14 good if one man died for the

18:32 of death he was going to d.

19:7 acc. to that law he must d.

21:23 this disciple would not d.

21:23 not say that he would not d.

6. to kill (*apokteinō*; 12/74)

5:18 all the harder to k. him

7:1 were waiting to take his life

7:19 Why are you trying to k. me?

7:20 Who is trying to k. you?

7:25 the man they are trying to k.

8:22 Will he k. himself?

8:37 Yet you are ready to k. me

8:40 you are determined to k. me

11:53 they plotted to take his life

12:10 made plans to k. Lazarus as

16:2 anyone who k.s you will think

18:31 no right to execute anyone

7. to perish (*apollumi*; 10/90)

3:16 shall not p. but have eternal

6:12 Let nothing be wasted

6:27 Do not work for food that spoils

6:39 that I shall lose none of all

10:10 to steal and kill and destroy

10:28 and they shall never p.

11:50 than that the whole nation p.

12:25 loves his life will lose it

17:12 None has been lost except

18:9 I have not lost one of those

8. to persecute (*diōkō*; 3/45)

5:16 the Jews persecuted him

15:20 If they persecuted me

15:20 they will p. you also

9. to be sick (*astheneō*; 8/33)

4:46 whose son lay sick at

5:3 a great number of disabled

5:7 "Sir," the invalid replied

6:2 he had performed on the s.

11:1 a man named Lazarus was s.

11:2 brother Lazarus now lay s.

11:3 the one whom you love is s.

11:6 heard that Lazarus was s.

10. sickness (*astheneia*; 2/24)

5:5 had been an invalid for 38

11:4 This s. will not end in death

11. to stone (*lithazō*; 4/8)

10:31 picked up stones to s. him

10:32 For which of these do you s.

10:33 We are not stoning you for

11:8 the Jews tried to s. you

12. stone (*lithos*; 6/58)

8:59 picked up stones to stone him

10:31 picked up stones to stone him

11:38 It was a cave with a s.

11:39 Take away the s.

11:41 So they took away the s.

20:1 saw that the s. had been

13. tomb (*mnēmeion*; 15/40)

5:28 in their graves will hear

11:17 had been in the t. for four

11:31 going to the t. to mourn

11:38 deeply moved, came to the t.

12:17 called Lazarus from the t.

19:41 and in the garden a new t.

19:42 and since the t. was nearby

20:1 Magdalene went to the t.

20:1 removed from the entrance

20:2 taken the Lord out of the t.

20:3 disciple started for the t.

20:4 and reached the t. first

20:6 and went into the t. He saw

20:8 the t. first, also went

20:11 bent over to look into the t.

D. Discipleship
(see also R. Teacher)

1. believe (*pisteuō*; 98/241)

1:7 through him all men might b.

1:12 to those who believed in his

1:50 You b. because I told you I

2:11 disciples put their faith in

2:22 Then they believed the Scr.

2:23 and believed in his name

2:24 But Jesus would not entrust

3:12 and you do not b.; how then

3:12 will you b. if I speak of

3:15 everyone who believes in

3:16 that whoever believes in

3:18 Whoever believes in him

3:18 but whoever does not b.

3:18 because he has not believed

3:36 Whoever believes in the Son

4:21 Believe me, woman, a time

4:39 from that town believed in

4:41 many more became believers

4:42 We no longer b. just because

4:48 you will never believe

4:50 man took Jesus at his word

4:53 all his household believed

5:24 and believes him who sent

5:38 you do not b. the one he

5:44 How can you b. if you accept

5:46 If you believed Moses

5:46 you would b. me, for he

5:47 But since you do not b.

5:47 how are you going to b.

6:29 is this: to b. in the one
6:30 we may see it and b. you
6:35 he who believes in me will
6:36 and still you do not b.
6:40 and believes in him shall
6:47 who believes has everlasting
6:64 some of you who do not b.
6:64 which of them did not b.
6:69 We b. and know that you are
7:5 brothers did not b. in him
7:31 crowd put their faith in him
7:38 Whoever believes in me, as
7:39 whom those who believed in
7:48 of the Pharisees believed in
8:24 if you do not b. that I am
8:30 many put their faith in him
8:31 To the Jews who had believed
8:45 you do not b. me! Can any of
8:46 truth, why don't you b. me?
9:18 The Jews still did not b.
9:35 Do you b. in the Son of Man?
9:36 Tell me so that I may b. in
9:38 the man said, "Lord, I b."
10:25 tell you, but you do not b.
10:26 but you do not b. because
10:37 Do not b. me unless I do
10:38 though you do not b. me
10:38 b. the miracles, that you
10:42 place many believed in Jesus
11:15 so that you may b. But let
11:25 He who believes in me will
11:26 whoever lives and believes
11:26 Do you b. this?
11:27 I b. that you are the Christ
11:40 if you believed, you would
11:42 they may b. that you sent me
11:45 Jesus did, put their faith
11:48 everyone will b. in him
12:11 and putting their faith in
12:36 Put your trust in the light
12:37 they still would not b. in

12:38 Lord, who has believed our
12:39 reason they could not b.
12:42 leaders believed in him
12:44 When a man believes in me
12:44 he does not b. in me only
12:46 no one who believes in me
13:19 you will b. that I am He
14:1 Trust in God
14:1 trust also in me
14:10 Don't you b. that I am in
14:11 B. me when I say that I am
14:11 or at least b. on the evid.
14:12 anyone who has faith in me
14:29 it does happen you will b.
16:9 because men do not b. in me
16:27 have believed that I came
16:30 This makes us b. that you
16:31 You believe at last!
17:8 and they believed that you
17:20 also for those who will b.
17:21 that the world may b. that
19:35 so that you also may b.
20:8 He saw and believed
20:25 side, I will not b. it
20:29 seen me, you have believed
20:29 seen and yet have believed
20:31 written that you may b.
20:31 and that by believing you

2. believing (*pistos*; 1/67)
20:27 Stop doubting and believe
3. disciple(s) (*mathētēs*; 78/260)
1:35 with two of his disciples
1:37 When the two disciples heard
2:2 and Jesus and his disciples
2:11 and his disciples put their
2:12 brothers and his disciples
2:17 His disciples remembered
2:22 his disciples recalled what
3:22 After this, Jesus and his d.
3:25 some of John's disciples and
4:1 baptizing more disciples than
4:2 baptized, but his disciples
4:8 His disciples had gone into
4:27 Just then his d. returned

4:31 Meanwhile his d. urged him
4:33 Then his d. said to each
6:3 and sat down with his d.
6:8 Another of his d., Andrew
6:12 he said to his d., "Gather
6:16 When evening came, his d.
6:22 not entered it with his d.
6:22 they [the d.] had gone away
6:24 neither Jesus nor his d.
6:60 On hearing it, many of his d.
6:61 Aware that his d. were
6:66 From this time many of his d.
7:3 so that your d. may see the
8:31 teaching, you are really my d.
9:2 His d. asked him, "Rabbi
9:27 Do you want to becomes his d.
9:28 You are this fellow's d.
9:28 We are disciples of Moses!
11:7 to his d., "Let us go back
11:8 "But Rabbi," they [the d.]
11:12 His d. replied, "Lord, if
11:54 where he stayed with his d.
12:4 But one of his d., Judas
12:16 At first his d. did not
13:5 began to wash his disciples'
13:22 His d. stared at one another
13:23 the d. whom Jesus loved
13:35 know that you are my d.
15:8 yourselves to be my d.
16:17 Some of his d. said to one
16:29 Then Jesus' d. said, "Now
18:1 Jesus left with his d. and
18:2 often met there with his d.
18:15 Simon Peter and another d.
18:16 The other d., who was known
18:17 You are not one of his d.
18:19 Jesus about his d. and his
18:25 You are not one of his d.
19:26 and the d. whom he loved
19:27 and to the d., "Here is
19:27 From that time on, this d.
19:38 Now Joseph was a d. of Jesus
20:2 the other d., the one Jesus
20:3 So Peter and the other d.

20:4 the other d. outran Peter
20:8 Finally the other d., who
20:10 Then the d. went back to
20:18 Mary Magdalene went to the
20:19 when the d. were together
20:20 The d. were overjoyed when
20:25 So the other d. told him
20:26 A week later his d. were in
20:30 in the presence of his d.
21:1 appeared again to his d.
21:2 of Zebedee, and two other d.
21:4 but the d. did not realize
21:7 Then the d. whom Jesus loved
21:8 The other d. followed in the
21:12 None of the d. dared ask him
21:14 Jesus appeared to his d.
21:20 the d. whom Jesus loved
21:23 that this d. would not die

4. fellow-disciple (*symmathētēs*; 1/1)
11:16 the rest of the disciples

5. to follow (*akoloutheō*; 19/89)
1:37 this, they followed Jesus
1:38 Jesus saw them following
1:40 who had followed Jesus
1:43 Follow me!
6:2 crowd of people followed
8:12 Whoever follows me will
10:4 his sheep f. him because
10:5 But they will never f. a
10:27 know them, and they f. me
11:31 they followed her, supposing
12:26 Whoever serves me must f. me
13:36 going, you cannot f. now
13:36 but you will f. later
13:37 Lord, why can't I f. now?
18:15 were following Jesus
20:6 Peter, who was behind him
21:19 Follow me!
21:20 Jesus loved was following
21:22 You must f. me

6. to learn (*manthanō*; 2/25)
6:45 learns from him comes to me
7:15 get such learning without

7. to remain, to stay (*menō*; 40/118)
1:32 as a dove and r. on him
1:33 Spirit come down and r.
1:38 where are you staying?
1:39 saw where he was staying
1:39 and spent that day with him
2:12 There they stayed for a few
3:36 God's wrath remains on him
4:40 they urged him to stay
4:40 and he stayed two days
5:38 nor does his word dwell in
6:27 for the food that endures
6:56 drinks my blood remains in
7:9 Having said this, he stayed
8:31 If you hold to my teaching
8:35 slave has no permanent place
8:35 a son belongs to it forever
9:41 can see, your guilt remains
10:40 Here he stayed and many
11:6 he stayed where he was two
11:54 Ephraim, where he stayed
12:24 remains only a single seed
12:34 the Christ will r. forever
12:46 should stay in darkness
14:10 the Father, living in me
14:17 lives with you and will be
14:25 spoken while still with you
15:4 Remain in me
15:4 and I will remain in you
15:4 fruit unless you r. in me
15:5 If a man remains in me
15:6 If anyone does not r. in
15:7 If you remain in me
15:7 and my words remain in you
15:9 Now remain in my love
15:10 you will r. in my love
15:10 and remain in his love
15:16 fruit that will last
19:31 not want the bodies left
21:22 If I want him to r. alive
21:23 If I want him to r. alive

8. to remember (*mimnēskomai*; 3/23)
2:17 His disciples remembered
2:22 his disciples recalled
12:16 glorified did they realize

9. to remember (*mnēmoneuō*; 3/21)
15:20 Remember the words I spoke
16:4 the time comes you will r.
16:21 she forgets [does not r.]

10. to remind (*hypomimnēskō*; 1/7)
14:26 will r. you of everything

11. unbelieving (*apistos*; 1/23)
20:27 Stop doubting and believe

E. Father/God

1. Father (*patēr*; 136/413)
1:14 who came from the F., full
1:18 who is at the F.'s side
2:16 turn my F.'s house into
3:35 The F. loves the Son
4:12 Are you greater than our f.
4:20 Our f.s worshiped on this
4:21 worship the F. neither on
4:23 worship the F. in spirit
4:23 worshipers the F. seeks
4:53 Then the f. realized that
5:17 My F. is always at his work
5:18 even calling God his own F.
5:19 what he sees his F. doing
5:20 For the F. loves the Son
5:21 For just as the F. raises
5:22 Moreover, the F. judges no
5:23 just as they honor the F.
5:23 Son does not honor the F.
5:26 For as the F. has life in
5:36 the very work that the F.
5:36 testifies that the F. has
5:37 And the F. who sent me
5:43 I have come in my F.'s name
5:45 accuse you before the F.
6:27 On him God the F. has
6:31 Our forefathers ate the
6:32 but it is my F. who gives
6:37 All that the F. gives me
6:40 For my F.'s will is that
6:42 Joseph, whose f. and mother
6:44 unless the F. who sent me
6:45 Everyone who listens to the F.
6:46 No one has seen the F. except
6:46 only he has seen the F.
6:49 Your forefathers ate the

237

6:57 Just as the living F. sent me

6:57 and I live because of the F.

6:58 Your forefathers ate manna

6:65 unless the F. has enabled

7:22 but from the patriarchs

8:16 I stand with the F., who

8:18 my other witness is the F.

8:19 Where is your f.?

8:19 do not know me or my F.

8:19 you would know my F. also

8:27 telling them about his F.

8:28 just what the F. has taught

8:38 seen in the F.'s presence

8:38 you have heard from your f.

8:39 Abraham is our f.

8:41 the things your own f. does

8:41 The only F. we have is God

8:42 If God were your F., you

8:44 You belong to your f., the

8:44 carry out your f.'s desire

8:44 a liar and the f. of lies

8:49 but I honor my F. and you

8:53 greater than our f. Abraham

8:54 My F., whom you claim as

8:56 Your f. Abraham rejoiced

10:15 just as the F. knows me

10:15 and I know the F.

10:17 The reason my F. loves me

10:18 I received from my F.

10:25 I do in my F.'s name

10:29 My F., who has given

10:29 snatch them out of my F.'s

10:30 I and the F. are one

10:32 great miracles from the F.

10:36 one whom the F. set apart

10:37 unless I do what my F. does

10:38 understand that the F. is

10:38 is in me, and I in the F.

11:41 Father, I thank you that

12:26 My F. will honor the one

12:27 Father, save me from this

12:28 Father, glorify your name

12:49 but the F. who sent me

12:50 just what the F. has told

13:1 world and go to the F.

13:3 Jesus knew that the F. had

14:2 In my F.'s house are many

14:6 No one comes to the F.

14:7 you would know my F. as

14:8 Lord, show us the F. and

14:9 seen me has seen the F.

14:9 say, "Show us the F."?

14:10 that I am in the F., and

14:10 that the F. is in me?

14:10 Rather, it is the F.

14:11 that I am in the F. and

14:11 and the F. is in me; or

14:12 because I am going to the F.

14:13 may bring glory to the F.

14:16 And I will ask the F., and

14:20 realize that I am in my F.

14:21 will be loved by my F.

14:23 My F. will love him, and

14:24 belong to the F. who sent

14:26 whom the F. will send in

14:28 I am going to the F., for

14:28 for the F. is greater than I

14:31 learn that I love the F.

14:31 what my F. has commanded me

15:1 and my F. is the gardener

15:8 This is to my F.'s glory

15:9 As the F. has loved me, so

15:10 as I have obeyed my F.'s

15:15 I learned from my F. I have

15:16 Then my F. will give you

15:23 hates me hates my F. as

15:24 hated both me and my F.

15:26 send to you from the F.

15:26 goes out from the F., he

16:3 have not known the F. or

16:10 because I am going to the F.

16:15 All that belongs to the F.

16:17 Because I am going to the F.

16:23 my F. will give you whatever

16:25 tell you plain about my F.

16:26 I will ask the F. on your

16:27 No, the F. himself loves

16:28 I came from the F. and

16:28 and going back to the F.

16:32 alone, for my F. is with me

17:1 Father, the time has come

17:5 And now, Father, glorify me

17:11 Holy Father, protect them

17:21 may be one, Father, just as

17:24 Father, I want those you

17:25 Righteous Father, though

18:11 drink the cup the F. has

20:17 not yet returned to the F.

20:17 I am returning to my F.

20:17 and your F., to my God

20:21 As the F. has sent me, I

2. God (*theos*; 83/1306)

1:1 and the Word was with G.

1:1 and the Word was G.

1:2 He was with G. in the

1:6 a man who was sent from G.

1:12 to become children of G.

1:13 will, but born of G.

1:18 No one has ever seen G.

1:18 but God the One and Only

1:29 Look, the Lamb of God

1:34 that this is the Son of G.

1:36 Look, the Lamb of God

1:49 Rabbi, you are the Son of G.

1:51 the angels of G. ascending

3:2 teacher who has come from G.

3:2 if G. were not with him

3:3 the kingdom of G. unless he

3:5 the kingdom of G. unless he

3:16 For G. so loved the world

3:17 For G. did not send his Son

3:18 name of G.'s one and only

3:21 has been done through G.

3:33 certified that G. is truthful

3:34 For the one whom G. has sent

3:34 speaks the words of God

3:36 for G.'s wrath remains on him

4:10 If you knew the gift of G.

4:24 God is spirit, and his

5:18 calling G. his own Father

5:18 making himself equal with G.

5:25 the voice of the Son of G.

5:42 have the love of G. in your

5:44 that comes from the only G.

6:27 On him G. the Father has

6:28 do the works G. requires?

6:29 The work of G. is this: to

6:33 For the bread of G. is he

6:45 will all be taught by G.

6:46 the one who is from G.

6:69 you are the Holy One of G.

7:17 my teaching comes from G.

8:40 truth that I heard from G.

8:41 only Father we have is G.

8:42 If G. were your Father, you

8:42 for I came from G. and now

8:47 He who belongs to G. hears

8:47 what G. says. The reason

8:47 you do not belong to G.

8:54 whom you claim as your G.

9:3 so that the work of G.

9:16 This man is not from G.

9:24 Give glory to G.

9:29 We know that G. spoke to

9:31 We know that G. does not

9:33 this man were not from G.

10:33 mere man, claim to be G.

10:34 I have said you are gods

10:35 If he called them "gods"

10:35 to whom the word of G. came

10:36 I said, "I am G.'s Son"?

11:4 No, it is for G.'s glory

11:4 so that G.'s Son may be

11:22 even now G. will give you

11:22 whatever you ask [of G.]

11:27 the Christ, the Son of G.

11:40 would see the glory of G.?

11:52 scattered children of G.

12:43 more than praise from G.

13:3 that he had come from G.

13:3 and was returning to G.

13:31 and G. is glorified in

13:32 If G. is glorified in him

13:32 G. will glorify the Son

14:1 Trust in G.; trust also

16:2 offering a service to G.

16:27 that I came from G.

16:30 that you came from G.

17:3 know you, the only true G.

19:7 claimed to be the Son of G.

20:17 and your Father, to my G.

20:17 and your G.

20:28 My Lord and my G.!

20:31 the Christ, the Son of G.

21:19 Peter would glorify G.

F. Feast

1. Feast (*heortē*; 17/25)

    2:23 Jerusalem at the Passover F.

4:45 Jerusalem at the Passover F.

4:45 had been there [at the F.]

5:1 Jerusalem for a f. of the

6:4 The Jewish Passover F. was

7:2 Jewish F. of Tabernacles was

7:8 You go to the F. I am not

7:8 yet going up to this F.

7:10 brothers had left for the F.

7:11 Now at the F. the Jews were

7:14 halfway through the F. did

7:37 and greatest day of the F.

11:56 Isn't he coming to the F.

12:12 that had come for the F.

12:20 up to worship at the F.

13:1 just before the Passover F.

13:29 what was needed for the F.

G. Glory/glorify

1. glory, honor, praise (*doxa*; 19/166)

    1:14 We have seen his g.

    1:14 the g. of the One and Only

    2:11 He thus revealed his g.

    5:41 I do not accept praise

    5:44 praise from one another

    5:44 to obtain the praise that

    7:18 to gain honor for himself

    7:18 works for the honor of the

    8:50 I am not seeking glory for

    8:54 glorify myself, my g. means

    9:24 Give g. to God

    11:4 No, it is for God's g.

    11:40 you would see the g. of God

    12:41 he saw Jesus' g. and spoke

    12:43 they loved praise from men

    12:43 more than praise from God

    17:5 with the g. I had with you

    17:22 I have given them the g.

    17:24 I am, and to see my g.

2. to glorify (*doxazō*; 23/61)

    7:39 had not yet been glorified

    8:54 If I g. myself, my glory

    8:54 is the one who glorifies me

    11:4 God's Son may be glorified

    12:16 after Jesus was glorified

    12:23 Son of Man to be glorified

12:28 Father, g. your name!

12:28 I have glorified it

12:28 and I will g. it again

13:31 is the Son of Man glorified

13:31 and God is glorified in him

13:32 If God is glorified in him

13:32 God will g. the Son in

13:32 and will g. him at once

14:13 the Son may bring glory

15:8 That is to my Father's glory

16:14 He will bring glory to me

17:1 Glorify your Son

17:1 that your son may g. you

17:4 I have brought you glory

17:5 And now, Father, g. me

17:10 And glory has come to me

21:19 which Peter would g. God

H. Judgment/judge

1. to judge, condemn (*krinō*; 19/114)

    3:17 world to condemn the world

    3:18 in him is not condemned

    3:18 stands condemned already

    5:22 the Father judges no one

    5:30 I j. only as I hear

    7:24 Stop judging by mere

    7:24 make a right judgment

    7:51 Does our law condemn

    8:15 You j. by human standards

    8:15 I pass judgment on no one

    8:16 But if I do j., my

    8:26 much to say in judgment

    8:50 and he is the judge

    12:47 I do not judge him

    12:47 For I did not come to j.

    12:48 There is a judge

    12:48 which I spoke will condemn

    16:11 and in regard to judgment

    18:31 and j. him by your own law

2. judgment (*krima*; 1/27)

    9:39 For j. I have come into

3. judgment (*krisis*; 11/47)

    3:19 This is the verdict:

    5:22 has entrusted all j. to

    5:24 will not be condemned

    5:27 him authority to judge

    5:29 will rise to be condemned

    5:30 my j. ist just, for I

7:24 make a right j.

8:16 my decisions are right

12:31 Now is the time for j.

16:8 and righteousness and j.

16:11 and in regard to j.

I. King/Kingdom

1. king (*basileus*; 16/115)

1:49 you are the K. of Israel

6:15 and make him k. by force

12:13 Blessed is the K. of Israel

12:15 see, your k. is coming

18:33 Are you the k. of the Jews?

18:37 You are a k., then!

18:37 right in saying I am a k.

18:39 release the k. of the Jews

19:3 Hail, k. of the Jews!

19:12 Anyone who claims to be a k.

19:14 Here is your k.

19:15 Shall I crucify your k.?

19:15 We have no k. but Caesar

19:19 THE K. OF THE JEWS

19:21 "The K. of the Jews," but

19:21 claimed to be k. of the Jews

2. kingdom (*basileia* (5/162)

3:3 no one can see the k. of God

3:5 no one can enter the k. of

18:36 My k. is not of this world

18:36 If it [my k.] were, my

18:36 But now my k. is from

J. Know

1. to know (*ginōskō*; 57/222)

1:10 the world did not recognize

1:48 How do you know me?

2:24 for he knew all men

2:25 for he knew what was in a

3:10 do you not understand these

4:1 The Pharisees heard that

4:53 Then the father realized

5:6 and learned that he had

5:42 but I know you

6:15 Jesus, knowing that they

6:69 We believe and know that

7:17 he will find out whether

7:26 really concluded that he is

7:27 But we know where this man

7:49 But this mob that knows

7:51 find out what he is doing?

8:27 They did not understand

8:28 then you will k. that I am

8:32 Then you will k. the truth

8:43 language not clear to you?

8:52 Now we know that you are

8:55 Though you do not know him

10:6 but they did not understand

10:14 I know my sheep

10:14 and my sheep know me

10:15 just as the Father knows me

10:15 and I know the Father

10:27 I k. them, and they follow

10:38 that you may know

10:38 and understand that the

11:57 that if anyone found out

12:9 crowd of Jews found out

12:16 did not understand all

13:7 You do not realize now

13:12 Do you understand what I

13:28 one at the meal understood

13:35 By this all men will know

14:7 If you really knew me

14:7 you would know my Father

14:7 From now on, you do k. him

14:9 Don't you know me, Philip

14:17 sees him nor knows him

14:17 But you know him, for he

14:20 you will realize that I am

14:31 the world must learn that

15:18 keep in mind that it hated

16:3 they have not known the

16:19 Jesus saw [knew] that they

17:3 that they may know you

17:7 Now they k. that everything

17:8 They knew with certainty

17:23 to let the world know that

17:25 the world does not k. you

17:25 I know you

17:25 and they k. that you have

19:4 to let you k. that I find

21:17 you know that I love you

2. to know (*oida*; 84/318)

1:26 stands one you do not k.

1:31 I myself did not k. him

1:33 I would not have known

2:9 He did not realize where

2:9 drawn the water knew

3:2 Rabbi, we know you are a

3:8 but you cannot tell [k.]

3:11 we speak of what we know

4:10 If you knew the gift of

4:22 worship what you do not k.

4:22 we worship what we do k.

4:25 I know that Messiah

4:32 food that you k. nothing

4:42 we k. that this man really

5:13 had no idea who it was

5:32 and I k. that his testimony

6:6 he already had in mind what

6:42 father and mother we know?

6:61 Aware that his disciples

6:64 For Jesus had known from

7:15 this man get such learning

7:27 But we know where this man

7:28 Yes, you know me

7:28 and you k. where I am from

7:28 You do not know him

7:29 but I know him because I am

8:14 for I k. where I came from

8:14 But you have no idea where

8:19 You do not know me or my

8:19 If you knew me

8:19 your would know my Father

8:37 I know you are Abraham's

8:55 Though you do not k. him

8:55 I know him

8:55 but I do know him and keep

9:12 I don't know

9:20 We know he is our son

9:21 see now [we don't know]

9:21 we don't know. Ask him

9:24 We k. this man is a sinner

9:25 sinner or not, I don't k.

9:25 One thing I do know. I was

9:29 We know that God spoke to

9:29 we don't even k. where he

9:30 You don't know where he

9:31 We k. that God does not

10:4 because they k. his voice

10:5 they do not recognize a

11:22 But I know that even now

11:24 I know he will rise again

11:42 I knew that you always hear

11:49 You know nothing at all!

12:35 does not k. where he is

12:50 I know that his command

13:1 Jesus knew that the time

13:3 Jesus knew that the Father

13:7 You do not realize now

13:11 For he knew who was going

13:17 Now that you know these

13:18 I know those I have chosen

14:4 You know the way to the

14:5 Lord, we don't k. where

14:5 so how can we k. the way?

15:15 servant does not know his

15:21 they do not k. the One who

16:18 We don't understand what

16:30 Now we can see that you

16:30 that you know all things

18:2 who betrayed him, knew the

18:4 Jesus, knowing all that was

18:21 Surely they k. what I said

19:10 Don't you realize I have

19:28 Later, knowing that all

19:35 He knows that he tells the

20:2 and we don't k. where they

20:9 still did not understand

20:13 I don't know where they

20:14 she did not realize that it

21:4 did not realize that it was

21:12 They knew it was the Lord

21:15 you know that I love you

21:16 you know that I love you

21:17 you know all things

21:24 We know that his testimony

K. Life

1. to give life (*zōopoieō*; 3/11)

5:21 dead and gives them life

5:21 even so the Son gives life

6:63 The Spirit gives life; the

2. to live (*zaō*; 17/140)

4:10 have given you living water

4:11 you get this living water?

4:50 You may go. Your son will l.

4:51 news that his boy was living

4:53 to him, "Your son will l."

5:25 and those who hear will l.

6:51 I am the living bread that

6:57 Just as the living Father

6:57 and I live because of the

6:57 will live because of me

6:58 this bread will l. forever

7:38 streams of living water

11:25 who believes in me will l.

11:26 whoever lives and believes

14:19 Because I live

14:19 you also will live

3. life (*zōē*; 36/135)

1:4 In him was life

1:4 and that life was the light

3:15 in him may have eternal l.

3:16 perish but have eternal l.

3:36 in the Son has eternal l.

3:36 the Son will not see l.

4:14 welling up to eternal l.

4:36 the crop for eternal l.

5:24 who sent me has eternal l.

5:24 over from death to l.

5:26 For as the Father has l.

5:26 the Son to have l. in

5:29 done good will rise to live

5:39 you possess eternal l.

5:40 to come to me to have l.

6:27 that endures to eternal l.

6:33 and gives l. to the world

6:35 I am the bread of life

6:40 shall have eternal l.

6:47 believes has everlasting l.

6:48 I am the bread of life

6:51 I will give for the l. of

6:53 you have no l. in you

6:54 my blood has eternal l.

6:63 spirit and they are l.

6:68 the words of eternal l.

8:12 will have the light of l.

10:10 come that they may have l.

10:28 I give them eternal l.

11:25 the resurrection and the l.

12:25 will keep it for eternal l.

12:50 command leads to eternal l.

14:6 and the truth and the life

17:2 he might give eternal l.

17:3 Now this is eternal life

20:31 you may have l. in his name

L. Light

1. to give light (*phōtizō*; 1/11)

1:9 that gives light to every

2. light (*phōs*; 23/73)

1:4 and that life was the l.

1:5 l. shines in the darkness

1:7 concerning that l., so

1:8 He himself was not the l.

1:8 as a witness to the l.

1:9 The true l. that gives

3:19 L. has come into the world

3:19 darkness instead of l.

3:20 does evil hates the l.

3:20 will not come into the l.

3:21 truth comes into the l.

5:35 that burned and gave l.

8:12 I am the l. of the world

8:12 will have the l. of life

9:5 I am the l. of the world

11:9 sees by this world's l.

11:10 stumbles, for he has no l.

12:35 have the l. just a little

12:35 Walk while you have the l.

12:36 Put your trust in the l.

12:36 while you have it [the l.]

12:36 you may become sons of l.

12:46 come into the world as l.

M. Love

1. to love (*agapaō*; 37/143)

3:16 For God so loved the world

3:19 men loved darkness instead

3:35 The Father loves the Son

8:42 you would love me, for I

10:17 The reason my Father loves

11:5 Jesus loved Martha and her

12:43 for they loved praise from

13:1 Having loved his own who

13:1 full extent of his love

13:23 disciple whom Jesus loved

13:34 Love one another

13:34 As I have loved you

13:34 so you must l. one another

14:15 If you l. me, you will obey

14:21 he is the one who loves me

14:21 He who loves me

14:21 will be loved by my Father

14:21 and I too will l. him and

14:23 If anyone loves me, he will
14:23 My Father will love him, and
14:24 He who does not love me
14:28 If you loved me, you would
14:31 world must learn that I l.
15:9 As the Father has loved me
15:9 so have I loved you
15:12 Love each other
15:12 as I have loved you
15:17 Love each other
17:23 and have loved them
17:23 even as you have loved me
17:24 because you loved me before
17:26 that the love you have for
19:26 the disciple whom he loved
21:7 disciple whom Jesus loved
21:15 do you truly love me more
21:16 do you truly love me
21:20 disciple whom Jesus loved

2. to love (phileō; 13/25)
5:20 the Father loves the Son
11:3 Lord, the one you love is
11:36 See how he loved him!
12:25 The man who loves his life
15:19 it would l. you as its own
16:27 Father himself loves you
16:27 because you have loved me
20:2 the one Jesus loved
21:15 you know that I love you
21:16 you know that I love you
21:17 do you love me?
21:17 Do you love me?
21:17 you know that I love you

3. love (agapē; 7/115)
5:42 do not have the l. of God
13:35 if you love one another
15:9 Now remain in my love
15:10 you will remain in my love
15:10 and remain in his love
15:13 Greater love has no one
17:26 the love you have for me

N. Send

1. messenger (apostolos; 1/80)
13:16 nor is a m. greater than

2. to send (apostellō; 28/132)
1:6 a man who was sent from God
1:19 Jews of Jerusalem sent
1:24 Pharisees who had been sent
3:17 For God did not s. his Son
3:28 not the Christ but am sent
3:34 the one whom God has sent
4:38 I sent you to reap what
5:33 You have sent to John and
5:36 that the Father has sent me
5:38 not believe the one he sent
6:29 in the one he has sent
6:57 as the living Father sent
7:29 came from him and he sent me
7:32 Pharisees sent temple guards
8:42 on my own; but he sent me
9:7 Siloam (this word means Sent)
10:36 and sent into the world
11:3 So the sisters sent word to
11:42 believe that you sent me
17:3 Christ, whom you have sent
17:8 believed that you sent me
17:18 As you sent me into the
17:18 I have sent them into the
17:21 that you have sent me
17:23 know that you sent me
17:25 that you have sent me
18:24 Then Annas sent him, still
20:21 As the Father has sent me

3. to send (pempō; 32/79)
1:22 back to those who sent us
1:33 one who sent me to baptize
4:34 the will of him who sent me
5:23 the Father, who sent him
5:24 believe him who sent me
5:30 but him who sent me
5:37 And the Father who sent me
6:38 the will of him who sent me
6:39 the will of him who sent me
6:44 unless the Father who sent
7:16 It comes from him who sent

7:18 honor of the one who sent
7:28 but he who sent me is true
7:33 go to the one who sent me
8:16 with the Father, who sent
8:18 is the Father, who sent me
8:26 But he who sent me is
8:29 The one who sent me is
9:4 the work of him who sent me
12:44 in the one who sent me
12:45 he sees the one who sent me
12:49 but the Father who sent me
13:16 than the one who sent him
13:20 whoever accepts anyone I s.
13:20 accepts the one who sent me
14:24 to the Father who sent me
14:26 whom the Father will s. in
15:21 know the One who sent me
15:26 whom I will send to you
16:5 going to him who sent me
16:7 but if I go, I will s. him
20:21 I am sending you

O. Sign(s)

1. sign(s) (sēmeion; 17/77; see also WORK)
2:11 first of his miraculous s.
2:18 What miraculous s. can you
2:23 people saw the miraculous s.
3:2 perform the miraculous s.
4:48 miraculous s. and wonders
4:54 second miraculous sign
6:2 saw the miraculous signs
6:14 saw the miraculous sign
6:26 saw miraculous signs but
6:30 What miraculous sign then
7:31 more miraculous signs than
9:16 do such miraculous signs?
10:41 performed a miraculous sign
11:47 many miraculous signs
12:18 given this miraculous sign
12:37 all these miraculous signs
20:30 many other miraculous signs

P. Sin

1. to sin (hamartanō; 3/42)
5:14 Stop sinning or something

9:2 Rabbi, who sinned, this man

9:3 man nor his parents sinned

2. sin (hamartia; 17/173)

1:29 takes away the sin of the

8:21 you will die in your sin

8:24 you would die in your sins

8:24 indeed die in your sins

8:34 everyone who sins is a

8:46 prove me guilty of sin?

9:34 You were steeped in sin

9:41 would not be guilty of sin

9:41 can see, your guilt remains

15:22 would not be guilty of sin

15:22 no excuse for their sin

15:24 would not be guilty of sin

16:8 in regard to sin and

16:9 in regard to sin, because

19:11 is guilty of a greater sin

20:23 forgive anyone his sins

3. sinner (hamartōlos; 4/47)

9:16 How can a sinner do such

9:24 We know this man is a s.

9:25 Whether he is a sinner

9:31 does not listen to sinners

Q. Son

1. Son/son (huios; 55/377)

1:34 that this is the S. of God

1:42 You are Simon son of John

1:45 Nazareth, the s. of Joseph

1:49 you are the Son of God

1:51 descending on the S. of Man

3:13 heaven—the Son of Man

3:14 the Son of Man must be

3:16 gave his one and only Son

3:17 God did not send his Son

3:18 of God's one and only Son

3:35 The Father loves the Son

3:36 Whoever believes in the Son

3:36 whoever rejects the Son

4:5 given to his son Joseph

4:12 as also did his sons and

4:46 whose son lay sick at

4:47 to come and heal his son

4:50 Your son will live

4:53 Your son will live

5:19 the Son can do nothing by

5:19 Father does the Son also

5:20 the Father loves the Son

5:21 even so the Son gives life

5:22 all judgment to the Son

5:23 that all may honor the Son

5:23 who does not honor the Son

5:25 the voice of the Son of God

5:26 granted the Son to have life

5:27 because he is the Son of Man

6:27 which the Son of Man will

6:40 who looks to the Son and

6:42 Is this not Jesus, the son

6:53 the flesh of the Son of Man

6:62 if you see the Son of Man

8:28 lifted up the Son of Man

8:35 a son belongs to it forever

8:36 So if the Son sets you free

9:19 Is this your son?

9:20 We know he is our son

9:35 believe in the Son of Man?

10:36 I said, "I am God's Son?"

11:4 God's Son may be glorified

11:27 the Christ, the Son of God

12:23 has come for the Son of Man

12:34 Son of Man must be lifted

12:34 Who is this "Son of Man"?

12:36 may become sons of light

13:31 is the Son of Man glorified

14:13 the Son may bring glory to

17:1 Glorify your Son

17:1 that your Son may glorify

17:12 the one [son] doomed to

19:7 to be the Son of God

19:26 Dear woman, here is your s.

20:31 the Christ, the Son of God

R. Teacher (see also D. Discipleship)

1. to teach (didaskō; 9/96)

6:59 He said this while teaching

7:14 and begin to teach

7:28 Then Jesus, still teaching

7:35 and teach the Greeks?

8:20 these words while teaching

8:28 what the Father has taught

9:34 how dare you lecture us!

14:26 will t. you all things

18:20 always taught in synagogues

2. teacher (didaskalos [Grk.]; 7/58)

1:38 (which means Teacher)

3:2 t. who has come from God

3:10 You are Israel's t.

11:28 The Teacher is here

13:13 You call me "Teacher" and

13:14 now that I, your Lord and T.

20:16 (which means Teacher)

3. teacher (rabb[oun]i [Aram.]; 9/17)

1:38 "Rabbi" (which means

1:49 Rabbi, you are the Son of

3:2 Rabbi, we know you are a

3:26 Rabbi, that man who was

4:31 Rabbi, eat something

6:25 Rabbi, when did you get

9:2 Rabbi, who sinned, this

11:8 "But Rabbi," they said

20:16 "Rabboni!" (which means

4. teaching (didachē; 3/30)

7:16 My teaching is not my own

7:17 whether my t. comes from

18:19 his disciples and his t.

S. Truth

1. true, valid (alēthēs; 14/26)

3:33 that God is truthful

4:18 just said is quite true

5:31 my testimony is not valid

5:32 testimony about me is valid

6:55 my flesh is real food

6:55 my blood is real drink

7:18 sent him is a man of truth

8:13 testimony is not valid

8:14 my testimony is valid

8:17 of two men is valid

8:26 who sent me is reliable

10:41 about this man was true

19:35 that he tells the truth

21:24 his testimony is true

2. true (alēthinos; 9/28)

1:9 The true light that gives

4:23 when true worshipers will

4:37 the saying . . . is true

6:32 the true bread from heaven

7:28 but he who sent me is true

8:16 my decisions are right

15:1 I am the true vine

17:3 the only true God

19:35 his testimony is true

3. truly (alēthōs; 7/18)

1:47 Here is a true Israelite

4:42 this man really is the

6:14 Surely this is the Prophet
7:26 Have the authorities really
7:40 Surely this man is the
8:31 you are really my disciples
17:8 They knew with certainty

4. truly (*amēn*; 50/127)
1:51 I tell you the truth
3:3 I tell you the truth
3:5 I tell you the truth
3:11 I tell you the truth
5:19 I tell you the truth
5:24 I tell you the truth
5:25 I tell you the truth
6:26 I tell you the truth
6:32 I tell you the truth
6:47 I tell you the truth
6:53 I tell you the truth
8:34 I tell you the truth
8:51 I tell you the truth
8:58 I tell you the truth
10:1 I tell you the truth
10:7 I tell you the truth
12:24 I tell you the truth
13:16 I tell you the truth
13:20 I tell you the truth
13:21 I tell you the truth
13:38 I tell you the truth
14:12 I tell you the truth
16:20 I tell you the truth
16:23 I tell you the truth
21:18 I tell you the truth

5. truth (*alētheia*; 25/109)
1:14 full of grace and truth
1:17 grace and t. came through
3:21 whoever lives by the t.
4:23 Father in spirit and t.
4:24 worship in spirit and t.
5:33 has testified to the t.
8:32 Then you will know the t.
8:32 the t. will set you free
8:40 the t. that I heard from
8:44 not holding to the t.
8:44 there is no t. in him
8:45 because I tell you the t.
8:46 If I am telling the t.
14:6 I am the way and the t.
14:17 the Spirit of truth
15:26 the Spirit of truth
16:7 But I tell you the t.
16:13 the Spirit of truth
16:13 guide you into all t.
17:17 Sanctify them by the t.
17:17 your word is truth
17:19 may be truly sanctified

18:37 to testify to the t.
18:37 Everyone on the side of t.
18:38 What is truth?

T. Witness

1. to witness, testify (*martyreō*; 33/76)
1:7 as a witness to testify
1:8 he came only as a w. to
1:15 John testifies concerning
1:32 John gave this testimony
1:34 I have seen and I testify
2:25 not need man's testimony
3:11 we testify to what we have
3:26 one you testified about
3:28 You yourselves can testify
3:32 He testifies to what he
4:39 the woman's testimony
4:44 himself had pointed out
5:31 If I testify about myself
5:32 is another who testifies
5:32 his testimony about me is
5:33 he has testified to the
5:36 testifies that the Father
5:37 me has himself testified
5:39 Scriptures that testify
7:7 I testify that what it
8:13 appearing as your own w.
8:14 my testimony is valid
8:18 I am one who testifies for
8:18 my other witness is the
10:25 miracles . . . speak for me
12:17 continued to spread the word
13:21 in spirit and testified
15:26 he will testify about me
15:27 And you also must testify
18:23 testify as to what is wrong
18:37 to testify to the truth
19:35 and his testimony is true
21:24 the disciple who testifies

2. testimony (*martyria*; 14/37)
1:7 He came as a witness to
1:19 Now this was John's t.
3:11 do not accept our t.
3:32 no one accepts his t.
3:33 man who has accepted it
5:31 my t. is not valid
5:32 his t. about me is valid
5:34 Not that I accept human t.
5:36 I have t. weightier than
8:13 your t. is not valid
8:14 my t. is valid, for I know
8:17 the t. of two is valid

19:35 who saw it has given t.
21:24 We know that his t. is true

U. Work

1. to work, labor (*kopiaō*; 3/23)
4:6 Jesus, tired as he was
4:38 what you have not worked
4:38 Others have done the hard w.

2. labor (*kopos*; 1/18)
4:38 the benefits of their l.

3. to work (*ergazomai*; 8/41)
3:21 has been done through God
5:17 is always at his work
5:17 and I, too, am working
6:27 Do not work for food that
6:28 do the works God requires
6:30 What will you do?
9:4 we must do the work of him
9:4 when no one can work

4. work (*ergon*; 27/169)
3:19 their deeds were evil
3:20 his deeds will be exposed
3:21 that what he has done
4:34 and to finish his work
5:20 even greater things than
5:36 For the very w. that the
5:36 and which I am doing
6:28 we do to do the works God
6:29 The work of God is this:
7:3 see the miracles you do
7:7 that what it does is evil
7:21 I did one miracle, and
8:39 you would do the things
8:41 doing the things your own
9:3 that the w. of God might
9:4 we must do the w. of him
10:25 The miracles I do in my
10:32 you many great miracles
10:32 For which of these do
10:33 not . . . for any of these
10:37 I do what my Father does
10:38 believe the miracles
14:10 in me, who is doing his w.
14:11 evidence of the miracles
14:12 will do what I have been
15:24 have seen these miracles
17:4 by completing the w. you

V. World

1. World (*kosmos*; 78/185)
1:9 was coming into the world

1:10 He was in the world
1:10 and though the w. was made
1:10 the w. did not recognize
1:29 away the sin of the w.
3:16 For God so loved the w.
3:17 send his Son into the w.
3:17 to condemn the w., but
3:17 to save the w. through him
3:19 Light has come into the w.
4:42 is the Savior of the w.
6:14 who is to come into the w.
6:33 and gives life to the w.
6:51 give for the life of the w.
7:4 show yourself to the w.
7:7 The w. cannot hate you
8:12 I am the light of the w.
8:23 You are of this world
8:23 I am not of this world
8:26 heard from him I tell the w.
9:5 While I am in the w.
9:5 I am the light of the w.
9:39 I have come into this w.
10:36 and sent into the world?
11:9 sees by this world's light
11:27 who was to come into the w.
12:19 Look how the whole w. has
12:25 hates his life in this w.

12:31 for judgment on this w.
12:31 now the prince of this w.
12:46 into the w. as a light
12:47 not come to judge the w.
12:47 but to save it [the w.]
13:1 to leave this w. and go
13:1 his own who were in the w.
14:17 The w. cannot accept him
14:19 Before long, the w. will
14:22 to us and not to the w.?
14:27 give to you as the w. gives
14:30 prince of this w. is coming
14:31 but the w. must learn that
15:18 If the w. hates you, keep
15:19 If you belonged to the w.
15:19 it [the w.] would love you
15:19 you do not belong to the w.
15:19 chosen you out of the w.
15:19 That is why the w. hates
16:8 convict the w. of guilt
16:11 the prince of this w. now
16:20 mourn while the w. rejoices
16:21 a child is born into the w.
16:28 Father and entered the w.
16:28 now I am leaving the w. and
16:33 In this w. you will have
16:33 I have overcome the world

17:5 before the world began
17:6 you gave me out of the w.
17:9 I am not praying for the w.
17:11 I will remain in the w. no
17:11 they are still in the w.
17:13 while I am still in the w.
17:14 and the w. has hated them
17:14 for they are not of the w.
17:14 any more than I am of the w.
17:15 take them out of the w. but
17:16 They are not of the world
17:16 even as I am not of it
17:18 As you sent me into the w.
17:18 have sent them into the w.
17:21 so that the w. may believe
17:23 the w. know that you sent
17:24 the creation of the w.
17:25 the w. does not know you
18:20 spoken openly to the w.
18:36 My kingdom is not of this w.
18:36 If it were [from this w.]
18:37 I came into the w., to
21:25 even the whole w. would not

Note: Since John 7:53–8:11 is judged not to have been part of John's original Gospel, the above listings do not include this portion.

Excursus 1
"Life" and "Light" in John's Gospel

"In him was life, and that life was the light of men" (1:4). This statement at the beginning of John's Prologue links the two important Johannine terms of "life" and "light." What is the relationship between life and light, and what are the roots of John's juxtaposition of these terms? It appears that the foundation is already laid in the Genesis narrative of God's creation of the world. As his first creative act by his word, God calls forth light (1:3–5). Later he places lights in the sky to separate between light and darkness (1:14–18). This light, in turn, makes it possible for life to exist. Thus on creation days 5 and 6, God calls forth living creatures in the water and on the land (1:20–31), culminating in his creation of man (2:7; 3:20). The tree of life and the tree of the knowledge of good and evil are set in the garden, linking life with obedience to God (2:9).

In John's creation theology, which explicitly links what was "in the beginning" (Jn 1:1; cf. Gn 1:1) with the incarnation of Christ, the above painted scenario forms the backdrop against which Jesus' coming is more readily understood. For man's sin had resulted in the loss of life, plunging humanity into moral darkness. The crying need was for human beings to be restored to life, "eternal life," and light, that is, liberation from the power of sin. What the Synoptic writers present in terms of God's kingdom, and what Paul develops in terms of justification, reconciliation, and so on, John grounds in creation realities that have been perverted through the fall and have now been restored in Christ. On a secondary level, parallels from the

Psalms suggest themselves as well, in particular a passage from Psalm 36:

> They feast on the abundance of your house;
>   you give them drink from your river of delights.
> For with you is the fountain of life;
>   in your light we see light (vv. 8–9).

One thinks here of Jesus' promise of living water (Jn 4:10–15), his promise of rivers of living water flowing out of people's innermost being (Jn 7:38), and of his promise of abundant life (Jn 10:10). As Jeremiah had lamented, people had forsaken God, "the spring of living water," and had "dug their own cisterns" (Jer 2:13; cf. 17:13). They must return to the Lord. Finally, light and life had become permanently associated in the common phrase "the light of life" (e.g., Job 3:20; 33:30; Pss 49:19; 56:13; Is 53:11; cf. Jn 8:12). The vision of restored, abundant life in God's presence is given final expression at the end of the Book of Revelation (22:1–2; cf. Ez 47:12).

Life and light are thus inextricably wedded in John's theology. Both attest to the fruit of Christ's coming into the world: new, eternal life made available through Christ's substitutionary death to "everyone who believes," and a will liberated by the truth that is again ready to love, obey, and trust. Jesus thus reenacts the event of creation on a cosmic as well as personal level; he fulfills the psalmists' longings; he makes possible the prophets' highest aspirations; and he paves the way for the fulfillment of the apocalyptist's vision of abundant, eternal life in God's presence.

Excursus 2
"The Jews" in John's Gospel

In recent years, the label "anti-Semitic" has frequently been attached to John's Gospel. What basis in fact has such an astonishing charge?

At the outset, one notices that John usually does not distinguish between the different parties within Judaism current in Jesus' day but lumps them all together under the epithet "the Jews." Thus the Sadducees, which enjoy considerable prominence in the Synoptics, are not mentioned in John's Gospel at all. And while there is the occasional positive or neutral reference, most uses of the term "the Jews" are demonstrably negative. Was the author of John's Gospel therefore anti-Semitic?

To begin with, the charge of anti-Semitism clearly involves anachronism. At the end of a century that has witnessed the murderous holocaust of the Jewish people by the hands of Hitler's Nazi Germany, it is of course not surprising that people are particularly sensitive to the appearance of anti-Semitic sentiments, even when this involves Scripture. What adds fuel to the fire is that the Bible has in fact been used in the course of history to justify anti-Semitism, and not even powerful Christian men such as the Reformer Martin Luther have been free from anti-Semitic tendencies. Hence the concern to expose any latent anti-Semitism wherever it can be found is certainly legitimate.

At the same time, it must be said that any such charge against a document whose writer (the apostle John) is a Jew, and whose major "hero" (Jesus) is a Jew (cf. 4:9), seems at the outset rather implausible. "A house divided against itself cannot stand," said Jesus, so what about John, the Jew, writing an anti-Semitic Gospel about the Jew Jesus? Also, every member of Jesus' inner circle, the twelve, was Jewish, and as the Johannine Jesus makes clear when talking to the Samaritan woman, "salvation is from the Jews"

(4:22). This hardly sounds anti-Semitic. Apart from this, there are frequent neutral reference to "the Jews," such as in the phrase "a Feast of the Jews" (e.g., 2:13; 5:1; 6:4; 7:2; 11:55) or with reference to a particular Jewish custom (e.g., 2:6; 19:40). The purpose here is simply to educate John's readers (which are not necessarily familiar with Palestinian Jewish customs) in this regard.

What, then, can be said about the negative instances of the phrase "the Jews" in John's Gospel (e.g., 5:16, 18; 7:1; 8:48; 10:31, 33; 11:8; 19:12)? The general answer is that, theologically, John places ultimate responsibility for Jesus' crucifixion squarely on the shoulders of the Jewish people as represented by their religious leadership, the Jewish ruling council (called Sanhedrin). In this context, the thrust of John's use of the term "the Jews" is not ethnic, it is salvation-historical. What John is seeking to forestall is Jewish presumption upon their religious heritage. For in John's analysis, the Jews, by claiming Abraham and Moses as their ancestors and the Scriptures (including their own traditions) as their own possession, fell into the sins of religious pride and prejudice that blinded their eyes toward their very own Messiah, that is, Jesus.

In this sense, Israel had become part of the "world" in that it rejected the God-sent Messiah (note the parallelism between 1:10: "*the world* did not recognize him" and 1:11: "his own [that is, *the Jewish people*] did not receive him"). This does not mean that the Jews rejected Jesus *without exception:* it has already been pointed out that all of Jesus' initial close followers were in fact Jews. Yet by pinning guilt for Jesus' crucifixion on the Jews, John makes clear that God's plan now had shifted: no longer was the primary locus of his saving purposes *the nation of Israel*, but rather *whoever believed that the Messiah was Jesus, whether Jew or not*, was a member of God's new covenant community.

In light of the rapid influx of Gentiles into the church, the paradoxical reversal had taken place—most of the Jews had become part of "the world," while many non-Jews (that is, Gentiles) had become part of God's people. But is this not exactly what was already promised by the Old Testament prophets? Yes, it is. Thus both Paul and Peter concur in quoting Hosea's statement, "I will say to those called 'Not my people,' 'You are my people'" (Hos 2:23; cited in Rom 9:25 and 1 Pt 2:10) with reference to the New Testament church made up of believing Jews and Gentiles alike. Now it is hard to see how Paul and Peter, too, would have been anti-Semitic.

There may be one further reason for John's lack of further differentiation among "the Jews": his location post-A.D. 70, when, subsequent to the destruction of the temple, the Sadducees had ceased to exist as a party, so that it was no longer meaningful to speak in such terms. By refraining from distinguishing between Pharisees and Sadducees among the Jewish leadership, John makes the important theological point that the Jewish nation at large, represented by its religious leadership, had rejected the God-sent Messiah. This John did not to humiliate un-

believing Jews or to slam the door of forgiveness in their faces. Rather, in order to lead them to faith, it was necessary that they be confronted with their guilt.

Peter did this, when, at Pentecost, he fixed his eyes squarely on his Jewish audience and said, "*you*, with the help of wicked men, put him to death by nailing him to the cross" (Acts 2:23). Paradoxically, therefore, John's Gospel, with its apparent harsh language regarding the Jews, is actually engaged (at least in part) in an effort at Jewish evangelism. For the period after A.D. 70 saw Jews grope for answers to the national catastrophe that had befallen them. Now John believed to have the answer: Jesus the Messiah, the new center of worship in place of the old sanctuary, the true meaning symbolized by the various Jewish festivals. For John, despite the Jews' rejection of their Messiah, Jesus was still holding out his hand, waiting to forgive them if they returned to him in repentance and faith.

Is John's Gospel anti-Semitic? No. Rather, the Jews in Jesus' day were anti-Jesus the Messiah and thus had become part of the unbelieving world. In order to remedy this tragedy, and in order to present Jesus as the Messiah the Jews had waited for so long, John wrote his Gospel.

Excursus 3
Asides in John

John 1:38 and 41 are examples of asides in John, instances where the evangelist seeks to clarify a given issue or undertakes to provide additional information to make an aspect of his narrative intelligible to his readers. In the case of 1:38 and 41, John simply translates an Aramaic expression for his readers, who, living in the diaspora, may not be familiar with these terms in the original language spoken by Jesus and his contemporaries. Here is a select list of Johannine asides grouped according to the kind of contribution made by these editorial comments of the evangelist. Note that this literary device enables John to distinguish between his narrative proper and his own clarifying comments while still helping his readers along as he sees fit. Note how translations such as the NIV customarily (though not in every instance) place these asides in brackets.

1. Translation of Aramaic or Hebrew terms:
   "'rabbi' (which means Teacher)" (1:38)
   "'the Messiah' (that is, the Christ)" (1:41; 4:25)
   "'Cephas' (which, when translated, is Peter)" (1:42)
   "'Siloam' (this word meant Sent)" (9:7)
   "Thomas (called Didymus)" (11:16; 20:24; 21:2)
   "a place known as the Stone Pavement (which in Aramaic is Gabbatha)" (19:13; note that this is actually not a translation but a different name for the same place; literally, "Gabbatha" means something like "the hill of the house")
   "the place of the Skull (which in Aramaic is called Golgotha)" (19:17)
   [Mary] "cried out in Aramaic, 'Rabbouni!' (which means Teacher)" (20:16)

2. Explanations of Palestinian topography:
   "Now there is in Jerusalem near the Sheep Gate a pool, which in Aramaic is called Bethesda" (5:2)

   "the Sea of Galilee (that is, the Sea of Tiberias)" (6:1)
   "Bethany was less than two miles from Jerusalem" (11:18)

3. Explanation of Jewish customs:
   "six stone water jars, the kind used by the Jews for ceremonial washing" (2:6)
   "(For Jews do not associate with Samaritans.)" (4:9)
   "Then came the Feast of Dedication at Jerusalem. It was winter" (10:22)
   "to avoid ceremonial uncleanness the Jews did not enter the palace; they wanted to be able to eat the Passover" (18:28)
   "This was in accordance with Jewish burial customs" (19:40)

4. References to Jesus' supernatural insight or foreknowledge of events:
   "But Jesus would not entrust himself to them, for he knew all men. He did not need man's testimony about man, for he knew what was in a man" (2:24–25)
   "For Jesus had known from the beginning which of them did not believe and who would betray him" (6:64; cf. 6:71; 12:4)
   "Jesus knew that the time had come for him to leave this world and go to the Father. . . . Jesus knew that the Father had put all things under his power, and that he had come from God and was returning to God" (13:1–3)
   "For he knew who was going to betray him, and that was why he said not every one was clean" (13:11)
   "Jesus, knowing all that was going to happen to him" (18:4)

5. References to characters or events mentioned earlier in the narrative:
   "Once more he visited Cana in Galilee, where he had turned the water into wine" (4:46; cf. 2:1–11)

"Then some boats from Tiberias landed near the place where the people had eaten the bread after the Lord had given thanks" (6:23; cf. 6:1–15)

"Nicodemus, who had gone to Jesus earlier and who was one of their own number" (7:50; cf. 3:1–2)

"the man who had been blind" (9:13, 18, 24; cf. 9:1–7)

"Then Jesus went back across the Jordan to the place where John had been baptizing in the early days" (10:40; cf. 1:28)

"Lazarus . . . whom Jesus had raised from the dead" (12:1–2, 9, 17; cf. 11:1–44)

"Caiaphas was the one who had advised the Jews that it would be good if one man died for the people" (18:14; cf. 11:49–51)

"One of the high priest's servants, a relative of the man whose ear Peter had cut off" (18:26; cf. 18:10)

"He was accompanied by Nicodemus, the man who earlier had visited Jesus at night" (19:39; cf. 3:1–2)

"Finally, the other disciple, who had reached the tomb first" (20:8; cf. 20:4)

"(This was the one who had leaned back against Jesus at the supper and had said, 'Lord, who is going to betray you?')" (21:20; cf. 13:23–25)

6. References to the fulfillment of Scripture or of Jesus' words:

"His disciples remembered that it is written: 'Zeal for your house will consume me'" (2:17)

"This happened so that the words he had spoken would be fulfilled: 'I have not lost one of those you gave me'" (18:9; cf. 6:29; 10:28; 17:12)

"This happened so that the words Jesus had spoken indicating the kind of death he was going to die would be fulfilled" (18:32; cf. 3:14; 8:28; 12:33)

"This happened that the scripture might be fulfilled which said, 'They divided my garments among them, and cast lots for my clothing.' So this is what the soldiers did" (19:24)

"Later, . . . so that the Scripture would be fulfilled, Jesus said, 'I am thirsty'" (19:28)

"These things happened so that the scripture would be fulfilled: 'Not one of his bones will be broken,' and, as another scripture says, 'They will

look on the one they have pierced'" (19:36–37)

7. References to a failure to understand:

"He did not realize where it had come from, though the servants who had drawn the water knew" (2:9)

"The man who was healed had no idea who it was, for Jesus had slipped away into the crowd that was there" (5:13)

"For even his own brothers did not believe in him" (7:5)

"They did not understand that he was telling them about his Father" (8:27)

"Jesus used this figure of speech, but they did not understand what he was telling them" (10:6)

"Jesus had been speaking of his death, but his disciples thought he meant natural sleep" (11:13)

"At first his disciples did not understand all this. Only after Jesus was glorified did they realize that these things had been written about him and that they had done these things to him" (12:16)

"but no one at the meal understood why Jesus said this to him. Since Judas had charge of the money, some thought Jesus was telling him to buy what was needed for the Feast, or to give something to the poor" (13:28–29)

"(They still did not understand from Scripture that Jesus had to rise from the dead)" (20:9)

"but she did not realize it was Jesus" (20:14)

"but the disciples did not realize that it was Jesus" (21:4)

8. Clarifications of the meaning of statements made by Jesus or others:

"But the temple he had spoken of was his body. After he was raised from the dead, his disciples recalled what he had said. Then they believed the Scripture and the words that Jesus had spoken" (2:21–22)

"For this reason the Jews tried all the harder to kill him; not only was he breaking the Sabbath, but he was even calling God his own Father, making himself equal with God" (5:18)

"He asked this only to test him, for he already had in mind what he was going to do" (6:6)

"(He meant Judas, the son of Simon

Iscariot, who, though one of the Twelve, was later to betray him)" (6:71)

"By this he meant the Spirit, whom those who believed in him were later to receive. Up to that time the Spirit had not been given, since Jesus had not yet been glorified" (7:39)

"His parents said this because they were afraid of the Jews, for already the Jews had decided that anyone who acknowledged that Jesus was the Christ would be put out of the synagogue. That was why his parents said, 'He is of age; ask him'" (9:22)

"Jesus loved Martha and her sister and Lazarus. Yet when he heard that Lazarus was sick, he stayed where he was two more days" (11:5)

"He did not say this on his own, but as high priest that year he prophesied that Jesus would die for the Jewish nation, and not only for that nation but also for the scattered children of God, to bring them together and make them one" (11:51–52)

"He did not say this because he cared about the poor but because he was a thief; as keeper of the money bag, he used to help himself to what was put into it" (12:6)

"He said this to show the kind of death he was going to die" (12:33)

"Isaiah said this because he saw Jesus' glory and spoke about him" (12:41)

"Jesus said this to indicate the kind of death by which Peter would glorify God" (21:19)

"Because of this, the rumor spread among the brothers that this disciple would not die. But Jesus did not say that he would not die; he only said, 'If I want him to remain alive until I return, what is that to you?'" (21:23)

9. Statements in relation to the Gospel tradition:
"Andrew, Simon Peter's brother" (1:40; cf. 1:41)
"(This was before John was put in prison.)" (3:24)
"(Now Jesus himself had pointed out that a prophet has no honor in his own country)" (4:44)
"Bethany, the village of Mary and her sister Martha. This Mary . . . was the same one who poured perfume on the Lord and wiped his feet with her hair" (11:1–2)

10. Numbering of events in the narrative:
"This was the second miraculous sign that Jesus performed, having come from Judea to Galilee" (4:54; cf. 2:11)
"This was now the third time Jesus appeared to his disciples after he was raised from the dead" (21:14; cf. 20:19, 26)

11. Other clarifying statements:
"although in fact it was not Jesus who baptized, but his disciples" (4:2; cf. 3:22)
"(His disciples had gone into the town to buy food.)" (4:8)
"Judas (not Iscariot)" (14:22)
"(The servant's name was Malchus.)" (18:10)

The literary device of asides enables John as the narrator to steer his readers to his desired conclusion (see esp. 6:60–71; 12:37–43; 20:30–31; 21:24–25). By these asides, the evangelist is able to remove ignorance on part of his readers with regard to terminology or topography, to alleviate the possible perception of inconsistency in his presentation of events, and to highlight important theological motifs such as people's misunderstandings or Jesus' supernatural foreknowledge of events. In the context of the triad of history, literature, and theology, the asides focus our attention on the literary dimension of John's Gospel, the way in which the evangelist carefully crafted his narrative (see also the self-references in 1:14; 13:23; 18:15–16; 19:35; 20:2–9; 21:7, 20–25). An understanding of this aspect of the Johannine narrative, too, will help us to develop a deeper appreciation for this remarkable Gospel.

Note: Three helpful essays on Johannine asides are Tom Thatcher, "A New Look at Asides in the Fourth Gospel," Bibliotheca Sacra 151 (1994): 428–39; John J. O'Rourke, "Asides in the Gospel of John," Novum Testamentum 21 (1979): 210–19; and Merrill C. Tenney, "The Footnotes of John's Gospel," Bibliotheca Sacra 117 (1960): 350–63.

Excursus 4
References to Time in John's Gospel

Both Jews and non-Jews counted time in the first century A.D. from sunrise (6 A.M.) to sunset (6 P.M.). As Jesus himself says, "Are there not twelve hours of daylight?" (11:9). Thus when the original Greek says, for example, "It was the tenth hour," that means that it was 4 P.M. (6 A.M. + 10 hours). In addition, people often thought of the twelve-hour day in terms of four segments of three hours each. In an age before wristwatches, it was often difficult to determine the exact time. Thus people would content themselves with estimating the hour by approximating the closest interval of three.

Here are references to time in John's Gospel (see also *Sidebar: The Coming of Jesus' "Hour"*):

1. "It was about the tenth hour" (1:39). Jesus' first two followers (one of them being Andrew) decide to stay with Jesus at about 4:00 P.M.
2. "It was about the sixth hour" (4:6). Jesus, tired from his journey through Samaria, took a break at Jacob's well at about 12:00 noon. This was also when the Samaritan woman came to the well in order to draw water. Presumably she had to come during the heat of the day because she was considered immoral (cf. 4:16–18) and thus socially ostracized.
3. "yesterday at the seventh hour" (4:52). The royal official's son was healed at about 1:00 P.M., the exact time at which Jesus had said to the official that his son would live (4:53; cf. 4:50).
4. "It was . . . about the sixth hour" (19:14; cf. 4:6). Jesus' Roman trial before Pilate concluded at about 12:00 noon. Compare with this Mark, who says that Jesus was crucified at around the third hour (15:25), no doubt a rough estimate (see above) and that darkness came over the land from the sixth until the ninth hour, with the hour of Jesus' death being the ninth hour, that is, around 3:00 P.M. (15:33).

Note: For fuller treatments of the references to the hour of Jesus' death in John and the Synoptics, see D. A. Carson, *The Gospel According to John* (Grand Rapids: Eerdmans, 1991), 604–5; and Craig L. Blomberg, *The Historical Reliability of the Gospels* (Leicester, U.K./Downers Grove: InterVarsity, 1987), 179–80.

Excursus 5

Misunderstandings in John's Gospel

John is united with the Synoptic writers in his recording of several "misunderstandings," frequently on part of Jesus' disciples. This is paralleled by the Marcan motif of "discipleship failure" (which is also found, albeit to a somewhat lesser extent, in Matthew and Luke). In John's case, however, the "misunderstandings" encompass a wide array of people and are occasionally coupled with another distinctive Johannine literary device, that of irony. Here, then, is a list of selected "Johannine misunderstandings":

- the Jews believe Jesus will rebuild the temple in three literal days (2:20)
- Nicodemus thinks Jesus is talking about a literal second birth (3:4)
- the Jews fail to understand the atonement Jesus would provide; they are puzzled about Jesus' giving them "his flesh" to eat (6:52)
- people's ignorance of Jesus' otherworldly origin (6:42; 7:27; 8:27)
- people's ignorance of Jesus' Bethlehem birth (7:41–42; cf. 1:45–46; 7:52)
- the Jews think Jesus is talking about literal descendance from Abraham while he is talking about spiritual offspring (8:31–39)
- the Pharisees fail to understand that Jesus is talking about spiritual blindness (9:40–41)
- the disciples fail to understand Jesus' parable of the shepherd and the sheep (10:6)
- when Jesus says Lazarus has "fallen asleep," the disciples take it literally; but Jesus had used the term "sleep" as an euphemism for death (11:11–13)
- Martha thinks Jesus is speaking of Lazarus's resurrection at the last day when Jesus is talking about raising Lazarus right then (11:24)

- only after Jesus' glorification do the disciples understand the significance of the events surrounding Jesus' triumphal entry (12:16)
- Peter fails to understand the significance of the footwashing (13:6–11)
- the disciples in the Upper Room fail to understand the significance of Judas's leaving the meal (13:28–29)
- Peter misunderstands Jesus' point about his inability to follow him at that time (13:36–38)
- Thomas and then Philip misunderstand Jesus' reference to his being "the way" and his having showed them the Father (14:5, 8)
- the disciples miss Jesus' point about the "little while" (16:17–18)
- Peter, by cutting off Malchus's right ear, shows that he still fails to understand Jesus' need to "drink the cup" the Father has given him (18:11)
- even at the empty tomb the disciples fail to understand from Scripture that Jesus had to rise from the dead (20:9)
- Mary Magdalene does not realize that the man she sees is the risen Jesus; instead, she thinks he is the gardener (20:14–15)
- likewise, the seven disciples who had gone fishing do not realize that whom they see is their risen Lord (21:4)

Frequently, the misunderstandings featured in John's Gospel hinge on people's taking literally what Jesus means figuratively. In other words, people fail to understand the underlying spiritual message Jesus seeks to impart. The scope of these misunderstandings encompasses "the Jews" as well as the members of Jesus' inner circle. Importantly, it is only Jesus' crucifixion and resurrection followed by the giving of the Spirit that removes the veil of spiritual understanding (cf. esp. 2:22: "after he was raised from the dead"; 12:16: "only after Jesus was glorified").

This constitutes a significant difference between later generations of believers (including us) and Jesus' first followers as depicted in the Gospels. For the New Testament makes clear that after the pouring out of the Spirit at Pentecost (cf. Acts 2)—the so-called mini-Pentecosts in Acts 8, 10, and 19 being no real exceptions—every person receives the Spirit upon trusting in Christ (e.g., Rom 8:9; 1 Cor 12:13). Unlike the original eleven plus Matthias and the larger circle of believers prior to Pentecost, there is no need to "wait for the Spirit" (Acts 1:8, 14). Hence there is also no clear parallel between our experience of Christian growth and the misunderstandings of Jesus' original followers. For living prior to Pentecost, these did not have the Spirit—but we do.

Thus the misunderstandings featured in John's Gospel (and the Synoptics) belong inextricably to the period of Jesus' earthly ministry prior to his "glorification." The fact that John notes these misunderstandings which hinge so palpably on the disciples' historical location prior to the crucifixion shows that this evangelist is indeed concerned not to blur the lines between the so-called historical Jesus and the early church's later belief in what has been called "the Christ of faith." While John displays a keen interest in the implications of Jesus' earthly ministry for later believers—in this he is united with Paul and the rest of the New Testament writers—he is careful to maintain the historical contours of his gospel. His interest in theology does not cause him to compromise the accuracy of his historical portrayal. For this the Johannine "misunderstandings" provide powerful evidence.

Note: For a detailed discussion of Johannine misunderstandings, see D. A. Carson, "Understanding Misunderstandings in the Fourth Gospel," *Tyndale Bulletin* 33 (1982): 59–91.

Excursus 6
Divine Necessity in John's Gospel

The little Greek word *dei* ("it is necessary"), used ten times in John's Gospel, carries a lot of theological weight. Often the implied subject of these expressions is none other than God himself who declares the necessity of certain things. Here is a list of things declared in John's Gospel to be (divinely) "necessary":

"You must be born again" (Jesus to Nicodemus; 3:7)

"the Son of Man must be lifted up" (3:14; cf. 12:34)

"He must become greater; I must become less" (John the Baptist and Jesus; 3:30)

Jesus "had to go through Samaria" (4:4)

"God is spirit, and his worshipers must worship in spirit and in truth" (4:24; cf. 4:20)

"As long as it is day, we must do the work of him who sent me" (9:4; cf. 4:34)

"I have other sheep that are not of this sheep pen. I must bring them also" (10:16)

according to Old Testament Scripture, "Jesus had to rise from the dead" (20:9)

The Baptist's ministry, Jesus' Samaritan (and later Gentile) mission, his ministry, crucifixion and resurrection, and spiritual rebirth as well as spiritual worship are all said to be divine necessities in John.

Excursus 7
Jesus as a Rabbi in John's Gospel

While Jesus is cast in John's Gospel as Son of God (1:34, 39; 5:25; 10:36; 11:4, 27; 20:31), Son of Man (1:51; 3:13, 14; 5:27; 6:27, 53, 62; 8:28; 9:35; 12:23, 24; 13:31), and the Christ (1:17, 20, 25, 41; 3:28; 4:25, 29; 7:26, 27, 31, 41, 42; 9:22; 10:24; 11:27; 12:34; 17:3; 20:31), the only way Jesus is shown to be actually addressed by his contemporaries is as Rabbi/Teacher (Grk. *rabbi* from the Hebrew/Aramaic; 1:38, 49; 3:2; 4:31; 6:25; 9:2; 11:8; 20:16) or Master/Lord (Grk. *kyrios*; 4:11, 15, 19, 49; 5:7; 6:34, 68; 9:36, 38; 11:3, 12, 21, 27, 32, 34, 39; 12:21, 38; 13:6, 9, 25, 36, 37; 14:5, 8, 22; 20:15, 28; 21:15, 16, 17, 20, 21).

This characterization (supported also by the Synoptic writers: cf. Mk 4:38; 5:35; 9:5, 17, 38; 10:17, 20, 35, 51; 11:21; 12:14, 19, 32; 13:1; 14:14, 45; Mt 8:19; 9:11; 12:38; 17:24; 19:16; 22:16, 24, 36; 26:18, 25, 49; Lk 7:40; 8:49; 9:38; 10:25; 11:45; 12:13; 18:18; 19:39; 20:21, 28, 39; 21:7; 22:11) proves that Jesus' contemporaries, disciples and otherwise, perceived Jesus first and foremost as a rabbi, a Jewish religious teacher. In keeping with this characterization, John depicts Jesus' relationship with his followers in terms of first-century Jewish teacher–disciple relationships.

As a teacher, Jesus provides his disciples (or others) with verbal instruction, often using a rabbinic style of argumentation. One such device is the argument from the lesser to the greater, which Jesus employs when talking to Nicodemus: "If I told you earthly things and you do not believe, how shall you believe if I tell you heavenly things?" (3:12). Or, as he tells the Jews, "But if you do not believe his [Moses'] writings, how will you believe my words?" When embroiled in the Sabbath controversy, Jesus retorts, "Now if a child receives circumcision on the Sabbath so that the law of Moses may not be broken, why are you angry with me for healing the whole man on the Sabbath?" (7:23).

Jesus' verbal instruction was supplemented by rabbinic-style didactic actions. This included his cleansing of the temple (2:13–22) and the footwashing (13:1–17). In everything, Jesus sought to set an example his disciples were to follow. As the sent Son of the Father, he exemplified absolute dependence, obedience, and faithfulness to his sender (e.g., 4:34; 5:23, 30, 36, 38; 6:38–39; 7:16, 18, 28; 8:26; 9:4; 12:44–45, 49; 13:20; 14:10b, 24). This stance, in turn, is in the end held up as the paradigm for his disciples' mission: "As the Father has sent me, I am sending you" (20:21).

Conversely, Jesus' disciples, in keeping with rabbinic precedent, are shown to follow their teacher wherever he went. They lived with him (e.g., 1:39; 3:22). They joined him at a wedding (2:1–12). They accompanied him when he healed the sick (4:43–54; 5:1–15; chs. 9 and 11) and fed the multitudes (6:1–13). During the farewell discourse, they were not afraid to ask him questions when they failed to grasp an aspect of his teaching (13:36–38; 14:5, 8, 22). This, too, coheres with the picture painted of first-century Jewish teacher–disciple relationships in the relevant sources.

Also in keeping with contemporary practice, Jesus' disciples are shown in John's Gospel to perform acts of service. They are sent to buy bread (4:8) and are asked to help provide food for the multitudes (6:5). At the feeding, they help Jesus to have the people sit down, distribute the food, and gather up leftovers (6:10, 12). Later, one of Jesus' closest disciples is entrusted with the care of his mother (19:26–27), while two of Jesus' disciples assume responsibility for his burial, another task customarily performed by a deceased teacher's disciples (19:38–42). Even the writing down of John's Gospel can be seen as the faithful discharge of one of the responsibilities of a disciple, the cultivation of his teacher's memory and teaching (21:24–25).

Interestingly, there are times when Jesus reverses the customary pattern of teacher and disciple for teaching purposes. One such instance is the footwashing, where Jesus assumes the role of a household slave and performs a task that was considered to be too menial even for disciples in his day (b. Ketub. 96a). Another example is (the risen!) Jesus' preparation of breakfast for his disciples on the shore of the Sea of Galilee (21:9–13). For food preparation, too, was part of the tasks of a disciple.

Notably, the depiction of Jesus as a rabbi is inextricably linked to his earthly ministry. This can be seen in the farewell discourse, which already anticipates the role Jesus will assume as the disciples' exalted Lord subsequent to his "glorification." At that time, Jesus will be the recipient of prayer and worship (e.g., 14:12–13). Also, more endearing terms are used for Jesus' followers, including "his own" (13:1), "children" (13:33; 21:4–5), "friends" (15:15), my own" (17:10), and even "brothers" (20:17).

In the end, it is clear that John presents Jesus as *more* than a rabbi. He is the preexistent Word-become-flesh. He is the signs-working Messiah, the Son of God who is himself God. He is the exalted Lord who is worthy of worship. Yet part of Jesus' "enfleshment" involved his assumption of the role of a Jewish religious teacher, a rabbi. So while he was certainly more than a rabbi, even a rabbi "with a difference," he was not less than a rabbi. This was acknowledged, not merely by his own disciples, but even by Nicodemus, "the Teacher of Israel" (3:2, 10).

One final thought: if the teacher–disciple pattern characteristic of Jesus' relationship with his disciples was in fact part and parcel of first-century Jewish culture, what does that mean for us in terms of contemporary application? It seems that we need not seek to copy slavishly in our culture what had its origin in another culture and another time. Rather, under the guidance of the Spirit, we are free to pursue appropriate patterns of discipleship in our day, remembering also that this is the age of the church, of the body of Christ, of which we all are members (e.g., Eph 5:30).

Note: The above is a sketch based on the following more extensive essay: Andreas J. Köstenberger, "Jesus as Rabbi in the Fourth Gospel," *Bulletin of Biblical Research* 8 (1998): 97–128. See also Andreas J. Köstenberger, "The Challenge of Systematized Biblical Theology: Missiological Insights from the Gospel of John," *Missiology* 23 (1995): 445–64.

Excursus 8

The So-called Seams (Aporias) in John's Gospel

Ever since the famous series of articles titled "Aporien im vierten Evangelium" [Aporias in the Fourth Gospel] by the German scholar E. Schwartz, which appeared in 1907 and 1908, there has been intense discussion of alleged "literary seams" in John's Gospel that, so it is argued, reflect traces of successive stages of redaction of the Johannine material. This redaction may, of course, have been performed by John on his own material in order to streamline it. Alternatively, it could have been undertaken by others after the apostle's death.

What immediately raises cautions against any such proposals, however, is the fact that John's narrative is remarkably uniform, as several detailed studies performed by the scholar E. Ruckstuhl (1951, 1991) have shown. This means, moreover, that any later redactor must have done his work rather clumsily, so that we today are able to identify "seams" that he (unsuccessfully, it appears) attempted to patch up. Of course, to call these alleged incongruities in style "seams" is already to beg the question. Let's therefore take a brief look at some of the most important passages to see whether they in fact constitute "seams" or not.

(1) "Jesus came into the land of Judea." In 3:22 the text appears to be saying that Jesus "came into the land of Judea." The problem is, he has been in Judea all along since attending a Passover festival from 2:23 to 3:21. Did it simply slip the author's (or redactor's) mind that Jesus had been in Judea all along? Apart from the unlikelihood of such a major blunder, it turns out that the solution lies close at hand. It is found in an alternate meaning of the word translated "land" above. In fact, this expression can (and here arguably does) mean "countryside." If this is correct, John simply indicates in 3:22 that Jesus now left Jerusalem and came "into the Judean countryside," as the NIV appropriately renders this phrase.

(2) The "second sign" referred to in 4:54. John 4:54 appears to refer to a "second sign" performed by Jesus. But if Jesus' turning water into wine at the Cana wedding (recorded in 2:1–11) was the first such sign, then what about the Jerusalem signs mentioned in 2:23 and 3:2? Again, the apparent incongruence evaporates when it is realized that the phrase "second miraculous sign" is further qualified in 4:54 by the addendum "having come from Judea to Galilee." In other words, John, by way of literary inclusion, links the two signs performed by Jesus in Cana of Galilee in order to constitute chapters 2–4 of his Gospel as a unit, Jesus' ministry circuit beginning and ending in Cana (cf. 2:11; 4:46: "once more he visited Cana").

(3) The sequence of chapters 5 and 6. In the present order, Jesus travels to Galilee via Samaria in chapter 4, is found in Jerusalem in chapter 5, and then is said at the beginning of chapter 6 to "cross to the far shore of the Sea of Galilee." Now it seems rather abrupt to say Jesus crossed over the Sea of Galilee when at the last occasion he was said to be in Jerusalem. Some creative minds (foremost the famed German scholar R. Bultmann) have suggested that chapters 5 and 6 should be reversed to straighten out John's account. In this case, it is argued, Jesus' works in Galilee are neatly combined in chapters 4 and 6, while Jesus' feats in Judea follow in chapters 5 and 7–11. The problem is, there is absolutely no evidence that John's Gospel ever circulated this way. Also, there is no need to force John into a straitjacket of recording everything in between accounts he chooses to select. Thus it may appear abrupt for Jesus to be in Jerusalem in chapter 5 and then "cross the Sea of Galilee" at the beginning of chapter 6. But this does not necessarily constitute evidence for an actual "seam" as is sometimes alleged.

(4) The pericope of the adulterous woman (7:53–8:11). Clearly, the pericope

of the adulterous woman interrupts the flow of the Johannine narrative. This is seen when the account is excised and 7:52 is followed immediately by 8:12. Here the simple answer is that we have here a floating narrative in search of a Gospel home (be it Luke or John) which was almost certainly not part of John's original Gospel in the first place.

(5) Mary's mention in 11:2. In John 11:2, Mary of Bethany is introduced as the woman who "poured perfume on the Lord and wiped his feet with her hair." The problem is, this account is not found in John's Gospel until the following chapter (12:1–8). But again, this may simply be an instance where John expects his readers to be familiar with basic Gospel tradition. Or had Jesus not said himself, "I tell you the truth, wherever the gospel is preached throughout the world, what she has done will also be told, in memory of her" (Mk 14:9; Mt 26:13)? Thus this passage is no different from John's introduction of Andrew as "Simon Peter's brother" in 1:40 when Peter is mentioned only in the following verses or John's reminder that "this was before John was put in prison" (3:24) when nothing of this sort had been mentioned previously in his Gospel. This is also why John can call Bethany "the village of Mary and her sister Martha" in 11:1. For Luke's Gospel had provided a memorable account of these two women (cf. Lk 10:38–42).

(6) "Come now, let us leave" (14:31). In 14:30, Jesus tells his disciples that he will not speak with them much longer. Then he says in the following verse, "Come, let's go." Stunningly, however, what follows is three more chapters of material (15–17)! Should 14:31 perhaps be followed immediately by 18:1, where it is said that Jesus left with his disciples and crossed the Kidron Valley? Again, the incongruence may merely be apparent. For the plausible suggestion has been made that Jesus and his followers indeed leave the Upper Room after 14:31 and that vineyards provide a suitable backdrop for Jesus' continued discourse in John 15 as he and his disciples have embarked on their walk.

(7) "None of you asks me 'Where are you going?'" (16:5). On the face of it, Jesus' statement in 16:5 seems to be in conflict with Peter's question in 13:36 and Thomas's similar query in 14:5. Some

have therefore sought to place 16:5 prior to 13:36 and 14:5 in the sequence of events. But we need not approach the text so mechanically. The solution may be that Jesus chided his followers for not *really* being interested in where he is going. In other words, they were too absorbed in self-pity and their own personal situation.

(8) The "ending" of 20:30–31. John 20:30–31 reads like the ending of the Gospel. Then why is there an additional chapter appended, with "another" ending added in 21:24–25? A close look suggests that chapters 20 and 21 cohere quite closely. Thus the numbering system employed in 21:14 ("the third time Jesus appeared to his disciples") presupposes the two previous resurrection appearances recounted in chapter 20. Also, chapter 21 provides the climax of Peter's relationship with the "disciple whom Jesus loved," which is developed in the Gospel from chapter 13 on, intensifying in chapters 18–20. It is therefore unnecessary to suppose that the transition from 20:30–31 to 21:1ff. constitutes a literary "seam." More likely, chapter 21, as an epilogue, corresponds structurally to John's Prologue in 1:1–18.

Our brief panoramic tour of some of the major alleged literary "seams" in John's Gospel has yielded the result that in each instance plausible—even probable—explanations can be given in favor of the coherence of the text as it stands. The solution may be text-critical (as in the case of the pericope of the adulterous woman), it may hinge on an alternative meaning of a given word (as in the instance of the term $g\bar{e}s$ in 3:22), or there may be other reasons why the Johannine narrative flows a certain way. At the end of the day, it is doubtful if there is even a single instance where we are driven to the conclusion that the text of John's Gospel as we have it reflects a genuine literary seam, an incoherence in the way the Johannine narrative is told.

Note: Compare the helpful article by Gary M. Burge, "The Literary Seams in the Fourth Gospel," *Covenant Quarterly* 48 (1990): 15–25; see also the same author's chapter 3 in *Interpreting the Gospel of John*, Guides to New Testament Exegesis (Grand Rapids: Baker, 1992).

Excursus 9

The Absolute "I Am's" in John's Gospel

Apart from Jesus' well-known seven "I am sayings," John's Gospel also features several important instances where the phrase "I am" is not complemented by a descriptive phrase of what Jesus *is*. Rather, Jesus merely claims to be "I am" *(egō eimi)*. Clearly these statements are also of crucial importance, since "I am" is the Old Testament name of God (cf. Ex 3:14–15; frequently in Is 40–66: e.g., 41:4; 43:10–13, 25; 45:18; 51:12; 52:6). At the same time, the phrase "I am" can simply mean "it is I" or, in more mundane terms, "it's me." Then again, in a work like John's where double entendre is commonplace, there may be instances where both meanings—Jesus appropriating the divine name *and* a simple self-identification—come into play.

Here are the major instances of the absolute use of "I am" in John's Gospel grouped according to the likelihood that they involve a divine self-reference on part of Jesus:

1. Virtually certain:

a. 8:58: "I tell you the truth, before Abraham was, I am!"—The Jews' reaction—they pick up stones to stone Jesus—makes clear that they took Jesus' statement as involving a claim to deity.

b. 18:5–6: "Who is it you want?" "Jesus of Nazareth," they replied. "I am he," Jesus said. When Jesus said, "I am he," they drew back and fell to the ground.—On one level, this is a simple self-identification—"It's me!" At the same time, the soldiers' response to Jesus' words indicates that they also involved a manifestation of his deity (a theophany).

2. Highly probable:

a. 6:20: "But he said to them, 'It is I; don't be afraid.'"—Again, on one

level this is a mere self-reference. But, as the preceding verse tells us, Jesus was walking on the water when he made this statement!

b. 8:24, 28: "If you do not believe that I am [the one I claim to be], you will indeed die in your sins"; "Then you will know that I am [the one I claim to be]."—The least that can be said here is that apart from insinuations of deity this would be a somewhat awkward statement, which makes a divine self-reference likely.

c. 13:19: "I am telling you now before it happens, so that when it does happen you will believe that I am He."—This is another emphatic declaration that appears to involve more than mere self-reference.

3. Possible:

a. 4:26: "I who speak to you am he" [that is, the Messiah].—Possibly the absolute use of "I am" here involves reference to deity. More likely, Jesus here merely affirms that he is the Messiah.

b. 8:18: "I am one who testifies for myself; my other witness is the Father, who sent me."—The reference is not dissimilar to 8:24, 28 (see above), so that divine self-reference cannot be ruled out.

Note: See also *Table 7.2: The Seven "I Am" Sayings.* For a full-fledged treatments of the Johannine "I am sayings," see Philip B. Harner, *The "I Am" of the Fourth Gospel* (Philadelphia: Fortress, 1970); David Ball, *"I Am" in John's Gospel*, JSNTSS (Sheffield: Sheffield Academic Press, 1996).

Excursus 10
Pilate's Uneasy Relationship with the Jews

The Jewish historian Josephus reports several clashes between Pontius Pilate (A.D. 26–36) and the Jewish population. One such incident involved Pilate's erection of statues of Caesar in Jerusalem. Since this is the first incident mentioned in the account of Pilate in both the *Jewish War* and the *Antiquities of the Jews*, it appears that the most likely date for this episode is A.D. 26/27, the first year of Pilate's procuratorship:

> Pilate, being sent by Tiberius as procurator to Judaea, introduced into Jerusalem by night and under cover the effigies of Caesar which are called standards. This proceeding, when day broke, aroused immense excitement among the Jews; those on the spot were in consternation, considering their laws to have been trampled under foot, as those laws permit no image to be erected in the city; while the indignation of the townspeople stirred the countryfolk, who flocked together in crowds. Hastening after Pilate to Caesarea, the Jews implored him to remove the standards from Jerusalem and to uphold the laws of their ancestors. When Pilate refused, they fell prostrate around his house and for five whole days and nights remained motionless in that position.
>
> On the ensuing day Pilate took his seat on his tribunal in the great stadium and summoning the multitude, with the apparent intention of answering them, gave the arranged signal to his armed soldiers to surround the Jews. Finding themselves in a ring of troops, three deep, the Jews were struck dumb at this unexpected sight. Pilate, after threatening to cut them down, if they refused to admit Caesar's images, signalled to the soldiers to draw their swords. Thereupon the Jews, as by concerted action, flung themselves in a body on the ground, extended their necks, and exclaimed that they were

ready rather to die than to transgress the law. Overcome with astonishment at such intense religious zeal, Pilate gave orders for the immediate removal of the standards from Jerusalem (*Jewish War* 2.169–174; a similar account is found in Josephus's *Antiquities of the Jews* 18.55–59).

Immediately following, Josephus recounts yet another clash between Pilate and the Jews:

> On a later occasion he provoked a fresh uproar by expending upon the construction of an aqueduct the sacred treasure known as *Corbonas;* the water was brought from a distance of 400 furlongs. Indignant at this proceeding, the populace formed a ring round the tribunal of Pilate, then on a visit to Jerusalem, and besieged him with angry clamour. He, foreseeing the tumult, had interspersed among the crowd a troop of his soldiers, armed but disguised in civilian dress, with orders not to use their swords, but to beat any rioters with cudgels. He now from his tribunal gave the agreed signal. Large numbers of the Jews perished, some from the blows which they received, others trodden to death by their companions in the ensuing flight. Cowed by the fate of the victims, the multitude was reduced to silence (*Jewish War* 2.175–177; cf. *Antiquities of the Jews* 18.60–62).

This account is in the *Antiquities of the Jews* immediately followed by the so-called *Testimonium Flavianum,* Josephus's account of the life of Jesus. This suggests that both of the above conflicts took place prior to Jesus' crucifixion. What the above related incidents suggest is that Pilate's relationship with the Jews got off to a more than rocky start. Also, it seems that in the end the Jews usually got their way, owing to their persistence and fierce religious commitment. At the same time,

Pilate's backing from Rome was extremely tenuous after the execution of his mentor Sajanus in A.D. 31, so that he was highly vulnerable to manipulation on the part of the Jews. This is underscored by the following incident that, occurring several years after Jesus' crucifixion, finally led to his dismissal. This time the background is a Samaritan uprising that had been brutally put down by Pilate. Josephus writes,

> When the uprising had been quelled, the council of the Samaritans went to Vitellius, a man of consular rank who was governor of Syria, and charged Pilate with the slaughter of the victims. For, they said, it was not as rebels against the Romans but as refugees from the persecution of Pilate that they had met in Tiranthana. Vitellius thereupon dispatched Marcellus, one of his friends, to take charge of the administration of Judaea, and ordered Pilate to return to Rome to give the emperor his account of the matters with which he was charged by the Samaritans. And so Pilate, after having spent ten years in Judaea, hurried to Rome in obedience to the orders of Vitellius, since he could not refuse. But before he reached Rome Tiberius had already passed away (*Antiquities* 18.88–89).

The account of this uprising sounds similar to the incident mentioned in Luke 13:1: "Now there were some present at that time who told Jesus about the Galileans whose blood Pilate had mixed with their sacrifices." The picture painted by these various narratives is that of Pontius Pilate as a ruthless, violent ruler torn hopelessly between his subjects and his Roman bosses. This historical sketch is helpful in understanding Jesus' trial before Pilate as recounted in John and the Synoptic Gospels.

Note: for further information on Pilate, see Helen K. Bond, *Pontius Pilate in History and Interpretation*, SNTSMS 100 (Cambridge: University Press, 1998). On Pilate's relationship with Herod Antipas, see Harold W. Hoehner, *Herod Antipas*, SNTSMS 17 (Cambridge: University Press, 1972).

Scripture Index

Subject Index

Andreas J. Köstenberger is professor of New Testament and Greek at Southeastern Baptist Theological Seminary. He is the author of *The Missions of Jesus and the Disciples according to the Fourth Gospel*. He is also the translator of the influential two-volume New Testament theology written by Adolf Schlatter.